$2—

FROM SILICON VALLEY
TO SINGAPORE

From Silicon Valley to Singapore

LOCATION AND COMPETITIVE ADVANTAGE
IN THE HARD DISK DRIVE INDUSTRY

David G. McKendrick

Richard F. Doner

Stephan Haggard

STANFORD UNIVERSITY PRESS

STANFORD, CALIFORNIA

Stanford University Press
Stanford, California

© 2000 by the Board of Trustees of the Leland Stanford Junior University

Library of Congress Cataloging-in-Publication Data

McKendrick, David G.
  From Silicon Valley to Singapore : location and competitive advantage in
the hard disk drive industry / David G. McKendrick, Richard F. Doner,
Stephan Haggard.
      p. cm.
  Includes bibliographical references and index.
  ISBN 0-8047-4152-2 (cloth : alk. paper) —
  ISBN 0-8047-4183-2 (paper : alk. paper)
    1. Data disk drives industry—Asia, Southeastern—Case studies.   2. Data
disk drives industry—United States.   3. Industrial location—Case studies.
4. Comparative advantage (International trade)—Case studies.
5. Competition, International—Case studies.   I. Doner, Richard F.
II. Haggard, Stephan.   III. Title.
HDJQ9696.27.A7852 M37   2000
338.4′76213976—dc21   00-058338

∞   This book is printed on acid-free, recycled paper.

Original printing 2000

Last figure below indicates year of this printing:
09   08   07   06   05   04   03   02   01   00

Contents

List of Figures   vii

List of Tables   ix

List of Disk Drive Related Abbreviations   xi

Acknowledgments   xiii

Part One. Introduction

1. Why Location Matters   3

2. Industry Background: Technology,
Competition, and Geographic Reach   16

Part Two. Location and Competitive Advantage

3. A Theory of Industry Evolution, Location,
and Competitive Advantage   37

4. Alternative Explanations for Industry Advantage   66

5. Global Shift and Competitiveness in Hard Disk Drives   87

6. Leveraging Locations: American Industry and
Its Southeast Asian Production System   119

Part Three. Case Studies

7. Singapore   155
WITH POH KAM WONG

8. Thailand   184

9. Malaysia   204

Part Four. Implications

10. Policy, Politics, and Location in Developing Countries   227

11. Globalization and Industrial Leadership   253

Appendixes

A. Industry Origins and Technological Evolution   275

B. An Innovator's Dilemma?   283

Notes   289

References   317

Index   341

Figures

2.1 Areal density growth 18

2.2 Average disk drive price per megabyte 19

2.3 Hard disk drive industry value chain 21

2.4 Hard disk drive firms worldwide, 1956–97 29

2.5 Industry revenue per drive 31

4.1 HDD and computer market shares 74

4.2 Captive disk drive revenue 78

5.1a Location of all U.S. disk drive firms in 1961 90

5.1b Location of all U.S. disk drive firms in 1970 90

5.1c Location of all U.S. disk drive firms in 1980 91

5.2a Location of all U.S. disk drive firms in 1985 93

5.2b Location of all U.S. disk drive firms in 1990 93

5.2c Location of all U.S. disk drive firms, 1995 94

5.2d Location of all U.S. disk drive firms, 1998 94

5.3a Location of the first ten producers of 5.25-inch form factors 96

5.3b Location of the first ten producers of 3.5-inch form factors 96

5.3c Location of the first ten producers of 2.5-inch form factors 97

5.4 U.S. HDD firm age and assembly in Southeast Asia 101

5.5 Average age of U.S. and Japanese HDD firms 102

5.6 Percent of U.S. and Japanese HDD firms in Southeast Asia 103

5.7 Distribution of production in U.S. and Japanese firms 108

5.8 HDD shipments by form factor, 1976–90 112

6.1   The HDD industry in Southeast Asia, 1982–85   122
6.2   The HDD industry in Southeast Asia, 1986–92   128
6.3   The HDD industry in Southeast Asia, 1993–98   135
6.4   Highest-capacity drive at each Seagate production location   144
11.1 Global industries and their geographic configuration   268

Tables

2.1	Annual unit shipments by form factor, 1976–98	26
2.2	Revenues by form factor, 1976–98	27
2.3	Market concentration, 1980–98	30
2.4	Worldwide market shares, 1998	32
3.1	Unpacking agglomeration economies: Clusters and their benefits	46
3.2	Dynamics of industry location and benefits: The HDD industry in Southeast Asia	60
4.1	IBM firsts in the HDD industry	80
4.2	The first ten entrants in new form factors plus surviving firms at the end of 1998	82
4.3	Disk drives with MR and GMR heads: Order of entry	83
4.4	Highest areal density	84
5.1	Timing and direction of overseas HDD assembly	99
5.2	Summary characteristics of firms assembling in Southeast Asia	107
5.3	Total noncaptive market share of firms producing in low-cost Asia	110
5.4	The market for 3.5-inch disk drives	113
5.5	Locations for HDD product development and assembly, 1999	116
6.1	Comparative wage rates in Southeast Asia	124
6.2	Labor force evaluation measure	125

6.3   Investment incentives in Southeast Asia   125

6.4   Physical infractructure in Southeast Asia   126

6.5   Comparative measures of project startup in Southeast Asia   131

6.6   Policies and institutions benefiting the HDD industry   132

6.7   Educational enrollments in Southeast Asia (latest
       available year)   137

6.8   Comparative R&D indicators   138

6.9   Industrial policy and institutional support in Southeast
       Asia   140

6.10   The geographic pattern of employment in Seagate,
       1981–98   146

7.1   Growth of Singapore's HDD industry, 1986–98   158

7.2   Leading suppliers to the HDD industry in Singapore   159

8.1   HDD and related firms in Thailand   185

8.2   Order of entry of HDD and related firms in Thailand   192

8.3   Real wages in Thailand, 1982–94   195

9.1   Growth of the HDD sector in Penang   205

9.2   Investment history in northern Malaysia: HDD major
       firms and suppliers   206

9.3   The second-tier of the HDD supply chain in Malaysia   208

10.1   The baseline policy environment   233

11.1   Industries and locational drivers   268

Disk Drive Related Abbreviations

CPU   central processing unit

FCB   flexible circuit board

FCBA   flexible circuit board assembly

HDA   head-disk assembly

HDD   hard disk drive

HGA   head-gimbal assembly

HSA   head-stack assembly

OEM   original equipment manufacturer

PC   personal computer

PCB   printed circuit board

PCBA   printed circuit board assembly

Acknowledgments

This book explores the links between U.S. global leadership in the hard disk drive industry and the concentration of American manufacturing operations in Southeast Asia. Truly a joint product, its design and writing were the result of many hours of conversation and long e-mails among the three authors. Nevertheless, the project's initial organization required a division of labor between the San Diego and the Southeast Asian teams.

The entire enterprise grew out of the efforts of Roger Bohn and Peter Gourevitch at the University of California, San Diego (UCSD), who submitted a proposal to the Alfred P. Sloan Foundation in 1995 to study the globalization of the hard disk drive industry. Without the early leadership of Bohn and Gourevitch, this book would not have been written. Joined by David McKendrick, they began to identify a number of important research questions, beginning with the deceptively simple "Where is the industry located?" Although just identifying the industry's location in 1995 required an enormous research effort, their analysis yielded an interesting empirical portrait of production and employment across the entire disk drive value chain (see Gourevitch et al. 1997, 2000). Bohn also co-authored several studies that helped us better understand some of the manufacturing issues challenging the industry (Terwiesch et al. 1997, Terwiesch and Bohn 1998, Terwiesch et al. 1999).

McKendrick followed up this initial wave of research by studying the evolution of competition, technology, and location since the industry's inception almost forty-five years ago. Many of the initial ideas for the book grew out of the working papers of McKendrick (1997, 1998, 1999), McKendrick and Hicken (1997), and Barnett and McKendrick (1998), some of which are accessible at http://www-irps.ucsd.edu/~sloan/. McKendrick directed the collection, compilation, and analysis of data on the entire population of firms in the disk drive industry as well as many parts of its value chain.

This effort would have been impossible without the assistance of Allen Hicken, John Richards, Guillermo Fornaresio, Gigo Alampay, Kyle Eischen, Yuko Kasuya, Richard Carney, Akie Shimatani, Katherine Wen, Jae-Young Yi, Bryan Garcia, and Jason Forse, all of UCSD. We are also grateful to Princess Mathews, the administrative coordinator at the university-based Information Storage Industry Center, for single-handedly managing all the support systems involved.

Although Richard Doner and Stephan Haggard directed the work on Southeast Asia, they could not have succeeded without the aid of an excellent group of collaborators. Early trip reports by McKendrick and Bohn based on a number of factory visits in Thailand, Malaysia, and Singapore were a first stab at understanding the regional production network. Read-Rite and Western Digital kindly allowed McKendrick to join a 1996 financial analyst tour of these factories. Poh Kam Wong from the National University of Singapore (NUS) was indispensable not only for his help with chapter 7 (which he co-authored) but in the genesis of the research approach used for Southeast Asia. He also secured financial aid from NUS, which partially supported the survey work reported in chapter 6. In Thailand, Doner worked with Peter Brimble (Brooker Group) and received terrific support from Brooker's Pattanan Woodkarn-Timm and Pranee Suriyan. In both Thailand and Atlanta, Bryan Ritchie of Emory University offered excellent research assistance for work that resulted in Doner and Brimble's (1998) study of the Thai disk drive industry. In Penang, Haggard worked with Lim Pao Li and Anna Ong and gained from the institutional resources provided by DCT Consulting, including the research assistance of Lim Wei Seong and Kang Beng Chin. The three collaborated on a history of the Malaysian disk drive industry (Haggard et al. 1998). Gwendolyn Tecson (1999) from the University of the Philippines and Gregory Noble (2000) from Australian National University produced excellent background studies on the Philippines and Taiwan respectively, providing the basis for the discussion of those two countries in chapter 10. These detailed country studies are also available at the web address listed in the previous paragraph. Barry Naughton of UCSD, an expert on China's economy, offered insights into the Chinese case based on his fieldwork there.

We also received assistance on the written versions of this research. Thanks go to William Barnett, Roger Bohn, Martin Kenney, Joyce Thompson, and James Porter, who shared incisive comments on the entire manuscript, and to Frank Mayadas, David Mowery, Gary Gereffi, Suzanne Stout, and Barry Naughton, who offered valuable feedback on parts of the manuscript or earlier versions of papers that preceded this book.

Several people in the industry went out of their way to help us in our work. Steve Luczo and Don Waite opened many doors for us at Seagate

Technology. Mark Geenen of TrendFocus; Dennis Waid of Peripheral Research Corporation; and Jack McLaughlin, publisher of *Rumors and Raw Data,* generously shared their knowledge of the industry. Joyce Thompson of Read-Rite, Dirk Thomas of IBM, Gunter Heine and Greg Martin of Seagate Technology, and Robert Katzive of Disk/Trend were gracious and patient about answering our seemingly unending questions. Above all, however, we would like to thank James Porter, president of Disk/Trend, who since 1996 has helped us understand both the history and current trends of the industry. Jim gave us open access to his extensive files as well as copies of his annual *Disk/Trend Reports,* on which so much of our analysis is based.

In addition, we are grateful to the many current and former disk drive managers and policymakers in the United States, Asia, and Europe whom we interviewed or corresponded with. In the United States, we have greatly benefited from conversations with Shashi Agarwal, Ralph Ahlgren, Chris Bajorek, Ami Bercowitz, Bob Blair, Leonard Bleininger, Sally Bryant, Jeff Burke, Scott Burton, Dave Caldwell, Colleen Cayes, Allen Cuccio, Steve Curtis, Phil Devin, Bisser Dimitrov, Dave Ernsberger, Hap Fisher, Harold Frank, Raymond Freeman, Jr., Ralph Funk, Gerry Gilbert, George Gray, Tim Harris, Al Hoagland, Gordon Hughes, Willi Jilke, Tom Kamp, Glenn Larnerd, Henry Lo, Pablo Luther, Dan Malueg, Denis Mee, Marshall Nathanson, Farid Neema, Steve Polcyn, Ken Potashner, Barry Schechtman, Ron Schmidt, Ted Siegler, Ronald Smith, Al Sniderman, Russell Stern, David Thompson, John Titsworth, Erwin Tomash, Stan Torchon, Jon van Bronkhorst, David Walling, and Blaine Zechenelly.

In Singapore, we are grateful to H. B. Chan, Joe Chen, Cheok Bin Yong, B. T. Chia, Stephen Chua, Richard Downing, Richard Ee, S. H. Goh, Edwin Gomez, C. C. Hang, Michael Khoon Heng Cheong, Harry Koh, S. H. Koh, Koh Whatt Hin, Y. S. Koh, K. L. Lee, L. C. Lee, Lee Eng Lock, S. C. Leong, Lim Ching Tong, David Lim, Kelvin Liu, Philip Loon Fu Yoon, Low Teck Seng, Vince Maestropietro, Ken Martini, Lothar Mork, Andrew Ng, K. L. Ng, Phung Huey Lin, Poon King Wang, Ron Rogers, Seah Peng Nee, Siew Teng Kean, Albert Sim, Valdew Singh, Soh Swee Hock, Mike Stears, James Tan, Kelly Tan, Teh Bong Lim, Thien Kwee Eng, S. C. Tien, Contance Wong, Yap Pau Lock, and Yeo You Huan.

In Thailand, we thank Teera Achariyapaopan, Sa-ard Banchirdrit, Bob Beaton, Jerrold Campbell, Javed Chaudhary, Mork Darakananda, Larry Eischen, Susumu Fujisawa, Kanokrud Glankwahmdee, Sadahiro Hariu, Ron Hensley, Shin Ichiro Hiroshima, Masamitsu Horike, Lyle G. Johnson, Sombat Kittisuphat, Tokio Kurinami, Samart Laicheewa, K. B. Lim, Rungruang Limchoopatipa, Tom Mitchell, Motoyuki Nagasaka, M. Nakazono, Norio Okumura, Soichi Okumura, Karn Osathanondh, Chakchai Panichapat, Sriprasad Prabhu, Dale Schudel, Okumura Soichi, Kwanjit Sudsawad,

John L. Sullivan, Robert Summers, Jirapannee Supratya, Masao Suzuki, Y. K. Teh, S. G. Tien, Nobuyuki Watanabe, and Y. M. Wong.

In Malaysia, we are grateful to Dominic Boudville, Scott Burton, S. K. Chan, Chang Kee Kwong, K. Y. Cheah, James C. K. Chuen, Foong Same Weng, John Foster, David K. K. Gee, K. Gopalan, Timothy Harris, Kenji Hirakawa, Ronnie Hong, M. Kataoka, K. H. Khoo, Lay Yok Hin, Simon Lee, Lim Heng Jin, Lim Wei Yee, K. C. Loh, Loh Soo Fung, K. M. Murugiah, Clement Ng, Victor Ng, Peter Quah, Phil Selser, Senator Dato' Chet Singh, Boonler Somchit, Tan Ghee Suah, Tan Thiam Seng, Bernard Tay, Alfred E. L. Teh, Ung Hock Lye, F. M. Wong, Yoon Chon Leong, and Yuen Teck Ping.

In Japan, we thank Norihito Aramaki, Ichiro Isozaki, Katsuhiko Kato, Yoshimasa Miura, seven managers who wish to remain anonymous, and nineteen additional companies that cooperated with phone, e-mail, and written requests for information about their disk drive histories.

In Europe, we thank David Antrich, Mike Caithness, Albrecht Doehler, John James Farguharson, Ulrich Frank, Hans Gatzen, Heinz Graichen, Axel Grüter, Jean-Michel Guillou, Peter Hammerschmid, Engelbert Hoermannsdoerfer, Brian King, Friedrich Kistermann, Jim Leslie, David Lockwood, Nigel Mackintosh, Jean-Jacques Maleval, Christian Maury, Jean Meneut, Karl Otto Reimers, Jean-Pierre Robinot, John Walker, Klaus Wattrodt, and Norman White.

This book would not have been possible without the generous financial support of the Alfred P. Sloan Foundation. For many years, Sloan has championed the idea that university research can create considerable social value by directing its attention to the study of specific industries. In this spirit, Sloan has underwritten the establishment of thirteen industry centers at American universities to study financial institutions, motor vehicles, trucking, airlines, semiconductors, retail food, textiles and apparel, managed care, pharmaceuticals, steel, powder metallurgy, construction, and our own Information Industry Storage Center. Because it is dedicated to a single industry, each center can examine in depth the range of challenges and issues confronting that industry and work closely with its managers and leaders. At the same time, an industry focus may lead to insights about the complex influences that shape business firms, the economy, and society in general.

In our own case, we are fortunate that Frank Mayadas and Hirsh Cohen, both of Sloan, had the wisdom to initiate research on industry globalization. We hope we have been able to live up to at least some of Sloan's expectations.

Finally, we thank our families for their forbearance and support.

Part **One**

INTRODUCTION

1 *Why Location Matters*

From the 1970s through the early 1990s, American corporations were assaulted by foreign competitors across a wide range of industries—from labor-intensive textiles and apparel to capital-intensive automobiles, steel, and shipbuilding, even to technology-intensive sectors such as semiconductors and computers. A rapidly growing trade deficit and anemic productivity growth called into question the ability of American industry to compete in international markets. Asian manufacturers, especially Japanese companies, appeared to pose a particular challenge to American industry and public policy, threatening the country with deindustrialization. Moreover, the challenge seemed deep and systemic: the American system of capitalism itself was seen as a liability. Asian forms of industrial organization and manufacturing, corporate governance, and industrial policy all pointed toward dominance in the battle for market share and economic growth. And in fact, industry after industry did lose significant worldwide market share to Japanese, Korean, Taiwanese, and other competitors from Asia.

The emergence of the "new economy" in the United States, the prolonged economic malaise in Japan, and the Asian financial crisis of 1997–98 now give such controversies and fears a dated ring. Nonetheless, even at the time a number of American industries offered a strong counterpoint to the pessimistic scenario. One of the most striking of these exceptions was the hard disk drive (HDD) industry.

In 1982, Seagate Technology, a three-year-old HDD startup located twenty miles south of Silicon Valley, began to assemble HDD components in Singapore, becoming the first firm in the industry to do so. Two years earlier, it had introduced the world's first HDD for the desktop computer. At the time, its main competition was the minifloppy, an inexpensive data storage device that contributed to the explosion in demand for personal computers. Because potential customers were extremely sensitive to price, Seagate would have to build its new drive cheaply to capture a larger share of the emergent data storage business. The small company won contracts from IBM to supply disk drives for the IBM PC-2 and later the PC/XT, but IBM was a demanding, even ruthless, customer. Although competition in the industry was not yet as severe as it would become when more firms entered, Seagate knew that IBM and other computer manufacturers would press relentlessly for lower disk drive prices in exchange for the promise of future orders for the rapidly growing PC market.

Seagate made a bold decision. Not only did it go abroad, but by 1984 it had shifted almost all disk drive assembly to plants it owned and operated in Singapore. In doing so, the company set in motion a dynamic that, within six years, transformed Singapore into the world's largest HDD assembler. A clutch of other small American disk drive makers followed Seagate's lead. Collectively, these industrial no-names—Tandon, Computer Memories, Maxtor, MiniScribe, Micropolis, Conner Peripherals, Microscience International, and others—completely upended the industrial status quo. As these small, young multinational corporations (MNCs) pioneered the industry's shift into Southeast Asia, some transformed themselves into large, successful firms. Seagate developed and used its Southeast Asian platform to become the world's largest disk drive producer; the largest private employer in Singapore, Thailand, and Malaysia; and China's largest exporter.

While these newcomers were building their base of operations in Southeast Asia, the American industry leaders—IBM, Burroughs, Hewlett-Packard, Memorex, and Digital Equipment—stuck with their existing locational strategy and continued to make disk drives in the United States and Europe. Not only did the newcomers drive all but IBM from the disk drive industry altogether, they also beat back a challenge from some of Japan's most formidable companies. Sony, Mitsubishi, Matsushita, NEC, and Hitachi appeared unstoppable in segment after segment of the electronics industry. They nonetheless discovered that manufacturing and exporting disk drives from Japan was no match for the operational clusters and supplier networks the smaller American firms had developed in Southeast Asia. By the mid-1990s, the remaining Japanese majors had moved significant production to Southeast Asia as well, although it was by then apparently too late to challenge seriously the dominance of their American counterparts.

Implicit in this sketch are a number of important developments in the global economy over the past two decades that have elevated the significance of location in corporate strategy. Exploiting advances in communications and transportation, firms have become more adept at coordinating activities dispersed across a number of international locations. At the same time, extensive deregulation and liberalization of trade and investment, particularly in former Socialist and developing countries, have dramatically increased the availability of possible investment sites and made it less costly to use them. Investment decisions are increasingly driven by efforts not only to lower costs or penetrate markets but also to gain access to an array of location-specific benefits that can complement and even develop the assets of the firm, such as specialized labor, clusters of critical suppliers, or strong research universities.

In seeking to exploit these assets, firms face competing locational pressures. Centripetal forces—such as scale economies and the advantages of proximity—push firms to concentrate value-added activities in a limited number of places. Yet centrifugal forces—such as the lure of lower factor costs, access to markets, or complementary assets—invite dispersion of activities across several locations. In many cases, succeeding in international competition requires companies to excel across a range of activities—R&D, assembly, logistics, service—that cannot be served by a single location, or even several locations, within the same country. For example, American firms typically seek to exploit knowledge-based assets that are concentrated in the United States and other developed countries or in regions with excellent research universities. But to realize efficiencies, these assets must often be coupled with low-cost inputs, including labor. These resources are more likely to be found outside the United States, Europe, and Japan.

This book examines the effect of location on international competition in the HDD industry, which, with sales of more than $30 billion in 1999, is dominated by American firms. American leadership has rested on the formation of two complementary industrial clusters. Fundamental research and product development have resided almost entirely within the United States, primarily in California. Manufacturing, by contrast, has internationalized but is concentrated in Southeast Asia. Locating initially in Singapore, the industry has spread over time into a network that spans Thailand, Malaysia, China, and the Philippines. A historical analysis of the industry since its inception more than forty years ago shows how location decisions have affected competition, competitive strategy, and industrial performance. Thus, we argue that the effective internationalization of production to locations in Asia played a key role in establishing the dominant competitive position of American firms.

How did Southeast Asia come to attract and retain investment in this industry? The answer is to be found in the dynamic interplay of factor endowments, competition, industry evolution, and public policy. While labor costs initially played a central role in luring firms to the region, other assets played an increasing role over time. The entry of American firms stimulated the development of complementary human resources, dynamic clusters of firms within countries, and networks between them—all of which further enhanced the competitiveness of the American industry. Rapid technological change and increasing competitive pressures forced the firms in the region to improve their operational capabilities and individual locations to improve their skill base. Government policy played a crucial role in locational decisions, not simply by creating an open business environment but also by actively fostering the local assets that contributed to firms' competitiveness.

The Argument

Industrial leadership derives from several sources (Mowery and Nelson 1999). Domestic demand, strong domestic suppliers, a university research base, availability of skilled scientists and engineers, government procurement, and government investments in basic research have all been invoked, singly or in combination, as necessary ingredients. While these factors clearly contribute to market advantage early in an industry's life, maintaining leadership can be problematic as new entrants appear, the industry diffuses to other countries, and domestic and international competition intensifies. Location—specifically, the establishment of operational clusters outside an industry's home base—can play a crucial role in preserving the competitiveness of national industry, complementing the industry's focus at home on the key functions of research, design and development, and marketing.

In hard drives, American firms led the way in organizing the industry into this particular geographic configuration. Initially, their shift abroad confirmed, at least in part, existing explanations of foreign investment that focus on market access, resource endowment and factor costs, and the nature of host country regulation and public policy. In addition, however, foreign investments create and leverage agglomeration economies and cross-border networks that provide additional advantages.

Our objective here is not simply to weight these five factors for one industry but to underline a more general dynamic through which the relative significance of these factors changes over time. Among these factors, we find that market access has had the weakest effect on investment decisions in the disk drive industry, and then only in the 1960s and early 1970s, when a few American companies sought access to the European market. But the logic that compelled these location decisions was undermined after Seagate Technology introduced a smaller, lighter, and cheaper disk drive in 1980.

This innovation introduced a new set of competitive pressures to the industry. Initially, subsequent investments predominantly focused on squeezing costs from the assembly process; the quest for low-wage production labor in particular played a crucial role in early investment decisions. This is not surprising, and if cheap factor costs were the main ingredient in industrial success, then our story would be unremarkable. The significance of low-wage labor, however, has not remained constant in the industry. If it had, we would find a highly footloose industry continually spreading to new low-wage sites. This has not been the case. Singapore was the first host to American investments in Southeast Asia; but as the city-state developed and wages rose, it continued to attract investment by offering other location-specific assets that complemented those of the U.S. disk drive industry. As a result, the industry did not continue to disperse but concentrated at key nodes.

Other factors besides labor costs were clearly shaping the emerging locational pattern. In fact, the industry's competitive requirements and the region's location-specific assets were co-evolving; the operational capabilities in Singapore in particular, but also in Thailand and Malaysia, grew to meet the HDD industry's increasingly challenging and complex manufacturing needs. Not only were cost pressures unrelenting, but by the mid-1980s HDD firms had to meet ever more stringent time-to-market schedules demanded by their customers, the PC manufacturers. Since the mid-1990s, firms have been required to compete across even more dimensions: cost, time-to-market, time-to-volume, and improvements in manufacturing yields.

In response, American firms reinvested in the region, developing agglomeration economies in operations. Economists and economic geographers have emphasized various externalities that arise from the collocation of firms, while sociologists and regional planners have examined how institutions within a given location can create trust and reduce transaction costs. A number of these studies have examined industrial districts, some with long histories (the Portuguese cork industry, the Swiss watch industry, the textile industry in northern Italy, and London's financial district) and others much more recent (Route 128, Silicon Valley).[1] Most analyses of industrial districts, however, assume that they are constituted primarily by culturally homogenous indigenous firms.

In fact, multinational firms are playing an increasingly important role in helping industrial regions and districts spring to life. During the early periods of an industry's development (as well as a given firm's life), there is a strong tendency for innovation and production to collocate at their place of origin. In the disk drive industry, as international competition intensified, the production and supporting activities that could be physically separated from product innovation were dispersed to lower-cost locations. At the same time, rather than dispersing across a wide spectrum of locations, these activities clustered in Southeast Asia. Innovative activities continued to cluster, but at the home-country locations with skills and resources more conducive to product development. The industry became organized into distinct technological and operational clusters.

Our analysis emphasizes not only agglomeration at several different investment sites but also the network that links firms operating at those sites. In the aggregate, we call this network a *regional production system*. Not only does leveraging multiple locations in an international network exploit the comparative advantage of different sets of locational assets, but it offers an industry a hedge against exchange rate shocks, labor shortages, and other supply disruptions. The strength of this system lies in the proximity of its constituent locations, which in the drive industry include Singapore, Thailand, and Malaysia. Like agglomeration economies, these operational networks—this regional production system—cumulate into a strong competitive asset.

Public policy and regulation are no less important to the competitiveness of industry; and they, too, were dynamic. In the early stages of the HDD industry's globalization, public policy mattered primarily by supporting (or impeding) the free movement of goods that is crucial to this industry and by providing various financial incentives that influenced profitability—a baseline set of policies that was a necessary condition for attracting the industry. Over time, however, a number of locations—but particularly Singapore—differentiated themselves by developing more sophisticated supporting policies that deepened local capabilities to meet increasingly demanding industry needs.

Our central empirical finding is that the American disk drive industry was much faster than its Japanese competitors at establishing and exploiting operational clusters outside its home base, influencing and benefiting from public policies in Southeast Asia, and developing regional networks that yielded further benefits. The nature of these advantages evolved with the industry, which itself became increasingly sophisticated. The ongoing fit between the operational requirements of American HDD firms and the region's abilities underscores the dynamic character of competitive advantage.

This difference between the American and Japanese industries was more important than differences in their industrial organization, capacity to innovate, other variations invoked to explain their relative performance, or the performance of national industries in international competition more generally. But this difference also raises questions. Why did American and Japanese firms behave so differently when facing the same competitive environment and technical requirements? Wouldn't the pressures of international competition drive firms toward the adoption of the same strategy regardless of their nationality?

Competitive behavior is strongly affected by a firm's national environment. Firms involved in global competition begin their lives under very different legal, social, and political environments and histories, all of which shape organizational forms, structures, and practices. There are, as Kogut (1992: 285) observes, "national organizing principles." While firms from different nations may eventually converge on some best practice, convergence may not happen quickly or automatically. Firms generally imitate the actions of others they judge to be salient; they develop mental models (Porac et al. 1995) about firms they consider their primary competitors. As firms begin to engage in international competition, they are most likely initially to monitor and learn from other firms from the same country. In this case, American disk drive firms mimicked the global strategies of other American disk drive firms, which were not salient to their Japanese counterparts.

But nationality is not the only way in which competitors classify one another. Firms also orient toward and consider the actions of other firms in the same strategic group. During the 1980s, for example, makers of desktop disk drives observed and responded to the actions of other desktop disk drive makers perceived as successful, not to the actions of the large firms making disk drives for mainframe computers. As illustrated in the sketch that opened this chapter, the MNCs most responsible for developing and leveraging locational assets in Southeast Asia did not conform to popular images of a multinational firm. Although most work on the internationalization of industry generally links it to the actions of large MNCs, we find that smaller and younger firms pioneered the industry's global shift. Silicon Valley upstarts such as Seagate Technology and Maxtor moved quickly to develop and exploit these low-cost locations, while established firms such as Digital Equipment and Hewlett-Packard were laggards. In fact, the globalization of operations was key to the growth and survival of once small and young firms. The speed and depth of American firms' move from Silicon Valley to Singapore was not a sign of weakness or a prelude to their exit from the industry but a factor central to their industrial leadership.

Our Approach

Despite the importance of location to competitive advantage, it is surprisingly difficult to find empirical work that links patterns of location, including the globalization of economic activity, to industry performance over time. In attempting this task, we have made a number of methodological choices. To begin with, we examine firms within an industry as opposed to larger aggregates that lump together diverse and often unrelated firms. We also seek to explain the performance of the U.S. industry as a whole as opposed to the performance of a particular firm or other outcomes such as innovation or urban and regional growth. We examine the industry from its inception rather than at a particular point and trace the development of the industry over time. Rather than focusing on only one or several locales, we track the location of all R&D and production sites globally. Finally, we differentiate between R&D and production, which have different geographic requirements.

This approach to industry analysis has at least three advantages over other studies of industries, globalization, or particular regions. First, it encompasses the entire population of firms that ever made an HDD. We also investigate almost all upstream firms that made two critical components (heads and media) and for the past eighteen years cover most firms in other parts of the value chain as well. This approach allows us to avoid the bias encountered in many industry studies that favor large firms and those that survive. We are thus able to capture how small firms pioneered and used locations to their advantage and to examine the sources of firm failure as well as success.

This approach also allows us to examine the strategic interactions and collective rationality of a set of organizations that face a similar environment, including locational choice. As Michael Porter has argued in *The Competitive Advantage of Nations* (1990), industry and industry segments are the best focus for analyzing competitive advantage because specialized and commercially valuable skills and technologies emerge from a competitive struggle within industries against foreign and domestic rivals.[2] We show that, in making a foreign investment decision, it matters to a firm whether a competitor, customer, or supplier has already invested abroad in a particular location.

A second virtue of tracing an entire industry through both space and time is that it captures the dynamics of industry location. We have identified the location of each HDD assembler—its R&D facilities and assembly plants—over the entire life of the industry. We also have detailed the history of the industry's movement into the major countries in Southeast Asia where production has located, including the buildup of supporting stages in the value chain. This portrait allows us to distinguish those activities that moved (assembly) from those that did not (product development). Analyses that focus only on manufacturing or R&D, the locations of a few of the largest organizations, or only some locations for a short period—no matter how intensively—can easily miss the changing role played by industry location in competition within the industry as a whole.

A third benefit comes from examining a high-tech sector such as the HDD industry. HDDs are the quintessential Silicon Valley industry, so often the subject of studies of regional development, strategic management, industrial districts, and economic geography. The industry was born in San Jose, California, and the region hosted more disk drive startups than any other place on earth. In fact, some say the region should have been named Ferrite Valley in honor of the magnetic materials used in disk drives before the emergence of semiconductors. The industry is among the most technologically innovative of the past fifty years. In sum, it would seem to fit perfectly the localized competition emphasized by researchers such as AnnaLee Saxenian (1994) in her influential study of Route 128 and Silicon Valley.

In fact, the industry has come to have two geographic faces. In addition to the remarkable innovations developed in a handful of locations in the United States, the industry came to be highly globalized in its operations. Moreover, foreign direct investment has been no less important in preserving the advantage of American firms than has the clustering of innovative activities in the United States. Our suspicion is that this is true of many other industries that are the subject of regional studies; these regions are in fact nested in a larger international industry structure. Studying industrial leadership in most industries, including disk drives, now requires understanding the causes and consequences of globalization.

Implications

Understanding the dynamic or evolutionary quality of globalization poses distinctive challenges for both policymakers and managers. From the point of view of managers, an improved understanding of the processes, forms, and outcomes of globalization offers important guidelines for corporate strategy and organization. Why are certain locations preferable to others? When should firms invest in some locations and avoid or disinvest in others? In making these decisions, managers need to be sensitive to the changing logic of globalization.

First, our study underlines the importance of adopting a nuanced view of costs. Many companies have sought to lower costs by relocating production facilities to low-wage, low-tax, or other low-cost-input locations, in part because these costs are easy to measure up front. But we show that locations with low wages and low taxes can be poor competitive platforms if they fail to generate agglomeration economies such as the emergence of suppliers and a production and managerial work force with industry-specific experience and skills. Many of the benefits of location are collective in nature. Individual firms benefit from the physical proximity of related firms, even competitors. Locating in an existing or developing cluster can lower total cost and improve time-to-market and time-to-volume production.

Second, and relatedly, managers must consider what corporate functions can be shifted offshore by asking what functions need to be proximate to one another. The experience of the disk drive industry shows how firms can separate product development, manufacturing, and a number of manufacturing processes over long distances and still thrive. At the same time, however, there is a certain logic to collocating activities that support manufacturing; *operational* clusters can be just as important a locational asset as *technological* ones.

Third, global strategy must harness the advantages of spreading activities across locations while capturing the innovation advantages of a home base.[3] American disk drive companies have successfully executed such a locational strategy; innovative activities have remained "sticky" in the United States.

Finally, managers need to be alert to the fact that the attributes of locations can change. Of course, investments made at one time must always adapt to and exploit those changes. But firms also play a role in the development of location-specific assets—for example, through training or vendor development programs or by helping governments implement public policies that contribute to firms' growth and competitiveness. The development of local capabilities of a variety of types—from skilled labor and suppliers to universities and other institutions—can complement the firm's assets.

Our study also carries lessons for policymakers on how to make their jurisdictions attractive to managers in high-tech commodity segments and to keep them attractive over time. Initial efforts to attract economic activity may or may not be successful in keeping those activities in place over the long run. Facilities close as well as open.

Firms in such globalized industries require an open trade and investment environment and a competitive trade infrastructure. But the provision of an open business environment does not obviate the need for industry-specific knowledge and policy. Early and systematic efforts to understand and attract a given industry, including important pieces of its value chain, can generate a critical mass of investments and corresponding agglomeration economies. Such economies make firms more permanent members of the community—more resistant to inducements offered by other jurisdictions and thus less footloose. First-mover advantages and the development of local capabilities are as salient for countries as for companies.

It is also important for policymakers to be cognizant of the activities of policymakers in neighboring countries. On the one hand, different jurisdictions compete for investment, and like firms are therefore rivals. On the other hand, proximate locations may have complementarities; policies initiated by one country or subnational government can have externalities for others, creating the potential for regional production networks to emerge among them. Regional cooperation agreements need to focus more attention on these possible complementarities and how to exploit them. By looking at one industry in detail, we are better able to make judgments about the efficacy of country strategies in attracting economic activity, forming production networks, and moving up in the international division of labor.

Our findings also cast doubt on some received wisdom about the capabilities of American firms, particularly in the electronics industry. One commonly held belief is that when Japanese and American firms compete in electronics, the American firms will survive by being better in technology and innovation, while the Japanese firms will excel at volume manufacturing and cost reduction. Once Japanese firms reach technical parity, American firms are likely to face overwhelming competition and are only likely to survive by subcontracting manufacturing to more competent, lower-cost producers. The decline of U.S. dominance in consumer electronics in the 1960s and 1970s and the survival of U.S. firms in the computer industry as a result of partnerships with Asian companies are often cited as proving these propositions.

Contrary to this characterization of American firms, those dominating the disk drive industry have done so not only through their design capabilities but also through their prowess in manufacturing. Throughout the history of the industry, global leaders have overwhelmingly assembled their own disk drives; almost every company that relied primarily or entirely on contract manufacturing did not survive for very long. American firms that dedicated themselves to manufacturing in fact became extremely good at it—and in one of the world's most cost-sensitive, high-volume businesses. But they did it not by clustering production close to innovation, not by forming industrial districts at home, but by managing long-distance technology and supply relationships and building up operational clusters abroad as well.

Plan of the Book

The book is organized into four parts. Part One (chapters 1 and 2) introduces our basic arguments as well as background about the disk drive industry. Chapter 2 explains what a disk drive is, describes the value chain for the product, and provides a brief history of the industry's origins.

It also offers an overview of the main technological and competitive forces driving the industry and a brief overview of its globalization.

Part Two (chapters 3–6) is the core of the book, outlining the basic theoretical argument and evidence on the link between location and competitiveness. Chapter 3 presents a framework that explicitly links location, including offshore production, to industry competitiveness. We outline the relationship between industry evolution and its geographic configuration, describe the main influences on industry location, emphasize the mechanisms that trigger changes in location over time, and explain how national differences in the use of overseas locations can create competitive differences. Since globalization is not generally viewed as a means for maintaining industrial leadership, chapter 4 addresses a number of competing explanations for industrial competitiveness. We show that none of these approaches, individually or collectively, fully accounts for the persistence of American leadership in the HDD industry and in particular the superior performance of American versus Japanese firms.

Chapters 5 and 6 provide detailed empirical support for the theoretical arguments in chapters 3 and 4. Chapter 5 describes the evolution of the industry's location since its inception, the dynamics leading to American firms' shift of manufacturing to Southeast Asia, and some of the ways in which this has sustained American leadership. It demonstrates that the U.S. industry's rapid and extensive shift of HDD assembly overseas enabled companies to push back a challenge from the Japanese HDD industry, which was very late in copying the U.S. locational strategy. Chapter 6 probes the nature of the location-specific assets that American firms developed and exploited in Southeast Asia and how they contributed to industry and firm competitiveness. A central theme is the evolutionary nature of these locational assets—specifically, the ongoing fit between the industry's changing and increasingly demanding manufacturing requirements and the region's growing capabilities. We emphasize the strong interaction of industry pressures, corporate strategies, and public policies and institutions and consider how lead firms knit diverse locations into a regional production system in Southeast Asia.

To demonstrate these points in more detail, part Three (chapters 7–9) provides case studies on the development of the HDD industry in three countries: Singapore, Thailand, and Malaysia. In each case, we trace the industry from its inception, including the investments of the majors and the development of complementary suppliers, and show how location-specific assets, including public policy, complemented the capacities of American firms and contributed to their success.

In part Four we step back to consider the broader implications of our empirical and theoretical story. Chapter 10 addresses the implications of our findings for public policy in developing countries. It examines the origins and effects of public policies and institutions against the backdrop of long-standing debates about the role of industrial policy in East Asia. Our study highlights the utility of a new generation of industrial policies that are quite different from the protectionist designs of the past. Chapter 11 concludes the book, looking forward to the future of the industry, revisiting the applicability of our findings to other industries, and drawing out lessons for public policy and corporate strategy.

2 Industry Background

TECHNOLOGY, COMPETITION,
AND GEOGRAPHIC REACH

Designing and manufacturing hard disk drives (HDDs) involve a rare combination of intense cost pressures, rapid technological change, value chain complexity, and short product cycles. Although the industry has not always been so dangerous, its technological and competitive challenges have dramatically intensified since the world's first desktop disk drive was introduced in 1980. In late 1999, Seagate CEO Steve Luczo characterized the industry as the "extreme sport" of manufacturing.[1]

Why have successful disk drive producers elected to play this difficult manufacturing game largely in Southeast Asia? To find the answer to this question, one must understand both the dynamics that have driven the industry over time and the location-specific assets that HDD firms have found and developed in the region.

This chapter examines the industry's challenges in innovation and manufacturing. We begin by considering disk drives and how they work and then outline the industry's value chain. Despite their small size, disk drives are made from numerous subassemblies and components, including wafers, sophisticated electronics, mechanical parts such as motors, and metal casings—a complex supply chain that struggles under constant technological pressure and increasingly stringent manufacturing requirements.

As the chapter shows, the industry's competitive environment has created extraordinary dynamism and tremendous market pressure, even when compared with the dizzying standards of other high-technology products such as semiconductor memory (see chapter 11). In addition to rapid technological change—and, in part, because of it—the industry is also subject to intense competition, extremely short product life cycles, and rapidly falling prices that have generated recurrent cycles of boom and bust. Under these conditions, success has required meeting a cumulative set of competitive pressures, including cost, time-to-market, time-to-volume production, and yield improvements.

Demands on disk drive producers have intensified significantly during the past two decades, and these pressures have had an important influence on the industry's geographic configuration. Thus, we conclude the chapter with a brief portrait of the extent of the industry's globalization, setting the stage for a more detailed exposition in subsequent chapters of the links between the American HDD industry's shift to Southeast Asia and industrial leadership.

Introduction to Disk Drives[2]

WHAT DO DISK DRIVES DO AND WHY ARE THEY SO IMPORTANT?

Computers are equipped with several kinds of memory, of which two are most critical for our purposes.[3] Main memory holds the data that the computer manipulates when it is in use; it consists of DRAM chips that can move data at the high speeds necessary to keep pace with the computer's logic circuits. But because the cost per megabyte of storage for semiconductor chips is high, an additional kind of memory, employing tapes or spinning magnetic disks, must be used for mass storage of data. While tape is cheaper than disks for storing data, it is much too slow for online processing. The online memory requirements for computers have become huge, and HDDs have emerged as the most efficient solution for storing large amounts of data at low—and declining—cost.

Consider the growth in the storage capacity of a drive. Capacity is determined by how many bits can be stored on a square inch of disk, otherwise known as the HDD's *areal density*. Figure 2.1 indicates the growth in areal density for two of the industry's technological and market leaders, IBM and Fujitsu, over the past forty years. Until 1991 areal density increased at an annual rate of 30 percent but grew by an astounding 60 percent per year between 1992 and 1997, faster than the rate of progress for semiconductors. In 1999 areal density increased an amazing 125 percent. This makes disk drives an unusual industry in the sense that technological change has actually accelerated, not decelerated, with industry age.

Rapidly increasing areal density has translated directly into dramatically falling prices that consumers pay for each megabyte of storage. As figure 2.2 shows, a little more than a decade ago the average per-megabyte cost of a disk drive was $11; in 1998 it was less than a nickel. The resulting capacity to store greater amounts of data at declining costs has made disk

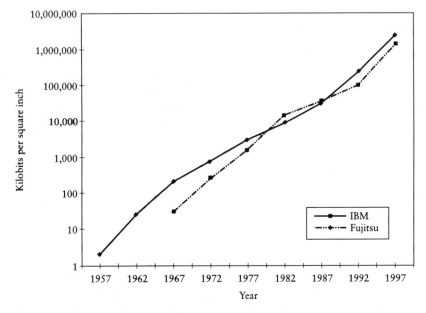

FIGURE 2.1. Areal density growth.
NOTE: The lines represent IBM and Fujitsu's highest-areal-density disk drives shipped in a given year.
SOURCES: *Disk/Trend,* various issues; Stevens (1981); and data supplied by Fujitsu.

drives a critical technology behind the spread of the Internet, permitting companies and individuals to offer and access the billions of web pages that now exist. In the future we are likely to use disk drives in a variety of other applications, including TV recording (replacing the VCR), home appliances, and automobiles.

HOW DO DISK DRIVES WORK?

A hard disk drive is a compact, electronically controlled, mechanical device. Some have compared its operation to that of a phonograph or a jukebox. Inside the case of a disk drive are one or more constantly spinning aluminum-alloy or glass platters arranged one on top of another in a stack. Driven by highly efficient motors, these disks can spin at rates of up to 15,000 revolutions per minute (rpm). Most disks in personal computers are just under 3.5 inches in diameter; disks inside notebook computers are almost 2.5 inches, and those in personal digital assistants and other handheld devices are 1 or 1.8 inches. When you enter computer commands through a keyboard or mouse, the hard drive's electromechanical

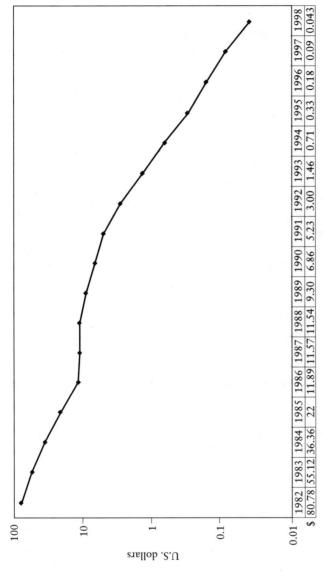

	1982	1983	1984	1985	1986	1987	1988	1989	1990	1991	1992	1993	1994	1995	1996	1997	1998
$	80.78	55.12	36.36	22	11.89	11.57	11.54	9.30	6.86	5.23	3.00	1.46	0.71	0.33	0.18	0.09	0.043

Year/Price

U.S. dollars

FIGURE 2.2. Average disk drive price per megabyte.
SOURCE: *Disk/Trend* (1988–98); representative prices for 5.25-inch drives from various trade journals for previous years.

actuator arm (much like a jukebox's tone arm) responds and moves to the proper place just one microinch (millionth of an inch) above the platter. Then the drive's read/write head—the recording head at the end of the arm—locates the information requested. The head "reads," or retrieves, the information and transfers it to the central processing unit (CPU), and the requested data either appear on the screen or are otherwise available for processing.

Disk drives operate on the basis of fundamental principles of magnetism. Hard drive platters (also known as disks or media) are coated with a magnetic material a few millionths of an inch thick. A disk drive uses read/write heads both to write to and to read from the surface of the disk. When writing, the head acts as a tiny electromagnet in which positive and negative pulses of current are translated into north and south magnetic poles on a rotating magnetic disk. When reading, the head senses magnetic fields from these poles and translates the alternating fields into positive and negative voltage pulses. These pulses become the bits of digital information stored on the disk. Although this head flies above the disk without touching it, it stays so close that even a particle of smoke is too large to fit between the head and the disk.

The data are recorded in tracks, or concentric circles, that are numbered from the outermost edge of the disk to the innermost. The hard drive is a random (as opposed to sequential) access device: it can retrieve stored data from anywhere on the disk in any order. HDDs store data on both sides of a platter because read/write heads are positioned on each side. The greater the number of platters, the greater the storage capacity. The drive actuator arm synchronizes all the read/write heads so that they stay in perfect alignment as they move together across the platter's surface. This arm can move from the outer to the inner edge of a disk and back fifty times per second. The seek time, which is the increment of time between the CPU request and the first byte of information being sent to the CPU, is roughly ten milliseconds.

According to the HDD industry association (IDEMA 1999), since the tracks on a platter are located only microinches apart and the heads are flying one microinch or less above the surface of the rapidly spinning disk, accurately positioning the read/write heads is comparable to flying a Boeing 747 only 0.025 inches above the ground while maintaining a course of flight directly over the center dividing stripe on a road. These almost unimaginably tight tolerances illustrate the daunting challenges of disk drive manufacture. Even the slightest contamination can cause the heads to touch the surface. If this impact is too severe, they will "crash," resulting in damage to the heads or data surface, lost data, and, in the most extreme cases, destruction of the drive. Because drives are tightly sealed to keep out contaminants, crashes are rare in today's advanced drives. But as one

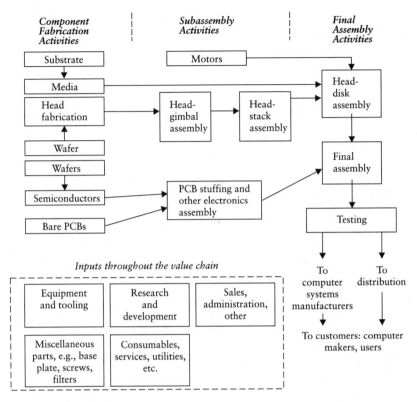

FIGURE 2.3. Hard disk drive industry value chain.
SOURCE: Adapted from Gourevitch et al. (2000).

U.S. drive producer, Western Digital, discovered in 1999, problems can still occur. Because foreign matter got onto parts before they entered the assembly area, the firm produced several bad batches of a particular model, causing users to lose data ("Western Digital" 1999). As this case illustrates, disk drives are extremely high-precision products. Even if final assembly is perfect, imperfections in specific components and subassemblies can lead to drive failure.

The Disk Drive Value Chain

The HDD is by far the most complex component in a personal computer in terms of moving parts, and its value chain is extremely differentiated.[4] Figure 2.3 illustrates the supply chain of physical components, noting in particular four main subchains: head subassemblies, media, motors, and electronics. Each has changed its manufacturing requirements over time as technologies have shifted. Other parts of the chain include sales and service, tools and equipment, and research and development. Contemporary producers have broken these steps of the value chain into many discrete pieces, analyzed the economics of each, and sought to locate them around the world at the most cost-efficient sites (Gourevitch et al. 2000).

CORE MANUFACTURING PROCESSES

Read/Write Heads. Read/write heads are the single most costly component of an HDD and have an enormous impact on drive design and performance. Heads are manufactured in stages, beginning with highly automated and technically complex wafer fabrication. Wafers are then machined into sliders, which are the tiny read/write elements. Slider fabrication has itself become more technology-intensive over time, moving from relatively simple milling of metal heads to vacuum photolithography and ion etching of wafers.

Each slider is then attached to a suspension, which is a small arm that holds the head in position above or beneath the disk. This process is called head-gimbal assembly (HGA) and has traditionally been a labor-intensive process, although steady shrinkage in the size of heads is forcing greater automation. Sets of HGAs stacked together for installation in a disk drive are called a head-stack assembly or HSA, modular units that include the required circuitry and actuators; this process has also been highly labor-intensive.

Platters, Media, or Disks. Platters, also known as media or disks, can be made of aluminum or glass, although approximately 90 percent are aluminum. Such media use thin film sputtering, a multistep batch-like process that involves the deposition of extremely thin, uniform layers of magnetic film onto a substrate. Typically, aluminum blank substrates are nickel-plated and polished; they then receive a magnetic layer (cobalt, chromium, and tantalum), on top of which is deposited a carbon overcoat and lubricant. As with heads, media are a high-technology and capital-intensive aspect of HDD production. A disk drive can contain as few as one to as many as fifteen disks stacked on a spindle to increase storage capacity.

Motors. A motor spins the media with extreme precision. Motors rotate the platters counterclockwise at speeds between 4,500 and 15,000 rpm. Motors, which include a shaft, a rotor, miniature ball bearings, and lubricants, are manufactured in Class 100 cleanrooms. One Japanese company, Nippon Densan (Nidec), has nearly 75 percent of the worldwide market share of HDD motors.

Electronics. Electronics include semiconductors and discrete components (including those designed specifically for disk drives), printed circuit boards (PCBs), and the flexible circuits or flexcircuits that connect the PCB to the rest of the HDD. The semiconductors include a read channel to store and retrieve data bits and a read/write preamplifier ("preamp") that amplifies the strength of the signals so that chips on the PCB can convert electrical impulses to a digital signal. Spindle and actuator motor controller electronics ensure that the platters spin at the correct speed and the actuator arms place the read/write heads over the precise spot on the platter. Interface electronics communicate with the system's CPU in the proper format. A microprocessor and associated memory chips oversee drive operations. For high-performance drives, an additional digital signal processor is required. All of these electronic components are typically mounted ("stuffed") onto PCBs in highly automated procedures.

Head–Disk Assembly. These four subchains constitute the major subassemblies of disk drives. Each subassembly is typically made in its own facility and all subassemblies are then brought together for final assembly, mainly in cleanrooms. The combined assembly of heads, actuator mechanism, disks, motor, and other components is often referred to as the head–disk assembly (HDA). The HDA is enclosed in a base casting or base plate, a single piece of aluminum that also provides a mounting for a PCB, which houses the electronics. A gasket between the base casting and the top cover acts as a seal to provide a contamination-free operating environment for the read/write heads. Once the HDA is assembled, it moves to a station for servo writing, an electromechanical technique to control the positioning of the head. The finished HDD then undergoes functional testing, which is automated, and manual rework if necessary.

Much of the HDA process is semi-automated, meaning that drives move along conveyor belts but most of the actual assembly involves manual labor. While automation would appear to generate higher yields than manual assembly, that advantage is bought at some cost in terms of flexibility: the ability to change products and ramp up and down quickly.[5] Nonetheless, the increasingly tight tolerances demanded of the industry are once again raising the question of the tradeoff between flexible but lower-yield manual processes and inflexible but higher-yield automation. Herein lies one of the challenges for the industry.

OTHER INTEGRAL ACTIVITIES

Sales, Service, and Management. In addition to the core manufacturing activities, the value chain includes steps that are outside the core flow of materials but nonetheless integral. Sales, service, and management are critical functions for an industry characterized by intense competition and rapid technological change. After-sales service involves value-added activities such as repair, operator training, and engineering support.

Tools and Equipment. The core manufacturing processes require process equipment; measurement and test equipment; and metal and plastic jigs, tools, and fixtures used in the assembly processes. Products in these categories are precise and sophisticated. Process equipment includes, for example, wafer slicing and slider grinding systems, physical vapor deposition systems for heads, and advanced robotics used in automated assembly lines for media processing. Even cleanrooms use advanced technologies to eliminate contamination. Test equipment includes systems for analyzing organic micro-contamination, scanning disk surfaces for defects, and measuring magnetic films on recording heads. Firms vary in their use of automation and their purchase versus in-house manufacturing of line equipment and tooling, but almost all test instruments are made by specialist suppliers.

Research and Development. In an industry known for its rapid technological change and breathtakingly short product life cycles, R&D has been of great importance. Through technology development, product design, process development, and pilot production, R&D has allowed disk drive producers to pack more data onto the disk while reducing the physical size of the drive and increasing the speed by which the data can be accessed. Here we note some of the more significant technological developments. (See appendix A for an overview of the industry's technical evolution.)

New materials and technologies have permitted heads to fly much closer to the media to increase the amplitude of a signal and pack bits more densely on the disk. Voice coil positioning technology, involving information prerecorded on a dedicated disk surface during manufacturing, has significantly reduced the time it takes the head to find information on a disk. New materials used in disk surfacing have further contributed to reducing the fly height of the heads by creating a smoother disk. Originally coated with a variation of the paint primer used for the Golden Gate Bridge, disks now use vastly improved coatings, substrates, and lubricants. Faster access times and data transfer rates have also resulted from faster-spinning disks driven by more powerful and sophisticated motors. Constant innovations and new materials—including the recent replacement of ball bearings with the hydrodynamic bearing technology used in gyroscopes—have increased disk rotation speeds from 1,000 rpm for the earliest drives to as fast as 15,000 rpm today. Finally, advances in electronics, especially innovations in semiconductors, have improved all aspects of disk drive performance. Taken together, these technological improvements have led to dramatic increases in performance and storage capacity.

These innovations have required comparable improvements in manufacturing. All stages of production, even those that are labor-intensive, now involve extreme cleanliness, tight tolerances, and precision equipment. In addition, rapid technological change makes the manufacturing process itself a moving target; it is one thing to develop a new product, quite another to manufacture it at high volumes. Frequent introduction of new products, with corresponding changes in components, can put enormous pressure on production teams. Drive producers and component firms speak of "losing the recipe" in assembly, which hurts manufacturing yields. These manufacturing challenges are difficult enough on their own, but they occur in the context of an incredibly competitive environment. Thus, although the market has grown dramatically, so has the intensity of competition.

Market Growth, Competition, and Globalization

MARKET GROWTH

The disk drive industry has been one of the fastest-growing in the world for a surprisingly long period. Measured by unit shipments, it has grown at a compound annual rate of 37 percent since 1976, when only 175,700 drives were shipped (see table 2.1). In 1998 almost 145 million were shipped. Desktop PCs consumed the majority of disk drives. Increasingly, then, success in the industry has required firms to achieve economies of scale.

Disk drives intended primarily for mainframe and minicomputer applications (between 6.5 and 14 inches in diameter) reached their peak in 1984, when almost 825,000 were shipped, falling to a negligible 1,500 in 1997. The first form factor for desktop computers, the 5.25-inch drive, quickly surpassed the larger form factors in units shipped in 1983, growing to 8.7 million units in 1988 before declining.[6] The most widely used disk drive in history, the 3.5-inch drive, appeared in 1983 and by 1989 surpassed the annual number of 5.25-inch drives shipped. In fact, 79 percent of all disk drives produced since the birth of the industry have been 3.5-inch drives. Disk drives for laptop (and later notebook) computers were introduced in 1988, with shipments reaching almost 18 million in 1998. Shipments of 3.5-inch and 2.5-inch drives continue to grow; demand for each has more than doubled since 1994. Smaller form factors (1.8 and 1.3 inches) have found a small market for specialized

TABLE 2.1

ANNUAL UNIT SHIPMENTS BY FORM FACTOR, 1976–98
(IN THOUSANDS)

Year	6.5–14"	5.25"	3.5"	2.5"	1.8" or less	Worldwide Total
1976	175.7	—	—	—	—	175.7
1977	235.2	—	—	—	—	235.2
1978	306.1	—	—	—	—	306.1
1979	386.3	—	—	—	—	386.3
1980	508.6	1.2	—	—	—	509.8
1981	649.2	51.5	—	—	—	700.7
1982	707.8	242.5	—	—	—	950.3
1983	744.8	1,214.9	5.0	—	—	1,964.7
1984	824.9	2,722.8	101.4	—	—	3,649.1
1985	788.4	3,637.9	428.7	—	—	4,855.0
1986	724.8	5,804.4	1,412.7	—	—	7,941.9
1987	700.9	8,162.3	4,328.7	—	—	13,191.9
1988	782.2	8,753.1	8,231.1	0.1	—	17,766.5
1989	639.0	8,306.2	13,210.8	24.5	—	22,180.5
1990	551.8	6,714.7	19,765.6	847.0	—	27,879.1
1991	425.3	3,041.1	26,036.4	3,085.5	1.0	32,589.3
1992	253.3	2,202.5	36,313.7	5,115.9	21.7	43,907.1
1993	180.0	1,278.1	43,954.4	6,287.9	157.2	51,857.6
1994	121.5	791.6	60,343.2	8,507.1	235.3	69,998.8
1995	14.2	706.8	77,775.8	10,637.8	418.8	89,553.4
1996	10.0	4,648.9	88,356.5	11,769.9	232.3	105,017.6
1997	1.5	5,628.3	109,647.2	15,018.0	203.1	130,498.1
1998	—	4,073.9	123,047.1	17,729.9	115.9	144,966.8

SOURCE: *Disk/Trend*, various issues.

applications, but their reduced storage capacities combined with their relatively high price limit their use.

The industry's revenue growth has been less impressive. In 1976, the first year for which comprehensive industry information is available, revenues were almost $1.9 billion (see table 2.2). The lion's share of industry revenue was generated from large-form-factor drives, which did not peak until 1988; only in 1990 did revenue from desktop disk drives exceed that generated by these larger form factors. But the PC revolution clearly had a major impact on the industry. From a standing start in 1980, the market for the 5.25-inch drives jumped to $62 million in 1981, reached almost $2 billion in 1984, and continued to grow until 1990 as their higher capacities made them attractive to some market segments. It took six years after their introduction in 1983 for revenues from 3.5-inch drives to exceed those from 5.25-inch drives. Total industry revenue peaked just shy of $32 billion in 1997 before declining to $30 billion in 1998.

TABLE 2.2

REVENUES BY FORM FACTOR, 1976–98 (IN MILLIONS OF DOLLARS)

Year	6.5–14″	5.25″	3.5″	2.5″	1.8″ or less	Worldwide Total
1976	1,876	—	—	—	—	1,876
1977	2,813	—	—	—	—	2,813
1978	3,457	—	—	—	—	3,457
1979	3,817	—	—	—	—	3,817
1980	5,180	1	—	—	—	5,181
1981	6,309	62	—	—	—	6,371
1982	7,160	243	—	—	—	7,403
1983	8,258	850	2	—	—	9,110
1984	10,014	1,811	42	—	—	11,866
1985	11,135	2,407	174	—	—	13,717
1986	10,581	3,573	604	—	—	14,757
1987	10,521	4,426	1,663	—	—	16,610
1988	12,118	4,669	3,637	n.a.*	—	20,424
1989	12,086	5,150	5,416	8	—	22,660
1990	11,674	5,163	8,510	231	—	25,578
1991	9,148	4,311	10,248	924	n.a.*	24,632
1992	6,604	4,175	12,190	1,576	6	24,550
1993	4,835	2,057	12,909	1,888	41	21,730
1994	2,465	1,359	16,648	2,706	54	23,231
1995	279	1,410	21,299	3,547	98	26,633
1996	102	1,244	23,501	3,917	56	28,819
1997	20	1,220	25,902	4,544	51	31,736
1998	0	741	24,434	4,866	36	30,077

SOURCE: *Disk/Trend*, various issues.
NOTE: Numbers may not add due to rounding. Dashes indicates that form factor had not yet been introduced. Revenues for 5.25-inch drives in 1980–82 are estimates based on unit shipments.
*n.a., Not available.

INDUSTRY COMPETITION

The combination of rapid technological change and product standardization has had profound implications for the nature of competition. Firms must not only keep up technologically but also face another grim reality: computer manufacturers and distributors make buying decisions largely based on price and the ups and downs of the computer industry business cycle. As a consequence, the industry is often whipsawed, with periods of rapid growth leading to overcapacity, followed by price wars, losses, and shakeouts. These dynamics are evident in an examination of technological competition and price pressures in the industry.

Technological Competition. Technological competition in disk drives is akin to running fast just to stay in place; no sooner does a company develop a new product than it must begin the development process anew. This kind of competition has occurred along several dimensions and, as we have shown, involves innovation in all major subcomponents. One challenge has been the miniaturization of drives—from 24-inch to 14-, 8-, 5.25-, 3.5-, and 2.5-inch drives. These changes in form factor have proven problematic for many manufacturers, and most firms have not survived the transition. They have had similar trouble keeping up with continuous product introductions *within* form factors. At least since the mid-1960s, when a wave of firms entered with less expensive copies of IBM products, continuous improvements to areal density have been a central feature of industry competition, putting firms on a treadmill to develop higher-capacity products.

Until the early 1980s, industry success meant being a fast follower of IBM: whenever IBM introduced a new generation of disk drives for its own mainframes and minicomputers, other companies joined the race to build their own, less expensive versions. But the introduction in 1980 of the 5.25-inch drive for personal computers created a different competitive dynamic. Competition in the desktop drive business was paced not so much by IBM (although it remained a technological leader in many ways) but by independent newcomers. The first few companies introduced disk drives holding five megabytes of storage. Soon new companies introduced ten-megabyte drives, then twenty-megabyte, and so on. New firms constantly introduced higher-capacity drives, while industry incumbents struggled to hang on and match the new rivals. The explosion in demand for PCs attracted new entrants, reaching a peak of eighty-five companies in 1985 (see figure 2.4).

This technological leapfrogging has created a market segregated between the early leaders, who were able to supply a "capacity point" in demand by the largest computer manufacturers, and the rest of the industry, which has had to divide up the secondary market of second-tier mainframe and minicomputer makers and the hundreds of small and medium-sized PC companies. Firms late to market with a new drive thus suffer a severe revenue penalty; if they are too late, they may find no customers and be forced either to absorb their development costs and start developing an even higher-capacity drive or to exit the industry altogether.

While being first to market was in many ways critical, first-to-volume production was often more important. Many new entrants have been among the first to introduce a drive with a particular form factor or capacity. But firms unable to ramp up to volume production effectively seldom received a second chance from computer vendors. As a result, survival in the disk drive industry has increasingly required the marriage of technological prowess to manufacturing ability.

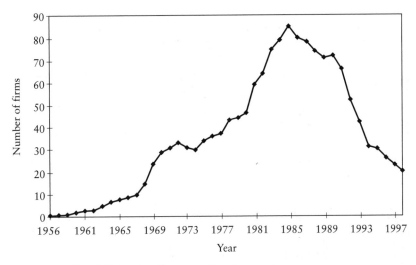

FIGURE 2.4. Hard disk drive firms worldwide, 1956–97.
SOURCE: Authors' calculations from various industry sources.

The difficulty of succeeding for very long in both product innovation and manufacturing is reflected in the industry shakeout that began in the late 1980s and has continued until today. Yet while shakeouts usually usher in eras of market concentration, the industry has been at least moderately concentrated throughout its history. Since the mid-1970s, the industry has operated as what economists consider a tight oligopoly, with the top four firms controlling more than 60 percent of the market (see table 2.3). At the same time, however, the composition of the oligopoly has changed as some of the new entrants grew to displace the leaders. The sole exception to the norm, as in so many other ways, is IBM, which is the only company to be in the top four in each year during this period. Since 1990, industry concentration has increased, but competitors have become more equal in their market shares (as measured by the Herfindahl-Hirschman index), suggesting relatively similar abilities among the top five or six leaders in product development, time-to-market, and manufacturing skills required for time-to-volume.[7]

Cost and Price Pressure. The industry's competitive intensity has limited the ability of the leaders to control pricing or the length of product life cycles. Periodic oversupply and constant price erosion are ways of life in the disk drive market. As in other industries, disk drive companies strive to avoid the pitfalls of the price-sensitive, high-volume, low-end of the market by differentiating products and moving into higher-capacity segments, such as drives for file servers and network storage. But historically,

TABLE 2.3

MARKET CONCENTRATION, 1980–98

Year	Industry Revenue (millions of dollars)	Four-Firm Concentration Ratio (%)	Herfindahl-Hirschman Index
1980	5,181.2	64	1,600
1981	6,370.6	62	1,662
1982	7,403.4	61	1,792
1983	9,112.2	63	1,827
1984	11,866.2	63	1,849
1985	13,716.8	69	2,430
1986	14,757.4	67	2,202
1987	16,610.4	64	1,962
1988	20,424.0	65	2,177
1989	22,660.3	67	2,124
1990	25,578.0	70	2,478
1991	24,632.0	70	2,424
1992	24,549.5	66	1,860
1993	21,729.8	65	1,660
1994	23,231.4	64	1,386
1995	26,632.9	68	1,472
1996	28,819.1	79	1,771
1997	31,736.3	76	1,630
1998	30,077.0	69	1,591

SOURCE: *Disk/Trend,* various issues.

firms have had little ability to sustain a product differentiation strategy. While one or two have been the capacity leaders for a year or two, trying to grab a more profitable position, no company in the history of the industry has survived solely by making small quantities of high-capacity drives. Firms fundamentally compete on price, which also means volume, and they face pressure to be first to market at that price.

Even so, first-to-market innovators typically hold only the slimmest of leads because other manufacturers generally introduce comparable products within a relatively short time. The likelihood of rapidly decreasing profitability over the life cycle of any given product provides a strong incentive for manufacturers to innovate. But the result is extremely short product cycles—currently estimated to be from six to nine months—and falling unit prices.

Figure 2.5 shows the drop in revenue per disk drive since 1977, when it was $12,000. In 1980, when the first 5.25-inch HDD was introduced, revenue per drive was still above $10,000. It dipped below $1,000 in 1990 and fell to just over $200 in 1998. Over the past decade, prices of completed 3.5-inch disk drives have been declining at a rate of 1 percent per week, prompting some managers to complain that they are in the fish busi-

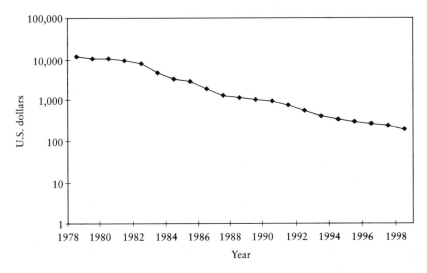

FIGURE 2.5. Industry revenue per drive.
SOURCE: *Disk/Trend,* various issues.

ness: products on the shelf begin to stink. Rapid product life cycles have led to discounting on older-generation drives, meaning that unit prices on disk drives fall about 50 percent a year: an eighteen-gigabyte drive selling at Fry's Electronics for $400 in 2000 will retail for $200 or even less in 2001. More recent pricing pressures have been caused by a dramatic shift to demand for sub-$1,000 PCs, which translates into orders for drives costing less than $80. Some entry-level PCs were being sold in early 2000 for $500, and low drive prices for that segment have pulled down prices for higher-capacity drives.[8]

To survive these kinds of pricing pressures, firms need to contain per-unit costs, focusing on both volume production and the reduction in the number and cost of components. As we will see, these strategies have had important implications for location and globalization. They create a vicious circle, however, as manufacturers scale up, build more than they can sell, and thus carry large inventories. In today's environment, with large economies of scale, the disk drive industry can profitably support only a limited number of manufacturers.

Price and cost pressures are further aggravated by the highly cyclical nature of the industry, as rising demand leads to overbuilding of production facilities, resulting in excess inventory. And we have noted, the industry's fate is tied to the PC market and the demand of PC makers for ever cheaper components. PC makers also change their requirements frequently and are poor forecasters, which prevents HDD companies from cutting their

TABLE 2.4

WORLDWIDE MARKET SHARES, 1998

	Revenues (millions of dollars)	Market Share (%)
U.S. firms		
IBM	8,161.9	27.1
Seagate	5,942.9	19.8
Quantum	3,717.2	12.4
Western Digital	2,871.9	9.5
Maxtor	2,408.2	8.0
Other	45.1	1.0
Total	23,147.2	77.8
Non-U.S. firms		
Fujitsu	3,021.9	10.0
Toshiba	1,848.7	6.1
Samsung	1,077.8	3.6
Hitachi	629.4	2.1
Other	87.5	0.3
Total	6,665.3	22.2
Total	30,075.7	100.0

SOURCE: *Disk/Trend*, 1999.

own production in a timely fashion. The resulting inventory overhangs typically take from one to three quarters to clear, eliminating most HDD profits. An overview of the past fifteen years, with commentary extracted from the business press, gives a flavor of the industry's volatility:

- *1983.* The disk drive market is one of the computer industry's hottest sectors.
- *1984–86.* A computer industry slump translates into a disk drive industry downturn.
- *1988.* A sudden slowdown in computer sales leads to severe price cutting, and three of the industry's leading independent companies (Micropolis, Seagate Technology, and Maxtor) struggle to survive.
- *1990.* After a shakeout in 1988–89, the hard drive market is extremely healthy with good growth prospects.
- *1991.* Worldwide recession leads to a slowdown in disk drive markets. Companies suffer through another quarter or two of what could be the worst time in the industry's history.
- *1992.* Disk drive makers are having a great year.
- *1993.* After last year's surge in demand, disk drive vendors ramped up production. They produced too many drives, however, and the ensuing price war left most companies battered.

And so it goes. Said one industry analyst in 1995, "Over all the years I can only find a one percent net profit in the industry" ("Seagate Is King" 1995). And in 1999 a leading industry analyst described disk drive markets as "chaotic," a "cyclical wasteland" driven by volatile pricing dynamics (Monroe 1999). This periodic bloodletting weeds out firms with insufficient resources to ride out these cycles; table 2.4 shows the survivors as of 1998. Caught in the middle of this competitive maelstrom, American firms have nonetheless maintained a worldwide share of 77.8 percent.

THE PUZZLE OF MANUFACTURING LOCATION

Surviving firms have successfully handled a number of pressures. In response to demanding and volatile markets, technology changes, and intense competition, they have reduced costs and moved technologically sophisticated products quickly to market and volume production. These pressures did not emerge all at once, but they came quickly and intensified over time. The ability to overcome them required strength in both R&D and manufacturing, which is where we encounter the puzzle of location.

The disk drive industry—composed almost entirely of American and Japanese companies for final assembly and its most sophisticated components—spans North America, Asia, and Europe, with some pieces of the production chain in Mexico. Despite this global reach, there are pronounced centers of concentration of two different sorts. Most product innovation and other advanced technology development, pilot production, administration, and marketing are clustered in the United States and Japan. In the United States, the HDD industry is centered in California, Colorado, and Minnesota. In Japan, the industry is clustered close to Tokyo. Today very little assembly and manufacturing remain in these two countries except for technically complex processes and specialized instruments and equipment that enable HDD firms to design and test components, make products, and monitor production.

Outside Japan and the United States, the production of components and their final assembly is also clustered, primarily in Singapore, Thailand, and Malaysia (among U.S. firms) and, more recently, in the Philippines (among the Japanese). There is a considerably smaller cluster in China, with some measurable activity in Europe, mainly in Ireland, Germany, and Hungary.

We can see this concentration of production if we consider the activity of American firms, which in 1998 made almost 80 percent of the world's HDDs. In that year, American firms assembled fewer than 1 percent of their drives in the United States and almost 70 percent in Southeast Asia; in 1985 almost all drives made by U.S. firms were assembled at home. In 1995, 29 percent of the employees who worked for American firms in the HDD value chain worked in the United States; 55 percent worked in Southeast Asia (Gourevitch et al. 2000). If just the three core stages of production are considered—fabrication and assembly of recording heads, production of magnetic disks, and final assembly of disk drives—the share of employment in Asia was even greater and that in America much smaller. One American disk drive company, Seagate Technology, is the largest employer in Thailand and Malaysia and the largest private-sector employer in Singapore. It is also the largest single exporter from China, with almost $1 billion in exports in 1998. Disk drives account for roughly 20 percent of Singapore's exports, and two American disk drive companies, IBM and Seagate, were the largest exporters in Thailand in both 1997 and 1998.

Today the Japanese disk drive industry appears almost as globalized as the American, with most assembly taking place in the Philippines. But such appearances hide crucial differences in both the timing of globalization and the degree to which firms have developed and exploited location-specific assets overseas. American HDD firms were not only much quicker than their Japanese counterparts to shift assembly and manufacturing to Southeast Asia but also embedded their activities more deeply into the fabric of host countries. The American style of globalization was profoundly different from the Japanese, and this has been central to maintaining the U.S. lead in the HDD industry. In part Two, we elaborate this theme, beginning with a model of how globalization—and location more generally—is a key ingredient in acquiring and sustaining competitive advantage.

Part Two

LOCATION AND
COMPETITIVE ADVANTAGE

3 A Theory of Industry Evolution, Location, and Competitive Advantage

The HDD industry is an exception to received wisdom about American industrial competitiveness. Like many industries that emerged in the twentieth century, it was initially dominated by American firms. Unlike the situation in other industries, however, the United States has never relinquished its leadership. Today, U.S. companies hold slightly less than 80 percent of a global market worth more than $30 billion. Luck has nothing to do with continued American dominance. Rather, American competitiveness has been sustained in large part by its early and extensive globalization of production. The establishment and exploitation of location-specific assets has given U.S. firms an evolutionary advantage.

This chapter illustrates the changing links between location and competitive advantage over time, using a basic model that shows where new industries have emerged and the initial sources of competitive leadership. Most entrants have started as single-plant operations, with product development and design generally collocated with production. Within countries, however, industry clusters tend to form, generating agglomeration economies that gradually provide firms with competitive advantages relative to those outside a cluster. During this period, the characteristics of the home base, including its industry clusters, are the single most important locational factor in the competitive advantage of firms.

Industry location, however, is highly dynamic. The benefits of keeping manufacturing operations within an existing cluster at home eventually diminishes relative to other opportunities, and a new locational logic emerges. Firms may decide to grow through geographic expansion, or new organizational or technological innovations may prompt firms to reconsider their existing locations. Competitive pressures may change, forcing firms to relocate production; or adjustments in the external environment, such as trade and foreign investment liberalization abroad, may open up additional locations for investment.

The value of a location thus depends not merely on conditions at one point in time but on a location's ability to continue to meet an industry's changing technological and organizational needs over time. Location-specific assets outside an industry's home base can meet both criteria, thus generating advantages at the industry level and complementing technological resources at home. Some of these advantages, particularly cheaper factor costs and market access, are well known. But we also emphasize three additional advantages: public policies that complement firm-specific assets; the formation of operational clusters, with their agglomeration economies; and international production networks that exploit multiple locations.

As chapter 6 details, Southeast Asia initially offered a combination of low factor costs and generic public policies such as tax holidays and liberal rules governing trade and investment. Over time, foreign investment, economic growth, learning, and changing public policies altered the nature of these locations. Local assets became more sophisticated and encompassed more industry-specific public policies that complemented firm-specific advantages and agglomeration economies. These diverse location-specific assets became linked into regional production networks that exploited the distinct advantages, including agglomeration economies, at each node.

Multinational corporations were central to the development of these location-specific assets. Locations were constituted by the evolving relationship between foreign firms and their local environment. Although domestic factor endowments, public policies, and ultimately political economy (see chapter 10) influence the nature of location-specific assets, none are wholly exogenous to firms' investment decisions. Although MNCs played a critical role in developing agglomeration economies and regional production networks, the surprising pioneers in this global shift were small, young American firms that leveraged these locations for their own benefit and, in the process, became exemplars for the rest of the American industry. By contrast, Japanese HDD firms ignored these early strategic moves for a decade and paid a high price.

But why would firms in the same industry but from different countries size up the competitive situation so differently? The reason, we argue, is that rivalry is socially constructed, and nationality is a powerful factor shaping how firms identify, monitor, and evaluate rivals. To compete successfully, managers must compare their firms with others and identify profitable sources of competitive advantage. These comparisons are embedded in the mental models corporate managers use to identify competitors, summarize their characteristics, and delimit market boundaries (Porac et al. 1995). Because industry competition begins as a highly local struggle, firms are primarily aware of other national competitors. As they global-ize, they initially monitor and respond to the behavior of other national enterprises. As a consequence, international convergence on a best prac-tice or strategy within an industry can take considerable time.

Because our model grew out of research on the evolution of the disk drive industry, readers might question its applicability to other industries. Indeed, location does depend to some extent on idiosyncratic aspects of an industry, the conditions under which it evolved, and the specific pressures and opportunities it faces in the environment. Nevertheless, our approach has wider import for at least two reasons. First, some of the competitive pressures operating in the HDD industry are also visible in other industries. Second, and more important, the logic we outline—of the general processes underlying industry location and the significance of locational decisions for industry and firm performance—can be extended to any industry, even if the nature of significant location-specific assets differ; we return to these themes in more detail in chapter 11.

The Spatial Emergence of Industry

An industry's geographic configuration always reflects some com-bination of firm entry, expansion, relocation, and exit. During an indus-try's early years, the pattern is driven largely by firm entry; but as the industry ages, expansions, relocations, and exits become more responsible for its geographic pattern. The spatial dimensions of industry growth parallel more general processes of industry evolution documented in a large number of industry studies. These studies have identified empirical regularities in the change of the number of firms in an industry over time based on fluctua-tions in firm entry and exit (see Hannan and Freeman 1989, Hannan and Carroll 1992, Klepper 1997, Carroll and Hannan 2000). Firm entry rates rise and then fall with increases in the number of firms in the industry, while exit rates decline and then rise with increases in the number of firms. These processes generate an inverted U-shaped pattern in the number of firms over time. As the number of firms in an industry grows, competition intensi-fies, new entry is deterred, the number of firms peak, exits increase, and the number of firms inevitably falls.[1]

Although initial entrants typically locate in a single country, the indus-try may soon diffuse to other countries. In hard disk drives, for example, Japan entered seven years after the United States, Europe twelve years after. Diffusion of the automobile industry happened even more quickly. Nev-ertheless, even with rapid global spread, competitive environments are likely to remain predominantly local for several years (Hannan et al. 1995, Barnett and McKendrick 1998). An industry's cultural images and technical information about it spread across countries more quickly than does competition, which historically has been constrained by political and physical factors. One implication is that competitive dynamics initially take place within a country, and firms pay more attention to the behavior of domestic competitors than to distant ones.[2] This domestic orientation has important consequences for subsequent global behavior and competitive advantage, an issue we return to at the end of the chapter.

Where does a new industry appear? Clearly, it does not emerge simultaneously in all 188 member states of the United Nations or even 10 percent of them. It is more likely that only a few countries will host the initial entrants; it is even possible that the industry will reside in only one country during its first few years. Several factors determine where a new industry emerges. The availability of necessary information, resources, and social and institutional support to identify and act on technological and economic opportunities varies across countries and affects the likelihood of firm entry. All else being equal, countries that value new venture formation or do not hinder entry into new branches of industry are more likely to be among the early hosts, and a business culture that rewards new economic activity is likely to be among the early entrants. Technological opportunities can also only be exploited by locations with the necessary skills (Nelson 1993, Dosi 1988), which organizations develop through internal efforts and absorption of knowledge from competitors, universities, suppliers, and customers. The character and quality of a firm's external environment and industry context thus have a strong influence on where industry emerges. Technology accumulates and develops in ways that reflect patterns of past technological abilities. New industries become populated by firms—whether *de alio* (from another industry) or *de novo* (new firms)—that are experienced with the technology and the problem to be solved. Since new industries have some grounding in existing ones, their initial location may resemble the patterns of their precursors.

INDUSTRY LOCATION WITHIN COUNTRIES:
CLUSTERING AND AGGLOMERATION ECONOMIES

Historically, industries have shown signs of both geographic dispersion and regional clustering during their early development. In the case of the U.S. automobile industry, for example, firms were widely dispersed (Ellinger 1977), but three clusters appeared early in the industry's development: in New England, the midwest, and the New York City area (Bigelow et al. 1997). Although Silicon Valley became the center for the semiconductor industry, important early entrants (Motorola, Texas Instruments, Philco,

General Electric, Hughes Aircraft, Sylvania) were dispersed across the United States ("Semiconductor Family Tree," July 8, 1968). Similarly, by 1970, HDD entrants were scattered from California to Massachusetts, with some clustered in the San Francisco Bay Area.

As with international diffusion, industry location within a country initially results from entry processes rather than relocations and exits. For de alio entrants, operations are likely to be located at or near an existing business. These firms operate from an established base where they have accumulated knowledge and complementary business assets. Although some entrepreneurs deliberately establish a startup in an advantageous location, new firms usually locate in the region where their founder lives.[3] Similarly, new firms are likely to spring up in the shadow of incumbents. Although the semiconductor industry may be the archetype, with Fairchild Semiconductor spawning a large number of startups in Silicon Valley (Hannan and Freeman 1989, Saxenian 1994), the same is true for software and other sectors. One study, for example, found that more than 50 percent of software startups in Washington State were formed by people previously employed in other software firms in the region (Haug 1991).

Where a firm establishes itself can affect its survival chances (Lomi 1995). In industries that compete nationally or internationally, one or more industrial clusters gradually begin to gain an evolutionary advantage. Not all locations hosting the industry continue to do so; firms residing in a region exit the industry, or the location may not attract additional entrants. Some locations, however, emerge with stronger competitors and also attract new entrants. New firm entry is important to the competitive strength of a cluster because it replenishes the location's knowledge stocks by introducing new technologies and business practices. Silicon Valley's dynamism and longevity is generally attributed to the entrepreneurial spinoff through which new technologies and industries emerged (Freiberger and Swaine 1984, Saxenian 1994, Cringely 1996, Kaplan 1999). Over time, these locations generate agglomeration economies, and isolated firms are more likely to exit, thereby diminishing the number of locations hosting the industry.

Agglomeration, or external, economies are a central part of industrial life and accrue to firms that locate close to one another. As Krugman (1993: 173) writes, "the best evidence for the practical importance of external economies is so obvious that it tends to be overlooked. It is the strong tendency of both economic activity in general and of particular industries or clusters of industries to concentrate in space." They exist when the net benefits of being in a location with other firms increase with the number of firms in the location (Arthur 1986). Under these circumstances, firms from the same industry continue to invest in the same location up to the point where the costs to the collocation of activities exceed the benefits. Companies can thus benefit from the physical proximity of a greater number of companies in the same activity, despite the tendency to think that this situation will create more local competition, drive up input costs, and make it more difficult to retain employees.[4]

Agglomeration economies enable proximate firms to be more innovative, seize opportunities faster, produce at lower cost, and respond to market changes more quickly than firms that are not clustered. Although difficult to measure (Audretsch and Feldman 1996, Hayter 1997), these economies result from any of three elements: a pooled market for workers with specialized skills; specialized intermediate inputs and services; or informational spillovers, including technological ones (Arthur 1986, Krugman 1991, Head et al. 1995, Hayter 1997).

While it is common to assume that the presence of a dense concentration of firms from the same industry is evidence of agglomeration economies, this is not strictly the case. Companies might select the same location for reasons having nothing to do with the presence of similar firms. They may merely have similar needs, such as inexpensive labor or adequate water or power supplies, or may benefit from the same public policies, such as tax breaks that have nothing to do with the presence of other firms in the value chain. Such firms do not form a cluster as we define it since there is no reason to believe that their common presence generates distinct external economies.

THE LOCUS OF INNOVATION AND OPERATIONS

Thus far we have described the geographic location of industry and the benefits of agglomerating without distinguishing among a firm's different activities. But in fact, aggregating tasks misses out on much that is important in the dynamics of location and the globalization process in particular. What tasks are clustered? This is an important but seldom-asked question because different tasks have different locational requirements. It is useful as well as realistic to distinguish between technological activities and operational ones (O'hUallachain 1989).[5] As an industry ages, the two sets of activities begin to have separate locational requirements that lead them to organize into overlapping but distinct geographic configurations.

During an industry's early development, firms are likely to collocate product development and manufacturing. At this point, products and processes are uncertain and undergo extensive experimentation, with products often being made in artisanal ways. At the plant level, producing more units generates experience in the manufacturing process and greater understanding of how to produce additional units even more cheaply—the learning-by-doing phenomenon. Feedback loops between product development and manufacturing can enable a firm to design and produce new products incorporating similar or related technologies at the same location and serve as a strong force to concentrate both sets of activities. These clusters thus become self-reinforcing for both innovation and methods of production, thus increasing their dominance (Pred 1965, Webber 1972). Theoretical models used to characterize the emergence of an industry cluster emphasize increasing returns, path dependence, and cumulative causation (see Arthur 1986, Krugman 1991).

But there is little reason to think that the agglomerative forces enhancing innovation and those making operations more efficient are the same. On the one hand, innovative activity, such as patenting, tends to cluster in places where knowledge spillovers are high (Jaffe et al. 1993, Audretsch and Feldman 1996); proximity facilitates the communication and absorption of highly contextual or uncertain knowledge. On the other hand, "production is remarkably concentrated in space" (Krugman 1991: 5) because economies of scale and lower-cost production are also achieved through clustering. Because these two sets of activities are subject to different locational requirements, they do not need to be in the same place. In fact, no single location may have the requisite assets to satisfy the competitive requirements of both sets of activities as an industry evolves. The skills to design something are not the same as those needed to make it. Silicon Valley is a center of innovation, but it is not a center of volume production. Indeed, over time we expect industries to organize themselves into separate technological and operational clusters.

Technological Clusters. Technological clusters are the collocation of activities that lead to the recognition of new market opportunities, the development of new technologies, and the design of new products.[6] They are places where innovation occurs (Powell and Brantley 1992, Jaffe et al. 1993, Storper 1993, Feldman 1994, Harrison et al. 1996). Technological clusters primarily form at an industry's home base and are perhaps the most long-lived industry locations. Their longevity or durability depends on new firm entry, repeated intra- and interfirm coordination in product design, and technological diffusion.

Although spinoffs contribute to a region's ongoing competitiveness, they do not explain why a firm continues to concentrate technical activity in a location for an extended period of time; one might expect a firm to search for less expensive R&D talent and shift product development work to a lower-cost area. In most industries, however, an enormous amount of tacit knowledge associated with product development makes these technology clusters durable. Especially in knowledge-intensive industries, in which product cycles are short, the overriding challenge is time to market. Firms that do not keep up pay a huge revenue penalty. At the same time, product designers must often make difficult tradeoffs regarding price and performance. Insight into this tradeoff comes with experience—knowing, for instance, how much functionality a firm can put into an integrated circuit and working with different suppliers to understand their capabilities. Thus, firms not only must incorporate new technology into new products but face enormous pressure to design them so they can be made inexpensively and quickly.

The importance of tacit knowledge is evident in two kinds of intra- and interfirm interactions that demonstrate how innovation occurs at the community level. The first involves design coordination between component makers and downstream assemblers. These close engineering-level relationships among stages in the value chain reflect the technical collaboration necessary for a component company to win a design-in for a particular product. Such collaboration involves intensive interaction during the design stages and the design and fabrication of new product prototypes. Recording heads producers, for example, work with disk drive firms to determine the performance characteristics required for heads to be used in a new design and develop customized heads for each program.

The second interaction involves coordination among designers of critical components that are brought together during assembly or subassembly. The commercial usefulness of any single technical advance by a component maker often depends on complementary technical progress by producers of other components. In disk drives, for example, the interaction between head designers and disk designers is important because disk drive storage capacity and performance are largely determined by the magnetic properties and interface of the recording head and disk.

In both kinds of design-to-design coordination, face-to-face interaction is necessary, and short product cycles mean that designers must interact almost continuously in preparation for new product introductions. Whether carried out within the firm or among independent suppliers, design teams in high-tech industries are usually interdisciplinary. In disk drives, they are comprised of chemists, chemical engineers, physicists, materials scientists, and tribologists (who study the head-disk interface and lubrication). The nonroutine but frequent nature of these interactions, combined with the need for highly specialized skills that often require field experience, constrains geographic dispersion of design and development. Thus, many drive designers say that the workers remain the same; they just shift periodically from company to company.

Finally, firms need to keep up with external technology developments, and diffusion of technical knowledge can be especially rapid and effective within industrial clusters. Although geography may not be as large a constraint in technological diffusion as it is in product development, certain kinds of information can be highly localized. "[M]ore rapid (or more complete) diffusion is arguably more likely to occur in places where there is a relatively densely packed community of organizations with shared interests in a particular innovation than in less institutionally rich or densely packed locales" (Harrison et al. 1996: 234).

Operational Clusters. Like many assembled products, disk drive firms make or acquire a wide variety of inputs: recording heads and head subassemblies, disks, motors, and electronics plus various lower value-added components such as base plates, magnets, and clamps. To the extent that the assembly or manufacture of these products is collocated, they constitute operational clusters based on the economies of proximity in input-output relations: lowered transport, logistics and packaging costs, speed of throughput, product changeovers, increasingly specialized process engineering and assembly labor, and economies of scale. Technological clusters are characterized by the development and dissemination of information critical to product innovation. Operational clusters facilitate the dissemination of manufacturing, assembly, or logistics methods as well as information on how to operate in a particular political and legal jurisdiction. Operational clusters may on occasion be sources of new product ideas, but their principal goal is to achieve operational efficiency; any new technologies they create are meant to improve production processes or supply chain management.

Clustering in operations offers several benefits. Indeed, operational clusters are typically what economists have in mind when they define economies of scale as a principal agglomeration externality (Krugman 1991, Paul and Siegel 1999). In this view, clustering facilitates specialization and scale, so that ancillary firms can spread their output across large local customers, and risk pooling, in which a concentration of suppliers constitutes a depot of specialized inputs such as components, services, or labor. Because firms can tap into common pools of labor, materials, and services from both the public and private sectors, assemblers have lower costs if they operate at a location with a large number of suppliers of differentiated inputs (Klimenko 1998). Using second-sourcing strategies, assemblers can drive down prices and obtain supplies in time to meet changing demand; and the development of backward links with suppliers and forward links with customers makes a given location even more attractive (Hoover 1971, Krugman 1991). Clusters of manufacturing operations also facilitate the diffusion of best practice through information spillovers, thereby making plants within the operational cluster more productive than those outside.

TABLE 3.1

UNPACKING AGGLOMERATION ECONOMIES:
CLUSTERS AND THEIR BENEFITS

Technological Clusters	*Operational Clusters*
Early identification of new technological or market opportunities	Lower transportation costs
New technologies or new products or services through greater numbers of start-ups or technological spillovers (e.g., personnel mobility)	Reduced transport time between stages in value chain
	Economies of scale in production
	Faster ramp up in production
Rapid product development (proximity in problem solving)	Pools of specialized labor: process engineers, technicians, procurement managers, experienced assembly workers
Availability of venture capital	
Pools of specialized and heterogeneous labor: programmers, electrical engineers, chemists, physicists, technical marketers, etc. (disk drive designers or servo engineers)	Rapid imitation of innovations in assembly, manufacturing, or logistics
	Monitor quality in supplier manufacturing process
Rapid imitation of product innovations	Lower inventory costs

SOURCE: McKendrick (1998).

Table 3.1 breaks down the different elements underpinning agglomeration economies. Each cluster achieves economies through pools of specialized labor, the proximity of suppliers, and information and technological spillovers; but the specific requirements of technological and operational clusters differ, as do the benefits derived from participating in each.[7]

The Dynamics of Industry Location and Mechanisms of Change

Models and empirical studies of agglomeration typically focus on why clusters persist, and certainly the HDD industry's technological cluster has been remarkably durable. Nevertheless, this approach to collocation and clustering raises a critical question: why would a firm embedded in an attractive operational cluster shift production elsewhere, seemingly forgoing the benefits of agglomeration? If agglomeration arguments have merit, we might have expected both HDD product development and assembly to have remained in Japan and the United States or to dissipate only gradually. As chapter 5 details, however, the HDD industry moved offshore very rapidly—initially to Singapore, later to Thailand and Malaysia, and most recently to the Philippines and China. To understand why, we need to analyze the dynamics of industry location.

So far in our discussion, we have viewed the location of individual firms (if not of the industry as a whole) as static: firms populate a landscape based on a combination of the location of precursor industries, regional skill levels, institutional environment, attraction to the presence of related firms, and the like. Over time, some locations prove more dominant than others, and industrial clusters emerge. But firms also change their location, either through relocations or the addition of new facilities. In their infancy they are attracted to one kind of area and repelled or merely ignorant of another. Over time, their locational preferences may alter. We need to understand at a general level why firms are motivated to exploit multiple locations in the first place and how the changing demands of the industry and investment decisions themselves generate demands for different location-specific assets.

CHANGE IN THE ENVIRONMENT

An industry's environment includes both global technological and regulatory changes as well as developments at specific locations that can be treated as exogenous to the industry. Among the international factors that affect the range of possible investment locations are technological advances in communications and transport, both of which enable greater dispersion of economic activity (Dicken 1998; also see chapter 5), and global and regional agreements that liberalize trade and investment.

Of particular relevance here are characteristics of locations that are subject to change over time. As Kuznets (1966), Chenery (1979), Balassa (1989), and others have pointed out, factor endowments change with the process of economic growth itself. As countries and the regions within them accumulate physical and human capital, the relative prices of these factors change. Thus, a firm that locates a piece of the value chain at one location at one point in time may later find the same location to be too expensive if factor costs rise without a commensurate rise in skills, agglomeration, or other advantages. As a result, a factor that initially was critical in attracting investment and reinvestment to a location can diminish in importance, a dynamic that played an important role in the development of the regional production system in Southeast Asia. MNCs are a central force in contributing to the structural adjustment of locations to technological and managerial changes in the global economy. Similarly, a country's public policies may evolve as a result of learning or political changes. Generic public policies can be transformed into more specialized ones offering greater benefits to industry, or restrictive policies may be liberalized.

While external events can trigger changes in the location of industry, so can an industry's internal dynamics. Although the specifics of these industry dynamics vary in important ways across industries, firm-level growth, technological change, and competitive pressures are the fundamental drivers affecting location decisions.

Firm Growth through Geographic Expansion.   In the spatial emergence of industry and initial clustering, the principal process driving industry location is firm entry, although some clustering results from relocations. But firms also add to their portfolio of locations through their efforts to grow. Firm growth can occur through expansion at an existing location or by licensing intellectual property to others.[8] At some point, however, growth from a single location reaches its limits, and the firm begins to consider growth through expansion into new geographic markets. The horizontal geographic spread of a firm is an important and widespread mechanism of growth (Penrose 1956, Chandler 1990). The geographic expansion of an industry as a whole is simply the aggregation of the decisions of firms to establish additional plants or facilities to serve new markets at lower cost or exploit resources or assets in different locations.

Technological Change.   Another basic influence on industry location is technological change (Markusen 1985), which often changes the basis on which firms compete. Product innovations can alter a firm's calculations about the most efficient place to manufacture or assemble. Miniaturization of a wide range of products, for instance, has changed the economics of location; products that once needed to be manufactured close to their markets can now be shipped over long distances. Product innovations in disk drives have had such an effect: 14-inch drives were large, heavy, and expensive to ship over long distances, while 5.25-inch drives were the size of a shoe box and could be shipped by airfreight at a fraction of the cost per drive; in 2000, the cost of air shipping a 3.5-inch HDD to the United States from Southeast Asia averaged between 1 and 2 percent of the product's cost.

  Product innovations can also change a firm's notions about where it needs to search for knowledge. For example, some research universities are centers of excellence in certain scientific fields, which may attract firms to locate nearby as a means to keep abreast of related technological developments.

  Changes in process technology also influence location decisions (Smith 1981). Improvements in plant-level understanding of manufacturing processes gradually allow the firm (and the industry) to replicate or relocate operations elsewhere, including abroad. At some point, manufacturing proximity to product development becomes less important than do other issues associated with location, such as closer proximity to suppliers or customers or the acquisition of lower-cost inputs (Vernon 1966, Teece 1976).[9] This can also be true when products are not yet standardized: even if product specifications are uncertain and changing, and not always followed in a straightforward way during manufacturing, a firm may nonetheless derive advantages from relocating production.[10] Conversely, the development of new manufacturing technologies, such as automation, not only makes high-wage, high-skill locations more viable but increases the need for proximity of various functions. In many manufacturing industries, tolerances become tighter as the industry matures and learns, so locations that cannot generate comparable improvements in skill level or support services risk losing such activities.

Technological change can thus induce new geographic arrangements. Nevertheless, as we have elaborated in our discussion of technological and operational clusters, it is critical to distinguish its effect among types of activity. In our view, technological change is more likely to lead to changes in the location of operations than in product innovation or design. Although many large U.S. firms engage in R&D overseas, innovation is still overwhelmingly concentrated at home (Patel and Pavitt 1991, Patel and Vega 1999). Product development may be less amenable to locational shift than manufacturing is because its effectiveness may depend on sharing tacit kinds of knowledge, making the product innovation process more difficult to fragment into component pieces. Thus, technological tasks may be stickier than operational ones; and in fact, innovative clusters in disk drives, particularly in California, have persisted long after manufacturing's shift to Southeast Asia.

Changing Competitive Pressures. While technological change introduces a new locational dynamic, so can changes in an industry's competitive pressures. Competition intensifies as the number of firms in an industry approaches its peak and is followed by an industry shakeout. As competitive pressures build, firms search for better ways to achieve performance targets, triggering other firms to engage in their own search in an incremental and self-reinforcing process: adaptation to rivals drives rivals to adapt and so forth.[11]

At the same time, however, every industry has its own competitive ecology with different degrees and kinds of competitive pressure that affect locational preferences. Industries under intense cost pressures, for example, develop a geographic configuration in an attempt to minimize overall costs. Where economies of scale are present, costs are minimized by concentrating production; where they are not, as in many labor-intensive or batch assembly processes, production may be dispersed across multiple locations. The physical characteristics of a product also affect locational preferences. Commodity industries such as cement are under intense cost pressures, but the product must be made where it is consumed because its low value-to-weight ratio makes shipping it costly.

In other industries, cost pressures may be less influential in location decisions; instead, industries may be under pressure to respond to diverse local needs. In general, industries that must respond to local market requirements, such as tailoring products for different tastes or standards, need to operate in more locations than do industries producing more scale-intensive or standardized products. In still other industries, the competitive ecology may be characterized by rapid technological change, which may encourage firms to keep manufacturing proximate to R&D because of the production problems associated with making new products. As industries evolve, some face conflicting pressures of cost *and* differentiation or cost *and* innovation.

As chapter 2 has shown, technological change has always been a competitive driver in the hard disk drive industry. By some measures, the industry has become even more innovative over time: rates of growth in areal density have increased, product cycles have shortened, and the number of new products introduced has increased. At the same time, cost pressures have intensified since the 1980s as computer companies increasingly demand cheaper disk drives. These pressures have made the industry reconsider its locational strategy, including where to locate different pieces of its value chain.

Globalization and Location-Specific Assets

It is impossible to develop a general theory of location that applies to all industries because their locational requirements differ. It is possible to state, however, that the environmental and industry-specific factors just outlined give rise to new locational dynamics over time as firms both exploit new locational opportunities and respond to various technological and competitive changes. Here, we explain the logic of one particular set of location decisions: those having to do with the globalization of manufacturing activities.

Theories of foreign direct investment have long considered location to be an influence on foreign direct investment activity. Scholars in the 1960s, particularly at the Harvard Business School (see Vernon 1966, 1974; and Wells 1972), emphasized locational variables in their work on multinational corporations. Economic theories of foreign direct investment have delineated the advantage of exploiting differing national endowments. In his eclectic theory of foreign investment, John Dunning (1974, 1981, 1993) identified location as one of three equally important variables in explaining foreign direct investment—"one leg of a three-legged stool" along with internalization of economic activity and ownership-specific assets (Dunning 1998: 45). Theories of the firm have similarly linked competitiveness to effective multinational behavior (Penrose 1956, Dunning 1971, Buckley and Casson 1976, Rugman 1981, Teece 1985, Chandler 1990).

Despite these efforts, the importance of location as a variable affecting the global competitiveness of firms has received insufficient attention.[12] When coupled with a firm's home-based assets, however, the location portfolio of firms becomes an important determinant of global competitive position (Dunning 1998). Although researchers applying options theory to the analysis of multinational investments (Kogut 1983, Kogut and Kulatilaka 1994) have come to similar conclusions about how a portfolio of locations may contribute to MNC competitiveness, there has been surprisingly little work on how these locational portfolios develop and shape competitiveness over time.

Studies of national industries or particular regions suffer from more serious weaknesses in their thinking about the influence of location on competitive advantage at the industry level. Comparative studies of industry have been motivated by the consequences of different national factors on international competition—measured, for example, by export performance from the home country (Zysman and Tyson 1983, Dertouzos et al. 1989, Porter 1990, Ahlbrandt et al. 1996, Mowery 1999, Mowery and Nelson 1999). Industry studies of developing countries have, of course, paid significant attention to the role of MNCs in national performance (Evans 1979, 1995; Newfarmer 1980; Grieco 1984; Bennett and Sharpe 1985; Gilpin 1987; Doner 1991; Gereffi 1994). But with few exceptions, the literature on the competitiveness of national industries has generally not considered the role that global investment plays in sustaining or reinforcing industry performance.[13] As we detail in chapter 4, even the most influential and extensive study of industry competitiveness, Michael Porter's *The Competitive Advantage of Nations,* downplays any competitive benefits of foreign investment, a striking lacuna given that whole industries, not just their largest firms, are producing an increasing portion of their value-added overseas (UNCTC 1992, UNCTAD 1997).

Location has also surfaced as a key concept in a growing literature on regions and industrial districts. In general, this research has explored location and its elements in much greater depth than have studies of the MNC (Piore and Sabel 1984; Oakey 1985; Goodman and Bamford 1989; Storper 1989, 1993; Saxenian 1991, 1994; Scott 1993; Appold 1995; Florida and Kenney 1990; Harrison 1992; Markusen 1996). Nevertheless, as we explain in more detail in chapter 4, this literature has suffered from a somewhat different disability. While multinational firms are increasingly at the center of developing and exploiting assets in different locations, much of the literature chooses cases in which multinationals are not relevant, such as crafts-based industries in Italian industrial districts, or ignores altogether the role of MNCs in constituting districts. To the extent that MNCs are seen to play a role, they function merely as branch plants or enclaves with few local ties (Markusen 1996).[14] Even the regional literature that refers to the MNC is restricted because it overlooks the multiregional nature of the international firm and the role that different locations play within a broader network that transcends but incorporates a variety of different regions.

In our view, the international performance of national industries can be improved or preserved through the effective exploitation of overseas locations. Foreign investment can complement an industry's home-base advantages. History offers some evidence that national firms in the same industry make similar foreign investment decisions and as a consequence share similar fates (both positive and negative) relative to competitors from other nations. In his seminal work on technological change, for instance, David Landes (1969) observes that the dyestuffs branch of German chemical industry was in third place behind Britain's and France's in the 1860s but only a decade later held more than 50 percent of the world market, growing to 90 percent by 1900, in part because of aggressive overseas expansion. In general, however, national industrial performance has not been linked explicitly to globalization of operations, and questions remain about its salience.

To make such a link, we begin by reviewing five features of location that can contribute to both firm and industry performance:[15]

- Factor costs
- Market access
- Public policy
- Agglomeration economies in operations
- International industry networks

FACTOR COSTS

Many researchers are beginning to play down the importance of access to generic factors such as low-cost labor in competitive advantage. Much of the world's investment takes place among advanced industrial states, which have similar factor endowments. Rather, specialized factors that tend to be less tradable and subject to imitation are driving investment decisions (Porter 1998).

While agreeing with the overall thrust of this argument and devoting considerable space to it later in the chapter, we believe that some manufacturing foreign direct investment is still motivated by a search for cheap labor and other factors. The search for lower factor costs, particularly for cheap labor, could be expected to disperse economic activity fairly widely across locations with abundant labor, of which there are many. The progressive liberalization of international trade and investment policies over the past twenty years has presented business with an even greater range of locations for labor-intensive activities.

In the disk drive industry, one might expect relatively simple, labor-intensive components to be sourced from a variety of low-wage locations, while more knowledge-intensive work, such as technology development, is scattered across countries where wages for engineers are the lowest. This pattern, however, does not fit the industry's evolution. The offshore movement of firms was initially motivated by cost considerations. But rather than being widely dispersed, assembly is heavily concentrated in a single region, Southeast Asia, and almost absent from locations with comparable or lower labor and land costs such as Latin America or Southeast Asia. Moreover, as costs have risen in certain locations, such as Singapore, firms have maintained and even expanded their presence.

MARKET ACCESS

Improving market access is one of the most compelling and oft-cited reasons to locate production abroad (Dunning 1993). Economists such as Allen Pred (1966) and Raymond Vernon (1966) have long emphasized that a large market can make it profitable to produce goods locally through foreign investment rather than export. Chandler (1990) has similarly observed that historically the large industrial enterprise began to serve large foreign markets through horizontal investments once domestic markets became saturated. Additionally, circumventing import controls has influenced the decision to produce abroad as well as the need to adapt or customize products for the local market.

With the growing liberalization of trade and changes in the cost of communication, logistics, and transport, there is some question about whether market access and proximity to customers will remain a compelling determinant of the location of production.[16] If the search for market access were the principal motivating factor behind foreign investment in disk drives, for example, we would expect assembly to be clustered in the countries assembling the vast majority of the world's computers or the largest consuming markets. Market access had some influence on overseas disk drive assembly during the industry's first twenty years, but its role is almost negligible in shaping contemporary patterns of HDD assembly. The world's largest markets—the United States and Japan—have very little HDD assembly, while Taiwan, also a leader in computer assembly, hosts no disk drive assembly. With a high value-to-weight ratio and with trade barriers falling, disk drives—and many other high-tech commodities—are easily and cheaply shipped by air throughout the world.[17]

PUBLIC POLICY

Public policy shapes the costs facing firms by structuring markets and market incentives. Taxes affect firms' profitability directly, as does the regulatory environment and a host of policies from education to trade and industrial policy. Public policy interventions are typically seen as skewing the geographic division of labor away from a direct factor cost model in one of two ways. First, investment might be drawn to a country by protection and other industrial policies aimed at fostering the local development of the industry; this pattern was visible in the early days of the European Community and in developing countries in the 1960s and 1970s. Second, regulation might be used to attract foreign investment through tax incentives in the context of liberal rules governing investment and trade; such a policy regime would similarly seek to attract investment but on very different terms.

The disk drive story offers little evidence of the first use of regulation. As chapter 10 will show, where such efforts have been tried, they result in either the industry's bypass of the country altogether or abject failure. In contrast, we find substantial evidence of the second sort of industrial policy. Singapore, Malaysia, and Ireland all actively courted the disk drive industry, and liberal trade and investment policies and particularly tax incentives played a powerful role in influencing firms' decisions.

We also find that the countries most successful in attracting and keeping the industry as its technological and other requirements evolved were not those that limited their efforts to arm's-length inducements and an inviting investment climate. In Singapore in particular, public policies evolved to include labor market measures, efforts to promote interfirm links, and targeted interventions aimed at supporting the industry. Other countries' policies supported clustering as well. The policies and programs especially designed to meet the particular competitive requirements of the disk drive industry go a long way to explain its rootedness in Southeast Asia (see chapters 6 and 10).

AGGLOMERATION ECONOMIES IN OPERATIONS

Just as agglomeration economies can emerge in an industry's home base, they can also develop abroad. Although initially they play a small part in an industry's globalization, agglomeration effects in offshore locations can over time complement those at home. Again, distinguishing between technological and operational activities can clarify this connection and reveal underlying relationships between industrial clusters and the global economy. As an industry evolves, it organizes itself into two distinct clusters—one centered around the activities needed to support innovation, the other supporting operations. Although the two clusters may be collocated early in an industry's life, their requirements and pressures differ. As a result, they may eventually possess two distinctly different geographic configurations.

How and where do agglomerations of offshore operations emerge? Some models of geographic clustering underscore the element of uncertainty and accident in location (Arthur 1986, Krugman 1991). Firms enter locations in sequence and choose a location based on the number of other firms already there and some random element. As the number of firms entering increases, one location emerges as the winner, largely because of the choices made by early entrants. In other words, processes of cumulative causation or self-fulfilling expectations lock in the initial pattern, and a spatial equilibrium sets in. Clustering occurs through historical accident, not because of the attributes of a particular location but because of luck.

As Martin (1999) points out, empirical evidence in support of this model is sparse. In fact, given that the dominant location of manufacturing in many industries has changed more than once, spatial equilibria do not appear to emerge (Rauch 1993). Institutions, public policies, local capabilities and infrastructure, and the nature of interfirm relationships all influence where agglomerations emerge in real historical time, how strong they become, and how long they last.

In the disk drive industry, economies associated with the clustering of operations became particularly large in Singapore but also emerged in Thailand and Malaysia. Their preeminence was not due to luck. On the contrary, these locations learned to make increasingly sophisticated disk drives even as competitive pressures mounted in the industry. As we show in chapters 6 and 10, the development of locational assets in these countries—and the ability of the disk drive industry to take advantage of them—was strongly affected by the character of their domestic institutions and public policies.

INTERNATIONAL INDUSTRY NETWORKS

While it is common knowledge that industry networks are important in the management and performance of firms, the concept of networks has been interpreted in various ways. The dominant approach treats them as a mechanism for governing transactions among and within organizations (Oliver and Ebers 1998, Podolny and Page 1998).[18] In this characterization, network forms of governance, as distinct from either the market or an internal hierarchy, can improve firm performance. Examples include the virtual or network firm and intermediate forms of organization such as strategic alliances, joint ventures, consortia, and long-term supply partnerships. In this conception, locational issues are largely irrelevant.[19]

The literature on industrial districts and regional studies reveals a second use of the network concept, adopting some of the language of the governance approach and emphasizing the fuzzy boundaries and repeated exchanges among firms and other organizations, such as trade associations and universities (Pyke et al. 1990, Saxenian 1994, Staber et al. 1996, Grabher and Stark 1997). Unlike the governance approach, this conception has a stronger spatial dimension. Interfirm networks are seen as the building blocks of subnational regional networks that support agglomeration economies. As we have noted, however, while location is a defining part of this view, the industry network is typically analyzed within the context of a relatively self-contained, small area within one nation and consists of small entrepreneurial firms. Thus, this conception is useful in understanding agglomeration economies but does not capture the growth of international production networks.

Our conception of network differs in some important respects from both the governance or the industrial cluster approaches. Like them, we view the industry network as a set of organizations that have developed recurring ties while serving a particular market. In contrast, however, we treat the network as a system of interrelationships that can cross national borders through the operations of leading multinational firms (Hakansson 1987, Dicken 1998). This modification highlights the advantages associated with leveraging the assets of multiple locations.

Just as clusters tend to form around related activities, so do network ties. It is unlikely, for example, that researchers grappling with the principles of magnetism in IBM's Almaden Research Laboratory interact with IBM's assembly facility in Thailand or its suppliers. Rather, they are likely to have much stronger links with university researchers in Silicon Valley or abroad. As with clusters, it is helpful to differentiate innovation networks, wherein the information exchanges are directed at technology creation, from production networks, which involve the exchange of goods and information directed at efficiency and quality of production. Given that international innovation networks are relatively thin in the drive industry, we concentrate primarily on international production networks.[20]

Governance and coordination in networks are largely performed by a cohort of multinational firms whose central feature is ownership of cross-border, value-adding activities. Governance in such systems can take a variety of forms, from vertically integrated firms coordinating the activities of some locations to arm's-length relationships with independent suppliers. Yet in either case, the MNC plays a distinctive part at the apex of the system. As we will see, local MNC managers and suppliers assume a coordinating role in these networks but function largely as an extension of MNC boundaries rather than as "a genuine spread of authority" (Amin and Thrift 1992: 575). With imperfect competition, the MNC is likely to be a more efficient coordinator of resources and capabilities than arm's-length markets are (Caves 1996) and is in a better position to both develop and leverage location-specific assets than purely domestic firms are. Because the MNC is likely to employ leading-edge organizational and technological processes, it is apt to be the prime source of spillovers to other firms, including backward links to suppliers and subcontractors.[21]

Our approach also stresses a different level of analysis. As we have seen, while research on industrial districts and clusters emphasizes the importance of location in industry advantage, its analytic focus is on a network operating within a subnational region or district—a boundary that is almost always artificial. In contrast, we focus on networks that operate across national borders and argue that their advantages accrue not only to the firm but to the national industry as well. In other words, when a national industry collectively engages in foreign investment, the benefits of networking that arise from coordination among multiple locations apply collectively to the industry level.[22]

Specifically, we see three benefits to an industry of an international network. First, the *locational heterogeneity* of international networks generates advantages by integrating different locations, each of which exploits the benefits of specialization. In disk drives, for example, one location can specialize in design of desktop drives, another in drives for notebook computers, still another will manufacture desktop drives, and a fourth will make notebook drives. Each separate location offers different capabilities to meet market requirements; overall, however, the industry benefits from the locational heterogeneity of the network.

Second, most organizational scholars and sociologists emphasize that *learning* is often the main benefit of the network form of organization, which encourages participating firms to acquire new skills or knowledge (Dore 1983, Powell 1990, Uzzi 1997, Podolny and Page 1998). This reasoning can be extended to the operations of the multinational firm. By increasing the diversity of knowledge sources, networks generate advantages that cannot emerge from locations in a single nation. For instance, an American firm might establish an R&D facility in Japan or Germany and thus tap into knowledge that differs from what is being generated in its U.S. facility. A company might establish manufacturing operations in Japan as a way to learn more advanced process engineering or just-in-time manufacturing systems; subsequently, the firm diffuses the innovation to other factories.

Third, *flexibility* is a network-level benefit that allows firms to reallocate resources quickly and smoothly in response to changing market conditions (Buckley and Casson 1998). The sustained increase in volatility in the international environment has led companies to search for more flexible ways to manage global operations. One solution is to create redundancy in operations. An MNC may operate a network of plants in different countries, substituting various sources of supply in response to short-term exchange rate movements, labor strikes, or other environmental shocks such as the devastating earthquake in Taiwan that interrupted the worldwide computer supply chain. Just as an MNC gains operational flexibility or redundancy through the location of subsidiaries (Kogut and Kulatilaka 1994), so does an international network provide an industry with the opportunity to coordinate plants flexibly across borders. An industry can mitigate some of its operating risk by creating geographic redundancy across various stages of production, thus increasing or decreasing production in specific locations depending on changing requirements. The production network implies the existence of multiple sources of information, components, and other capabilities that redound to the benefit of the industry as a whole.

Network Tradeoffs and the Role of Proximity.   Each of these international network benefits comes at some cost. In the concept of network as we have defined it—the knitting together of diverse locations across borders—greater locational heterogeneity, diversity of knowledge sources, and flexibility imply more locations and thus greater geographic dispersion, which in turn implies higher coordination costs.

As an illustration, consider the importance of speed in production networks. One of the largest competitive challenges faced by firms and industry is speed of execution at competitive costs. Better information flow and improved coordination of resources among network members can generate savings in cost and time. But the importance of speed in international competition implies that the geographic spread of the network should in fact be minimized. Geographic dispersion in the value chain can slow lead times, product ramp-up, and throughput. Speed in general is facilitated when stages of production are adjacent. Ease of transport to and from all the locations employed at the adjacent stage maximizes speed, as do exchanges conducted among people who share a language and culture. Thus, the requirement for speed should tend to concentrate activity at locations that have particular advantages in that respect—one reason why economic activity can be geographically dispersed yet concentrated in locations that are relatively sticky even if their costs appear higher.

Clearly, there are network tradeoffs; and a balance must be struck between too much and too little locational heterogeneity, learning, and flexibility in both types of networks. One way of solving this problem and achieving a balance is to develop networks in geographically proximate clusters of countries. Proximity reduces the time involved in managerial oversight, facilitates rapid resource exchanges, and lowers transportation and coordination costs. This may be more desirable, however, in production networks, in which transportation, production, and coordination costs are relatively high, than in innovation networks, although the richness of information content sometimes requires face-to-face interaction (Frohlich and Oppenheimer 1998).

This is precisely the pattern of the disk drive industry, in which a number of discrete operational clusters are tied into geographically proximate networks in Southeast Asia. As chapters 6 through 9 detail, Singapore, Thailand, and Malaysia, and more recently China and the Philippines, have offered complementary yet relatively proximate locational assets that the major HDD firms have tied together and leveraged into a network that serves the industry's need for low costs, flexibility, and rapid ramp-up. We call this geographic configuration a *regional production system*.

THE CO-EVOLUTION OF INDUSTRY
REQUIREMENTS AND LOCATIONAL ASSETS

The investments of American HDD firms in Southeast Asia have not only transformed the geography of the industry but completely altered the kinds of assets leveraged at each location. While cheap labor and tax benefits offered the initial impetus for American investment, they did not remain the primary contribution to U.S. competitiveness. Constantly chasing cheaper factors would have nullified any initial advantage, as Porter (1990, 1998) has observed. But American firms reinvested in the region, stimulated the formation and growth of local suppliers, and created strong operational clusters that complemented the technological clusters at home. Although public policy played an important complementary role, American MNCs were the central force behind the construction of the HDD industry in Southeast Asia.

Industry competition—and thus its manufacturing requirements—has gone through three phases since 1980, when the first desktop disk drive was produced. During each period, the industry's competitive requirements became more demanding. Table 3.2 summarizes these changing competitive dynamics, the role of Southeast Asia in drive assembly, and the precise locational assets the region provided to American firms.

TABLE 3.2

DYNAMICS OF INDUSTRY LOCATION AND BENEFITS: THE HDD INDUSTRY IN SOUTHEAST ASIA

Period	Competitive Pressures	Southeast Asia's Role in Disk Drive Assembly	Country-Specific Assets			Regional Production System
			Singapore	Thailand	Malaysia	
1980–1985	Cost	Produce new product in the United States Transfer mature product to Singapore	Labor costs Generic incentives Non-industry-specific infrastructure Preexisting managerial and technical personnel	Labor costs Generic incentives Proximity to Singapore	—	Modest heterogeneity benefits
1986–1992	Cost Time-to-market	Ramp new product in the United States, transfer to Singapore for volume production after process has been stabilized Mature product later transferred from Singapore to Thailand and Malaysia	Moderate agglomeration effects (specialized labor, intermediate inputs) Some industry-specific incentives Generic incentives	Preexisting managerial and technical personnel Labor costs Proximity to Singapore	Preexisting managerial and technical personnel Labor costs Proximity to Singapore	Strong heterogeneity benefits Moderate flexibility benefits
1993–present	Cost Time-to-market Time-to-volume Yield improvement	Pilot production in the United States, products transferred directly from the United States to Southeast Asia for ramp	Strong agglomeration effects (specialized labor, intermediate inputs, technological spillovers) Strong industry-specific incentives Proximity to Thailand and Malaysia Generic incentives	Generic incentives Moderate agglomeration effects (specialized labor; intermediate inputs) Proximity to Singapore and Malaysia Labor costs	Generic incentives Moderate agglomeration effects (specialized labor; intermediate inputs) Proximity to Singapore and Thailand Labor costs	Strong heterogeneity benefits Moderate flexibility benefits

During the first phase (1980–85), the industry was obsessed with cutting costs, largely by squeezing labor rates and reducing tax liabilities. Disk drive quality was not as high as it is today, and firms could realize considerable savings from having lower-paid employees rework defective drives. In addition, firms began to squeeze costs out of their components by developing a set of indigenous suppliers for making relatively basic parts. Most industry activity was concentrated in Singapore, with Thailand beginning to host the most laborious tasks and feeding the output back to Singapore.

Competition intensified in the second phase (1986–92) as the desktop disk drive became a more common feature of personal computers. Cost pressures remained a central competitive driver, but firms also began to compete more vigorously to get design wins with computer manufacturers, which required faster time to market. In 1986 exits began to exceed entries into the HDD industry; a dramatic shakeout had begun, driven by a combination of cost and time-to-market pressures. While original equipment manufacturers (OEMs) such as IBM and Apple were important disk drive customers during the first phase, only 25 percent of desktop computers came equipped with hard drives; the add-on market (in which consumers buy drives directly from dealers) was a larger part of the business. In contrast, during the second phase, large OEMs assumed a greater role. Virtually all 32-bit computers (for example, Apple's MacII and Compaq's DeskPro 386) had hard drives, and disk drive firms began to focus much more on selling disk drives directly to these OEMs. Unlike dealers, OEMs generally required state-of-the-art products and imposed more demanding time-to-market cycles on HDD firms as well as thinner profit margins.[23]

Rather than shifting production to even lower-wage locations in response to these new pressures, American firms reinforced their commitment to Southeast Asia as their subsidiaries and suppliers learned how to meet these requirements efficiently. Singapore began to generate some agglomeration economies, while Thailand and Malaysia offered U.S. firms an increasingly skilled technical labor force for doing more sophisticated subassemblies. The three countries together represented an interdependent system, with most drives being assembled in Singapore, which was fed by subassemblies from its neighbors. Proximity to Singapore minimized coordination and transportation costs.

The most recent phase, roughly beginning in 1993, finds firms in the industry competing along multiple dimensions: unrelenting pressure on costs, time to market, as well as time to volume and yield improvement. Manufacturers compete for contracts with even fewer major customers such as Compaq, Dell, Hewlett-Packard, and Apple. Economies of scale have became even more critical, along with better quality control, faster ramp (o–2 million drives in a quarter for one product, with larger firms offering several products concurrently), and better control over the supply chain. Profit margins increasingly depend on achieving high manufacturing yields and uninterrupted access to high-quality components.

During this phase, the U.S. HDD industry has developed operational clusters in all three Southeast Asian countries, each generating at least moderate agglomeration economies. Singapore continues to stand apart: it produces the highest-performance disk drives, has the deepest process engineering skills, hosts the most suppliers, and offers the strongest institutional base. By the time the Japanese HDD firms copied this strategy by developing their own production system centered on the Philippines, they had merely preserved their small share of the worldwide market.

In sum, Southeast Asian operational clusters and their integration into a production system have emerged to complement U.S.-based technology development. Product innovation usually grabs most of the credit for industrial leadership, but manufacturing programs must also be capable of rapid change to new products with fast, smoothly executed production ramps. The U.S. disk drive industry has developed strong operational assets in Southeast Asia with the ability to evolve quickly to new products. As much as product innovation, this regional production system has sustained American industrial leadership in disk drives.

Location and National Differences in Industrial Competitiveness

Clearly, the American disk drive industry implemented an incredibly effective locational strategy and reaped the corresponding benefits. But why did the Japanese industry take so long to imitate that strategy? We argue that firms in a given industry in one nation behave differently from their foreign competitors, which can lead to different competitive outcomes. So why do these firms respond differently to the same environmental, technological, and competitive changes?

We believe that an industry's competitive dynamics are shaped by both the strategic focus of firms in an industry and the mental models they develop to interpret and make sense of the competitive environment. Typically, a new locational strategy will be pioneered by only a small set of national firms sharing some similar characteristics. Through processes of competitive mimicry, firms from the same nation initially adopt similar global strategies (in our case, overseas assembly); but over time the industry as a whole converges on the same strategy. By contrast, late adopters are likely to share similar characteristics regardless of nationality; in hard disk drives they were larger, older, and more diversified firms. As a result, first-mover advantages apply both to the firms that pioneer the new location strategy and the national industry of which they are a part.

What explains such mimetic behavior? One important mechanism that motivates mimicry and appears to account for the early and rapid shift of the American disk drive industry to Southeast Asia is observational learning of salient competitors. As one industry pioneer told us, "everybody follows everybody in our industry."[24] Observational learning explains why imitation within industries takes place even when it is unclear whether there is any communication among the adopters or when the sources of information are diffuse (Greve 1995).

Which firms are salient to others? The answer is not simply the best performers; social aspects of organizational life and mental models also determine the patterns of mimicry (Porac et al. 1989, Porac et al. 1995, Nath and Gruca 1997, Greve 1998). When making decisions, managers group organizations that are similar along important dimensions (such as size, sales growth, or products offered), monitor these organizations (Porac et al. 1995, Greve 1998), and define unique product positions in relation to them.[25] Indeed, organizations are likely to mimic only their salient competitors because of overreliance on information about them (Porac et al. 1989, Greve 1996).[26]

Nationality—even regional proximity—also shapes mental models and determines which firms are salient. A variety of empirical evidence suggests cross-national differences in the direction and timing of foreign investment. National level data on outward foreign investment show that firms from the same country tend to invest in neighboring countries or in those with which they have close political or cultural ties (UN 1993). For instance, Davidson (1980) found that 30 percent of American foreign investment before 1975 went to the culturally similar countries of Canada, Great Britain, and Australia. Bartlett and Ghoshal (1989) have also noted the persistence of national characteristics in the global strategies of firms in the same industry. Hu (1995) contends that differences among national qualities are likely to be more important than are differences among firms based in the same country; thus, national advantages usually outweigh firm-specific ones.

These findings suggest that strategic behavior cannot be explained entirely by reference to technological and economic factors; in response to pressures for locational change, firms in the same industry but from different countries will behave differently. Managerial ideologies, cultural norms, or historical residues limit the repertoire of an organization's choices and channel behavior. Therefore, as a nation's firms begin to extend their operations internationally, they carry with them national business practices and principles (Dunning 1993, Kogut 1993).

Behavioral differences in internationalization can have competitive consequences. In the first stage, global strategy favors one nation's firms over others. While imitation of the "right" strategy is an obvious way for competitors to undermine an initial advantage, inherited organizational structures, practices, and relationships constrain their ability to adopt superior practices quickly. Because these kinds of practices are difficult to observe directly or are strongly interdependent with other routines, they take much longer to diffuse across national borders than do more observable phenomena such as product innovations (Armour and Teece 1978, Kogut 1991). The result can be differences in timing and direction of strategic action: one nation's industry develops a more effective strategy relative to its competitors from another nation. Because of factors such as agglomeration economies and the development of networks, those advantages can be difficult for second movers to match.

This is precisely what we observe in the disk drive industry. As we explain in chapter 5, not only did the American industry globalize extensively, it did so much earlier than its Japanese competitors. The firms that led the shift abroad were similar along several dimensions: they made the same kinds of disk drives, were of similar size and age, and often came from California. Close geographic proximity and a shared strategic focus tended to heighten their awareness of each other, while the business press and financial analysts began to associate Southeast Asian production with success and came to expect American HDD firms to conform with that industry model.

By contrast, Japanese firms appeared to follow a different competitive logic. Not until the mid-1990s did the surviving Japanese firms copy the U.S. location strategy. Conversations with Japanese managers and a reading of the business press suggest three reasons for this late response. First, although aware of the U.S. move offshore, Japanese managers not did not necessarily consider the U.S. pioneers to be viable competitors; it took a few years before Seagate and other new American disk drive firms began to be salient to the Japanese. Rather, key strategists in Japanese firms identified other Japanese HDD firms as their immediate rivals. Second, Japanese industry continued to follow a model that emphasized the importance of producing close to the customer. In fact, several firms began to produce drives in the United States at the same time U.S. firms were moving production to Southeast Asia. While this logic might have been compelling in the era of large-diameter disk drives, it was completely inappropriate for the production of desktop disk drives. Finally, Japanese managers also had a sense that souring U.S.-Japan trade relations might lead to the establishment of trade barriers against Japanese disk drives; as in other industries, Japanese production in the United States was thought to mitigate that threat.

The American HDD industry thus maintained its leadership position by being first to shift assembly offshore to lower-cost locations, where it quickly constituted operational clusters and cross-border networks that leveraged the location-specific assets of Singapore, Malaysia, and Thailand. Although American firms have not generally been known for their manufacturing capabilities, the location-specific assets that U.S. disk drive companies developed in Southeast Asia enabled them to dominate the low-margin, high-volume segments—the price and capacity points most in demand by users of personal computers. But to demonstrate the hypothesized link between location and competitiveness, particularly between the United States and Japan, it is first necessary to consider other explanations of national competitiveness.

4 Alternative Explanations for Industry Advantage

The role of location in the competitive performance of national industries in international markets has received considerably less attention than have other explanations, especially those focusing on interfirm relationships, intrafirm organization, industrial policy, and innovation (Dertouzos et al. 1989, Porter 1990, Hollingsworth et al. 1994, Ahlbrandt et al. 1996, Mowery 1999, Mowery and Nelson 1999). These studies have advanced our understanding of the factors shaping industrial evolution and leadership, especially when compared with traditional explanations centering on comparative advantage and national factor endowments (Nelson 1996). Yet any perspective that neglects the globalization of manufacturing cannot offer an overarching explanation of industry advantage. Most internationally competitive industries are now globalized, led by multinational enterprises with a range of overseas assets. Certainly, globalization is not the only, or even the most important, variable contributing to international competitive advantage; but any theory that ignores it is seriously incomplete.

Nevertheless, testing alternative perspectives on the competitiveness of specific industries is problematic, raising a number of issues of commensurability. Research has been conducted at the firm, industry, and sector levels as well as at different levels of spatial aggregation such as the subnational region and nation. National advantage is sometimes cast in terms of the performance of an industry or a sector (for example, "the Japanese consumer electronics industry is competitive," "the U.S. computer industry is the leader," "U.S. high-technology sectors dominate European high-technology sectors"), sometimes in terms of firms ("U.S. firms are more innovative than European firms," "Toyota is more productive than Ford"), and sometimes in terms of regions ("Silicon Valley is more entrepreneurial and innovative than other subnational regions are"). Measures of competitiveness naturally differ depending on the unit chosen: the performance of regions and nations are measured by wage rates or growth, while profitability, labor productivity, market share, or survival rate are more relevant for firms and industries.

Despite these inconsistencies, each theoretical perspective should offer at least an implicit explanation for national competitive position at the industry level. We divide these competing explanations into five categories—first-mover advantage, national characteristics, industrial organization, innovativeness, and industrial policy—and focus on how each explains the position of American firms vis-à-vis their Japanese rivals. Does American dominance in disk drives result from its first-mover advantage relative to its foreign competitors? From its distinct embeddedness in its home market? From greater or lesser degrees of vertical integration in the core stages of production and distribution? From its superior innovativeness? From a more supportive set of industrial policies? Although each explanation has merit in other contexts, none accounts for the nation's almost forty-five-year dominance in the disk drive industry. Rather, as chapter 5 elaborates, globalization has been a critical and underappreciated factor in maintaining American competitiveness in the industry, and we suspect that it is important in other industries as well.

Industry Life Cycles and National Embeddedness

The first-mover advantages associated with industry life cycles and the national bases for competitive advantage are two central and related explanations for industrial success. Neither, however, effectively accounts for the sustained competitiveness of the American disk drive industry.

FIRST-MOVER ADVANTAGE: INDUSTRY AND PRODUCT LIFE CYCLES

Many scholars attribute both firm and industry competitive advantage to first-mover advantages. Two life cycle models have been developed to explain how competitive advantage is created and maintained—one for industries, the other for firms. The two are related, but the distinction between them is not always explicit. Researchers often use the terms *industry* and *product* interchangeably, although they are very different units of analysis.[1]

The product life cycle theory of foreign direct investment, introduced by Raymond Vernon (1966) and extended by several of his colleagues (such as Wells 1972), identified three stages in a product's life: an early stage, a maturing product, and a mature product in an advanced stage of standardization. The model's essential prediction is that while the newest and most innovative products are made at home, the manufacture of products embodying older technology tends to shift abroad. During the initial stages of a product's life, the innovator has a monopoly position and faces little pressure to produce in lower-cost locations. As demand grows abroad, the innovator initially serves foreign markets through exporting and later initiates foreign production. Eventually, foreign competitors are able successfully to imitate these mature products. But as long as the innovator (the United States, in Vernon's depiction) continues to bring out new products at the home base, it can maintain its leadership in a specific industry over time.

Although Vernon (1979) later repudiated most features of this model, it has had tremendous staying power.[2] During the exploratory stage, the market grows rapidly, many firms enter, and product innovation is fundamental. Output growth is still high during an intermediate stage; but entry slows, existing producers experience a shakeout, product innovation declines, and production processes become better understood. The mature stage signals considerable slowing in output growth, entry declines even further, market share stabilizes, innovations are less significant, and marketing and manufacturing techniques become more refined. A key finding is that the first entrants capture the greatest share of the market and earn the greatest return (Klepper 1996).

For our purposes, these models raise two questions. One is whether their stylized characterization fits the evolution of the disk drive industry; the other is whether they explain competitive advantage. Unfortunately, the product life cycle model does not capture the history of the disk drive industry very well, where innovation has in fact accelerated during the past decade. As chapter 2 showed, component technology introduced in 1991 increased disk storage capacity (areal density) to a 60 percent annual growth rate from a historical rate of just under 40 percent; and from 1997 to 1999 it grew at a rate of more than 100 percent. In addition, product life cycles have gotten even shorter, less than nine months for some products. As Vernon (1979) was among the first to recognize, shortening product life cycles lend a certain quaintness to the long maturation period for products specified in the earlier model. In addition, disk drives are now directly ramped up in overseas locations; there really is no home-based manufacture for even the newest and most innovative products.

The second issue is the ability of such models to explain industry competitiveness. The original product life cycle model was intended to explain why the United States was the leader in so many industries. But as it evolved, the theory came to represent a story about first-mover advantage: nations and firms that are early entrants derive an initial and sustainable advantage through strong path dependencies and increasing returns (Klepper 1996, 1997; Nelson 1996; Krugman 1991). The model typically stops at the point where foreign competition enters the picture, but its proponents generally adopt the view that industry dominance starts to erode once it begins to face significant challenges from foreign competitors (Klepper 1997). The decline in leadership seemed to fit a large number of American industries: automobiles, steel, professional and scientific instruments, consumer electronics, and telecommunications (Nelson and Wright 1994, Nelson 1996).

Although life cycle models do not fully specify the conditions under which a leader becomes a follower, the disk drive industry appears to fit the story of a first-mover who is grabbing an advantage, at least during the early stages. But the industry has confounded the prediction that a foreign challenge or a shift in location necessarily undercuts industrial leadership. American disk drive companies maintained their leadership in the face of challenges from Japanese producers dating to the 1980s. Moreover, the U.S. industry's collective shift of assembly to Southeast Asia was not evidence of industrial decline; on the contrary, that shift sustained rather than undercut American dominance.

NATIONAL AND REGIONAL FOUNDATIONS OF COMPETITIVENESS

With its focus on the characteristics of a nation's or subnational region's economic system, the literature on industrial districts and clusters pays explicit attention to the role of location in competitiveness. Both Michael Porter (1990, 1998) and the research of industrial sociologists and regional scientists on industrial districts emphasize that competitive advantage is created and sustained through a highly localized process of accumulating skills and technologies. Both streams of research have identified critical processes at work behind industry competitiveness. But their geographic scope is unnecessarily narrow and typically misses the international setting in which regions are nested.

Porter (1990) argues that the home base is an industry's principal source of competitive advantage. Internationally competitive industries are based in only a few nations, and "most successful national industries comprise groups of firms, not isolated participants" (10). Four interrelated features of the home nation affect the international success of national industry: factor endowments; demand conditions; supporting industries; and firm strategy, structure, and rivalry. These factors create the context within which a nation's firms emerge and compete, and nations succeed in particular industries because their home environment is the most conducive for accumulating and upgrading skills over time.

While Porter emphasizes the national sources of industrial competitiveness, regional scientists and industrial sociologists have located the elements of industrial success in subnational regions or industrial districts (Piore and Sabel 1984, Sforzi 1989, Best 1990, Storper 1993, Saxenian 1994, Markusen 1996, Paniccia 1998). Industrial sociologists emphasize that once new industries emerge in particular places, industrial expansion is likely to be confined to the original or neighboring sites (Harrison et al. 1996). Socially and politically embedded networks of cooperation among small and medium-sized enterprises, based on a heritage of skills and capabilities, can help industries compete successfully in national and international markets. Local production systems show that even traditional industries can find niches in a ruthlessly competitive world. Firms in parts of Germany, Italy, and Silicon Valley tend to draw on local knowledge and relationships to create new markets, products, and applications. Interorganizational cooperation and trust in these locales appear more efficient than do arm's-length transactions and more flexible than what we find in large organizations.

According to both Porter and the industrial sociologists, competitiveness derives from national or subnational embeddedness and relationships among organizations in an industry or related cluster of industries. Both approaches implicitly discount the benefits to industry of operating internationally. While Porter clearly acknowledges that multinationality can be an important ingredient in industry competitiveness (1990: 53–67), his case studies emphasize the importance of home-based advantages and largely ignore industry's development and exploitation of overseas locations.[3] More recently, Porter (1998: 11) has addressed globalization explicitly—largely to dismiss it:

It has been widely recognized that changes in technology and competition have diminished many of the traditional roles of location. Resources, capital, and other inputs can be efficiently sourced in global markets. Firms can access immobile inputs via corporate networks. It is no longer necessary to locate near large markets.

It is natural, perhaps, that the first response to globalization was to pursue these benefits by shifting activities to low cost locations. However, anything that can be efficiently sourced from a distance has been essentially nullified as a competitive advantage in advanced economies. Global sourcing mitigates disadvantages but does not create advantages. Moreover, global sourcing is normally a second-best solution compared to a cluster.

Although there is little doubt about the importance of an industry's home region and nation and the power of industrial clustering, this emphasis on the national bases of advantage is unnecessarily restrictive. It also ignores the dynamic quality of location. Locations can be developed and leveraged, and both low- and rising-cost locations can be developed into important competitive assets. In fact, leveraging locational assets outside the home base can be critical not only to sustaining the initial advantages conferred by a favorable home base but to offsetting unfavorable trends in the home base, such as rising costs, as international competition intensifies.

FIRST-MOVER ADVANTAGE AND EMBEDDEDNESS RECONSIDERED: EVIDENCE FROM DISK DRIVES

It is one thing to describe the analytic limitations of these perspectives but quite another to offer empirical evidence on the relative significance of first-mover advantages and local embeddedness for American leadership. Nevertheless, an analysis of the ties between disk drives and computers can underscore the limitations of these perspectives.

One possible explanation for the success of the American HDD industry that fits with the home base and first-mover models is American success in the computer industry. At first glance, this explanation seems reasonable. When IBM shipped the first rigid disk drive to a customer in 1956, the United States was already the world's dominant computer producer and exporter. Although Europe contributed enormously to the technical development of the early computer industry, American firms led the world in computer installations; and many of these same companies developed their own hard disk drives. General Electric, Control Data, Burroughs, and Digital Equipment followed IBM's entry into hard disk drives in the 1960s and 1970s. Some independent companies, such as Bryant Computer Products and Data Products, also emerged in the early 1960s to develop disk drives for sale to computer manufacturers that had not yet made their own—notably Sylvania, RCA, Honeywell, and Univac. In the late 1960s, after IBM had secured its position as the dominant mainframe maker, a new wave of independent companies emerged to make disk drives that were plug-compatible with IBM systems: Memorex, Potter Instrument, Marshall Data Systems, and Information Storage Systems. Without incurring IBM's R&D expenses, the plug-compatible companies were able to offer disk drives identical to or better than IBM's at a much lower price. Plug compatibility was not limited to IBM systems but extended to those made by other computer manufacturers as well.

A parallel trend was evident in Japan and Europe, although on a smaller scale. In Japan, the principal computer companies made their own disk drives: NEC, Fujitsu, Hitachi, and Toshiba all entered in the mid to late 1960s. Only in the 1970s did Japanese companies attempt to market disk drives to non-Japanese customers in the U.S. market; until then the size of the market for Japanese computers limited the market for their disk drives. A smaller domestic market also meant that fewer independent Japanese disk drive companies (namely, Hokushin Electric Works) entered in the 1970s as alternative sources of supply.

In Europe, Siemens and Philips made disk drives for their own computer systems, while BASF produced for the OEM market. Data Recording Instruments (DRI) and Sperac, a French maker of peripherals, which later merged into Compagnie Internationale pour l'Informatique, did both OEM and captive production.[4] In Eastern Europe, COMECON designated DZU of Bulgaria as the principal disk drive supplier for all computers in the region, and it became the most vertically integrated producer in the world. Only in rare cases did European disk drives find their way into American or Japanese computer systems.

Thus, throughout the 1960s and 1970s, the relative positions of the U.S., Japanese, and European disk drive industries could be explained by the market share of their respective national computer industries, which were their primary customers.[5] During the 1970s, captive production remained the largest channel for disk drives, although the relative importance of the original equipment market grew. Led by Control Data, Diablo Systems, CalComp, and Memorex, the OEM segment reached $631 million in 1979, still well below the $2.8 billion associated with captive production (*Disk/Trend* 1980). In 1979, American firms had 81.1 percent of the global HDD market, Japan 14.3 percent, and Europe the remainder. Between them, IBM and Control Data controlled 30 percent of the market.

Up to this point the story conforms to an explanation of competitive advantage through domestic demand, increasing returns, and path dependence: the large U.S. market for mainframe computers, and later minicomputers, gave American disk drive firms an unassailable long-term advantage. But it does not account for the divergence in the fortunes of the American disk drive and computer industries after 1980, when both came under greater global competitive pressures.

A watershed event was the 1981 debut of the IBM PC, the dominant design in the industry for many years (Langlois 1992, Anderson 1995). In addition to setting the standard for what a desktop computer should look like, it featured an open architecture that attracted the entry of not only some of IBM's established mainframe and minicomputer rivals but de novo startups that set out to manufacture IBM clones. Although Compaq and Dell were two of the most important American entrants, many of the new clone makers emerged outside the United States, especially in Taiwan, Korea, and Japan. Daewoo, Epson, Hyundai, Acer, and scores of smaller companies collectively dispersed the production of computers. As a result, the global market share of U.S. computer makers steadily eroded during the 1980s and early 1990s. Whereas U.S. firms held an estimated 88 percent of the worldwide computer market in 1983, their share fell to about 56 percent by 1992 (including mainframes). Over the same period Japanese market share in the industry increased from 8 to 30 percent.[6]

The same open architecture that attracted the new clone manufacturers stimulated entry into peripheral equipment. Whereas mainframe and minicomputer manufacturers made many of their own peripherals and components, the assemblers of personal computers outsourced almost all of their production. Even more dramatically, Japanese, Korean, and Taiwanese producers of keyboards, floppy disk drives, monitors, DRAMs, and motherboards displaced U.S. firms as market leaders in peripherals and components. The Japanese also led in a related data storage technology—optical disk drives (CD-ROM, DVD-ROM, and CD/DVD writable drives), a $7 billion market of which the United States has a less than 1 percent share.

Given these trends and the development of national clusters of computer-related capabilities in these countries, one might have expected Asian countries and their companies to erode the American position in hard disk drives. After all, much the same competitive dynamics faced the HDD industry as it sold drives to the PC industry. Disk drive firms are subject to intense cost pressures, and there was considerable entry from Japanese, Korean, and Taiwanese firms as well as a few from Europe. Between 1980 and 1998, nearly one hundred new entrants exploded into the market, resulting in intense competition and shakeouts. By 1996 fewer firms were making disk drives than at any time during the previous twenty years (see figure 2.4). The HDD landscape was littered with the graves of once prominent American companies—Priam, PrairieTek, Conner Peripherals, MiniStor, and Hewlett-Packard, all of them leaders at one time or another in certain market segments or technologies.

But while most of the rest of the American computer peripherals industry largely vanished during this period, its HDD industry remained dominant in the face of competition from Asia and Europe.[7] Although U.S. firms exited, so did those from other countries, including Mitsubishi, Matsushita, Rodime (the first firm to introduce the 3.5-inch disk drive), Olivetti, BASF, Sony, Philips, and Siemens. Asian and European PC makers bought HDDs from U.S. firms. South Korea, for example, depended almost entirely on American companies to meet the HDD requirements of its major PC exporters such as Samsung Electronics, Hyundai Electronics, Goldstar, Daewoo Telecom, and Trigem Computer ("Korea," July 19, 1991). In Europe, PC companies such as Amstrad also purchased American disk drives. Compared with the computer industry, the American HDD industry held a roughly steady 75 percent of the global market throughout the

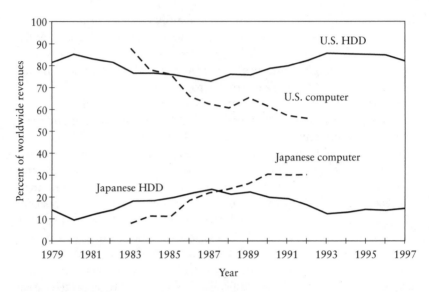

FIGURE 4.1. HDD and computer market shares.
SOURCES: *Disk/Trend,* various issues; *Datamation,* various issues.

1980s, only to see it rise above 80 percent by 1992 (see figure 4.1). By 1995 U.S. global market share reached 85 percent, where it had been in the early 1970s.

In sum, the market share for American computer manufacturers fell throughout the 1980s, the American floppy drive industry practically disappeared, and the world increasingly turned to non-American suppliers of other computer components and peripherals. Nonetheless, American firms continued to be the overwhelming source for hard disk drives. Thus, although it is clear that the drive industry owed its birth to the American computer industry, a first-mover, path-dependence argument is severely deficient given the fate of other computer peripherals and components. The advantages associated with first movers and cumulative capabilities were not the same as those that sustained the American drive industry through the competitive challenge of the 1980s and early 1990s.

Form of Industrial Organization

Another research stream explains differences in competitive advantage in terms of the style of industrial organization—that is, whether industries are organized via the market, internalized within vertically integrated firms, or constructed within a network of closely associated firms.

In his study of economic growth in Britain and France, for example, Kindleberger (1964) claimed that British industry was eclipsed by Japan and West Germany because it was more likely to be organized into separate, independent companies. Similarly, Chandler (1990) located the success of the modern industrial enterprise, epitomized by its American form, in the rise of the multidivisional firm.

Style of industrial organization was similarly invoked to explain Japanese competitive advantage in the 1980s and early 1990s. The Japanese, it was argued, were more competitive in large part because of the nature of their interfirm *keiretsu* relations.[8] Japanese industry was less vertically integrated than American firms were and had closer interfirm relations and greater cross-ownership, which facilitated better coordination among stages of production and lower transaction costs (Aoki 1988, 1990; Gerlach 1992; Teece 1992). In contrast, American institutional traditions made such cooperation difficult, pushing toward more costly vertical integration (Dertouzos et al. 1989, Hill 1995). According to Aoki (1990: 3), Japan's industrial organization was "key to an understanding of Japan's industrial performance."

Given American success in the disk drive industry, of course, the Japanese could not have had a superior organizational form, at least in that industry. Was there, by contrast, something about the American form of industrial organization that sustained U.S. advantage in the HDD industry? Were U.S. firms successful because they followed a different strategy toward vertical integration than their Japanese competitors did, one better suited to the demands of this technology-intensive yet price-sensitive industry? In fact, we find that national style of industrial organization did not have much effect in competitive position one way or the other.

BACKWARD INTEGRATION: COMPONENTS AND HDD ASSEMBLY

For the industrial organization argument to hold, we must first establish that Japanese and American disk drive firms practiced different methods of organizing production and delivery. We focus on three of the most important disk drive components: the recording heads that read and write the data; the disk to which data are written and stored; and the motor used to rotate the disk. We also consider the extent of contract assembly of disk drives. In none of these areas do Japanese and American firms diverge substantially in their extent of vertical integration.

In contrast to the microcomputer industry (see Langlois 1992), vertical integration has been an important, although not universally implemented, strategy for HDD firms. We compared backward integration since 1983 into three components (heads, media, and motors) for a sample of twenty-eight firms, including both surviving firms and those that exited the industry. (Of the twenty-eight, nine were still producing HDDs in 1998.) Ten of the firms were Japanese, with the remainder from the United States. The degree of backwards integration, measured by the number of components manufactured, was compared in five different years. Although the comparison showed that backward integration has clearly been an important strategy in the industry and has become more prevalent over time, the extent of vertical integration across Japanese and U.S. firms was fairly similar.[9]

In-house assembly of HDDs has also been the dominant model in the industry, regardless of nationality. While contract assembly relationships have been used, they have never accounted for a large share of total production. Of the more than one hundred firms that shipped disk drives under their brand names between 1976 and 1998, only twenty used contract assemblers. The majority that engaged contract assemblers did so because they were small or competed in niche segments. The important exceptions to the general model are Quantum and IBM. Roughly 30 percent of all disk drives shipped in 1997 were done on a contract basis for these two firms. All of Quantum's disk drives are assembled by Matsushita-Kotobuki-Electronics, while IBM has used a Thai subcontractor, Saha-Union, to assemble 2.5- and 3.5-inch drives, an operation that IBM tightly controls.

Nevertheless, when viewed historically, contract assembly has played a relatively insignificant role. With the exception of the Quantum-MKE connection and IBM's recent use of Saha-Union, the vast majority of units shipped have come from HDD companies' own factories. All leading firms except Quantum have maintained a strong manufacturing capability. IBM, for example, makes most of its drives at its own facilities in a second plant in Thailand and in Hungary and Singapore. Moreover, most of those performing contract work have themselves been HDD firms rather than specialist assemblers. Several of those who contracted work to others also engaged in contract assembly themselves, including IBM. Interestingly, many American disk drive firms have performed contract assembly. Of the companies that have contracted all assembly to others, only Quantum survives.

Despite the dominant theme of in-house assembly and the general trend toward backward integration into critical components, there is certainly interfirm variation in the levels of integration. There does not, however, appear to be any systematic difference in this regard between leading Japanese and American firms. Highly integrated firms exist on both sides of the Pacific: for example, Seagate, IBM, Fujitsu, and Hitachi make both heads and disks in house (although not all are self-sufficient). In addition, a number of Japanese and American firms once only assembled HDDs without integrating upstream into heads or media. Those that never integrated into heads or disks were typically the smallest firms in the industry and remained small until they exited. The majority of firms in both countries have stood somewhere between these two extremes, producing one key HDD component.

Moreover, the closest observable interfirm relationships appear to be *between* American and Japanese firms: Quantum and MKE, IBM and NEC.[10] At the component level, the top three independent media companies are Komag (United States), Showa Denko (Japan), and Mitsubishi Chemical (Japan) (TrendFocus 1999b). For recording heads, TDK (Japan) and its Hong Kong subsidiary, SAE Magnetics; Read-Rite (United States); and Alps Electric (Japan) are the three largest independent producers (TrendFocus 1999a); and none has an equity relationship with any HDD producer.

FORWARD INTEGRATION: COMPUTER SYSTEMS

If differences in the extent of backward integration appear negligible, are there differences between Japanese and American firms in forward integration into computer assembly? It is true that a view of the industry in 1999 reveals that virtually all of the surviving Japanese HDD firms make computers, while none of the American firms except for IBM do. But this misses much of the industry's history. Throughout the 1970s and 1980s, many of the largest American HDD manufacturers were computer makers: IBM, DEC, Burroughs (later Unisys), Control Data, and Hewlett-Packard. Conversely, numerous Japanese companies began to make HDDs during the 1980s but did not make computers: for example, Alps Electric, Otari Electric, TEAC, Tosoh, and Fuji Electric.

Nonetheless, conventional wisdom in the industry holds that the Japanese HDD industry has been at a competitive disadvantage due to its heavy reliance on captive sales. This dependence tends to slow the speed and degree of innovation since captive drive makers may not be subject to the same competitive pressures as noncaptive firms are. A former Maxtor president and chief executive also noted that "the history of computer systems manufacturers in most instances has been that building peripheral products like disk drives is not a core business that can generate volume and economies of scale to be cost competitive" ("Seagate/Imprimis Deal," August 21, 1989). Finally, captive HDD manufacturers find it difficult to sell drives to outside computer firms: "To enter into a large OEM relationship with a disk drive company means disclosing future computer plans. Most large OEM computer companies would prefer not to disclose those plans with a competitor" ("Seagate/Imprimis Deal," August 21, 1989).

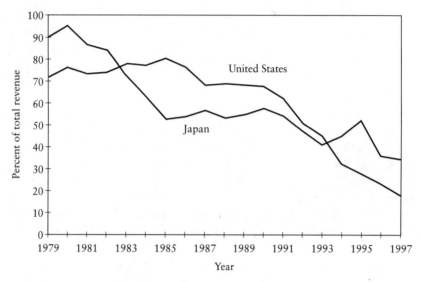

FIGURE 4.2. Captive disk drive revenue.
SOURCE: *Disk/Trend,* various issues.

While the captive market has indeed been whittled away, the perception of Japanese companies as overreliant on internal sales can be challenged on at least two fronts. First, as we will discuss later in the chapter, captive sales have not made Japanese firms notably slower to innovate than successful American HDD firms are. Second, the Japanese HDD industry has not been more reliant on captive sales than the Americans are. Historically, there has been little difference between the two; if anything, the opposite has been true. Figure 4.2 compares the share of captive revenues in total revenue for American and Japanese industry, showing that between 1983 and 1993 captive sales accounted for a slightly higher percentage of total HDD revenue among American firms than among Japanese. Only for before 1983 and since 1994 is it possible to argue that the Japanese have been more reliant on captive sales. In either case, the differences are too small to provide a compelling account of competitive advantage.

In sum, it is unlikely that variation in mode of organizing among U.S. and Japanese firms is responsible for sustained U.S. dominance in the HDD industry. In fact, there has been little difference in the style of industrial organization between the American and Japanese industries. They are remarkably similar in degree of vertical integration, and some of the strongest ties have been between Japanese and American firms. Therefore, national style of industrial organization, as traditionally framed, cannot account for competitive differences. Yet as the rest of the book argues, there was an important organizational difference between American and Japanese firms in their development and exploitation of locational assets. Americans developed and exploited these assets abroad, including their use of cross-border networks, more effectively than the Japanese did.

Innovative Capacity

If industrial organization does not differentiate Japanese and American firms, perhaps their capacity to innovate does. One stream of research emphasizes the importance of country-specific institutional context in shaping national technological capabilities—so-called "national systems of innovation" (Lundvall 1992, Nelson 1993). Yet while the conception is useful for explaining a nation's technological specialization and national economic performance, the national innovation systems approach does not explain differences in performance across industries. For example, it notes that innovative performance requires strong and competent firms, innovative effort (in-house R&D), domestic rivalry, and a pool of technically literate workers—factors present in both the Japanese and American disk drive industries.

A second and related body of scholarship draws more specific distinctions between the innovative style and capabilities of Japanese and American firms, arguing that Japanese firms possess a number of organizational, incentive, and communication advantages over their western counterparts that are conducive to innovation (Aoki and Rosenberg 1987, Aoki 1990). Because of close contacts between R&D and other units in Japanese companies, "research undertaken [is] more commercially relevant and the introduction of a new product into the production and marketing stages [is] faster" (Odagiri and Goto 1993: 107; Mansfield 1988). According to this view, Japanese firms are stronger in testing and redesign and better at small product modifications based on careful engineering (Imai et al. 1985), making them well adapted for innovations along a predictable technological trajectory.

Relative to their American competitors, however, the links between scientific research and invention are weaker in Japanese firms. They are less flexible in gathering specialists from different disciplines and thus may be weaker in interdisciplinary research and the introduction of radically new products. While they are adept at "the better known, closer-at-hand technologies," Japanese firms are less likely to choose "bolder, riskier, and more visionary technologies" that lead to pivotal new products or process technologies (Okimoto and Nishi 1994: 201).

Can U.S. success in the industry be explained by firms' greater innovative capabilities in riskier, leading-edge technologies? Certainly, IBM was

TABLE 4.1

IBM FIRSTS IN THE HDD INDUSTRY

	Model	Year	MB*	Disks	Disk Size (inches)
First disk drive	IBM RAMAC	1956	5	50	24
First disk drive with air bearing heads	IBM 1301	1962	28	25	24
First disk drive with removable disk pack	IBM 1311	1963	2.68	6	14
First disk cartridge drive	IBM 2310	1965	1.024	1	14
First disk pack drive	IBM 2311	1965	7.25	6	14
First disk drive with ferrite core heads	IBM 2314	1966	29.2	11	14
First track following servo system	IBM 3330-1	1971	100	12	14
First disk drive with low-mass heads, lubricated disks, sealed	IBM 3340 Winchester	1973	70	4	14
First disk drive with thin film heads	IBM 3370	1979	571.4	7	14
First 8-inch hard disk drive**	IBM 3310	1979	64.5	6	8
First disk drive to use MR heads and PRML	IBM 681	1990	857	12	5.25
First disk drive with GMR heads	IBM Deskstar GPS	1997	16,800	5	3.5

SOURCE: Quantum Corporation web page based on information in *Disk/Trend*, various issues.

*MB, megabytes.

**Microscience International also introduced an 8-inch drive at the same time.

the technological fountainhead for the industry, spawning many firms and continuing to demonstrate remarkable technological leadership.[11] As table 4.1 shows, IBM established the industry and introduced many key innovations: the first removable disk pack drive; the Winchester standard; the first drive with ferrite, thin-film, magneto-resistive (MR) and giant MR (GMR) heads; and the first eight-inch disk drive for minicomputers. More than any other institution, the firm displayed engineering brilliance in overcoming critical technical constraints.

Nonetheless, the co-evolution of technology and competition in the HDD industry confounds conventional wisdom about differences in Japanese and American innovative capability in two ways. First, Japanese firms have been stronger than theory would predict in technologically advanced new products. One measure is the shift to different form factors (see appendix B). The movement from 14- to 8- to 5.25-inch disk drives and then to 3.5- and 2.5-inch drives reflects distinct product generations. While IBM was first to introduce the 14- and 8-inch form factors, young entrepreneurial firms rather than older incumbents have since led the way. One might thus expect Japanese firms to lag behind their American competitors in the shift to new form factors, and at first glance this seems to be the case. Table 4.2 lists the order of entry into 5.25-, 3.5-, and 2.5-inch disk drives. Seven of the first ten companies to introduce 5.25-inch drives were American, led by Seagate in July 1980. Two were European (Rodime and Olivetti), but only one was a Japanese firm (Nippon Peripherals). By the end of 1982, thirteen more firms had begun shipping 5.25-inch drives, seven of which were Japanese, including Fujitsu and Hitachi. In 1983, fourteen more firms made the shift to 5.25-inch drives, five of them Japanese. Thus, from 1980 to 1993 only thirteen of forty-one HDD firms that shipped 5.25-inch drives were Japanese, and these firms were a year or more behind in introducing the drives. Nevertheless, among firms that still made disk drives through the end of 1998, the Japanese were quicker than most of their U.S. counterparts in making the move to 5.25-inch drives. While Seagate was the first to introduce 5.25-inch drives, Fujitsu, Hitachi, and NEC shipped them before or concurrently with Quantum, Maxtor, Micropolis, and IBM.[12]

The story was similar in the shift to the 3.5-inch form factor. In this case, the first HDD firm to ship the new drives was Rodime, a European company, in September 1983. The next three firms to ship, however, were American—Microcomputer Memories, Microscience International, and MiniScribe—all of them shipping in 1984. The first Japanese firm to ship was Nippon Peripherals in February 1985. In fact, the first nine firms to ship 3.5-inch drives have since exited the industry. The first surviving HDD firm to ship 3.5-inch drives was Hitachi in June 1985, with NEC, Fujitsu, and Quantum following close behind. As with the transition to 5.25-inch drives, Japanese firms were quicker to make the shift to 3.5-inch drives than were almost every U.S. firm that is a leader today. IBM did not introduce the drives until May 1986, Seagate until the third quarter of 1987. Maxtor did not make the move until 1988. Thus, while the Japanese were behind the first movers into 3.5- and 5.25-inch drives, most of whom were from the United States, they introduced these new form factors before today's most successful American HDD manufacturers did.[13]

Japanese firms have also led in incorporating advanced technology into their disk drives—specifically, the new thin-film MR recording heads. As discussed in chapter 2, MR heads are designed to read media with very high recording densities and thus account for the growth in areal density to an annual rate of 60 percent between 1990 and 1997. Because the switch to MR heads requires corresponding changes in media and electronics technologies, and because they are very difficult to make, many companies were

TABLE 4.2

THE FIRST TEN ENTRANTS IN NEW FORM FACTORS PLUS SURVIVING FIRMS AT THE END OF 1998

Order of Entry	Firm	Country	First Shipment 5.25-inch*	Order of Entry	Firm	Country	First Shipment 3.5-inch*	Order of Entry	Firm	Country	First Shipment 2.5-inch*
1	**Seagate**	U.S.	July 1980	1	Rodime	U.K.	September 1983	1	PrairieTek	U.S.	4Q 1988
2	Tandon	U.S.	December 1980	2	Microcomputer Memories	U.S.	March 1984	2	JVC	Japan	4Q 1989
3	International Memories	U.S.	1Q 1981	3	MiniScribe	U.S.	3Q 1984	3	Conner Peripherals	U.S.	1Q 1990
4	Rodime	U.K.	June 1981	4	Microscience International	U.S.	4Q 1984	4	Areal Technology	U.S.	2Q 1990
5	Computer Memories	U.S.	2Q 1981	5	LaPine Technology	U.S.	February 1985	5	**IBM**	U.S.	4Q 1990
5	Rotating Memory Systems	U.S.	2Q 1981	5	Nippon Peripherals	Japan	February 1985	6	Fuji Electric	Japan	March 1991
7	Olivetti	Italy	September 1981	7	Hewlett-Packard	U.S.	March 1985	7	**Western Digital**	U.S.	1Q 1991
8	Texas Instruments	U.S.	3Q 1981	8	Alps Electric	Japan	April 1985	8	**Toshiba**	Japan	April 1991
8	MiniScribe	U.S.	October 1981	9	Tandon	U.S.	April 1985	9	**Quantum**	U.S.	June 1991
10	Nippon Peripherals	Japan	October 1981	10	**Hitachi**	Japan	June 1985	10	**Seagate**	U.S.	2Q 1991
11	NEC	Japan	May 1982	11	NEC	Japan	July 1985	11	**Maxtor**	U.S.	4Q 1991
16	Fujitsu	Japan	July 1982	16	**Fujitsu**	Japan	October 1985	13	**Fujitsu**	Japan	1Q 1992
16	Hitachi	Japan	4Q 1982	22	**Plus (Quantum)**	U.S.	October 1985	16	**Hitachi**	Japan	May 1994
18	Quantum	U.S.	April 1983	31	**IBM**	U.S.	May 1986	17	**NEC**	Japan	4Q 1994
24	Maxtor	U.S.	2Q 1983	33	**Seagate**	U.S.	3Q 1987				
24	Toshiba	Japan	2Q 1983	33	**Toshiba**	Japan	3Q 1987				
31	IBM	U.S.	July 1984	45	**Maxtor**	U.S.	3Q 1988				

SOURCE: *DiskTrend*, various issues.

NOTE: **Boldface** companies were in operation as of December 31, 1998. 1Q, First quarter; 2Q, second quarter; 3Q, third quarter; 4Q, fourth quarter.

* All first shipment dates refer to fixed HDDs.

TABLE 4.3

DISK DRIVES WITH MR AND GMR HEADS: ORDER OF ENTRY

Company	MR Heads	Company	GMR Heads
IBM	May 1991	IBM	December 1997
Fujitsu	February 1994	Toshiba	May 1998
Seagate	First quarter 1994	Hitachi	June 1998
Hitachi	June 1994	Fujitsu	September 1998
Quantum	October 1994	NEC	1998*
Hewlett-Packard	Fourth quarter 1995	Western Digital	January 1999
NEC	First quarter 1996	Maxtor	March 1999
Micropolis	December 1996	Quantum	April 1999
Maxtor	Fourth quarter 1996	Samsung	June 1999

SOURCE: *Disk/Trend,* various issues.
*Month not available.

slow to commit resources to the new technology, choosing instead to try to increase capacity through conventional technologies.

Stylized notions of American and Japanese innovative capabilities suggest that U.S. firms are more likely to move first into smaller market segments with more sophisticated technology while ceding market segments dominated by older technology to firms from other countries. Thus, in disk drives we might expect American firms to lead the way into MR and GMR technology. Similarly, some argue that Japanese drive designers are likely to push technological improvements using the inductive thin-film technology with which they are familiar rather than shift to complex MR and GMR heads. In one sense this is true: IBM invented MR and GMR technology, entering the market with MR heads almost three years before the nearest competitor and six months ahead with GMR. Yet three of the next six companies to introduce disk drives with MR heads were Japanese, as were the next four companies to introduce drives with GMR (see table 4.3).

Moreover, a look at areal density reveals Japanese technological strength. Areal density (the amount of data that can be squeezed onto a given space of a disk) encapsulates in one indicator a company's ability to bring together head, media, and flying-height technologies and is a major feature of the technology race in hard disk drives. As table 4.4 shows, the Japanese are among the leaders in areal density. The table ranks firms according to their disk drives with the highest areal density as of May 1997 and June 1999 (*Disk/Trend* 1997, 1999). Although this ranking changes frequently (the newest product on the market always seems to embody the highest areal density), the illustration nonetheless demonstrates Japanese innovativeness.[14] In 1997, IBM was clearly far ahead, although three of the top five were

TABLE 4.4

HIGHEST AREAL DENSITY (MEGABITS PER SQUARE INCH)

May 1997		June 1999	
Company	Areal Density	Company	Areal Density
IBM	2,638.0	Hitachi	6,299.0
Hitachi	2,013.0	Toshiba	5,833.0
Quantum	1,646.0	IBM	5,693.0
Toshiba	1,308.0	Western Digital	5,476.0
Fujitsu	1,300.0	Fujitsu	5,129.0
Maxtor	1,193.0	Seagate	5,094.0
Seagate	1,108.0	Maxtor	4,984.0
JTS	1,008.0	Samsung	4,950.0
Micropolis	959.2	NEC	3,741.0
Samsung	884.0	Quantum	3,454.0

SOURCE: *Disk/Trend* (1997, 1999).

Japanese. By 1999, however, Hitachi and Toshiba had shipped products with the industry's highest areal density, followed by IBM.

Despite these signs of strength, Japanese firms have also been weaker than theory might predict in some areas. Within a given form factor, technology has evolved in ways that should have given the Japanese an advantage. All companies have technology roadmaps: technological progress has moved along well-known paths, and firms have solved well-known puzzles within form factors, especially in the technological development of disk drives employing inductive thin-film heads and disks (although MR and GMR heads have now almost completely displaced inductive). In 1979, IBM was the first company to ship disk drives with thin-film inductive heads; drives with thin-film media appeared four years later. Innovations in areal density over the next decade involved improvements to these two increasingly understood technologies. Thus, Japanese firms might have been expected to advance more quickly along this technological trajectory while simultaneously obtaining cost advantages through more efficient manufacturing. But the reverse is true. American firms dominated this largest segment of the disk drive market and made adaptations to the basic technology.[15] In this way, they have been most responsible for extending the life of inductive head technology, which innovation theory does not predict.

In sum, according to a number of key measures, there is little evidence that the Japanese are less innovative than successful American companies are. They have not been far behind their U.S. competitors on the technological frontier and even introduced advanced new products before leading U.S. companies did. While innovation has been necessary for all companies to stay in the game, it has not been a sufficient condition. Differences in innovative capability are, at best, an incomplete explanation for the U.S. industry's sustained competitive performance.

Industrial Policy

An enormous body of research claims that industrial policy has made an important difference in industrial success across countries and industries, particularly in Asia (Johnson 1982, Amsden 1989, Wade 1990). Both Japan and most of the East Asian economies have pursued sector-specific industrial policies at some stage, which proponents argue have resulted in industrial catch-up in a variety of industries (Lall 1996). Nevertheless, whatever the merits or demerits of these arguments in other sectors (and they are hotly contested), industrial policy has had little to do with our story. The hard disk drive industry has not been the focus of public policy in either the United States or Japan. Although in the late 1980s some American firms worked to acquire the kind of policy support then going to the semiconductor industry, little resulted from those efforts.[16] Only since the mid-1990s have both Japan and the United States dedicated small amounts of public monies in support of the data storage industry (McKendrick 1999). While these changes may contribute to future variation in outcomes, industrial policy has not yet had a direct effect on the evolution of the industry.[17]

That said, public policy has certainly benefited the American HDD industry in countries hosting U.S. investment—particularly Singapore, Thailand, and Malaysia. While these policies played a role in inducing the shift in the industry's geographic center of gravity to Southeast Asia, they consisted of a new generation of policies quite different from the protectionist designs of the past. We take up this theme again in chapters 6 and 10, where we consider the implications of our findings for long-standing debates about the role of industrial policy in East Asia and the rest of the developing world.

Conclusion

First-mover advantages and innovation contributed to American success in the disk drive industry, which was built by successful computer firms and thus able to achieve an early lead over European and Japanese drive manufacturers. In addition, innovation and some degree of vertical integration have been necessary conditions for industrial performance. Yet taken together, differences among American and Japanese companies along these dimensions do not appear substantial enough to explain the persistence of U.S. leadership in the industry. Japanese companies have been innovative in important ways, and both American and Japanese companies exhibit similar levels of vertical integration.

5 Global Shift and Competitiveness in Hard Disk Drives

While vertical integration, innovation, and initial home-based advantages contributed to the competitiveness of American HDD firms, those pieces do not reveal the whole picture. The missing puzzle piece is location, which has helped sustain U.S. dominance, particularly during the industry's early and extensive globalization. In documenting the industry's history and spatial evolution, we find that the locus of innovation and production has diverged over time. Innovation remains rooted at a few sites in the United States; but disk drive technology, markets, and firm competition have changed since the introduction of the personal computer, when American firms moved production abroad more quickly and completely than did their Japanese counterparts. The American HDD industry, led by relatively young, small multinational firms, developed an important operational cluster in Southeast Asia (centered first in Singapore and later in Malaysia, Thailand, and elsewhere in the region) that enabled them to excel at efficient, high-tech production (see table 3.2). Thus, an examination of the industry's global shift offers not only a geographic portrait of activity but an explanation for success.

The Changing Geography of the Disk Drive Industry

INDUSTRY ORIGINS AND DIVERSITY OF LOCATION: THE FIRST TWENTY-FIVE YEARS

The disk drive industry took a decade to develop recognizable clusters. In the United States, activity was initially quite geographically dispersed. By the late 1960s, industry clusters appeared first in northern and southern California and later in Massachusetts and Minnesota. Similarly, Japanese firms took a decade to cluster around Tokyo. In contrast, Europe never attracted sufficient entrants to generate a homemade cluster, although a few American firms eventually opened branch plants in Europe to gain access to that market. In all cases, however, firms generally collocated production and innovation during the industry's first twenty-five years.

A variety of captive and independent firms entered the U.S. disk drive business between 1956 and 1980. Most were computer system manufacturers and diversified industrial enterprises, some were specialists in peripherals or other types of magnetic storage, but few were de novo startups. All can be classified into one of three groups.

The first group consisted of computer systems manufacturers. In the early 1950s, IBM's San Jose lab was searching for a capacious storage device because the company was lagging behind Remington Rand, which had announced magnetic drum storage for its Univac File Computer in 1954. IBM responded with the first prototype disk drive, which was delivered to a customer site in June 1956. In June 1957, the first production unit came off the line (Bashe et al. 1986). IBM's drive was an immediate commercial hit, and other systems manufacturers judged that they needed to make disk drives to be competitive. By the early 1970s, General Electric, Control Data, NEC, Hitachi, Fujitsu, Honeywell, Burroughs, NCR, and Toshiba had all begun to make drives to bundle with their mainframe systems. Their data storage activity usually collocated with their systems development: GE in Arizona, CDC in Minnesota, Burroughs and NCR in southern California, and Digital Equipment in Massachusetts.[1]

The second group of entrants included machinery and computer peripheral companies serving computer system manufacturers that had not yet made their own disk drives. These firms placed a wide variety of different technological bets, experimenting with various disk and recording head technologies. They were also geographically dispersed. Bryant Computer Products (Michigan) and Data Products (initially in Minnesota but later moving to southern California) were the first two companies to enter the industry after IBM. While IBM's first drive used 24-inch disks, Bryant's were 39 inches and Data Products' 31 inches. Other early entrants in this group came from northern California (Friden) and Massachusetts (Anelex). In Europe, Sperac, a creation of France's Plan Calcul, and Data Recording Instruments (England) served their national computer firms.

The third group consisted of second-generation producers of disk drives. Engineers and managers from IBM left to start their own companies, others reverse-engineered IBM drives, and some firms relied on technology transfer agreements with existing players.[2] ISS and Memorex, two significant IBM spinoffs in northern California, made drives completely plug-compatible with IBM's and even improved on the performance of IBM's products. A set of second-generation firms from the electronics and defense industries generally reverse-engineered IBM disk drives. Many of these firms were located in southern California, which after World War II became the home of many technology companies, especially aerospace and defense firms. The western part of the San Fernando Valley into southern Ventura County was often seen as a smaller version of what became known as Silicon Valley, but disk drive activity also emerged in Orange County, south of Los Angeles. Century Data Systems, Marshall Industries, Pertec, and Data Products were four prominent disk drive companies with headquarters and product development in southern California.

Although northern and southern California hosted the most HDD production, a great many other places had some disk drive activity. The two most successful entrants outside of California were Control Data and Digital Equipment Corporation. Control Data was for many years the leader in OEM production and the source of Minnesota's present-day capabilities in magnetic recording. Digital Equipment was one of the most successful of the captive drive makers, for many years second only to IBM, with operations in Massachusetts and later Colorado. General Electric invested in storage technology in Arizona, moving it to Oklahoma City in the late 1960s.[3] Potter Instrument of Melville, New York, leveraged its know-how in tape drives to enter the disk drive business. Although a leader in magnetic drum storage, Univac had a brief and unhappy experience designing disk drives for its mainframes at its Blue Bell, Pennsylvania, facility.[4] Storage Technology, an IBM spinoff that originally made tape drives, helped establish Colorado as a center for data storage technology.[5]

The Collocation of Technology Development and Production, 1960–80. Figures 5.1a through 5.1c show the headquarters location of all American firms producing disk drives between 1961 and 1980 (in ten-year increments).[6] As we have seen, location was initially dispersed, although the five largest HDD producers between 1960 and 1980 were somewhat less dispersed, with the majority based in California. Led by IBM, the captive disk drive companies came to dominate the industry by 1980, when they captured 77 percent of worldwide revenue. IBM alone accounted for 33 percent, followed by Burroughs, Control Data (which led in the OEM market), and Digital Equipment. Whether measured by number of firms or revenue, disk drive activity was well spread across the United States. Almost all production was also carried out in the United States, usually in the same location as product engineering and development. Scale economies for the large diameter drives encouraged concentration of production in one location, and product development was similarly proximate to assembly among European and Japanese producers.

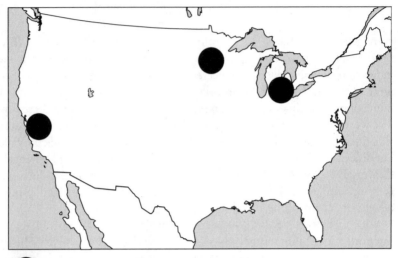

● = 1 firm (33 percent of total)

FIGURE 5.1a. Location of all U.S. disk drive firms in 1961.
SOURCE: Authors' data.

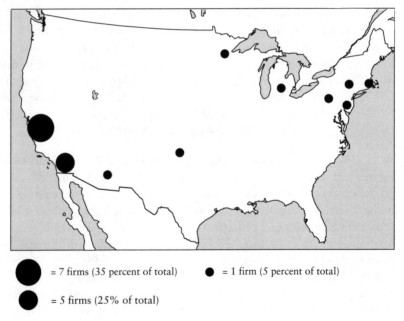

● = 7 firms (35 percent of total)   ● = 1 firm (5 percent of total)

● = 5 firms (25% of total)

FIGURE 5.1b. Location of all U.S. disk drive firms in 1970.
SOURCE: Authors' data.

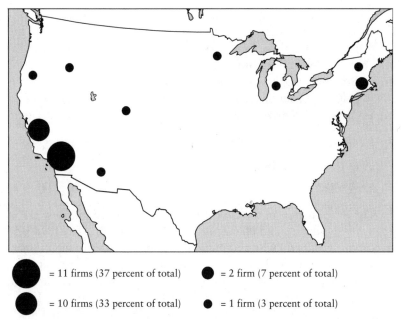

● = 11 firms (37 percent of total)   ● = 2 firm (7 percent of total)

● = 10 firms (33 percent of total)   ● = 1 firm (3 percent of total)

FIGURE 5.1C. Location of all U.S. disk drive firms in 1980.
SOURCE: Authors' data.

Nevertheless, high transportation costs should have encouraged dispersion of assembly to locations closer to overseas markets for firms seeking to expand internationally. Disk drives introduced before 1980 were very large and expensive. The original IBM disk drive had fifty 24-inch platters, although the company switched to a 14-inch diameter in 1963, which became the de facto standard for almost twenty years.[7] In the late 1960s, Control Data offered a disk drive that was three feet deep, six feet tall, ten feet wide, weighed 1,000 pounds, stored fifty megabytes, cost $300,000, and needed a crane to deliver it to any customer residing above the first floor. Even the IBM 3380, a 14-inch-diameter Winchester disk drive introduced in 1981, stood almost six feet high and four feet wide and deep. Moreover, the minimum efficient plant size was small by today's standards. The number of HDDs built for mainframes and minicomputers numbered less than 100,000 annually during the early 1970s, and only 500,000 disk drives were shipped in 1980 (*Disk/Trend* 1981). Century Data Systems, for example, one of the leading OEM producers during the early 1970s, produced only five hundred drives per month.

Only the largest companies assembled drives or manufactured components overseas. During the 1960s and 1970s, the largest overseas markets were in Europe, where IBM, Burroughs, Control Data, and Memorex established assembly facilities.[8] In fact, of the forty-six U.S. entrants into the industry before 1980, these four were the only companies that assembled drives abroad: IBM in Germany; Burroughs in Scotland, Canada, and the growing Brazilian market; Control Data in Germany; and Memorex briefly in Belgium.[9] Among Japanese and European companies, only BASF (Germany) assembled drives overseas, making 8-inch Winchester drives in Los Gatos, California.

NEW MARKETS, FIRMS, TECHNOLOGIES, AND LOCATIONS

The introduction of the desktop computer ushered in a new era in the disk drive industry and changed the logic of location. The IBM personal computer, in particular, and the subsequent explosion of the PC market in the 1980s drove demand for mass production of small storage devices. As discussed in chapter 2, floppy disk drives initially met this need; but shoebox-sized 5.25-inch hard drives—"little trifles," as one IBM engineer called them—rapidly displaced floppies as the PCs' principal mode of storage.[10]

Initially, producers of smaller disk drives, like their predecessors, collocated technology development and assembly. But PC makers increasingly exerted pressure on HDD firms to cut prices. While these firms often tried to innovate as a way to differentiate themselves and avoid strong price competition, the strategy proved ephemeral. American, but not Japanese, disk drive firms began to shift assembly overseas to achieve lower costs. At the same time, the relentless pace of innovation tended to concentrate technological development into a few clusters. Among American firms, HDD production was largely concentrated in Southeast Asia by 1990, while technological development was clustered in northern and southern California, Colorado, and Minnesota. By contrast, Japanese HDD firms continued to collocate drive design and production in Japan, making a short-lived effort to assemble drives in the United States. The locational choices of American firms gave them a considerable competitive advantage.

Figures 5.2a through 5.2d show the location of all U.S. HDD firms between 1985 and 1998. Between 1980 and 1985, forty companies entered the industry. Because many of the companies that pioneered the new desktop market were spinoffs of incumbent firms that made larger disk drives (especially IBM), these new firms set up business in the same region. Few new entrants, however, were spinoffs from Control Data (Minnesota) or Digital Equipment (Massachusetts), the other market leaders during the 1970s. Throughout the 1980s, new entry therefore occurred primarily in northern

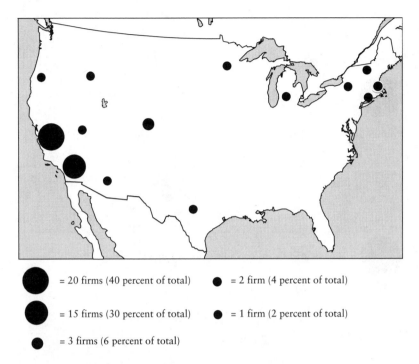

⬤	= 20 firms (40 percent of total)	●	= 2 firm (4 percent of total)
⬤	= 15 firms (30 percent of total)	●	= 1 firm (2 percent of total)
●	= 3 firms (6 percent of total)		

FIGURE 5.2a. Location of all U.S. disk drive firms, 1985.
SOURCE: Authors' data.

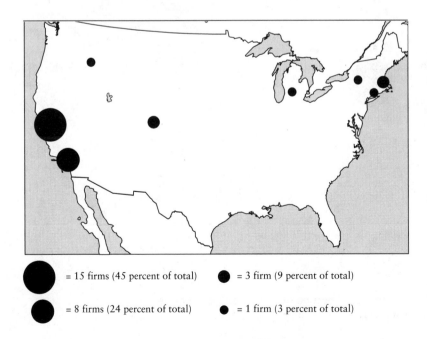

⬤	= 15 firms (45 percent of total)	●	= 3 firm (9 percent of total)
⬤	= 8 firms (24 percent of total)	●	= 1 firm (3 percent of total)

FIGURE 5.2b. Location of all U.S. disk drive firms, 1990.
SOURCE: Authors' data.

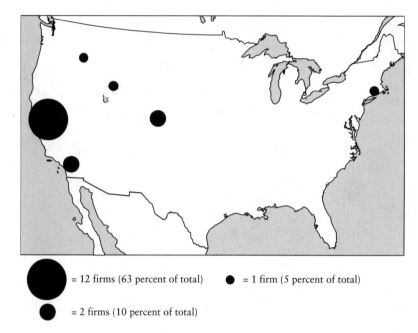

FIGURE 5.2c. Location of all U.S. disk drive firms, 1995.
SOURCE: Authors' data.

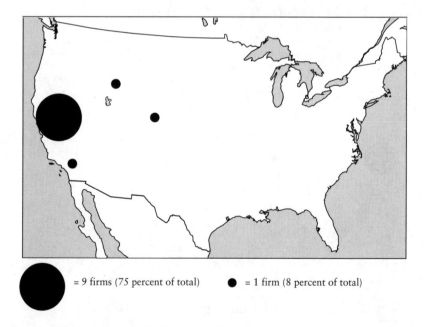

FIGURE 5.2d. Location of all U.S. disk drive firms, 1998.
SOURCE: Authors' data.

and southern California (with some activity in Colorado), with the result that drive development and manufacturing gradually became more concentrated in those regions. Interestingly, these rapidly growing new companies were largely independents and began to displace the large, captive drive manufacturers. By 1991, the five largest companies had headquarters in northern California: IBM, Seagate Technology, Quantum, Conner Peripherals, and Maxtor.

In the United States, California—and Silicon Valley in particular—eventually became the technological center. Of course, IBM gave birth to the industry in northern California; but relative to other regions, new firm entry replenished California's strength through the introduction of new technologies. The founders of many initial 5.25- and 3.5-inch entrants had worked in product development and marketing for other disk drive firms located in northern California.[11] While fewer in number, most early entrants in southern California—Tandon, Computer Memories, Peripheral Technology, Microcomputer Memories—were founded by engineers with experience at other southern California disk drive firms, including floppy disk drive companies.[12] Figures 5.3a through 5.3c show that the pioneers of smaller disk drives came primarily from these two regions.

Technological clustering has been reinforced by the interaction of design groups within the value chain. For example, media maker, Komag of San Jose, California, and Read-Rite, a head manufacturer in Milpitas, California, collaborated in March 2000 to reach 50.3 gigabits per square inch areal density. This is the industry's highest density yet.[13] Nidec, the spindle motor manufacturer, has four design centers in the United States, each in the same location as HDD product development: San Jose, California (for the Silicon Valley firms); Longmont, Colorado (Seagate and Maxtor); Oklahoma City (Seagate); and Minneapolis (Seagate).

Through the first half of the 1980s, assembly of small disk drives occurred in locations proximate to product development. Although assembly was scattered geographically by the end of 1983, it was still overwhelmingly located at the manufacturer's home base. Virtually all HDD production in 1983 was concentrated in two countries: the United States (72.3 percent of shipments) and Japan (12 percent of shipments). With almost 5 percent of global shipments, Europe produced more disk drives than did the rest of Asia (other than Japan). Home-based production remained the dominant strategy for American, Japanese, and European firms, with U.S. firms producing nearly 93 percent of their drives in the United States and Japanese firms producing all of theirs in Japan.

Some HDD firms, however, began to consider offshore production. PC makers were putting enormous cost pressures on their HDD suppliers just as a wave of new HDD entrants was emerging. For many young companies, winning early contracts from computer makers was a make-or-break sit-

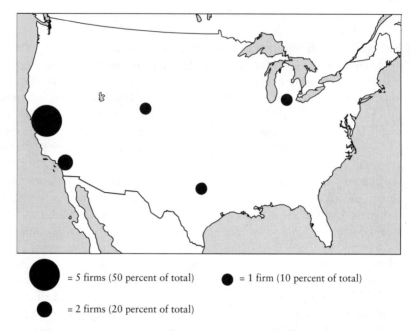

= 5 firms (50 percent of total)   = 1 firm (10 percent of total)

= 2 firms (20 percent of total)

FIGURE 5.3a. Location of the first ten producers of 5.25-inch form factors.
SOURCE: Authors' data.

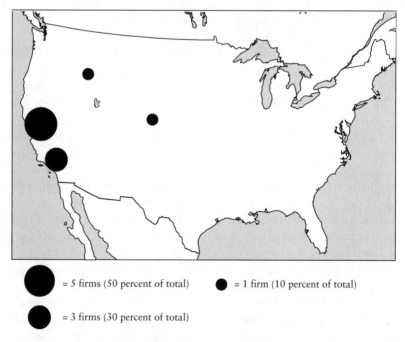

= 5 firms (50 percent of total)   = 1 firm (10 percent of total)

= 3 firms (30 percent of total)

FIGURE 5.3b. Location of the first ten producers of 3.5-inch form factors.
SOURCE: Authors' data.

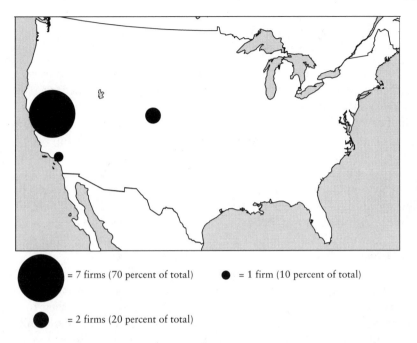

= 7 firms (70 percent of total)　　　● = 1 firm (10 percent of total)

= 2 firms (20 percent of total)

FIGURE 5.3C. Location of the first ten producers of 2.5-inch form factors.
SOURCE: Authors' data.

uation. As the largest PC producer, IBM, in particular, had enormous leverage. In 1982, it paid $600 for each 5.25-inch drive it purchased; in 1984 it bought about 1 million 5.25-inch drives at $400 each ("Smaller Business Computers," June 4, 1984). Although some HDD firms did not think such price cuts were sustainable, others were less sanguine. Hoping to lower its operating costs, Seagate was the first to take production to a low-cost offshore location, starting in Singapore with subassemblies in 1982 and final assembly in 1983. Singapore was then a relatively low-wage country with some experience in the manufacture of electronic components. In the early 1980s, for example, its Economic Development Board encouraged U.S. disk drive companies to invest by advertising that an assembly job paying $5 to $6 an hour in California typically pays only $1 an hour in Singapore. Companies such as Seagate, Computer Memories, and others thus discovered they could reduce the share of labor cost in assembly from almost 25 percent to 5 percent while significantly cutting unit costs.

In sum, American disk drive companies increasingly concentrated their technological resources in California, but a handful of pioneers realized they could physically separate volume manufacturing from product and process development. Manufacturing had begun its move offshore.

A SHIFT IN PRODUCTION'S CENTER
OF GRAVITY, 1983–90

The experiences of Seagate, Tandon, and Computer Memories in Southeast Asia began to influence other American HDD firms. In particular, Seagate's successful Singapore facility spurred several other producers to adopt a similar cost-based location strategy. According to Seagate's president, the company's transportation costs had soared; and communication between U.S. engineers and foreign plants was difficult, as was controlling quality ("Seagate Goes East," March 16, 1987). But company sales jumped from $51 million in 1982 to $222 million in 1983 (its first full year of Singapore-based assembly) and $302 million in 1984, establishing Seagate as the leader in desktop disk drives. Computer Memories also experienced rapid growth, with sales jumping from $41 million in 1983 to $150 million in 1985.

Table 5.1 shows the movement of overseas disk drive assembly among firms with headquarters in the United States, Japan, and Europe. Many American firms followed Seagate's lead and chose Singapore as their first overseas manufacturing site. In addition to Computer Memories and Tandon, both Maxtor and MiniScribe began to ship drives made in Singapore plants in 1984, followed by Micropolis (1986), Conner Peripherals (1987), and Cybernex Advanced Storage Technology (1987). In 1992, soon after they were established, Integral Peripherals and MiniStor also began to ship from Singapore; and American HDD companies opened overseas facilities in other low-cost Asian locations such as Taiwan (Microscience and Priam in 1987) and Hong Kong (Ampex in 1983).

Gradually, a dramatic change in the locus of assembly took place. Manufacturing in low-cost assembly locations in Asia, particularly Southeast Asia, became the norm among a large proportion of American firms. As chapters 6 through 9 detail, the desirability of locating in Southeast Asia increased with the number of American firms that found it advantageous to do so, thus becoming a collective phenomenon. By 1990 Singapore was the world's largest producer of hard disk drives, accounting for 55 percent of global output as measured in unit shipments. The rest of Southeast Asia accounted for only 1 percent of final drives, but significant operational clusters were emerging in parts of the value chain (for example, in head-gimbal and head-stack assembly) in Thailand and Malaysia.

At the same time, however, the firms that moved abroad during this period shared similarities beyond nationality. Every American assembler that went to Asia made desktop disk drives, and almost all also made only the smaller form factors. Companies that made larger disk drives for mini-computers and mainframes were much less likely to shift, even if they also

TABLE 5.1

TIMING AND DIRECTION OF OVERSEAS HDD ASSEMBLY

Year	U.S. Firms	Location	Japanese Firms	Location	European Firms	Location
As of 1982	Burroughs	Scotland, Brazil, Canada, Mexico				
	Control Data	Germany				
	DEC	Germany				
	IBM	Germany, England				
1983	Ampex	Hong Kong				
	Computer Memories	Singapore				
	Hewlett-Packard	England				
	Quantum	Puerto Rico				
	Seagate Technology	Singapore				
	Tandon	India				
	Tandon	Singapore				
	Vermont Research	England				
1984	IBM	Japan			Rodime	United States
	Maxtor	Singapore				
	Miniscribe	Singapore				
1985	Microscience International	Singapore				
1986	Micropolis	Singapore	Fujitsu	United States		
	Tandon	Korea				
1987	Connor Peripherals	Singapore	NEC	United States	Rodime	Singapore
	Control Data	Singapore				
	Cybernex	Singapore				
	Microscience International	Taiwan				
	Priam	Taiwan				
	Seagate Technology	Thailand				
1988	IBM	Brazil				
	Unisys	Singapore				
	Western Digital	Singapore				
1989	Kalok	Philippines				
	SyQuest	Singapore				
1990	Connor Peripherals	Malaysia				
	Connor Peripherals	Scotland				
	Microscience International	China				
1991	PrairieTek	Singapore	Fujitsu	Thailand		
			Xebec	Philippines		
1992	Integral Peripherals	Singapore	Toshiba	United States		
	MiniStor	Singapore				
1993	Conner Peripherals	China				
1994	DEC	Malaysia				
	Hewlett-Packard	Malaysia				
	JTS	India				
	Quantum	Malaysia				
	Western Digital	Malaysia				

(*continued*)

TABLE 5.1
(continued)

Year	U.S. Firms	Location	Japanese Firms	Location	European Firms	Location
	SyQuest	Malaysia				
1995	Avatar	Thailand	Hitachi	Philippines		
	IBM	Singapore	NEC	Philippines		
	IBM	Hungary				
	Seagate Technology	China				
	Seagate Technology	Ireland				
1996	Iomega	Malaysia	Toshiba	Philippines		
	IBM	Thailand	Fujitsu	Philippines		

SOURCE: Authors' calculations from industry sources.
NOTE: Dates refer to start of production, not plant construction or announcement of the decision. Table excludes subcontracting arrangements.

made the smaller drives. In addition to specializing in desktop drives, the early adopters of the global strategy were generally medium-sized and relatively new to the industry at the time of their move. Seventy-five percent fell into the middle third of the size rankings at the time they started up production in Southeast Asia: Seagate was the twenty-second-largest company when it began to ship from Singapore, with Tandon ranked twenty-fifth and Computer Memories twenty-seventh. Similarly striking was the disparity in age between early and late adopters of the Southeast Asia assembly strategy (see figure 5.4). Until 1994, when the older disk drive manufacturers made the move, the average age (duration in the HDD industry) of the firms assembling drives in Southeast Asia was below that of the rest of the American industry.

While American firms with similar organizational characteristics and strategic focus tended to adopt the Southeast Asian assembly strategy during this period, comparable Japanese firms did not. In fact, their revealed global strategies could not have been more different. Not one of the new Japanese entrants into the desktop market (those that made drives *only* for the desktop) copied the American strategy, nor did any Japanese assembler make the move. After entering the market in 1985, for example, Fuji Electric, JVC, Seiko Epson, and Alps Electric all confined their manufacturing to Japan. And while the average duration of American and Japanese firms in the HDD industry was similar, not a single new Japanese entrant copied its American counterparts (see figure 5.5). By 1990, eight years after the first HDD was produced in Singapore, American firms assembled two-thirds of their disk drives in Southeast Asia. In contrast, Japanese companies assembled almost none there and only 2 percent in the

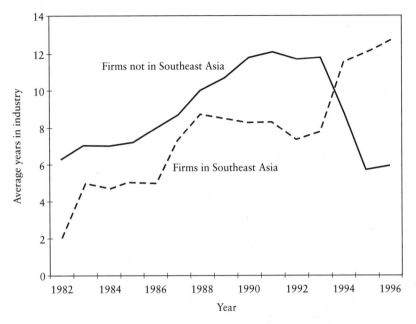

FIGURE 5.4. U.S. HDD firm age and assembly in Southeast Asia.
SOURCE: Authors' calculations from industry sources.

rest of Asia. Instead, they continued to manufacture predominantly in Japan, where they produced 95 percent of their disk drives.

As a group, Japanese firms clearly hesitated to abandon a strategy that appeared to be working: that is, exporting from Japan. In 1984, for example, TEAC Corporation was shipping almost 60 percent of its output to the United States. Even as late as 1989, both Matsushita and Hitachi invested in Japanese manufacturing capability for 3.5-inch drives, judging that applying more automation to drive assembly would enable them to overcome the otherwise higher costs of manufacturing in Japan. As the yen strengthened against the dollar and they turned their attention abroad, the United States, not Asia, was the site of their first overseas manufacturing investments. Fujitsu opened a U.S. plant in 1986, NEC followed in 1987, and Toshiba entered in 1992. At one point, Fujitsu reportedly intended to manufacture nearly all of its disk drives in the United States ("'Made in Japan' Tag," December 9, 1985). Toshiba explained that its strategy in HDDs was proximity to the market—to respond to market needs more effectively by designing and building products closer to the markets where they are sold ("Toshiba Develops Disk Drive," August 6, 1991). Thus, compared with American firms, Japanese companies pursued a strategy more consistent with industries under less cost pressure.

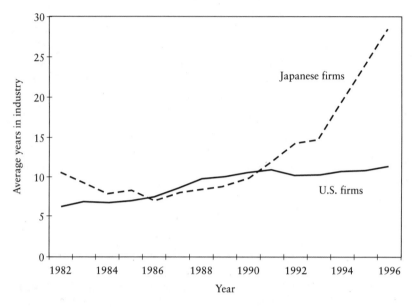

FIGURE 5.5. Average age of U.S. and Japanese HDD firms.
SOURCE: Authors' calculations from industry sources.

Analyzing the share over time of U.S. and Japanese HDD firms with facilities in low-cost Asia highlights these differing national strategies. As figure 5.6 shows, U.S. firms invested in low-cost Asia much earlier than did
their Japanese counterparts. By 1989, more than one-third of U.S. companies had facilities in Asia, almost all specializing in desktop products,
while none of the Japanese were assembling in the region. Only in 1996
did the share of Japanese companies in Asia (outside of Japan) exceed the
U.S. share, by which time all surviving Japanese companies had adopted
the dominant strategy.

What processes were at work in these collective national behaviors during
the early stages of globalization? A look at the American industry suggests
that strategic mimicry occurred through several mechanisms. First, American desktop drive makers assessed the competitive environment by learning from the experience of the American floppy disk drive (FDD) industry,
which had rapidly lost the market to the Japanese. HDD firms were
keenly aware of the growing competitiveness of offshore suppliers of
FDDs; during the early and mid-1980s the business press was publishing
regular articles about the large cost advantages that Japanese FDD manufacturers had over the Americans ("U.S. OEM Vendors Fight," July 7,
1986). Moreover, requirements for success in the desktop market seemed
to play directly toward Japanese strengths: sophisticated manufacturing

FIGURE 5.6. Percent of U.S. and Japanese HDD firms in Southeast Asia.
SOURCE: Authors' calculations.

processes for the production of extremely precise and reliable mechanisms at very low cost. Motivated by these reports and concerns, many
American companies believed they needed to go abroad to put off what
appeared to be an inevitable Japanese challenge.

Second, and most commonly, American HDD firms observed and imitated other desktop drive producers, primarily those that were successful,
relatively new to the industry, and of similar size. Firms monitored the actions
of their direct competitors through reports in the business press and feedback from a plethora of financial and business analysts, thus keeping
abreast of companies such as Seagate, Computer Memories, and Maxtor,
which grew much more rapidly than the industry average after their shift
to Southeast Asia. For example, Priam moved production from San Jose
to Taiwan in 1987, citing the examples of its major competitors, which had
gained competitive advantage over Priam because of their overseas operations ("Priam Goes Offshore," October 1, 1987). Moreover, many of these
young, medium-sized firms were physically proximate in the United States,
making them easy to watch and hence more salient to one another. Of the

seventeen firms that went to Southeast Asia between 1982 and 1990, ten had headquarters in Silicon Valley.

Third, among those that competed in the desktop drive segment, several went to Southeast Asia because their founders and other key executives had previous experience there. Several de novo HDD firms were founded by ex-employees of companies that had already gone abroad, and they chose a similar global strategy. Two prominent examples are Finis Conner's Conner Peripherals and Syed Iftikar's SyQuest. Conner, one of the founding members of Seagate, left the company in 1984. By the time he left, Seagate had been producing drives in Singapore for two years and had also set up subassembly operations in Thailand. Conner then served a brief stint as CEO of Computer Memories, which, like Seagate, was producing drives in Singapore. When he took the job, he cited the firm's Singapore facility as one of Computer Memories' key remaining resources ("The Checkered Past," October 31, 1988). After a short tenure, Conner left Computer Memories and went on to found Conner Peripherals in 1986. Almost immediately he moved to establish low-cost manufacturing facilities overseas, beginning volume production of disk drives in Singapore in 1987.

Syed Iftikar, also a co-founder of Seagate, left the company in 1982 to found SyQuest, just as Seagate made its first investment in Singapore. Soon after establishing SyQuest, Iftikar announced his intention to begin assembling drives in Singapore in 1983 ("The *Business Times* Reports," March 17, 1984). Technical problems with its product, however, forced the company to postpone its move until 1989. Within two years, half of SyQuest's seven hundred employees were located in Southeast Asia ("Syed Iftikar," June 3, 1991).

Finally, personnel movements influenced the adoption of a Southeast Asian manufacturing strategy. The HDD industry is highly incestuous, and in several cases senior employees who had worked for companies with activities abroad were lured away by other companies seeking to move overseas. One example is PrairieTek, which opened a facility in Singapore in 1991 after hiring away from Micropolis the manager who had planned and overseen its operations in Singapore and Thailand ("PrairieTek Selects Edwin Heacox," November 5, 1990). Like PrairieTek, MiniScribe moved production to Singapore after bringing on board a former Texas Instruments employee with extensive experience in setting up new plants and managing manufacturing in Singapore.

In contrast to the American experience, the Japanese HDD industry interpreted the environment differently and followed a different strategic logic. Through 1985, Japanese firms benefited from a strong dollar but began to complain about the strong yen as early as 1986 and had every incentive to move assembly offshore. Japanese executives noted that their disk drives were not as price-competitive as they had been ("U.S. OEM Vendors Fight," July 7, 1986); Seagate was undercutting their prices by 15 percent with drives shipped from Singapore ("Seagate Goes East," March 16, 1987), and Conner Peripherals announced that it had strong sales to the computer divisions of NEC and Toshiba ("How Conner Peripherals Races to Market," May 14, 1990). Ironically, in 1986 both Fujitsu and NEC shifted the production of other cost-sensitive components to Singapore because of the strong yen ("Singapore: Electronics," November 3, 1986). Still, no company, including new Japanese entrants into the desktop market, decided to shift drive assembly to lower-cost Asian locations. Instead, both Fujitsu and NEC set up assembly in the United States. As a Fujitsu executive commented in 1987, referring to the company's efforts to reduce its costs by 50 percent, "it is cheaper to build drives in the U.S. for export than in Japan" ("Fujitsu Execs," May 18, 1987). He made no mention of Southeast Asia. Although Japanese companies were aware of the U.S. production shift to Southeast Asia and the resulting competition in their domestic market, they did not follow suit.[14]

Why did the Japanese miss this early opportunity? One possibility is that mechanisms driving the adoption of the emergent global strategy among U.S. firms were absent or weak in Japan. No Japanese incumbent had spun off a new HDD firm, nor did employees job-hop among companies. A senior manager in Fujitsu's disk drive operations could not remember a single engineer who was hired from a competitor; instead, the company preferred to hire new university graduates.[15] Only one company that specialized in disk drives was ever formed (a joint venture of two existing HDD companies), and one company that made disk drives had a small equity stake in another. But neither the joint venture firm nor the affiliate invested in Southeast Asia. In general, although Japanese companies monitored one another's behavior as well as their American competitors', only their Japanese competitors were salient to their investment decisions.

INDUSTRY CONVERGENCE ON
SOUTHEAST ASIA, 1990–97

With high-volume, low-priced, and low- to medium-capacity drives, cutting costs was paramount. For American companies, Southeast Asia was clearly the location of choice. Their strategy increasingly confined the Japanese to niches in the high-capacity segments—a surprising switch since the Japanese have traditionally excelled in high-volume, low-cost manufacturing. Eventually, however, American success forced the Japanese to follow. Between 1991 (when Fujitsu began production in Thailand) and 1996, all of the principal Japanese HDD firms gradually shifted manufacturing to Southeast Asia, specifically the Philippines. But their lag in doing so placed them behind the American leaders.

By 1991, Fujitsu had reached the maximum capacity of its Yamagata, Japan, HDD facility and was searching for ways to expand production capacity ("Thailand: Fujitsu Slashed Local Production," January 3, 1992). In addition to expanding its Japanese facilities and investing in the United States, as it had done in the past, the company decided to manufacture drives in Thailand, retooling an existing facility for production of low-capacity 3.5-inch drives ("Fujitsu Will Produce," February 28, 1991). In response to the market downturn, however, it stopped all Thai production shortly thereafter.[16] In 1994, Fujitsu restarted Thai HDD assembly and by the end of 1995 was doing nearly all of its volume manufacturing at that facility and a new one in the Philippines. The CEO of Fujitsu Computer Products of America cited the move to Southeast Asia as one of the prime factors behind the company's rapid growth in 1996, when Fujitsu doubled its worldwide hard drive revenues and enjoyed a 123 percent growth in unit shipments ("Fujitsu Ranked the Fastest Growing," June 17, 1997).

NEC, Hitachi, and Toshiba soon joined Fujitsu overseas. NEC completed its own HDD facility in the Philippines in 1995 and increased its offshore production to 75 percent of total HDD output ("NEC Hard Drive Disk Plant," October 9, 1995). In 1995, Hitachi also made its first HDD investment in the Philippines, and by 1998 it had 90 percent of its 2.5-inch disk drive production there and was planning to make all 3.5-inch drives there as well.[17]

What finally drove adoption of the global strategy among Japanese firms? In an important respect, these late movers behaved just like their older American competitors, which were also slow to shift assembly to Southeast Asia. IBM, Unisys (the old Burroughs and Memorex drive operations), DEC, and Hewlett-Packard had all competed in the pre-desktop era. Like the Japanese, each also competed across multiple form factors throughout the 1980s (and in some cases into the 1990s), including the smaller form factors. More important, each relied to a considerable extent on an internal market. As captive sales as a share of total sales diminished, each made a greater commitment to assemble in lower-cost locations. Their internal market concealed the higher operating costs of assembling in "legacy" locations.[18]

While these shared characteristics delayed adoption of the emergent global strategy, firms differed in the direction of their globalization once they decided to move production offshore. While the Japanese followed one another to the Philippines (specifically, the island of Luzon) Control Data, DEC, Hewlett-Packard, Unisys, and IBM all drew on the infrastructure and personnel that American disk drive manufacturers had already constructed

TABLE 5.2

SUMMARY CHARACTERISTICS OF FIRMS ASSEMBLING IN
SOUTHEAST ASIA

	1982–1990		1991–1996		Profile of late adopters (1991–1996) in 1989	
	United States	Japan	United States	Japan	United States	Japan
Number of adopters	17	0	10	6	5	5
Noncaptive firms	15	0	7	2	2	1
Captive firms*	2	0	3	4	3	4
Small drive producers	12	0	10	4	2	1
Large and small drive producers	5	0	0	2	3	4
Small	1	0	4	2	1	1
Medium	12	0	3	2	0	1
Large	4	0	3	2	4	3
Younger than average	14	0	6	2	1	1
Older than average	3	0	4	4	4	4

SOURCE: Authors' calculations.
*Any captive sales.

in Singapore, Thailand, and Malaysia. Nationality still influenced location decisions.

Table 5.2 summarizes the characteristics of the firms that shifted assembly to Southeast Asia. American HDD firms were the early movers into Southeast Asia. They tended to compete in the same market segments (small disk drives for the OEM market), were of similar size (medium) and age (young), and emulated successful firms with similar characteristics (Seagate, Computer Memories, MiniScribe). Of course, none of the new Japanese entrants to the desktop market mimicked the moves of American firms competing in the same market segment. The firms late to Southeast Asia tended to be older and larger, were operating across market segments, and had a degree of captive sales.

As figure 5.7 shows, by 1995 more than 70 percent of the word's disk drives were produced in Southeast Asia, generating nearly 61 percent of the industry's revenues.[19] HDD production in the United States fell to 5 percent of world shipments that generated less than 9 percent of world revenues, while production in Japan fell to 10 percent of shipments and 13.3 percent of revenue. By 1995, Japanese firms had greatly increased their presence in Southeast Asia, producing nearly 55 percent of their HDDs in the region. Virtually all of their remaining drive production was still

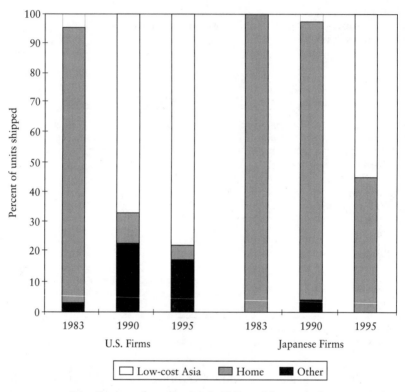

FIGURE 5.7. Distribution of production in U.S. and Japanese firms.
SOURCES: *TrendFocus,* various issues; *Disk/Trend,* various issues; McKendrick and Hicken (1997).

located in Japan—45 percent compared with 13 percent still located in the United States and Japan for U.S. firms.[20] By the mid-1990s, then, the geographic distribution of Japanese assembly had begun to resemble the American distribution. Nevertheless, the damage had already been done, and Japanese firms were left playing catch-up.

THE VALUE CHAIN FOLLOWS

Because of continued investment in the region, nearly every part of the HDD value chain is now produced in Southeast Asia in some quantity, reinforcing the area's preeminence as the center of HDD and components production. Seagate offers a good illustration of continued investment in the region. In almost every year since its initial investment in 1982 the company has reinvested in Singapore—upgrading existing facilities or building new ones. It has also invested heavily in Thailand and Malaysia in upstream activities such as motors, heads, and printed circuit board assemblies (PCBA) and has recently opened plants in Indonesia (PCBA) and China (HDDs). Today it is the largest private employer in both Singapore and Thailand and among the largest in Malaysia.

Independent manufacturers of critical components such as media and heads have also moved into the region, further reinforcing it as the industry's production region of choice. The first head makers to invest were Applied Magnetics and National Micronetics, following closely on the heels of early HDD investment in 1983. Read-Rite, another head company, opened or acquired facilities in Thailand and Malaysia in 1991. The first media maker to locate production outside the United States or Japan was Domain Technology, which began a disk-finishing operation in Singapore in 1988. Komag and StorMedia invested in Malaysia and Singapore, respectively, in 1993 and 1995. Hoya Media was the first Japanese media company to invest in Southeast Asia, opening a Singapore plant in 1996. As of 1995, 93 percent of the firms that make heads or head assemblies had plants in Asia (outside of Japan), while 86 percent of the firms had plants in Southeast Asia. Among media producers, 42 percent had plants in Asia (outside of Japan) in 1995, while 33 percent were producing in Southeast Asia.

Suppliers moved into Southeast Asia because of their ties to existing customers (Seagate, in particular), who encouraged a range of them to invest in Singapore, Malaysia, or Thailand. These suppliers included Domain, StorMedia, Hoya Media, and Komag (disks); National Micronetics, Read-Rite, and Applied Magnetics (heads); Nidec, Sankyo Seiki, and Minebea (motors); Xolox in voice coil actuators; 3M and Smartflex Systems in flex circuits; Magnecomp in suspensions; and Innovex in head wiring assemblies. Read-Rite, for instance, moved the bulk of its manufacturing to Thailand because it was selling more than 80 percent of its products to HDD firms in the region.

Singapore's role as a disk drive center was further consolidated through Seagate's efforts to identify a number of local entrepreneurs to make metal parts and components for the drive: base plates, covers, surface treatment, and circuit board assembly. Both Seagate and Conner Peripherals used the contacts of their local management teams to encourage indigenous investments in these activities. As chapter 7 explains, this local supporting industry was an increasingly important part of the larger industry's technical infrastructure.

The concentration of supplier activity in Singapore and its ties to auxiliary operations in Malaysia and Thailand attracted late followers such as Unisys as well as new HDD entrants. Such agglomeration economies and network benefits were clearly present by 1990. For instance, Integral Peripherals, a maker of 1.8-inch disk drives, selected Singapore as its manufacturing site because of not only the supporting industries available

TABLE 5.3

TOTAL NONCAPTIVE MARKET SHARE OF
FIRMS PRODUCING IN LOW-COST ASIA

Year	Market Share (percent)
1982	3
1983	16
1984	20
1985	19
1986	31
1987	55
1988	61
1989	60
1990	63
1991	70
1992	69
1993	66
1994	83
1995	94
1996	98

SOURCE: *Disk/Trend,* various issues, and authors'
calculations.

but also the possibility of expanding its manufacturing into neighboring countries ("Integral Peripherals," August 26, 1991). Similarly, Hewlett-Packard, a late mover to Southeast Asia, cited the fact that most of the industry's suppliers had moved into Southeast Asia—in some cases, right up the street from the firm's new Malaysian facility ("HP Boise Knows," April 30, 1996). That proximity enabled Hewlett-Packard to minimize its costs and supply lines for raw materials and components.

The value chain is not completely organized along national lines. Japanese suppliers such as Nidec and producers of substrates do the bulk of their business with American companies, and suppliers of other nationalities have converged on Southeast Asia as well. Nonetheless, there remains a distinctly national dimension to the pattern of globalization. Japanese HDD assemblers and their suppliers moved offshore roughly in tandem, which reinforced the attractiveness of the Philippines as an assembly site. Among others located there, Nidec make spindle motors, Hitachi Metals and TDK make heads, Sumitomo Special Metals makes voice coil motors, while Tsukuba Philippine Die-casting and Mette make base plates (Tecson 1999). By contrast, American suppliers have mostly ignored the Philippines. Seagate produced some of its own heads there, but its facility was located far from the cluster of Japanese majors in Luzon.

In sum, American HDD assemblers initiated the move to Southeast Asia, and much of the value chain followed. By 1995, more than 60 percent of global employment in the industry, including upstream activities, was in Asia outside of Japan (Gourevitch et al. 1997). After a decade of investment by both multinationals and local supplier firms, low-cost Asia has become the region of choice. The technical imperatives of the industry ultimately led to a convergence of American and Japanese strategic posture, as shown by the market share of firms adopting a low-cost assembly strategy (see table 5.3). By 1987, five years after an HDD firm first invested in low-cost Asia, noncaptive firms assembling there controlled 55 percent of the market as measured in revenue terms. By 1996, the market share for HDD firms with assembly facilities in Asia had increased to 98 percent.

GLOBAL STRATEGY AND NATIONAL ADVANTAGE

The American industry's early move into Southeast Asia both initiated and coincided with the dramatic shift in competitive logic to low-cost, high-volume manufacturing. Despite recent Japanese movements into Southeast Asia, the American industry has been able to sustain its advantage. Although by 1995 Japanese industry had increased its proportion of total assembly in Southeast Asia to nearly 55 percent, it was still below the almost 78 percent produced there by U.S. industry.[21]

During the late 1970s and early 1980s, Japanese firms were cutting into the American lead in larger disk drives; U.S. market share in eight-inch disk drives, which were first introduced in 1979, was cut to 48 percent in 1983 and 37 percent in 1985 (*Disk/Trend,* various years). Many industry observers predicted the same result in the desktop segment. The business press reported Japanese threats to take the 5.25-inch market and export the small drives to the United States "in significant numbers" ("Winners and Losers," December 1983: 197).

But shifting assembly to Southeast Asia turned back this challenge, initially in 5.25-inch drives and then in the exploding high-volume market for 3.5-inch disk drives in the late 1980s (see figure 5.8). In the low-capacity end of the 5.25-inch market, the segment most vulnerable to entry by low-cost producers, companies that assembled in Southeast Asia (primarily Seagate, Tandon, Computer Memories, MiniScribe, and International Memories) shipped 56 percent of all units in 1983, 64 percent in 1985, and 86 percent in 1987. Although in 1985 U.S. assemblers in Southeast Asia held only 5 percent of the market for high-capacity drives, by 1987 that share reached 71 percent as Micropolis, Control Data, and Priam began to produce there.

Although many of the leading incumbents were late into the 3.5-inch segment (falling behind Fuji Electric, NEC, Hitachi, JVC, and Fujitsu, for

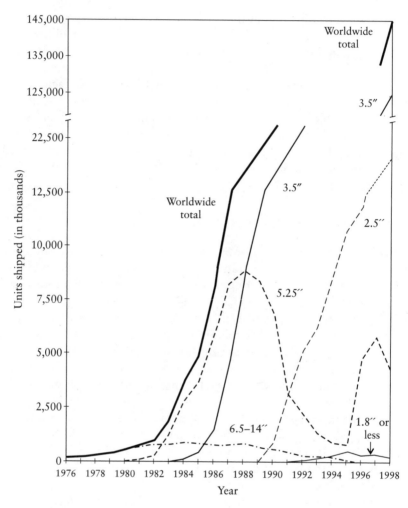

FIGURE 5.8. HDD shipments by form factor, 1976–90.
SOURCE: *Disk/Trend*, various issues.

example), their Southeast Asian base of operations enabled them to out-produce their competitors once they began to ship. During this period, America's leading desktop producers—Seagate, MiniScribe, Conner, Quantum, Maxtor, and Western Digital—extended U.S. dominance. It took three years for the U.S. industry to claim more than 50 percent of this market (see table 5.4), a share built largely by drive makers with low-cost 3.5-inch drive production capability in Southeast Asia. Although each of these leading independents, except MiniScribe, trailed the Japanese in the introduction of 3.5-inch drives, the strategy allowed American industry to claim 90 per-

TABLE 5.4

THE MARKET FOR 3.5-INCH DISK DRIVES
(IN THOUSANDS OF UNITS)

Year	Captive Shipments	Noncaptive Shipments	Total 3.5-inch Shipments	Noncaptive Shipments as Percent of Total	U.S. Market Share of Noncaptive (percent)
1983	0	2	2	100	0
1984	0	67	67	100	11
1985	23	339	361	94	45
1986	250	1,108	1,358	82	56
1987	1,565	2,703	4,268	63	61
1988	2,310	5,899	8,209	72	71
1989	3,620	10,692	14,311	75	74
1990	3,564	16,336	19,900	82	82
1991	3,866	22,170	26,036	85	90
1992	3,972	32,342	36,314	89	92
1993	3,904	39,368	43,272	91	94
1994	4,364	55,980	60,343	93	95
1995	4,623	73,153	77,776	94	93
1996	4,679	83,678	88,357	95	84
1997	5,069	104,579	109,647	95	81

SOURCE: *Disk/Trend*, various issues.

cent of the noncaptive market by 1991. Companies' success depended on their ability to ramp up low-cost, high-volume production in Southeast Asia where, with the exception of Quantum, they assembled the overwhelming majority of their 3.5-inch drives. By contrast, independent Japanese firms did not make a similar move abroad. Only after foreign firms purchased two U.S. HDD firms in late 1995 did the American share of this market dip below 90 percent.

The organizational experiences of Conner Peripherals, Seagate Technology, and MiniScribe illustrate how assembly in Southeast Asia gave the U.S. disk drive industry a competitive advantage. Each company became a leader in 3.5-inch drives, and each relied on production in Singapore to expand market share.

Conner Peripherals entered the industry at the right time with the right product and customer and made it in the right place—Singapore. Although it entered more than three years behind the first firms in the 3.5-inch market, its entry coincided with the explosive demand for computers using new 32-bit microprocessors. It also had the right customer, Compaq Computer, which contributed some initial equity capital. With a secure lead customer (Compaq bought 90 percent of the firm's first year's output) and a more innovative and higher-performance product than his competitors',

Finis Conner chose to open a Singapore assembly facility because he was aware that an inexpensive cost structure was critical to winning more lucrative high-volume OEM contracts. Thus, with good timing, a good product, and a low-cost assembly location, Conner achieved immediate success: the company became the fastest-growing firm in history, recording $1 billion in sales only four years after its founding. By 1990, it became the dominant disk drive supplier to NEC and Toshiba even though NEC had shipped its first 3.5-inch drive two years before Conner and Toshiba only a few months after ("Conner Peripherals Could Become the Fastest Growing," May 1, 1990). Although low-cost production in Singapore and later Malaysia was not the only reason for Conner Peripherals' success, it was a necessary condition.

By contrast, in 1983 MiniScribe was "dying on the vinyl," according to its vice president of manufacturing ("Miniscribe's Far East Secret," March 6, 1989). Hit hard when a large customer terminated its contracts, the company made an overnight decision to build drives in Singapore. The decision saved the company, according to the manufacturing vice president. Its Singapore base enabled it to become the top producer of 3.5-inch drives in 1988 and among the top five in 1989. Although the company collapsed in 1990 amid allegations of fraud, it had by then contributed to U.S. leadership in the 3.5-inch market.[22] MiniScribe failed, as have 90 percent of the companies that ever made hard disk drives, but the move to Singapore gave it a four-year lease on life.

Seagate, the 5.25-inch pioneer, fell behind Conner, MiniScribe, and the leading Japanese companies in the introduction of 3.5-inch drives and had been missing market windows in the mid-1980s for its 5.25-inch products. According to the company's CEO, Seagate was waiting for the market to develop before applying its high-volume production capacity, which approached 12,000 drives a day ("Suppliers Ramp Up," December 1, 1986). Nevertheless, the industry's transition to 3.5-inch drives occurred faster than it had expected, catching it a bit flat-footed. But once Seagate moved, the huge cost advantage it enjoyed by producing in Southeast Asia quickly enabled it to reestablish a leadership position in this segment. It ranked second in unit shipments by 1988 and became the volume leader in 1991. The company's low-cost, high-quality Southeast Asian base of operations proved an enormous advantage. Not only were its labor costs lower, but local supplier firms also lowered the cost and reduced time spent in putting together equipment, tools, fixtures, and machinery that enable fast ramp-up of new products. According to Seagate's president and CEO, "what we have done in Singapore could probably not have been done anywhere else" ("Why Seagate Set Sail," June 1, 1988).

LINKING TECHNOLOGICAL CLUSTERS TO
OPERATIONAL CLUSTERS

One result of an overseas move is that product development is geographically separated from volume manufacturing and, among industry leaders, by great distances (see table 5.5). As we have seen, pockets of technical sophistication developed in the United States (the Los Angeles area, Silicon Valley, Minnesota, and Colorado), Japan (near Tokyo and Osaka), and to a lesser extent in Europe (Great Britain, the Netherlands, France, and Germany).[23] Underpinning American exploitation of locational assets has been the ability of these centers to manage long-distance relations between themselves and operational clusters. One advantage of the early move overseas was to give U.S. firms time to learn how to manage international product and technology transfer.

Typically, U.S. companies conduct pilot production proximate to product development because of the importance of interacting with design teams during initial assembly. They also form product transfer teams consisting of product developers and process engineers from both the United States and the volume manufacturing facility. A product transfer team might include as many as sixty people, who stay with the product from pilot through overseas ramp-up before the local manufacturing group takes over responsibility for volume assembly.

Terwiesch et al. (1999) has examined the new product transfer process of one American disk drive firm. The goal of the transfer was to meet certain targets regarding yields, testing time, process-induced failures, and downtime. As with any transfer, unexpected problems occurred, requiring multiple changes to the product and process. For example, after transfer and during the first two weeks of ramp-up, yields were well below their target. But they quickly improved through better understanding of the problems as well as supplier improvements; and by the third week of ramp, target yields were reached much faster than they had been during any previous ramp. Such an efficient transfer thus hastened the payback of investment in new product design.

Terwiesch et al. (1999) attributed much of the company's success in ramp-up to the organization of the transfer process. The U.S. development facility conducted pilot production and engineering for cost reduction, quality, and product improvement, while the Singapore facility performed all HDD assembly (ramp-up and stabilization) and tests. On the basis of these functional responsibilities, the company formed new product introduction (NPI) groups in both the United States and Singapore to manage the transfer. The complete process involved many small steps over the course of nearly eighty days.[24] Fifteen members of the Singapore team arrived in

TABLE 5.5

LOCATIONS FOR HDD PRODUCT DEVELOPMENT
AND ASSEMBLY, 1999

Company*	Research and Product Development	Assembly
IBM	California New York Japan	Singapore Thailand Hungary
Seagate	California Colorado Singapore Oklahoma Minnesota Pennsylvania	Singapore China Malaysia Oklahoma
Quantum	California	Japan** Singapore** Ireland**
Fujitsu	Japan Colorado	Japan Philippines Thailand
Western Digital	California Minnesota	Singapore Malaysia
Maxtor	California Colorado	Singapore
Toshiba	Japan	Japan Philippines
Samsung	South Korea California	South Korea
Hitachi	Japan	Japan Philippines

SOURCE: Authors' calculations from SEC filings and various
industry sources.
*Firms listed in order of 1998 HDD revenue.
**Contract manufacture by Matsushita-Kotobuki Electronics.

the United States fifty days before the official transfer date, joined approximately one month before the date by twenty-four Singaporean operators
to be trained on the pilot line. A few days before the transfer, all Singapore
team members were sent home, along with eleven American personnel who
would participate in the installation and calibration of test and production
equipment. Two days before the transfer, one Singapore production line was
tested. On the transfer date, the U.S. and Singapore teams communicated
by video conference to discuss the list of items involved in the transfer and
then to transfer responsibility to the Singapore team.[25] Once the transition
had officially occurred, another ten Americans joined the team in Singapore

and stayed until all problems involving their expertise were solved; a few stayed as long as twenty days. By exchange of personnel, transfer of physical and software tools, and considerable face-to-face and electronic communication, the organization effectively overcame the most serious problems normally attributed to the physical distance between development and manufacturing.

An important reason for the success of the American model is that both the technology and the assembly process co-evolved. In the 1980s, the efficiency of transfer and ramp-up over long distances was not as critical to success as it later became; much of the cost pressure was relieved by using cheaper and less-skilled labor, and the number of products to be transferred were few. By the early 1990s, product cycles were much shorter and new product introduction more frequent, with competition centering more on ramp speed than it ever had before. Much of the operational skill underlying fast ramp and volume production thus accumulated in Singapore rather than the United States (see chapters 6 and 7). Therefore, even if close proximity between development and manufacture made sense in principle, shifting assembly back to the United States was not a practical solution. Firms had to master the transfer process, and the survivors became very good at it. At the same time, design itself had to improve to make these products easier to transfer and make. Although firms varied in their ability to minimize adjustments to products that might otherwise require substantial changes in tooling for the assembly process, products and processes in general change much less from one generation to the next.

Thus, companies have accumulated skills in design, transfer, and ramp-up as well as increased the quality of Singapore's and Malaysia's locational assets, thereby facilitating technology transfer and rapid ramp-up to volume manufacture. The HDD industry has developed a large base of skilled professionals in the region with specialized industry knowledge (see chapters 7 through 9). Because the Malaysian and Singaporean governments have been aggressive in offering complementary services such as rapid investment approvals, access to land, and labor training programs, there appears to be little loss in product yields or volume output but considerable cost savings. As product cycles shorten, ramping up has become even faster in Asia. In 1995, Western Digital ramped up production from 0 to 750,000 units within three months ("Western Digital's Burger Speaks Out," December 4, 1995). In 1996, Quantum/MKE went from 0 to 7 million disk drives in nine months ("Seagate Technology Keen to Expand," April 25, 1996). As one manager explained, "the costs of transfer and coordination are paid with just one day of high volume manufacturing."[26] Terwiesch et al. (1999: 23) found the cost of transfer between the United States and Singapore to be $300,000—"less than the value of one day of steady-state output" of the new product.

Similar processes operate among suppliers. An example is Xolox of Fort Wayne, Indiana, which designs and makes actuators. The technical center in Indiana provides product/process development, early-stage production, tool design build, coil winding, computer numerically controlled machining, and overmolding and insert molding. Xolox Malaysia produces molded actuator assemblies using prequalified tooling and processes from the technical center. According to the company, close cooperation has eliminated any problems associated with the transfer and ramp to high-volume production.

Coordinating technical activities with volume manufacturing across national boundaries has thus become standard practice for the industry. The model for American firms is design and pilot production in the United States, fast ramp-up in Singapore and Malaysia, and matured products and process transferred to Thailand or China. Firms that have not adopted this organizational model or have executed it poorly have left the industry.

Conclusion

During the disk drive industry's first twenty-five years, technological development and production were collocated and carried out primarily at a firm's home base. Gradually, a few industry clusters emerged in the United States (California, Minnesota, and Colorado) and Japan (Tokyo and Osaka). During the 1980s, however, changes in markets, technology, and competition increasingly forced American firms to produce disk drives abroad. The advent of the personal computer led to the demand for small form factor disk drives, and firms were under strong pressure to reduce their prices. In response, a few relatively young, small American firms shifted assembly offshore, and their success led other American producers to mimic their move. By the late 1980s, the American HDD industry had formed two distinct kinds of clusters: technological ones in the United States and operational ones in Southeast Asia. In contrast, the Japanese industry continued to maintain production in Japan until 1995.

The timing, direction, and scope of globalization allowed American firms to retain industrial leadership in hard disk drives. Early adoption enabled the industry to move down the learning curve in overseas assembly while accumulating effective capabilities in managing internal and external international links in the value chain. American firms were able to learn the organizational technology of international coordination, thereby benefiting from economies of specialization and horizontal communication. While their activities were dispersed, they were concentrated in key regions: research and development in the United States, labor-intensive assembly in low-cost Asia, and somewhat more skilled assembly in Singapore.

6 *Leveraging Locations*

AMERICAN INDUSTRY AND ITS SOUTHEAST
ASIAN PRODUCTION SYSTEM

Beginning in the mid-1980s, the disk drive industry became globally dispersed yet regionally concentrated, with Southeast Asia emerging as the favored location for overseas manufacturing. The shift was led by relatively young, small American firms specializing in the manufacture of desktop disk drives. Through competitive mimicry, these new MNCs first clustered in Singapore and then spread their operations to Thailand and Malaysia, developing and attracting supporting firms in a way that transformed Southeast Asia into the industry's worldwide manufacturing center. How and why did clusters of disk drive activity develop here as opposed to other regions? How and why were they transformed into a regional production system? Most important, how did these developments contribute to the competitiveness of American industry?

In making locational decisions, managers sought to match their production, technology, skill, and cost needs to an available portfolio of possible locations. Three factors influenced their decisions: factor costs, government policy, and agglomeration economies. Drawing on what we believe is a complete investment history of assemblers and major suppliers in the region, we detail the industry's evolution in Singapore, Thailand, and Malaysia in three periods: 1982–85, 1986–92, and 1993–99, examining how each location attracted investment and contributed to firms' competitiveness. We consider not only developments at each location but the relative position of each location vis-à-vis competitor sites and how those positions evolved over time into a regional production system.

As table 3.2 has shown, the reasons for American investment in the region changed as competitive pressures intensified. Between 1980 and 1985, cost cutting was the competitive driver, especially for firms producing smaller disk drives. Those investing in Singapore in the early 1980s did so to exploit low wage rates, government tax breaks, and a liberal trade and investment regime.[1] Market access was unimportant and agglomeration economies absent.

During 1986–92, competition intensified with the proliferation of the PC, meaning that HDDs became increasingly common. Although cost pressures were as strong as ever, if not stronger, PC manufacturers expected more predictable and faster time to market. American firms responded not by shifting to other locations but by reinvesting in the region, which included developing a strong supplier base. Gradually, a critical mass of companies emerged in Southeast Asia, including a range of supporting industries, so that by 1990 three-fourths of the parts needed to produce a disk drive could be purchased in Asia ("Why American High Tech Firm Recruits," June 25, 1990; "Plugging into an Asian Goldmine," May 3, 1993). These investments began to generate modest agglomeration economies in Singapore, while tapping into an increasingly skilled labor force in Malaysia and Thailand. As the region became an interdependent system, public policies evolved to offer more targeted benefits.

Beginning in 1993, competitive pressures again intensified. Not only were disk drive firms subject to unforgiving cost and time-to-market pressures, but time to volume and yield improvement became critical competitive drivers pushing the industry to improve its control of the supply chain. Despite rising costs for labor and land, Singapore remained the linchpin of the regional production system, and operational clusters emerged in Thailand and Malaysia.

Small, young American multinational corporations led the development of locational assets in the region and were also responsible for integrating each location into cross-national production networks. At the same time, the region was transformed into an interdependent production system, with activities in one country complementing and linked to those of its neighbors. Although at one level the regional production system simply emerged from the cumulation of discrete investments, these investment decisions were not independent of the actions of others. Rather, location decisions were affected by the experiences of competitors and suppliers as well as each company's portfolio of prior investments.

This system conferred benefits on the industry beyond those contributed by any single location. First, linking differently endowed locations meant simple but important gains; their proximity facilitated this link and thus helped meet the industry's need for low costs and rapid ramp-up. Second, the system offered the American industry flexibility in placing similar activities in more than one location, while proximity minimized the costs of redundancy. The U.S. disk drive industry was more competitive than the Japanese not just because it assembled drives in Singapore but because it also located complementary pieces of the value chain in nearby Thailand and Malaysia.

The regional production system proved to be a source of industrial leadership as difficult to imitate in its own way as any national innovation system (Nelson 1993). If American firms globalized production only as a means to exploit cheap labor and tax benefits, they would have been unable to meet the changing requirements of the industry, which became more competitive, more sophisticated, and more demanding of its manufacturing and assembly operations (see chapter 2). Competitive dynamics required that the locations at which firms made disk drives evolved and developed in line with industry requirements. Southeast Asia did that.

The Initial Phase, 1982–85

Figure 6.1 illustrates the beginning stages of the regional production system. In 1982, there were no industry suppliers in Southeast Asia; U.S. and Japanese manufacturers sourced almost all of their components domestically or from each other. Seagate pioneered production in Singapore, the first Asian production site outside of Japan, and began to define the aggressive cost-cutting ethic that has come to characterize the industry. Seagate's phenomenal success, and the fact that it shifted all assembly to Singapore by early 1985, triggered the mimicry outlined in chapter 5, with Maxtor, MiniScribe, Microscience International, and others following Seagate's lead. Although there were no local suppliers when Seagate arrived, growing demand contributed to their formation and growth in Singapore.

In addition to leading the way into Singapore, Seagate initiated the industry's move into neighboring countries. The firm's third investment in the region was in Thailand, which produced labor-intensive HGA/HSA subassemblies that were then shipped to Singapore for final assembly. California-based National Micronetics opened a Singapore facility to supply Seagate, and Applied Magnetics opened a new facility in Singapore to serve the needs of the other assemblers locating there.

LOCATIONAL ATTRIBUTES: LOW FACTOR
COSTS AND GENERIC POLICIES

Why Southeast Asia? Consider the range of options confronting the American industry in the early 1980s, when cost pressures were leading pioneer firms to consider offshore assembly. Neither Japan nor Western Europe offered any help in lowering the industry's wage bill, and Eastern

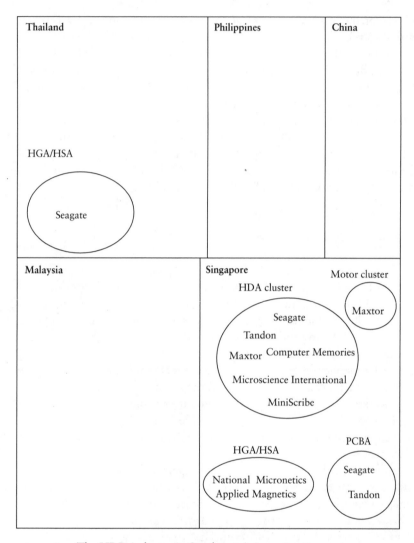

FIGURE 6.1. The HDD industry in Southeast Asia, 1982–85.

Europe was still socialist.[2] The countries of South Asia, despite substantial technical and engineering capabilities and low-wage labor, continued to pursue inward-looking development strategies, only occasionally experimenting with export processing zones. Not until the 1990s did reforms in India begin in earnest. Latin America was just entering the prolonged instability of the debt crisis. Its larger countries such as Brazil were still pursuing import substitution industrialization strategies, even in their computer industries. Few areas in Latin America away from the U.S.-Mexican border industrialization, or *maquila,* program could meet the requirements of adequate infrastructure as well as liberal trade and investment rules. With a prior history of successful offshore investment in electronics, East and Southeast Asia became the most likely locations for the disk drive industry to explore.

The dominant explanation for American offshore investment in Southeast Asia combines factor costs with generic elements of the policy environment. American HDD firms initially went offshore to tap pools of cheap but well-educated labor and were encouraged to do so by the provision of generic infrastructure and credible, arm's-length economic policies: stable macroeconomic policies, free trade or free trade zones, liberal rules governing foreign direct investment, and generous investment incentives.

Factor Costs. Table 6.1 provides an overview of the evolution of labor costs from the early 1980s to the mid-1990s in East and Southeast Asia, showing the region's labor cost advantages vis-à-vis the United States. Singapore certainly offered much lower wages than the United States did in 1983 and in subsequent periods. And as we saw in chapter 2 (and as the Singapore case will show), the PC revolution placed extreme cost pressures on drive makers; indeed, IBM's cost-cutting pressure on Seagate prompted the firm's first investments into Singapore. Yet compared with other locations in the region, Singapore was no bargain: hourly wage rates in neighboring countries were anywhere from 10 to 57 percent of those in Singapore in 1983 and 1985, and wage comparisons became less favorable over time.

In addition to watching labor costs, firms must attend to a range of other factors that impinge directly and indirectly on profitability. Although a number of production processes in the industry demand relatively unskilled labor, quality is an important consideration that, in turn, is strongly affected by government investment in education and training. Along this dimension, Singapore stood out in the early 1980s. Table 6.2 evaluates the comparative quality of the labor force as conducted by Business Environment Risk Intelligence (BERI). Composite scores are based on criteria such as productivity, workers' attitudes, technical skills, and the legal framework. BERI ranked Singapore's labor force best in the world over the fifteen years covered, with Malaysia, Thailand, and Indonesia following far behind. In addition, Singapore had a talented pool of managers and engineers with experience in the electronics industry, which facilitated the startup of assembly operations.

Generic Policies: Trade and Investment, Incentives, and Infrastructure. Government policies and infrastructure also play important roles in firms' decision making. Policies toward foreign direct investment and

TABLE 6.1

COMPARATIVE WAGE RATES IN SOUTHEAST ASIA

	1983	1985	1988	1990	1993	1995
Hourly Wage Rate for Manufacturing (U.S. dollars)						
Singapore	1.49	2.47	2.67	3.78	5.38	7.33
Thailand	0.43	0.54	0.62	1.03	1.25	1.41
Malaysia	—	1.41	1.34	1.39	1.74	2.01†
Philippines	0.59	0.55	0.74	1.02	1.07	—
Indonesia	0.13	0.3*	0.38	0.60	0.92**	—
United States	8.83	9.54	10.19	10.83	11.74	12.37
Wage as a Percent of U.S. Manufacturing Wage						
Singapore	17	26	26	35	46	59
Thailand	5	6	6	10	11	11
Malaysia	—	15	13	13	15	16
Philippines	7	6	7	9	9	—
Indonesia	1	3	4	6	8	—
United States	100	100	100	100	100	100
Wage as a Percent of Singapore Manufacturing Wage						
Singapore	100	100	100	100	100	100
Thailand	29	22	23	27	23	19
Malaysia	—	57	50	37	32	27
Philippines	40	22	28	27	20	—
Indonesia	9	12	14	16	17	—

Annual Wages for Manufacturing (including supplements, U.S. dollars)

	1985	1990	1994
Singapore	7,290	10,839	17,794
Thailand	2,392	3,522	4,917
Malaysia	3,375	3,240	4,555
Philippines	1,257	1,802	2,857
Indonesia	921	674	1,001

SOURCES: ILO, various issues; U.S. Department of Labor, various issues; UNIDO (1996).
*1986.
**1992.
†1994.

trade are in many ways a fundamental explanation of the historical pattern of investment in the region. Table 6.3 provides a comparative index of investment incentives in Southeast Asia from 1983 to 1997, focusing on a range of tax measures including holidays, accelerated depreciation, and other more targeted tax incentives for specific activities, such as exports, R&D, and capital expenditures.

Singapore was among the most generous countries in East Asia—and in the developing world, for that matter—in the investment incentives it offered to "pioneer" firms. These incentives took the form of tax breaks that went directly to the bottom line. For example, the city-state offered tax holidays for a defined period. As long as they did not repatriate their

TABLE 6.2

LABOR FORCE EVALUATION MEASURE

Country	1980	1990	1995
Singapore	81	77	79
Thailand	39	49	52
Malaysia	48	51	54
Philippines	60	58	57
Indonesia	47	42	44

SOURCE: Lall (1998: table 15).

TABLE 6.3

INVESTMENT INCENTIVES IN SOUTHEAST ASIA

Country	1983	1988	1993	1997
		Index		
Singapore	31	32	32	32
Thailand	21	19	21	21
Malaysia	26	27	26	27
Philippines	14	18	19	19
Indonesia	10	10	10	11
	Index Relative to Singapore's (percent)			
Singapore	100	100	100	100
Thailand	68	59	66	66
Malaysia	84	84	81	84
Philippines	45	56	59	59
Indonesia	32	31	31	34

SOURCES: Bardai (1993), Gosh (1996), Business Monitor International (1995, 1997a, 1997b, 1997c), Campbell (1985), Ernst and Young (1990, 1992a, 1992b), Malaysian Industrial Development Authority (1992), Manasan (1996), NTRC (1986), Nolan (1996), OECD (1994), Peat Marwick (1987), and Price Waterhouse (1985, 1986a, 1986b, 1988, 1989, 1990, 1993, 1994, 1996a, 1996b, 1996c).
NOTE: Eleven incentives were combined to form an index of investment incentives. Values for each incentive range from 0 for no incentive to 3 for the best in the region. The incentives include tax holiday, accelerated depreciation, reinvestment tax credits/allowances; K goods tax allowance/exemption/credit; other tax reductions/credits/exemptions; losses carried forward; losses carried forward from tax holiday period; R&D incentives; import duties and taxes; export duties; and exchange controls. The highest possible score is 33.

TABLE 6.4

PHYSICAL INFRASTRUCTURE IN SOUTHEAST ASIA

Element of Infrastructure	Singapore	Thailand	Malaysia	Philippines	Indonesia
1983					
Electrical generating capacity*	2,691	6,028	3,273	5,634	6,232
Electricity production**	3,618	381	857	412	85
Electric power transmission and distribution losses†	6	11	10	13	20
Telephone main lines per 100 people	28.78	0.93	4.82	0.94	0.32
1988					
Electrical generating capacity*	3,371	7,872	4,902	6,582	10,830
Electricity production**	5,045	595	1,103	412	149
Electric power transmission and distribution losses†	4	10	11	18	17
Telephone main lines per 100 people	36.10	1.85	7.37	0.97	0.47
1990					
Electrical generating capacity*	3,400	10,771	5,037	7,021	12,919
Electricity production**	5,809	795	1,326	447	196
Electric power transmission and distribution losses†	3	11	9	19	16
Telephone main lines per 100 people	38.89	2.37	8.93	0.98	0.59
Percentage of failed local calls	21	2	5	18	33
1993					
Electrical generating capacity*	4,513	13,861	6,857	7,464	15,915
Electricity production**	6,598	1,109	1,852	417	267
Electric power transmission and distribution losses†	5	8	9	16	12
Telephone main lines per 100 people	43.40	3.82	12.32	1.32	0.99

SOURCE: World Bank, World Development Report, various years.
*In thousand kilowatt hours.
**Kilowatts per capita.
†Percent of output.

earnings, small firms such as Seagate could defer most of their tax payments, effectively lowering the cost of investment for these rapidly growing MNCs. Singapore's effort to attract foreign direct investment was the centerpiece of the city-state's entire development strategy after 1967; only over time did other countries in the region seek to emulate the Singapore standard with respect to investment incentives. Nevertheless, the relative rankings of countries on this score have proven surprisingly stable. Singapore enjoyed first-mover advantages in providing incentives and has continued to maintain its advantages in this area, even as it has extended more targeted incentives to the industry.

Thailand established a relatively liberal policy toward foreign investment in 1970 and accelerated incentives for export-oriented investment in the 1980s, while during the 1970s Malaysia undertook liberalizing measures and Penang developed export-processing zones. But the country's ability to attract firms in the drive industry was partly hamstrung in the first half of the 1980s by the industrial policy ambitions of the new Mahathir government, which helps explain why Malaysia did not appear as attractive as Thailand when American firms first began to scout the region.

Despite widespread English-language proficiency and a relatively strong educational system, the Philippines was mired in low growth and political uncertainty during the late Marcos years of the early 1980s. That uncertainty extended into the Aquino administration, which undertook major political reforms but proved unwilling, unable, or both to liberalize foreign investment and trade.

The hierarchy in physical infrastructure was largely the same as for labor quality. As table 6.4 illustrates, the rank ordering broadly follows GNP per capita: Singapore leads in the efficiency of basic services such as electricity and telephone lines, followed by Malaysia, Thailand, the Philippines (depending on the indicator), and Indonesia. Singapore holds a commanding position over the entire period in basic areas such as electricity production per capita, the efficiency of its electricity production (a reasonable proxy for reliability of service), and telephone lines per one hundred people (a reasonable proxy for the depth of telecommunications infrastructure more generally).[3]

The Shift in the Center of Production, 1986–92

In the late 1980s and early 1990s, Singapore, Malaysia, and Thailand—and, to a much lesser extent, the Philippines—attracted more firms across the value chain, and the regional production system became more complex (see figure 6.2). The region began to reflect somewhat different degrees of specialization: Singapore became entrenched as the center for disk drive assembly; Malaysia emerged as a specialist in heads and PCBAs; while Thailand produced a more catholic mix of heads, disk drives, and motors.

In Singapore, the initial set of drive firms attracted a second wave of American assemblers, including Conner Peripherals, Micropolis, Ministor, and Western Digital, making the city-state the worldwide center for assembly by 1990. As chapter 5 has shown, these firms were supported by multinational suppliers and a growing number of small Singaporean suppliers. A cluster of printed circuit board assemblers also developed.

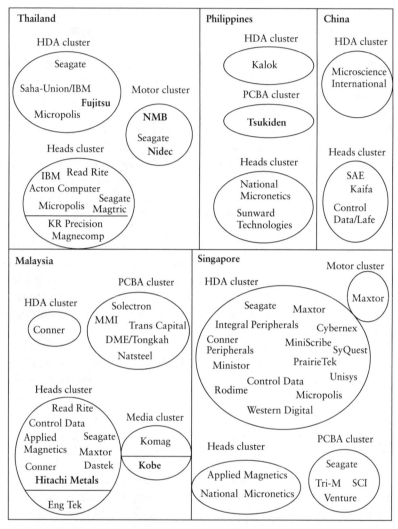

FIGURE 6.2. The HDD industry in Southeast Asia, 1986–92.
NOTE: Horizontal lines within circles separate HDD suppliers (above line) from their own components suppliers (below line). **Boldface** names are Japanese companies.

During this period, the Thai pole began to emerge both in disk drive assembly and in upstream activities that supported Singapore. Several important assemblers came into Thailand to produce low-end desktop drives, including Seagate, Micropolis, and IBM (through a subcontract with Saha-Union, a Thai conglomerate). Among the Japanese, only Fujitsu attempted drive assembly during 1991, but it quickly stopped production in Thailand during the global industry downturn and did not restart volume assembly there until 1994. Thailand also became a volume assembler in heads: both Seagate and Read-Rite had large operations there, and by 1991 Read-Rite was the largest independent maker of heads in the world. These investments attracted other stages in the value chain—specifically, the production of spindle motors—as well as second-tier suppliers to the heads producers such as suspension makers.

Malaysia also emerged as an important part of the production system, with its greater Penang region playing a role different from both Singapore's and Thailand's. While those countries hosted disk drive assembly, Malaysia focused until 1991 almost entirely on heads. Maxtor, which for a time assembled its own HGAs and HSAs, was Penang's first investor in the industry. Control Data (CDC), at the time the largest OEM producer of heads in the world, came to Malaysia the same year. When CDC sold its drive and heads operations to Seagate a year later, Seagate made several additional investments in heads capacity in northern Malaysia, transforming itself into the world's largest heads producer. Penang attracted expansions from the other two large independent heads firms (Applied Magnetics in 1989, Read-Rite in 1991) and Dastek, a small thin-film heads maker, in 1990. HDD assembler Conner Peripherals entered in 1989, initially to assemble heads for shipment to its Singapore facility. By 1991, Malaysia hosted the most important firms in the thin-film heads market.[4] In the early 1990s, its scope of activities broadened to include disks; PCBAs; and a second-tier supply base for actuators (which position the heads over the disks), turned parts, and tooling. Conner expanded into disk drive assembly, and by the early 1990s Malaysia accounted for 30 percent of Conner's HDD production.

During this period, American disk drive firms and heads manufacturers ventured into the Philippines and, by the early 1990s, into China. But production in these two countries accounted for a tiny fraction of the industry's output during this phase.[5] National Micronetics, a major heads supplier, invested in the Philippines; but without a major HDD assembler to anchor production, the country played only a minor role in the industry. Heads operations in China similarly accounted for a small share of worldwide output when compared with Malaysia and Thailand.

THE DRIVERS OF LOCATION: POLICY
LIBERALIZATION AND THE APPEARANCE
OF INDUSTRY CLUSTERS

During the second half of the 1980s, time to market became a more pressing issue as computer makers absorbed an increasing share of drive output and sought to find the "sweet spot" of highest customer demand. As a consequence, locational requirements became more demanding, and operational clusters emerged to satisfy them.

Factor Costs and the Dispersion of Investment to Thailand and Malaysia.   During this phase, drive firms and suppliers remained attentive to labor costs. Although rising wages in Singapore were an important motive for the extension of industry networks into Thailand and Malaysia, the factor cost story does not fully explain the geographic pattern of investment and the evolution of the regional production system. For example, while China had low labor costs and the Philippines was competitive with both Malaysia and Thailand, neither attracted many HDD-related activities until the 1990s. Moreover, Singapore, the high-cost site, continued to attract investment.

This pattern reflected the increasing importance of time to market and shortened product cycles, making proximity to suppliers a key element in solving production problems and changing to new products quickly. In addition, many HDD companies made a substantial investment in automating production at their Singapore facilities. At another level, Singapore's continued dominance reflected the growing significance of the industry's need for specialized labor—managers and engineers—in facilitating the spread into new locations.

The Role of Policy.   The timing of policy changes appears to be a significant factor in the timing of new HDD investments in the region, as Malaysia and the Philippines demonstrate. In the Philippines, the Aquino administration faced great difficulty in undertaking a modest revision in laws governing foreign direct investment, remaining preoccupied with the political issues surrounding a transition to democratic rule. In Malaysia, however, the liberalization of rules governing direct investment after the recession of 1985 expanded the ability of local development authorities to attract capital. As a result, the country, and particularly Penang, relived the success it had enjoyed during the 1970s.

In addition, countries' general incentive regimes differed with regard to implementation, the extent to which incentives could be tailored to individual firms' needs, and host country demands with respect to technological upgrading. Table 6.5 offers insight into policy implementation: the extent to which incentives capture the cost of doing business. Measures include the length of time spent to get project approval, the number of government officials necessary for securing approval, and the amount of total project cost expended on facilitating the application procedures. Data are only available for the early 1990s, but they are a stark reminder that statutory incentives do not necessarily correspond to the actual costs of doing busi-

TABLE 6.5

COMPARATIVE MEASURES OF PROJECT STARTUP IN SOUTHEAST ASIA

	Singapore	Thailand	Malaysia	Philippines	Indonesia
Length of Time to Get a Project Application Approved (percent of applications)					
Less than 3 months	80	15	24	18	10
3–6 months	10	50	39	46	45
More than 6 months	10	35	37	36	45
Number of Government Officials to See or Correspond with before Application Is Approved (percent of applications)					
1–3 people	75	8	27	18	15
3–10 people	15	69	58	46	35
More than 10 people	10	23	15	36	50
Amount of Project Cost Spent to Facilitate Application in Country (percent)					
Less than 3 percent	85	58	64	32	25
3–6 percent	5	23	29	27	40
More than 6 percent	10	19	7	41	35

SOURCE: Macpherson (1992).

ness. The rankings are surprisingly consistent with other measures: Singapore far outperforms the other locations in terms of the efficiency of government, followed by Malaysia and Thailand.[6] This ranking roughly corresponds to the industry's movements during the period, with the Philippines and particularly Indonesia less efficient and largely left out.

Industry-Specific Measures. Not only did Singapore deliver on its promises rapidly, but the Economic Development Board (EDB) was able to tailor general incentive packages to the needs of particular firms. Singapore was also far ahead in developing industry-specific programs such as encouraging automation at a time when Malaysia and Thailand were only beginning to adopt and implement more attractive generic policies. For some time, the EDB has had professional staff devoted solely to monitoring the HDD industry and its major foreign suppliers.

Through the Penang Development Corporation (PDC), Penang emulated Singapore in some important respects—for example, in the provision of high-quality infrastructure in the economic processing zones. The PDC also worked to match foreign firms with local suppliers, broker the application process with the central government in Kuala Lumpur, and provide specialized training. Nevertheless, its scope for policy action was limited by the control that Kuala Lumpur exercised over most major policy instruments, such as tax policy and investment incentives. Unlike the Singaporean case, local policy did not rest on a deep understanding of the industry.

TABLE 6.6

POLICIES AND INSTITUTIONS BENEFITING THE HDD INDUSTRY

Year	Singapore	Malaysia	Thailand
	Labor Market		
1982–85			
1986–92	Magnetic Technology Center		
1993–present	Data Storage Institute (DSI, 1996, formerly Magnetic Technology Center): e.g., in-house seminars, visiting experts, M.Sc. program in magnetics at National University of Singapore; IDEMA (1999): courses leading to Certificate in Storage Competence	IDEMA (1999): courses leading to Certificate in Storage Competence (offshoot of Singapore course)	IDEMA (1999): courses leading to Certificate in Storage Competence (offshoot of Singapore course)
	Technology Diffusion and Development		
1982–85			
1986–92	Magnetic Technology Center; Research & Development Assistance Schemes; Research Incentive Scheme for Companies		
1993–present	DSI; Innovation Development Scheme (EDB, 1996); Gintic Institute of Manufacturing Technology (1993) devoted to promotion of enabling technologies; Center for Advanced Media Technology (1997) for storage media R&D	Kulim High Tech Park (late 1990s)	
	Local Vendor Development		
1982–85			
1986–92	Local Industry Upgrading Program (LIUP, 1986); Small Industry Finance Scheme	Vendor Development Program (1988); Industrial Technical Assistance Fund (1990) for small and medium industries	
1993–present	LIUP; Promising Local Enterprises Program (PLE, 1995)	Malaysian Technology Development Corporation (1993)	

The Thai experience on all these dimensions fell at the other end of the continuum. Bureaucratic problems delayed policy initiatives; the Board of Investment lacked the personnel and knowledge of the industry; and the country's liberal investment and trade regime was grafted to a protectionist set of arrangements for indigenous producers, limiting links to foreign-owned disk drive producers.

Table 6.6 captures some of the emerging differences in industry-relevant public policies: labor market development and worker training, technology diffusion and development, and local vendor development and the promotion of links between foreign invested firms and local suppliers. Again, cross-national differences are marked; the countries differ in not only the existence or quality of programs but also HDD firms' level of involvement in designing and implementing the policies concerned.

Singapore was the first country to establish an institution—the Magnetics Technology Center (MTC)—devoted to the hard drive industry. The MTC provided laboratory infrastructure to facilitate applied research in process technologies and helped expand Singapore's HDD-specific technical work force. The Local Industry Upgrading Program (LIUP) helped expand the local supplier base and by 1992 linked disk drive assemblers with nearly twenty firms. Such suppliers were also able to tap into several financing schemes, such as the Small Industry Finance Scheme, to purchase process equipment (Tan 1994/95: 99–100). Moreover, most of the suppliers occupied JTC factories or industrial buildings made by the government.

Two additional features strengthened the efficiency of Singapore's policy support. First, the LIUP and MTC initiated projects only in response to and in cooperation with disk drive firms. Second, these efforts were influenced by a broader and more explicit industry cluster development strategy. Through its Strategic Economic Plan, formulated in 1991, the government explicitly viewed the disk drive industry as part of two broader clusters: precision engineering and information technology (MTI 1991: 126–29).

Agglomeration Economies. Combined with heterogeneity in factor costs and skills across neighboring countries, these policies contributed to some industrial clustering. Beginning in the mid-1980s, an operational cluster began to form in Singapore. Not until the late 1980s, however, did agglomeration economies emerge involving a wide variety of intermediate inputs, types of specialized labor that enabled firms to ramp up product quickly and reduce time to market, and some interfirm learning within the cluster. Clusters appeared somewhat later in Thailand and Malaysia (in the late 1980s, primarily in the heads complex), with agglomeration economies evident only in the early 1990s through the development of specialized labor and the presence of local suppliers.

Consolidation, 1993–99

By the early 1990s, the industry's geographic configuration had been completely transformed: within a decade, Southeast Asia had become the operational center of the HDD industry worldwide. Competition also became more pronounced, which hardly seemed possible to industry participants. Not only did firms compete in terms of cost and time to market, but product cycles became even shorter, and firms began to face pressure to reach volume production much faster as well as to improve yields. Competition thus occurred along more, and more demanding, dimensions than it ever had before; and not many firms survived. This phase coincided with the emergence of six or seven leading companies and a sharp reduction in the overall number of assemblers and suppliers throughout the value chain.

While Singapore, Malaysia, and Thailand remained at the core of the American production system, Japanese companies finally began to move assembly offshore, transforming the Philippines into their operational cluster (see figure 6.3). Among the assemblers still operating in 1998, almost all had extended their operations to new sites in the region. IBM added facilities in Singapore and Thailand, Western Digital added one in Malaysia, and Seagate added a second Chinese facility to the one it had inherited with its acquisition of Conner Peripherals.

Despite rapidly increasing wages, Singapore retained its position as the center of disk drive assembly as measured by unit shipments, and it developed a cluster of media manufacturers as well. In disk drives, it attracted IBM and MKE/Quantum, the industry's second- and third-largest producers. In media, Seagate, one of the industry's two largest producers, made Singapore its principal facility outside of California.

The two other established poles in the region continued to attract investment and consolidate their positions in the regional production system. Malaysia remained relatively more specialized in PCBA and media than were other locations, and Thailand was more specialized in motors. Both countries were major sources for heads and became more important sources for low- and medium-capacity drives, largely displacing Singapore in these segments.

Northern Malaysia attracted a substantial cluster of HDD companies, including Castlewood, the newest firm to enter the industry. Although DEC, SyQuest, and Hewlett-Packard had exited the industry by 1998, Seagate's Malaysian factory had gained responsibility for launching the company's desktop drives. Malaysia also received additional investments in media soon after Komag's entry, including Fuji Electric, Japan's largest disk producer, and Showa Aluminum, a disk substrate maker. Seagate remained the

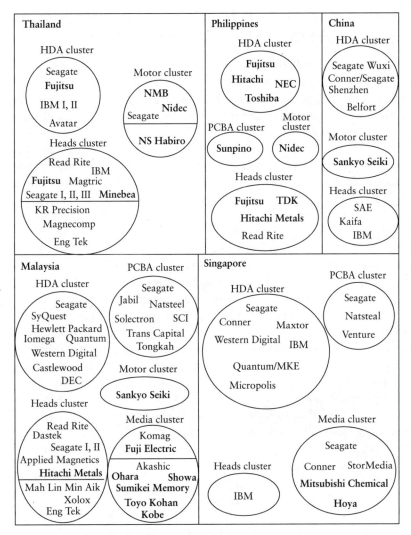

FIGURE 6.3. The HDD industry in Southeast Asia, 1993–98.
NOTE: Horizontal lines within circles separate HDD suppliers (above line) from their own components suppliers (below line). **Boldface** names are Japanese companies.

major heads player in Malaysia (producing all of Seagate's sliders), followed by Applied Magnetics and Read-Rite, the latter importing HGAs from its Thai facility to assemble into HSAs.[7] The second-tier supply base deepened through the entry of a clutch of Singaporean firms making base plates, covers, and other machined parts.

Thailand attracted some new HDA, hosted efforts by IBM and Fujitsu to use the country as a global assembly platform for both drives and heads, received some precision metalworking capacity from Malaysia (actuators from Eng Teknologi), and attracted new entrants to supply the motor cluster. IBM made Thailand its primary disk drive assembly site, accounting for approximately two-thirds of its unit shipments.[8] Fujitsu, in an attempt to regain the leadership it showed during the early and mid-1980s, made Thailand its primary volume production site for 3.5-inch drives and its only site for 2.5-inch drives, also investing to increase its HSA capacity.[9] Thailand maintained its position as the center of motor production with the presence of Seagate, Nidec, and NMB as well as bearing suppliers.

China began to attract additional HDD-related investments. Shenzhen had long drawn the low end of heads assembly (Kaifa and Lafe, two Hong Kong–based companies that largely did contract work); but the move by Seagate, and to a lesser extent IBM, signaled the country's potential. Seagate was China's largest single exporter among MNCs operating there in 1998, with $1 billion in exports. To date no other major assembler has followed.

During this phase, the surviving Japanese majors made a concerted push into the Philippines, accompanied by their principal suppliers, to match the locational advantages of the American assemblers. Nidec started motor production in 1997, TDK and Hitachi Metals expanded in heads assembly, and Sunpino Technology followed in PCBA as did several ancillary Japanese suppliers. These firms invested explicitly to supply their Japanese customers, exporting little to American firms in the region. Among American firms, only Read-Rite remained in the country.

THE DRIVERS OF LOCATION:
INDUSTRY-SPECIFIC POLICIES AND
AGGLOMERATION ECONOMIES

The regional production system continued to expand into low-cost areas, motivated by the same concerns that drove initial investment into Singapore. Yet despite remaining the highest-cost location in the regional division of labor, Singapore not only held on to its investment but continued to attract new investment into the 1990s, even from industry leaders such as IBM. In 1985, wages in Malaysia were 57 percent of those in Singapore; in 1995, they were 27 percent, falling even further with the crisis of 1997–98. Thus, while factor costs were important, they did not account for the continued deepening throughout the region.

Underlying these anomalies is a core characteristic of the HDD industry. While hard disk drives are indeed commodities, they are high-tech ones

TABLE 6.7

EDUCATIONAL ENROLLMENTS IN SOUTHEAST ASIA
(LATEST AVAILABLE YEAR)

| | Enrollment Ratios (percent of age group) | | | Tertiary Enrollment in Technical Fields (numbers and percent of population) | | | | | |
| | | | | Math/Computers | | Engineering | | Core Technologies* | |
Country	P**	S**	T**	Number	Percent	Number	Percent	Number	Percent
Singapore	107	68	46†	1,420	0.05	13,029	0.47	15,730	0.56
Thailand	87	49	21	—	—	51,949	0.09	90,994	0.15
Malaysia	93	61	10	4,557	0.02	12,693	0.07	26,026	0.14
Philippines	111	80	27	5,609	0.01	201,701	0.29	224,754	0.33
Indonesia	115	45	9	13,117	0.01	205,086	0.11	240,597	0.13

SOURCE: Adapted from Lall (1998: table 12).
NOTE: The enrollment ratio can be higher than 100 because children older than those normally enrolled in primary school are also attending.
*Core technical subjects are natural science, math, computing, and engineering.
**P, Primary schooling; S, secondary schooling; T, tertiary schooling.
†Includes enrollment in advanced vocational schools (polytechnics). If this is excluded, Singapore's tertiary enrollment ratio is 27 percent.

whose sales are based on quality, time to market, and time to volume as well as price. Given this mix of requirements, the costs of labor and other factors are important considerations but not the only ones. Firms must consider the availability of skilled labor (managers, engineers, and technicians), industry-specific industrial policies, and agglomeration economies. As with differences in factor endowments and generic government policies, these location-specific assets also varied across the region, contributing to the functioning of the regional production system.

Human Capital and Infrastructure Improvements. Owing to the industry's shift toward lower costs and quicker time to market, firms have developed even more sophisticated needs for human capital and infrastructure. Table 6.7 illustrates the growing attraction of more specialized workers, engineers, and managers. As the table shows, Singapore clearly outdistances Malaysia and Thailand with regard to enrollment ratios in general tertiary education and in technical fields such as math and computers, engineering, and core technologies. The contrast is even greater when R&D effort and the commitment to generating scientists, engineers, and technicians are considered (see table 6.8).

The industry's infrastructure requirements have also expanded as market volatility, changing consumer demand, and technological change com-

TABLE 6.8

COMPARATIVE R&D INDICATORS

Country	Year	Scientists and Engineers per Million Population	Technicians per Million Population	Expenditure for R&D as Percent of GNP
Singapore	1995	2,728	353	1.1
Thailand	1995	119	40	0.1
Malaysia	1992	87	88	0.4
Philippines	1992	157	22	0.2
Indonesia	1995	—	—	0.1
Brazil	1995	168	59	0.6
Mexico	1993	157	105	—

SOURCE: Unesco, Statistical Yearbook (1999), table 3.1.

pel firms to adopt inventory management practices such as "just in time." These practices require demand-responsive infrastructure and services that include not only traditional ones such as affordable and reliable power and water supplies (very important in particular segments, such as media), transport and communication networks, and efficient customs authorities but also intermediaries such as electronically linked freight forwarders and warehousing that themselves constitute value-added services (Peters 1998). As we discuss in later chapters, relative to Singapore and Malaysia, Thailand is weak in both traditional and more advanced infrastructure needs, including trade administration, transport, and telecommunications. In addition, Thailand lacks supplier development schemes, which accounts for the nation's much weaker indigenous supply base.

Industry-Specific Policies: National Differences Emerge. Cross-national differences in the policy environment are most obvious when we examine governmental capacity to initiate and sustain industry-specific policies. Singapore has expanded its Magnetics Technology Center into the Data Storage Institute, which has basic research and training capabilities as well as close links with the National University of Singapore (NUS) and industry. These initiatives continued to be supported by the EDB's broader policy of cluster development, including its effort to attract disk media companies. In addition, Singapore hosted the region's first industry-specific training program sponsored by the International Disk Drive Equipment and Materials Association (IDEMA), the California-based industry association. The program subsequently expanded to Penang and Thailand.

In Penang, HDD firms have been active users of generic electronics courses offered by the Penang Skills Development Center (PSDC), which has been key to the growth of the semiconductor industry. Moreover, the PSDC's members (the firms) play a central role in defining curricular needs. Until mid-1999, however, none of the courses were dedicated specifically to the drive industry, nor did the institute offer any courses aimed only at workers from drive firms.[10] In contrast, Thailand has almost no incentives or institutions for training relevant to either the electronics industry in general or the HDD industry in particular.

The situation is roughly similar with regard to suppliers, although it is important to note how public policies and institutions have built on market-driven processes. In both Singapore and Penang, the industry has developed a number of local suppliers; and public policies and institutions (for example, Singapore's Local Industry Upgrading Program and Penang's PSDC) have encouraged their close coordination with disk drive clients.[11] Conversely, Thailand has made few efforts along these lines, with the result that the country has almost no indigenous suppliers to the industry.

Simply outlining the existence of various programs does not necessarily mean that firms use or value them. From a survey of thirty-seven firms, we have comparable data on the role of public policy from the perspective of suppliers. The survey included thirteen firms in Singapore (all indigenous), fifteen in Penang (six indigenous), and nine in Thailand (only one owned by local shareholders). Although the firms are in different segments of the value chain, they broadly reflect the differences in the overall supplier bases in the respective countries.

The surveys confirm the significant differences we have already noted in the public policy environment of the three countries. First, compared with their Penang and Thai counterparts, a larger proportion of Singaporean supplier firms reported that they received government assistance (see table 6.9) and were offered a much broader array of assistance schemes. A sizable number of Singaporean firms used R&D and innovation investment incentives, personnel training, technical assistance schemes, and industry upgrading schemes; their Malaysian and Thai counterparts used none. In addition, a larger percentage of Singaporean suppliers have established relationships with local universities and research institutes compared with their Penang and Thai counterparts.[12]

Agglomeration Benefits.   Eventually, investment by HDD firms, their suppliers, and the second-tier supply chain created significant agglomeration economies. The small, young multinational firms from the United States mimicked one another in expanding offshore, investing in the development of a local supply base as well as a pool of managers and engineers who accumulated extensive experience in the manufacture of hard disk drives. Rapidly growing firms such as Seagate Technology, Maxtor, and Western Digital have continued to reinvest in the region to achieve economies of

TABLE 6.9

INDUSTRIAL POLICY AND INSTITUTIONAL SUPPORT IN SOUTHEAST ASIA

Singapore		Malaysia		Thailand	
Type of Support	%*	Type of Support	%*	Type of Support	%*
Tax incentives for R&D and innovation	23.1	Pioneer status	33.3	Zone 3 Board of Industry incentives	44
Tax incentives to aquire capital equipment	61.5	Reinvestment allowance	6.7	Zone 2 Board of Industry incentives	56
Relationship with local university or public research institute	61.5	Relationship with local university or public research institute	13.3	Relationship with local university or public research institute	11
Tax incentives to depreciate capital equipment	53.8	Overall tax relief	6.7		
Tax incentives for personnel training/hiring	46.2				
Overall tax relief	30.8				
Small Industry Technical Assistance Scheme	69.2				
Research Incentive Schemes	30.8				
Innovative Development Assistance Scheme	23.1				
Participation in LIUP	38.5				

SOURCE: Authors' survey.
*%, Percentage of firms receiving support.

scale and rapid production ramps. The industry-specific policies and related institutions just outlined also influenced the development of agglomeration economies riding on this wave of investment but also shaping it. Not surprisingly, Singapore hosted a more developed operational cluster that generated much greater agglomeration economies than elsewhere.

How have these agglomeration economies worked in the HDD industry in Southeast Asia? We focus here on two distinct channels: externalities that arise in the labor markets and those related to a group of multiple and proximate suppliers. The agglomeration economies associated with the labor market arose from the fact that new entrants benefited from the development of relatively specialized managerial, engineering, and even skilled operative labor markets as a result of prior HDD investment. The availability of workers, experienced technical personnel, and plant facilities helped the industry meet its requirements for quick plant startup at low cost. Increasingly, firms hired workers with experience in the industry, which became even more important as drives became more sophisticated. As many managers have told us, making disk drives requires a great deal of art, even as the process becomes routine: problem solving always continues, and "recipes" can be lost.

How do the countries compare with respect to the development of these labor market externalities? As the first site for foreign direct investment in the region, and with an even longer history in related electronics activities, Singapore has accumulated a deep pool of managerial and engineering workers with industry-specific skills, which makes the country attractive as a location for ramp-up and the production of high-end drives but also for process innovation and even some product development. Singapore's highly developed educational system combines support for in-house and state-supported training programs, offsetting, at least to some extent, the costs of rising wages.[13]

In Penang, prior electronics investment coupled with more active training programs involving groups of electronics firms has also created a deep pool of managerial and engineering capabilities and skilled labor. These skills contributed to extensive in-house process innovation in the 1990s and the location of certain process-related R&D and specialized functions, such as Quantum's repair facility. Collaborative training programs have helped upgrade this skill base, mimicking to some extent the highly institutionalized educational infrastructure in Singapore.

Although less developed than Singapore and Penang, Thailand has a long history of general electronics as well as HDD-specific investment, which has generated a reliable pool of engineers and semiskilled workers capable of ensuring stable operations in labor-intensive subassemblies of changing products such as HGA and spindle motors. In addition, proximate groups of disk drive and other electronics firms engage in systematic exchanges of information about pay rates, minimum wage issues, bonus and incentive plans, and other human resource issues.

Agglomeration effects arising from the presence of a pool of suppliers have been strongest in Singapore, followed by Thailand and Malaysia. Firms have benefited from supplier proximity in their ability to meet changing demand quickly through a shortened supply chain and in resolving unanticipated problems while achieving timely ramp-up and -down. By the late 1980s, the supplier base in Singapore was quite developed, representing almost every part of the value chain. Its collocation with the HDD firms gave both sets an enormous advantage: multiple customers for suppliers gave them the opportunity to develop economies of specialization and reach economies of scale, while firms had multiple suppliers of the same input to drive down costs. Thailand shows more modest evidence of agglomeration effects in motors and heads, while Malaysia enjoyed similar agglomeration economies for a while in the relationship between HDD assemblers, on the one hand, and HSA and PCBA suppliers, on the other.

Drive assemblers have had access to the broadest pool of specialized suppliers in Singapore, in part because it was the industry's first location. In tandem with the expanding drive producers, a supply base grew up in Singapore, including producers of parts and components (PCBAs, base plates, covers, actuator arms, and connectors), as well as services (equipment repair, cleanroom accessories, tool and die production, machining, casting, surface treatment, and inventory control). On the one hand, they formed a depot of specialized suppliers with distinct cost advantages; indeed, the high costs and reluctance of U.S. suppliers to move abroad gave local suppliers a critical opportunity. But at least some of these firms, such as tool and die makers, have facilitated process innovation, while others, such as PCBA and actuator arm producers, have contributed to component upgrade.

Since it has never been a major center of drive assembly, Penang appears anomalous. As chapter 9 details, however, this view privileges the present over the past. At several points, major assembly investments were made, particularly by Conner; and with them came strong efforts to build local suppliers, particularly in PCBA and actuators. Conner also played a role in internationalizing the operations of Singapore-based companies, and other Singapore-based assemblers benefited from proximity to lower-cost suppliers in Malaysia. In addition to creating depot effects, this supply base meant that several specialized process engineering firms with extensive industry experience could leverage into new areas, such as providing services to new media producers.

Thailand has offered HDD companies an extensive complex of suppliers of inputs into heads and spindle motor assembly. In both cases, Seagate initiated this supplier base as a way to avoid holdup by a single supplier; but it has also allowed assemblers to benefit from fast delivery since these firms focus almost solely on the drive industry. Moreover, the proximity of larger suppliers has facilitated problem resolution in the production process, particularly in volume production.

Agglomeration economies arising through technological spillovers have been less evident. In the case of an operational cluster, benefits are typically generated through the development of specialized knowledge about production processes. The presence of multiple suppliers and assemblers facilitates the spread of information in ways that enable the industry to meet demands for cost minimization, time to market, time to volume, and improved yields. Singapore again stands out in this regard, with many instances in which information about processes has diffused from one firm to another. Such technological spillovers have been less common in Malaysia and Thailand.

In sum, Singapore has clearly stood at the apex of the operational clusters developed by American MNCs in Southeast Asia. By 1990, it hosted more suppliers producing more disk drives than anywhere else in the world and had the most developed supplier base and most specialized cadre of managers and engineers. With these benefits, Singapore generated significant agglomeration economies, which, combined with ambitious and effective public policies, gave American firms enormous advantages over their Japanese competitors. While Thailand and Malaysia also offered the American industry key cost and agglomeration advantages, their development into operational clusters depended in part on their proximity to Singapore; they were part of a system of production that originated in and centered on Singapore.

American Industry's Regional Production System: Locational Heterogeneity and Operational Flexibility in Southeast Asia

Singapore, Thailand, and Malaysia each provided specific benefits to American firms that shifted over time in response to developments within the industry and the countries in question. In addition to the advantages derived from producing in a single country (such as agglomeration economies in Singapore), the American industry gained from operating at the regional level. The three major Southeast Asian producers fit into an interdependent production system that gave these firms an advantage over their Japanese counterparts.

EVOLUTION OF THE SEAGATE REGIONAL PRODUCTION SYSTEM

As an example, consider Seagate Technology, which developed and leveraged the assets of these three locations into its own regional production system. A microcosm of the American industry in Southeast Asia, Seagate illustrates how the regional production system worked. The company's experience also serves as a warning about the dangers of leveraging too many locations. As we argued in chapter 3, too much locational heterogeneity, flexibility, or redundancy can make a production system unwieldy and costly.

Figure 6.4 illustrates how Seagate used different locations to make different kinds of disk drives, showing the most capacious drive assembled at each location in each year. Within two years of beginning drive assembly in Singapore, Seagate was making its highest-capacity disk drives there. Although the company began to assemble drives in Thailand in 1987, Singapore and Thailand played two distinct roles. Singapore received new drives from the United States, ramped them up to volume production, eliminated bugs, and stabilized yields. Once the process had matured, Seagate saved on costs by

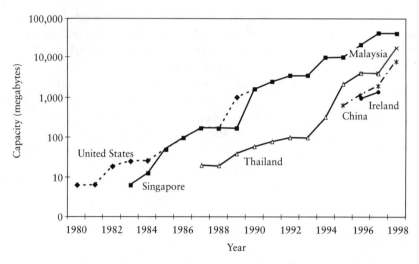

FIGURE 6.4. Highest-capacity drive at each Seagate production location.
NOTE: Seagate began producing HDD in Malaysia in 1996 and made HDD in
Thailand through 1997. The curves for the two countries converge in 1996–97.
SOURCE: Authors' caculations from industry sources.

transferring the mature product from Singapore to Thailand for its end-of-
life manufacture. For example, when Singapore began to make 168.5-mega-
byte drives in 1987, Thailand made the older model 20-megabyte drives, which
were still the most prevalent HDD used in small computers. Similarly, in 1990,
after Seagate had absorbed Control Data's HDD operations and shifted all
assembly offshore, Singapore made Seagate's highest-capacity drive (1.65 gigabytes), while Thailand made the older 60-megabyte models.[14]

Until 1995, only Singapore and Thailand assembled Seagate drives, with
Singapore doing the more skill-intensive processing.[15] Twice a day, after Thailand completed head-disk assembly, the drives were flown to Singapore for
final assembly and test. Merely focusing on low costs, however, was no longer
a viable strategy in the early 1990s. During the 1980s Seagate had been able
to sacrifice time to market in exchange for high-volume, low-cost production; but the industry's requirements had changed, and Seagate paid a heavy
price for being late to the market. To reduce the time-to-market cycle, the
company restructured its U.S. engineering department, and its Southeast Asian
operations responded. As chapter 5 has shown, Seagate was late to market
with a 3.5-inch disk drive but subsequently caught up and offered a full menu
of products. The company began to equal the time-to-market pace of its competitors—at lower cost. As our country studies show, the relatively close proximity of Seagate's operations within the region and those of its suppliers
facilitated the time-to-market strategy.

In 1995, the company opened assembly plants in China and Ireland as a hedge against potential constraints on market access to China and Europe. Moreover, through its 1996 acquisition of Conner Peripherals, Seagate inherited drive assembly operations in Singapore, Malaysia, and China as well as Italy (which the company quickly closed).

As time-to-volume pressures mounted and with too much capacity in the industry, Seagate found itself with too many HDD assembly plants. It closed its Ireland facility (evidence once again that consumers were unwilling to pay even slightly more for drives built in their region), moved drive assembly from Thailand to Singapore, and consolidated its three Singapore plants into one massive operation.[16] Each remaining location played a distinct role. Singapore remained the core of Seagate's drive operations, making the company's most advanced disk drives and performing the most demanding process and product engineering outside the United States. Singapore was also responsible for product development and production of Seagate's successful low-cost drive for the sub-$1,000 desktop PC market. Malaysia was responsible for Seagate's desktop products (which by 1998 included the assembly of a 28-gigabyte drive), receiving products directly from the United States for production. China was used in ways that took advantage of its lower labor costs, making the drives that were initially launched in Malaysia and Singapore.

The geographic proximity of Seagate's other stages of production supported drive assembly. Table 6.10 shows the geographic configuration of the company's employment since 1981, illustrating how it benefited from both the heterogeneity of assets offered by different countries and the flexibility of locating some activities in more than one country. In the early 1980s, the company's focus was on Singapore, where it began PCBA and drive assembly; by 1984, Singapore accounted for more Seagate employees than the United States did. But the company quickly used Thailand to assemble its heads. Keeping the most labor-intensive activities in Thailand but the engineering-intensive activities in Singapore leveraged the assets of both locations while minimizing oversight and coordination costs.

As Seagate grew, it expanded its operations in Southeast Asia, again pairing Thailand's cheaper labor with Singapore's more skilled engineering. It opened a second PCBA plant in Singapore and reinvested in its Thai heads assembly operations, adding a plant to make HGAs in 1989. As Seagate became more vertically integrated, it shifted additional stages to Thailand (in particular, motor production) and transferred motor technology to two Japanese firms in order to meet voracious demand. These firms nurtured the growth of firms supplying parts, making Thailand Seagate's motor supply center. In 1989, with HDA, motor, HGA, and HSA operations concentrated in Thailand, Seagate's Thai employment surpassed Singapore's to become

TABLE 6.10

THE GEOGRAPHIC PATTERN OF EMPLOYMENT IN SEAGATE, 1981–98

Year	Total	United States	Singapore	Thailand	Malaysia	Indonesia	China	Europe
1981	1,000	1,000						
1982	1,600	1,200	400					
1983	2,350	1,300	1,000	50				
1984	4,100	1,600	1,700	800				
1985	4,200	1,000	2,000	1,200				
1986	9,500	1,000	5,000	3,500				
1987	14,300	1,300	8,000	5,000				
1988	28,450	2,300	14,000	12,000				150
1989	35,150	9,000	10,500	14,000	1,000			650
1990	39,950	11,000	12,000	15,200	1,500			250
1991	40,550	9,500	12,400	16,600	1,500	300		250
1992	43,450	9,500	12,400	16,600	3,700	1,000		250
1993	43,250	9,000	13,000	16,000	4,000	1,000		250
1994	54,050	9,500	13,900	22,000	7,000	1,000		650
1995	65,200	9,500	15,000	26,000	12,000	1,500	500	700
1996	91,850	11,000	18,000	34,000	20,000	1,500	5,000	2,350
1997	106,150	9,500	19,400	44,000	23,500	1,500	5,100	3,150
1998	88,750	9,000	15,000	39,000	18,000	1,500	4,000	2,250

SOURCE: Authors' estimates from SEC filings and industry sources.
NOTE: For 1989, employment includes Control Data acquisition; 1996 includes Conner acquisition. U.S. numbers include overseas marketing and sales staffs not otherwise captured. Numbers are generally for mid-year. In cases where figures were unavailable, they have been interpolated.

the company's principal component production and subassembly center, a pattern that persists today. By the late 1980s, Seagate had also helped to develop a range of local suppliers in Singapore, which possessed greater experience in electronics manufacturing than Thailand did. These local firms cut component costs by 40 percent or more over what Seagate had been paying to import them from the United States or Japan. By the late 1980s, although the company was vertically integrated, Seagate was buying far more components in the region than it was making ("Hard Times for Hard Drives," November 15, 1988).

By the early 1990s, Seagate's regional production system had become even more self-sufficient, with multiple suppliers (including in-house production) in Singapore, Thailand, and Malaysia. The Control Data acquisition gave the firm a powerful new capability in thin-film heads along with an assembly plant in Malaysia. Seagate expanded production with investments of $100 million per year in 1989–91, most of it in Southeast Asia; and from 1994 to 1996, it added additional heads machining and assembly capacity ("Market Share Moves," December 24, 1990; "Asia's Hard

Drive," March 18, 1994). Not only did the company benefit from the heterogeneity of locational assets, but it had more sourcing options across the region that increased its flexibility. Seagate made sliders, HGA, and HSA in Malaysia as well as HGA and HSA in Thailand and had added PCB assembly in Indonesia and Malaysia to complement its Singapore PCBA operations.[17] The firm also sourced base plates, actuators, and other components from a range of suppliers in Singapore and Malaysia, many of which it helped to develop.

This geographic configuration of activities has offered Seagate a number of advantages over the course of its history. In the early 1980s, its operations in Singapore and Thailand were a key reason for its position as low-cost leader in the HDD business. It won critical high-volume production orders from IBM, which was making its own desktop drives at its Rochester, Minnesota, plant. Because of its locational choices, Seagate was thought to have a minimum 20 percent cost advantage in producing the same 20-megabyte drive that IBM was producing ("IBM PC AT Plan," April 29, 1985).

As it became more vertically integrated in the late 1980s, Seagate's locational heterogeneity gave it even greater cost advantages, making it perhaps the lowest-cost producer of heads in the world. According to Seagate's CEO, since 1983, the company has "improved its cost/performance ratio by nearly 2,000 times, making it the lowest cost producer of heads in the industry. Since the start of production, the cost of the heads has been reduced by a factor of 25 times and the areal density of the heads has increased 75 times" ("Seagate's Recording Head Operations," November 1, 1994). Since heads subassemblies are a significant part of a disk drive's bill of materials, this has given Seagate tremendous competitive advantages. Proximity among facilities has also reduced the company's supply line, giving it more control over delivery times.

As labor rates become relatively less important to competitive success (although they are not trivial) and time to volume more critical, Seagate has begun to reconsider the geographic configuration of its operations. Instead of considering only the cost of a particular component or process, the company has asked whether a given location can meet the industry's time-to-volume pressures. In some cases, it has been making components that are more costly to move than to manufacture, and the physical separation can delay schedules. Following a cyclical downturn in the industry in 1997, Seagate started to consolidate manufacturing and R&D operations. It closed a number of operations in Ireland and the United States and minimized the number of plants making the same part.[18] In late 1999, it even considered bringing together HGA and HSA, and perhaps HDA, under one roof to improve speed of operations. Such consolidation, however, can also reduce the benefits associated with locational heterogeneity and operational flexibility.

Proximity within Seagate's regional production system has been important from the perspectives of cost, speed, and flexibility or redundancy, enabling the company to capture significant economies in coordination, transport, component, labor, and other managerial costs. Singapore has been Seagate's manufacturing headquarters, with the highest product and process engineering skills. Lower labor costs in Thailand have made it Seagate's center of assembly, and proximity to Singapore has reduced the company's supply lines and given it more control over delivery. Malaysia has responsibility for assembling desktop drives and transferring product to China. Malaysia is also Seagate's global center for the machining of sliders, which are then sent to Thailand for assembly. China does not yet have the skill to do what Malaysia does; in essence, it plays the role that Thailand once played—making mature drives. The Chinese system still needs time to produce engineers and managers that can set up and manage a leading-edge HDD facility.[19]

THE EVOLUTION OF THE U.S. INDUSTRY'S
REGIONAL PRODUCTION SYSTEM

Seagate's experience is a microcosm of the American HDD industry in the region. Although the mix of factor cost and skill, policy incentives, and agglomeration economies at each location contributed to the success of the firms producing there, the industry also benefited from the regional production system as a whole: the heterogeneity of location-specific assets and flexibility in sourcing from multiple locations. These two factors, of course, can be found across a wider, more geographically distant set of countries. Nevertheless, in this case they were achieved through use of proximate locations in Southeast Asia that enabled the industry to meet its requirements for cost, quality, speed, and volume.

First, there were simple but important gains from trade among differently endowed production sites. In contrast to industrial districts or regions within countries, the heterogeneity of locational assets in Southeast Asia gave American firms a portfolio of investment sites across countries that matched both production needs and firms' evolving capability to manage such networks.

The countries of East and Southeast Asia occupy different positions on the development ladder—with Singapore most advanced, down through Malaysia (especially Penang), Thailand, and the Philippines, to even lower-cost locations in Indonesia and, most recently, China. As a result, the region provides investors with a range of both factor costs and competencies that is congruent with the industry's stringent and evolving production requirements, including the flexibility to shift operations quickly if necessary. A look at these activities and competencies reveals their great diversity: skill-intensive, specialized services (product failure analysis, process engineering, cleanroom services); sophisticated capital- and technology-intensive production processes (sputtering disks or ion milling of recording heads); specialized and precision metalworking (casting, machining, surface treatment for tool and die, specialized components); routine but nonetheless advanced high-volume manufacturing (printed circuit boards and board stuffing); volume metal machining and mechanical processes (base plates, motors, turned parts); and labor-intensive subassemblies (head-gimbal and head-stack assembly); and final assembly itself.

As figures 6.1 through 6.3 illustrate, this range of capacities is spread across the region roughly in line with national levels of development. Singapore has clearly been the leader in more skill-intensive and specialized operations and decision making, although these are also apparent in Malaysia, Thailand, and the Philippines. In contrast, Indonesia and China have specialized in labor-intensive assembly and subassembly operations (Seagate's experience notwithstanding). Singapore still is the leader in the production of high-performance drives, process engineering, product engineering, and regional administration. Thailand is the center for motor production, heads assembly, and the assembly of mobile or notebook disk drives. Malaysia bridges the two, with a mix of drive assembly, heads machining, PCBA, and media. This hierarchical division of labor is neither strict nor rigid. The American industry made investments, supported by government policies, that developed local capacities over time. Both Thailand (IBM) and Malaysia (Seagate) are sites for high-volume assembly of new products and no longer merely receive mature products for their end-of-life production. Overall, however, the industry has benefited from a portfolio of locational assets within the region, with Singapore at the apex.

Second, the countries offered opportunities to build redundancy into the system. In the late 1980s, many companies had difficulty obtaining an orderly supply of components, so they qualified multiple sources. Although that process mitigated some of the risk, an additional advantage came from geographic redundancy in component sources, minimizing shocks associated with exchange rate or other changes in cost, plant-level problems in production, or labor shortages. The industry could thus increase or decrease production in specific locations depending on changing requirements.

This option was not well developed until 1986–92 (see figure 6.2), when the industry began to benefit from multiple suppliers across the region, especially in the heads assembly complex. HDD assemblers had their choice of suppliers in Thailand and Malaysia in particular, but even in Singapore and the Philippines. The Singapore plants of Conner Peripherals, Maxtor, and Western Digital sourced heads from Applied Magnetics facilities in both Singapore and Malaysia. National Micronetics shipped HGAs and HSAs to companies in Singapore from its plants in the Philippines and Singapore. Similarly in PCBA, both Malaysia and Singapore serviced drive assembly operations throughout the region.

After 1993, the pattern extended to disks and, to a lesser extent, motors (see figure 6.3). As the world's largest independent supplier of media, Komag's Malaysia operations supplied all of the major assemblers in Singapore, Malaysia, and Thailand, including Seagate, which often used the company as a second source. But Singapore also emerged as an important source, with StorMedia, Mitsubishi Chemical, and Hoya supporting Western Digital, IBM, Quantum/MKE, SyQuest, and Integral Peripherals. Although Thailand was the major producer of motors, customers could also source them from Malaysia and Singapore. Micropolis, Maxtor, Western Digital, and Conner, among others, sourced heads from both Malaysia (Dastek, Read-Rite, Seagate, Applied Magnetics) and Thailand (Read-Rite).

A portfolio of capacities and the option to source from multiple locations, however, would not be sufficient to meet the drive industry's requirements for rapid time to market if the system were too geographically dispersed. Regional proximity facilitated the rapid and frequent movement of key personnel, managers, technicians, skilled labor, and information within and among firms. Such exchanges are important to ramp-up, debugging, and management of quality problems, including last-stage program qualification and decisions about returned materials. Of course, it is surprisingly hard to pin down a precise spatial meaning of the term *proximity* when describing cross-national ties. Is "proximate" within a two-hour plane ride? One manager told us that it was important for him to be able to visit a supplier and be back in his office by the next morning at the latest; certainly, this was possible within the region. Of course, the advantages of proximity must be balanced by the need for access to diverse cost structures and the quality of supply chain management. As one CEO in Singapore told us, "I would prefer to have everything next door," although he quickly noted that there were severe cost constraints to doing so. The key point is that in Southeast Asia, this tradeoff is mitigated by the relative proximity of a diverse array of possible investment sites.

At the simplest level, such proximity lowers transport and communication costs, permitting rapid shipment of equipment, parts, and components; personnel; and information from diverse locations. The industry's success in ramping up new products quickly has resulted in part from its ability to shop for tooling and other equipment throughout the region and obtain it within a month.[20] The ability to obtain parts from proximate locations allows better quality control and more choice in the range of suppliers.

Although this discussion of gains from heterogeneous and proximate locations implies a relatively top-down exchange, the flow of relevant information is not just down from the lead firm but also up from or across the supply chain, whether that chain is vertically integrated or consists of other foreign or local suppliers. American MNCs gave their local managers a remarkable amount of autonomy, especially during the early years, when the firms were small and had little international organizational structure. Firms relied on local managers to not only find or develop local suppliers but identify additional investment sites and coordinate interplant activities within the region.

The American use of location-specific assets has been remarkably meritocratic. U.S. firms allowed—even pushed—local managers and engineers to learn. Seagate's expansion into Thailand was the result of knowledge and decisions by Singaporean managers. Conner's Singaporean managers started up new factories in China. Indeed, the management of regional production by personnel from within the region has been a distinguishing feature of the American HDD system since Seagate's initial investment in 1982. To a much greater extent than Japanese firms (at least to date), American firms have exploited the knowledge embodied in local personnel in constructing and maintaining their corporate networks.

In sum, when compared to other possible mixes of regional production sites, Southeast Asia provides a fairly heterogeneous mix of cost structures and capabilities that are relatively proximate. The regional system evolved from a simple source of cheap factors to one that also provides what John Dunning (1998: 48) calls "complementary value-added activities." As the U.S. industry constructed the system, it reaped both network and location-specific benefits from it. Regionally based managers increasingly leveraged this proximate hierarchy of location-specific assets in ways that contributed not only to lowering costs but to the flexibility required to meet short product life cycles, rapid technological innovation, and shifting market demand.

Part **Three**

CASE STUDIES

7 Singapore

with Poh Kam Wong

Singapore's and America's disk drive industries grew up together. This may sound odd since the U.S. disk drive industry was already twenty-five years old when Seagate made its first investment in Singapore. But as we have argued, American success has been due largely to its ability to produce large volumes of drives cheaply and quickly. Singapore was the place where the industry learned that lesson: growth in the industry's scale of production coincided with Singapore's growth as an operational cluster. In 1983, when Seagate started assembling drives in Singapore, 26,000 was the average number of drives each firm in the industry assembled that year. Ten years later, in 1993, each firm averaged 1.2 million drives. In 1998, the number had jumped to 7.2 million. While the United States has been the source of new product technology, Singapore became the industry's manufacturing center of excellence.

Singapore was the first site for American HDD investment in Southeast Asia, and despite rapid changes in the industry's structure since the early 1980s, has continued to be its dominant Asian location. Between 1986 and 1996, Singapore still consistently accounted for 45 to 50 percent of the global shipment of HDD units, dipping below 40 percent only in 1997. This commanding share does not take into account the surge in media production after 1996 nor the multifaceted role Singapore plays in the regional production system.

The industry's concentration in Singapore during the past eighteen years is all the more remarkable given that the city-state's economy has experienced a significant increase in wage and land costs relative to its regional neighbors. Between 1989 and 1997, average nominal wages in the HDD industry rose by 5.2 percent per year (Economic Development Board, various years). But productivity growth was nearly double that (11 percent), far outstripping productivity growth in manufacturing as a whole (7.9 percent).[1] Understanding how the industry was able to sustain such high labor productivity growth can help explain Singapore's continuing dominance in HDD production and its contribution to the competitiveness of the American industry.

This chapter traces the evolution of the industry in Singapore, outlining how it grew quickly from a simple assembly platform to the center of offshore Asian production for American firms. Not only has Singapore continued to play an important role in hard drive assembly (particularly high-end drives), but the country has also been central in the development of the regional production system. Singapore-based managers influenced investment and sourcing decisions that extended the value chain outward to neighboring countries, while retaining the city-state's status as a regional headquarters, logistics hub, and center of the industry's process engineering talent. By the end of the 1990s, the HDD cluster in Singapore encompassed media manufacturing and associated fine chemicals; flex-circuit manufacturing; and even drive design, associated chip design services, and R&D activities.

Why Singapore? From the outset, firms locating in Singapore benefited from the local capabilities connected with the city-state's experience in the electronics industry. Singapore had strong managerial and engineering talent among people who worked for American MNCs such as National Semiconductor and General Electric. Moreover, initial investments were strongly motivated by lowering costs, particularly production labor and tax costs. Even more important in the long run was the development of agglomeration economies specific to the disk drive industry, which resulted from the interplay of MNC efforts and government policies.

With disk drive assembly, American multinationals introduced a new type of manufacturing to the city-state, one that required more precise machining and faster response times than did the consumer electronics segments in which Singapore was then engaged. Gradually, American disk drive firms created a cadre of managers, engineers, technicians, and operators with industry-specific skills; today, HDD companies in Singapore are populated by people with a wealth of experience from their prior work with other disk drive companies. Assemblers also stimulated the development of an internationally competitive local supplier base in a wide range of supporting industries, including precision engineering, printed circuit board assembly, automation equipment design, and other manufacturing process engineering services. The development of engineering capabilities and supporting industrial know-how not only reinforced Singapore's competitiveness as an HDD assembly hub but helped attract more technologically advanced activities over time.

The Singaporean government played a central role in attracting the MNCs and the development of local capacity. Public policy initially focused on attracting multinationals by offering generous, generic incentives. Over time, and with industry input, the government gradually moved toward more targeted policies and the development of new institutions, pioneering a market-friendly industrial policy that sharply distinguished it from Malaysia and Thailand.

The Development of the HDD Industry in Singapore

In a pattern later followed by Malaysia and Thailand, Singapore began its HDD-related manufacturing operations in subassembly work. But unlike its two neighbors, which had fewer skills in engineering and management, Singapore quickly attracted investments in disk drive assembly from several U.S. firms. As table 7.1 shows, output value grew nearly sixfold from S$3.4 billion in 1987 to S$19.6 billion in 1997, while employment increased from 21,500 to 36,300. Value added per worker doubled over this period. The number of disk drives shipped from Singapore-based HDD makers increased from 3.8 million units in 1986 to 52.2 million units in 1998; the average compound growth rate for 1987–97 was 18 percent. Although Singapore's share of global output declined to 36 percent in 1998, its share in terms of value is undoubtedly higher since it produces higher-end drives than its neighbors do. By the mid-1990s, Singapore was extending its reach up the value chain as a number of firms began to use the country as a site for design activities. Also remarkable is the fact that, with one exception, all HDD majors that ever established operations in Singapore continued their operations in Singapore for as long as they were in the industry.

The growth of drive assembly stimulated the development of a wide range of supporting activities in Singapore: printed circuit board (PCB) making and PCB assembly (PCBA) operations; die casting; metal stamping; precision machining and plating of various mechanical components such as base plates, covers, and actuator arms; connectors; and automation and cleanroom design services (see table 7.2). Some of these activities subsequently moved offshore—in some cases, following customers. Nevertheless, their presence in Singapore still remains strong, and many are listed on the Singapore stock exchange. Singapore also attracted a number of foreign component suppliers, such as Adaptec (connectors), Nidec (drive motors), and FerroTec (sealants). The most significant of these suppliers were involved in disk media and chemicals in the mid-1990s. By 1997, four major disk media companies had established operations in Singapore: Hoya, Seagate Media, StorMedia, and Mitsubishi Chemicals.

TABLE 7.1
GROWTH OF SINGAPORE'S HDD INDUSTRY, 1986–98

Year	N*	Output (millions of dollars)	Units Produced (millions)	Exports (billions of dollars)	Number Employed	Labor Force per Establishment	Value Added (millions of dollars)	Value Added per Worker (dollars)
1986	—**	—	3.8	1.9	—	—	—	—
1987	7	3,359.00	6.1	3.3	21,516	1,788	1,231.00	57,213
1988	8	3,920.00	8.6	4.9	21,532	2,692	1,326.00	61,583
1989	12	5,340.91	10.1	5.5	25,425	2,119	1,417.54	55,754
1990	13	7,354.76	14.9	7.2	28,335	2,180	1,841.91	65,005
1991	12	7,063.98	14.7	7.0	27,691	2,308	1,780.48	64,298
1992	15	8,266.86	20.8	9.0	28,695	1,913	2,237.81	77,986
1993	11	8,918.74	23.2	9.5	25,923	2,357	2,106.69	81,267
1994	13	11,281.68	32.3	11.1	30,178	2,321	2,761.92	91,521
1995	12	13,899.11	40.3	13.5	31,629	2,636	2,891.76	91,427
1996	12	17,559.39	47.4	16.6	37,305	3,109	3,866.60	104,184
1997	10	19,624.45	49.7	17.7	36,263	3,626	4,654.82	128,363
1998	—		52.2	18.4	—	—	—	—

Average Growth per Year (percent)

	Output	Employment	Value Added	Exports
1987–97	19.3	5.4	14.2	18.3
1991–97	18.6	4.6	17.4	16.7

SOURCES: Wong (1999a) from the Economic Development Board, Report on the Census for Industrial Production, various years; Trade Development Board, *Singapore Trade Statistics*, various years, for units and exports.

NOTE: All dollar amounts refer to Singapore dollars. Numbers include optical disk drives, but because their output is so small, they are in effect only for HDD. See Wong (1999a).

* N, Number of establishments.

** —, Not available.

TABLE 7.2

LEADING SUPPLIERS TO THE HDD INDUSTRY IN SINGAPORE

Precision Machining, Tool and Die
Uraco
MMI
CAM Mechatronic
Seksun
Heraeus Precision
Measurex
Brilliant
Swiss Precision
Spindex Precision
Kinergy
Wearnes Precision
BJ Industries
D'MAC
Disk Precision
Getech
Bi-Link Metal Specialities (United States)
Leksun Industrial
Polymicro
Sin Yuh
TNK Precision
TPK Precision
Westpoint Precision
Turntech Precision
Norelco Precision
Tata Precision
Miyoshi Precision
Alantec
Comport Asia
Honson Works
Advanced Materials Tech.

Metal Stamping
JC Metal
Amtek Engineering
Fine Components
Cheung Woh Metal Works
Oaktech Industries
Metal Component Engineering
Stamping Technology

Electroplating
ACP Metal Finishing
Chan Metal Finishing
Micro-Team

Moulding and Die Casting
Fu Yu
First Engineering
Armstrong
Hi-P Tool and Die
Dynacast (Great Britain)
Maxplas
Pioneer Die-Casting
Chosen Holdings
TPW

PCB/FCB
Gul Tech
M-Flex
Smart Flex System
Flexgate
3M (United States)

PCBA/FCBA
Natsteel Electronics
Venture Manufacturing
SCI (United States)
Flextronics
Tri-M
PNE Micro Engineering
Asian Micro
Speedy-Tech
Dyna-mech Electronics
Graphics Electronics

Spindle Motors and Components
Nidec (Japan)
Ferro-Tec (Japan)

Automation and Test Equipment
Excel Machine Tools
Dai Huat
Getech
Hongguan Technologies
MHE
Whyetech
Laser Research
AnA Mechatronics
Gregory System

Cleanroom Design and Engineering
Supersymmetry
Perdana

Media
Mitsubishi Chemicals (Japan)
StorMedia (United States)
Hoya Magnetics (Japan)
Seagate Media (United States)
Conner Peripherals (United States)

Connectors
Adaptec (United States)
Berg Electronics
Ultro Technology
Methode (United States)
Molex (United States)
AMP (United States)

Integrated Circuits, Magnets and Other Electronic Components
Ugimagnetics (United States)
ASJ
AMD (United States)
Silicon Systems (United States)

Heads
Applied Magnetics (United States)
National Micronetics (United States)

SOURCES: Wong (1999a), Tan (1994/95), and various press accounts.

INITIATING A CLUSTER, 1982–85

In 1982, Seagate began the first HDD-related assembly operation, three years after the company was founded in the United States.[2] According to a Seagate co-founder (its senior vice president of operations at the time), the company decided to relocate component production and eventually entire drive assembly from Scotts Valley due to the "high cost, marginal quality and poor availability of labor" in the United States.[3] At one time he had been the procurement manager for Fairchild, where he had developed a good knowledge of the manufacturing capabilities of countries in Asia. Seagate's decision narrowed down to three locations: Korea, Hong Kong, and Singapore. One reason for choosing Singapore was the responsiveness and incentives of the government. The manager contrasted the experience in Singapore with Hong Kong: "I did not feel that the infrastructure was there in Hong Kong to help a small company like ours. In contrast, we were received by Economic Development Board (EDB) officers at the airport, and they took us to see all kinds of manufacturing plants and to talk to the CEOs of these companies." Generous investment incentives quickly followed.

As the comment about Seagate's California workforce suggests, the availability of cheap, disciplined manufacturing labor played a central role in the company's initial decision to consider Singapore. From the beginning, however, Seagate was interested in more than the availability of operatives. Although there was no supply base ("Nothing" said the former senior vice president for operations), Seagate knew they could be built. Singapore had managerial talent, skilled labor, and a wealth of small companies from the city-state's longer involvement in the electronics industry. Although disk drives were more technically challenging (had tighter tolerances) than any product local suppliers were then making, Seagate was confident that a supply base could be developed.

The first local manager hired to head Seagate's Singapore operation had worked in the United States for IBM. He built his senior management team by recruiting a number of friends who had experience in electronics, although only one had ever seen a disk drive. Among them were a manager from General Electric Singapore, who became financial controller, and a lecturer at the electronics engineering school at the National University of Singapore, who became chief engineer. The new chief engineer in turn brought in a number of his former engineering students. The brother of Seagate's first Singapore manager, who was recruited to move head-stack assembly from Singapore to Thailand (the first step in Seagate's development of an overseas production network), had experience working for National Semiconductor in Thailand.

Through contact with the EDB, Seagate was able to locate a local mechanical and electrical engineering consulting firm to help quickly redesign and retrofit an existing factory space vacated by NEC. Seagate initially sourced basic components for shipment to the United States, in large part because the local team had no money to start manufacturing.[4] The first components were printed circuit boards from local board shops, which were debugged, tested, and burned at the new Singapore facility. Seagate then sourced a metal frame that held a disk drive; a part that cost $6 in the United States could be acquired locally for $1.50.

From such humble beginnings grew both a firm and the industry's main operational cluster. Based on this initial success, Seagate soon decided to shift production to take advantage of relatively low wages and the discipline of Singapore's workers. Its first components were PCB assembly and headstacks. In mid-1982, it began taking all its printed circuit board kits to Singapore, starting assembly in thirty days. Although Seagate attempted to outsource PCBA, local suppliers were unable to meet the company's standards. Subcontractors may have had a great deal of experience doing PCBA for use in a variety of products, but they had a difficult time maintaining the quality required for disk drives; nearly 10 percent were returned for rework. Deciding it needed more control, the company brought PCBA in house, followed by HSA.

Seagate started assembling disk drives in Singapore in early 1983, and IBM, then Seagate's largest customer, qualified the plant. IBM liked what it saw, finding both quality at the end of the line and operator quality high. Within a year, productivity, as measured by the number of drives produced per earned hour, was also higher in Singapore than in California, as were yields.[5] Although the extant capabilities of local managers and engineers played a role in this success, the company also found that it had to build new skills.

Disk drive assembly introduced an entirely new kind of manufacturing to Singapore. Many companies in Southeast Asia, including Singapore, could build a thousand units of various components in a day, but none were doing it in a cleanroom. Contamination skills, heads-disk interface skills, and precision machining to tight tolerances were not available in Singapore in the early 1980s. Although Seagate repeatedly urged its U.S. suppliers to follow it to Singapore, few did.[6] All the tooling and fixtures had to be brought from California.

To reduce the cost of final assembly, Seagate's local managers enlisted the help of the EDB in identifying a number of local entrepreneurs who could make metal parts and components: base plates, covers, and surface treatment. A number of the firms that moved into this business can be traced back to the German camera maker, Rollei, which created a significant pool of experienced precision engineering technicians. After Rollei closed its Singapore operations in 1981, some of these technicians set up their own precision tool and die operations in hopes of servicing the new electronics MNCs that were beginning to invest in Singapore.[7] These local suppliers eventually proved capable of making precision parts and components to Seagate's satisfaction and experienced rapid growth as the firm's assembly operations expanded.

Seagate's initial move to Singapore in 1982 and its success in sourcing and doing PCBA and HSA had a demonstrated effect on its competitors, a few of which initiated drive assembly at roughly the same time. Tandon and Computer Memories (CMI) both began assembly in Singapore in 1983. Like Seagate, CMI's largest customer was IBM; in fact, CMI was the sole supplier of drives for IBM's PC AT and was under pressure to cut prices. CMI doubled employment and added capacity at its Singapore facility between the end of 1983, when it started production, and early 1985 ("Say IBM Injects $6M Loan," December 31, 1984). Now drive firms were beginning to see that assembly in Southeast Asia was the way to squeeze costs, and the early leaders were soon followed by Maxtor, MiniScribe, and Microscience International in 1984 and 1985. According to Maxtor's president, Singapore offered "a fine labor pool and a growing technology base. . . . Additionally, the government of Singapore is highly committed to the computer industry and has offered Maxtor some very attractive incentives" ("Maxtor Corporation Will Produce," June 20, 1983).[8] But other than making proprietary spindle and actuator motors in its Singapore facility, Maxtor sourced few components locally and established offices in Taiwan and Japan to procure inputs.[9]

In sum, a combination of labor costs, attractive incentives, and a diverse pool of managerial and engineering labor were important in attracting Seagate. Although the HDD majors saw the potential for developing a local supplier base and began to source basic components in Singapore, cost reductions were primarily achieved through labor savings, tax holidays, and sourcing components from elsewhere in East Asia.

MIMICRY AMONG AMERICAN ASSEMBLERS, 1986–92

Over the next five years, a second wave of major new HDD investments came to Singapore; all but Rodime of Scotland were American. These firms were motivated by the advantages that Seagate and Maxtor seemed to have gained from being in Singapore. Maxtor had more than doubled its output between 1984 and 1985 and had attracted additional venture capital, while Seagate was the low-cost volume leader. Although the most significant makers of small-format drives entered Singapore during this period, the reinvestments of Seagate and Maxtor were equally important for the development of the operational cluster.

Among new investors, Conner Peripherals, the fastest-growing company in industry history, may have been the most important. Conner and Singapore were perfect complements: Conner developed innovative products rapidly in the United States; Singapore provided the powerful combination of rapid plant startup, rapid time-to-volume production, scale economies, and low cost.

Conner's decision to recruit a local manager to head the new operation in Singapore illustrates the growing significance of local managerial and engineering talent to American drive companies.[10] Before joining the company, this manager had worked for Fairchild in Singapore and subsequently established a reputation among American electronics MNCs for his ability to start up operations in Singapore, including National Micronetic's Singapore plant in 1982, the country's first slider and HGA facility. The ability to set up operations quickly was particularly important to Conner Peripherals, which wanted to move the company's new 20-megabyte, 3.5-inch drive to market as early as possible. Conner's new manager worked with the EDB to get quick approval for pioneer status tax incentives and was able to bring the Singapore operation to volume production within three months by hiring both new engineers and technicians and some he had met in his previous positions. Trained at Conner's San Jose plant, these engineers oversaw equipment transfer and proposed changes to the factory layout to improve the manufacturing process flow. By 1989, within two years of startup, Conner was producing close to 80 percent of its global output value in Singapore.

Although the scale of Seagate's and Conner's operations set them apart, other HDD assembly investments during the second half of the 1980s were also able to achieve fast ramp-up of production because of the ready availability of technical skills, government assistance in securing land and facilities, the ease and generosity in securing investment incentives; and the growing number of local suppliers. Rodime, for example, which pioneered the 3.5-inch drive format, came to Singapore in 1987. Relying on managers and engineers from Tandon, it was able to ramp up production quickly and inexpensively by sourcing HSA, PCBA, and base plates from local suppliers.[11] The managing director of MiniScribe hired a local human resources manager with industry experience to poach engineers from existing plants, while Western Digital relied on engineers from Seagate. Both firms also exploited the location's facility advantages. MiniScribe leased a ready-made facility from Jurong Town Council (JTC), a government statutory board responsible for developing industrial land for leasing and sales to manufacturing companies, and with the help of EDB and Western Digital acquired an existing facility once belonging to Tandon.

Micropolis selected Singapore for the availability of cheap, skilled manpower, the high standards of local supporting industries, and the availability of low-cost raw materials ("Micropolis Corp. of the US," March 20, 1986). Initially, it made its older-model drives in Singapore, but Micropolis's CEO found that within several months employee productivity in Singapore matched California's, at lower cost ("Labor Relations," September 1, 1986). Although such productivity comparisons can be misleading since U.S. workers had to debug and stabilize production and then ramp to volume before products were transferred to Singapore for end-of-life assembly, this perception became common among U.S. managers. Within a year, Micropolis started to shift production of its highest-capacity drives to Singapore, forgoing the volume manufacturing stage in the United States ("Investment Surges," February 24, 1988).

Control Data entered HDD assembly activities in Singapore for similar reasons, although its managers also cited proximity to Asian customers as a motive. While the rise of OEM sales of disk drives to emerging Asian PC makers did make a regional operation more attractive, the vice president of operations for the company's Data Storage Products Group said, "Many other factors also led to the decision to locate in Singapore, including a stable and supportive economic, social and government environment, an experienced disk drive manufacturing work force and existing manufacturing facilities to ensure fast start-up" ("Control Data to Begin," June 17, 1987). The plant's four-month startup time was a company record ("Why Seagate Set Sail," June 1, 1988).

As for Seagate and Maxtor, both deepened their commitment to Singapore. In 1986, Seagate announced it would build a second PCB assembly plant employing surface mount technology, thus becoming the country's biggest employer in the manufacturing sector, with 5,000 employees. Two years later it became the largest private employer in the country—larger than Singapore Airlines. With its 1989 acquisition of Control Data's disk drive business, Seagate became the world's largest drive maker. From Control Data the company inherited a Singapore disk drive plant and important recording heads assembly operations in Malaysia.[12] For its part, Maxtor ended 1989 with three plants in Singapore that produced 97 percent of the company's drives and employed 2,300 people.

CONSOLIDATION AND THE SHIFT
TO HIGH-PERFORMANCE ACTIVITIES,
1993 TO THE PRESENT

Despite rapidly rising costs in Singapore, new HDD investments continued into the mid-1990s; and by 1996, all six of the largest HDD companies in the world had established a significant manufacturing presence in Singapore. Investments during this period included both new entrants and incumbent expansion. Among the new entrants were established drive makers such as IBM and Matsushita Kotobuki Electronics (MKE), the manufacturing partner of Quantum, as well as startups such as Myrica, Integral Peripherals, and MiniStor. In addition, Seagate, Conner, Western Digital, and Maxtor expanded operations.

Given rising local costs, why were investments continuing? The major reason related to Singapore's maturation as an operational cluster. During the early 1990s, firm success increasingly came to depend on time-to-volume considerations. High-end disk drives became extraordinarily complex, and no other location possessed the depth of engineering resources to make them. Singapore also assumed a more explicit role in developing and managing the regional production network, functioning as a transfer station for the introduction of new product. Finally, the country began to diversify into new niches, including media, drive design, and other branches of data storage.

As the industry began to focus on time to market and reliability in the late 1980s, it converged on Conner Peripherals' model of product development, launch, and transfer. Fashioned by a Conner co-founder and its chief code writer, the idea was to take a product, bring it to maturity, and then pass it off to a lower-cost production site. At Conner, this three-step process meant that products were designed and initially produced (about two hundred drives) at the company's R&D facility in Longmont, Colorado.[13] They were then passed on to San Jose, California, for early volume production, including debugging, documentation, and development of testing procedures. Engineers who understood the factory then "cooked the product," bringing it to maturity (with a target yield) before transferring it to Singapore for high-volume production. Although the process sounds cumbersome, it was quite effective.

In 1992–93, however, the customer environment changed: customers no longer accepted an immature product (the one produced in San Jose) but needed more reliability and faster launch time. In response, Conner introduced the direct launch from the United States to Singapore. As a consequence, Singapore became important to the industry in a way that differed qualitatively from its previous status: it became the place where drives were debugged, tested, and initially launched. Once demand had stabilized and hitches in starting a new production line were ironed out, the product was transferred for production to other plants such as those in Malaysia and China. As Conner's senior vice president of its Singapore operations observed, "Singapore is the only place where we can take a new product and ramp up production volumes in a very short period of time" ("Conner to Mass Produce," January 29, 1993). After acquiring Conner in 1996, Seagate retained this approach. Because the Singapore organization understood everything about drive manufacture and could contribute to yield improvements directly rather than waiting for yields to be stabilized in the United States, the company could eliminate the transfer phase; the factory learned from production of the first unit.

This kind of capability was important to firms not yet in Singapore, those for whom fast plant startup was critical. IBM, for example, considered several alternative locations, including Thailand, where it had subcontracted HDD assembly since 1991 and subassembly since 1989 (see chapter 8). But Singapore was most attractive from an overall cost perspective: the logistics infrastructure allowed tight inventory management, the technical infrastructure was deep, and the government moved quickly.[14] In early 1994, IBM decided to move lines from San Jose, California, and Mainz, Germany, to Singapore and by early 1995 had ceased all drive production in the United States. Although the EDB facilitated "green lane approval" for fire, building safety, and power, and the Jurong Town Corporation set up a Class 100 cleanroom in just two months, IBM cited the technical infrastructure—the high level of technical expertise and the corresponding ability to start and then quickly ramp up production—as a key factor in its decision.

Singapore's ability to ramp quickly also directly benefited new firms such as MiniStor Peripherals and Integral Peripherals, for whom startup times were critical. Given the manufacturing capabilities in Singapore, both companies eschewed home-based assembly altogether; and by keeping pilot production and ramp to volume in Singapore, both achieved a fast start. According to Integral Peripherals' vice president of operations, who had been director of Seagate Singapore for three years, "Singapore offers Integral access to a broad vendor base as well as highly skilled technical staff and operators. All material, tooling and staffing are on schedule to meet capacity by year end" ("Integral Peripherals Signs Lease," January 10, 1992; "Integral Peripherals to Make World's Smallest Disk Drive," August 26, 1991).

Reinvestments by major incumbents reflected similar motives. Western Digital undertook an aggressive expansion plan, investing in 1995 to boost capacity and enable its local operation to handle new drive technology such as magneto-resistive heads. Maxtor, which had planned to open a second facility in China, changed its mind and decided to expand in Singapore. And in 1997, Seagate opened a $100 million plant, which became the company's largest single disk drive facility, with a total floor space of 1 million square feet and the capacity to make about 40,000 disk drives a day—a signal of Seagate's continued endorsement of Singapore as its most critical location outside of the United States.

In addition to providing speed and skill, Singapore became the manufacturing center for the industry's highest-performance drives—high-end server drives made by IBM and Seagate. (While Western Digital, Fujitsu, and others make server drives, they are less sophisticated.) Although Singapore had been the locus of high-capacity drive production since the late 1980s, server drives are an order of magnitude more complex to make than are drives of an earlier generation: they have more disks, more heads, more complex electronics, greater variation in interfaces, and consequently lower yields.[15] The coordination challenges are also more demanding. High-end server customers demand a small lot and different interface configurations, and components have less commonality. Because customers also pay a premium for these drives, they are even more demanding about service and delivery times.

In addition, the manufacture of server drives requires a greater depth of engineering skill. The engineering team needs to understand not only how to make a drive but also how it works. Failure analysis skills are important sources of feedback for how to design a better drive. In high-end server drives, the possible sources of failure are larger; engineers may get one part right but identifying the entire reason for failure is more complex. Server drive assembly also requires more technical support for equipment doing servo (head positioning) and merge (head-disk assembly). In a number of specialized skills—drive and test code development, optimization of read-write/servo circuits, motor controls, custom-tailored specifications, and the development of advanced error correction code algorithms—Singapore's engineering capabilities are unmatched in the region. Development of this skill base did not happen overnight and is hard to replicate.

Both Seagate and IBM make all of their high-end server drives in Singapore precisely for these reasons. Some 70 percent of disk drives produced at Seagate's Singapore plant are high-end drives; the plant was designed exclusively to make them, and all volume production is done there. According to IBM managers, high-end disk drives for the server market require a combination of skills and costs that only Singapore can meet. Thailand and China "may be able to do desktop, low end mobile, and HSA. But Singapore combines high competence *and* affordable labor costs."[16] When it entered the server market in 1996, Western Digital opened a new plant in Singapore despite earlier investments in Malaysia.

Finally, Singapore retained a strong presence in the industry by gradually diversifying into other products and functions. In 1995, five disk media companies announced they would invest in Singapore, including two HDD assemblers (Seagate Technology and Conner Peripherals) and three independents (Hoya, Mitsubishi Chemical Infonics, and StorMedia). Local production grew rapidly, rising from a negligible share of total world shipments in 1995, when the first plant opened, to 20.7 percent in 1997, making Singapore among the leading locations for disk media production in the world.

The Evolution of Supporting Industries in Singapore

Although the presence of a supporting industry base has played an important role in both attracting and holding the HDD majors, it first had to be developed. With the support of the Singapore government and through their procurement efforts, American multinationals built the most well developed operational cluster in Asia outside of Japan. Within a few years of its arrival, Singaporean firms offered the industry almost every component it needed except for heads, disks, motors, and chips, which were designed and made by U.S. or Japanese corporations. By 1990, local firms offered printed circuit boards (PCB) and flex-circuit boards (FCB) manufacturing; PCB/FCB assembly and contract manufacturing; precision engineering services such as die casting; metal stamping; tool and die; mold making; precision machining and plating of various mechanical components such as base plates, covers, and actuator arms; and cleanroom design services, automation equipment, input/output cards, and connectors.

When the first American firms began operations in Singapore, most local firms were incapable of meeting the tight tolerances demanded by the industry; American firms imported components primarily from the United States, Japan, Hong Kong, and Taiwan. In building its line, for example, MiniScribe had to source in Hong Kong and Taiwan because tool and die was a problem, as were PCBs.[17] A number of entrepreneurs, however, who recognized disk drives as a fast-growing business opportunity, were cultivated by Seagate and Maxtor and later encouraged by the government to invest in machinery. Seagate, in particular, believed that "developing suppliers is part of our business," according to a member of the original team.[18] Initially, it bought turned parts and PCBs in Singapore. Tandon sourced base plates and actuators from Uraco and BJ Industries, two local firms that had supplied Tandon in the floppy disk drive business. In 1985, Micropolis began to source a few components and tooling from Singapore, even though it had not yet assembled there. The bulk of the contracts were awarded to Flextronics (Singapore), a subsidiary of Flextronics of the United States, for PCBA; but two Singaporean suppliers, Precision Casting and Lam Soon Engineering, provided tools. By 1987, some 80 percent of mechanical parts were sourced locally, and Singapore emerged as a hub for important mechanical parts.

After it entered in 1987, Conner Peripherals contributed to the strength of the local supply base by starting a local vendor development program. Together, Conner and Seagate shipped almost 10 million drives in 1989, most of which were made in Singapore. These two companies offered an enormous market for local precision engineering firms such as CAM Mechatronic and Uraco, who received a tremendous boost from orders for base plates and covers. Conner also supported the contract manufacturing industry by outsourcing PCBA to Tri-M, Natsteel Electronics, and SCI and cultivated the development of local cleanroom design by giving Perdana Consulting major plant expansion contracts.[19] Conner was the first customer of MMI Holdings, which makes base plates, covers, disk clamps, actuator arms, and voice coil motor assemblies and is now listed on the main board of the Singapore stock exchange. Founded in 1989, MMI initially made actuators for Conner. The first batch, however, was scrap; the company did not even understand how to read the specs. After Conner gave MMI another chance, the company eventually made 20,000 actuators a month and became a captive supplier.[20]

The development of the local supply base was not limited to local firms; HDD assembly activities also stimulated the growth of foreign suppliers and induced new ones to enter. Foreign heads and disk suppliers were important entrants. Applied Magnetics heads assembly plant in Singapore grew so quickly that by 1988 it accounted for 30 percent of the company's total output ("Sales of Magnetic Heads," February 14, 1989). Singapore, however, also has one of the largest concentrations of production of connectors and input/output cards in the world, including Adaptec, AMP, Berg, Molex, and Methode. Although some of these firms were established before the HDD industry expanded in Singapore, all have been major suppliers to the industry. In the late 1990s Nidec started spindle-motor production and design activities in the city-state, having already done motor subassembly on nearby Batam Island in Indonesia. A number of U.S. makers of flex-circuits, including 3M, also established a strong presence in Singapore; and foreign firms were present in machine tools, resins, and a variety of other products.

As table 7.2 shows, more than one hundred supporting industry firms in Singapore have been significant suppliers to the HDD industry. Precision engineering services account for the largest group: machining of actuators (E-blocks), metal stamping of base plates and covers, and associated activities such as surface treatment and die casting. Nearly all these firms are local. Another important group does PCBA, which is primarily local but also includes some foreign firms (such as SCI). Three of these local PCBA firms (Venture, Flextronics, and NatSteel Electronics) now rank among the top ten electronics contract manufacturers in the world.

Although many of these firms were initially established to serve other electronics industries in Singapore, a significant number started with the HDD industry, particularly those in the precision engineering sector. Of the approximately twenty precision engineering and contract manufacturing firms that have grown large enough to be listed on the Singapore exchange during the past eight years, about two-thirds benefited significantly from supplying the industry at key stages of their corporate growth. Over time, most have diversified into other electronics manufacturing and assembly industries; but several, including MMI and Brilliant, remain heavily dependent on the HDD industry.

Singapore's Emergence as a Regional Base

The Singapore operations of the major firms played a role in the internationalization and regionalization of the industry by inducing other firms to come to Singapore or neighboring countries and serving as a base for the development of regional production networks. American MNCs gave Singaporean managers and engineers the freedom and responsibility to make a range of important decisions, and they responded by moving into or inducing production in Thailand and Malaysia.

The original Seagate team in Singapore initiated the regionalization of the industry, shifting head-stack assembly out of Singapore into Thailand (see chapter 8). Much of this regionalization was overseen by Singapore managers. One of the company's original Singaporean hires was responsible for setting up Seagate's Far East engineering facilities, including those in Thailand, and putting together the seventy-five-person engineering organization. In 1986, Seagate made him vice president of engineering for Seagate's Far East operations, responsible not only for research, development, and process engineering for disk drive operations in the region but for the company's extensive subassembly operations as well.[21]

At Conner Peripherals, the same local manager who had helped to get the company set up in Singapore orchestrated Conner's move into Penang, convinced Singapore-based suppliers to follow, and developed a handful of local, Malaysian suppliers. All of Conner's key suppliers went to Penang (CAM, Tri-M, Natsteel Electronics, and MMI) and eventually supplied part of Conner's Singapore operation from Penang as well. This local manager was also responsible for Conner's support of a new PCBA firm (Trans-Capital) and setting up Conner's assembly plant in Shenzhen, China, in 1992, relying on his experienced Singaporean managers and engineers to help supervise the transfer and training process.[22]

For Seagate, Conner, and Western Digital, Singapore became a transfer station where new drives were first ramped to volume production before being transferred to other plants as they reached maturity. Only after the Singapore plant had tooled up the assembly process lines for the new drive products and achieved process stability for volume production were the drives sent to be assembled in the other plants. Even then, the other facilities continued to receive technical support from Singapore process engineers in tooling design and equipment transfer.

During Seagate's expansion of drive assembly activity to Thailand, Singapore played a significant transfer station role. The Thailand HDA plant assumed responsibility for assembling the older, more mature products, with some of the process equipment being transferred from the Singapore plant. The Singapore plant was also the first to undertake automation in specific production stages, stabilizing them, and then transferring the tooling designs to the Thai plant. As we have mentioned, with the acquisition of Conner, Seagate adopted the Conner practice of ramping drive transfer directly from the United States into Malaysia; but Singapore remains the transfer station for one family of drives now made in China.

In 1994, Western Digital began to convert its Malaysian integrated circuit assembly and test facility into a disk drive manufacturing plant to increase production. The Malaysian facility was intended to make the company's more mature disk drive products, which were initially launched in Singapore ("Western Digital Opens," October 12, 1994). Western Digital uses the Singapore operation as a process development resource for the Malaysian plants.

Reinforcing Singapore's role in the regionalization of the production system are the investments of many of the local precision engineering firms and contract manufacturers, particularly in Malaysia but also in China. MMI, NatSteel Electronics, Venture Manufacturing, Elec & Eltek, Brilliant, CAM, Gul Tech, Armstrong Industrial, Uraco, Seksun, and Measurex have all made investments outside of Singapore to support their disk drive customers.

Explaining Singapore's Contribution to American Success

In this account of the development of the HDD industry in Singapore, we have invoked a number of causal arguments to explain the pattern of investment over time and how it benefited the U.S. industry. Here, we attempt a more systematic look at factor costs and supply conditions, agglomeration economies of industry-specific skills, supporting infrastructures and information spillovers, and government policy. In addition, we examine how the balance of these factors changed as technology shifted and the industry evolved.

FACTOR COSTS AND SUPPLY CONDITIONS

In the early 1980s, Singapore, Hong Kong, and possibly Taiwan provided the best mix of factor endowments for HDD assembly activities in Asia; not only did they have well-trained, disciplined, and inexpensive labor, but the workforce had prior exposure to electronics assembly work. Our interviews with managers show that the price pressures of the PC revolution meant that the search for low-cost labor was a paramount consideration among early entrants.

Low wages and rents, no taxes, availability of labor, plus managers who knew how to source lower-cost parts in the region were critical advantages for Seagate and the other pioneers in Singapore. These firms made explicit comparisons between wage rates in Singapore and the United States but not necessarily among Asian countries. MiniScribe emphasized that labor costs in Singapore were about 25 percent of U.S. labor costs ("MiniScribe, Others," July 13, 1987). Seagate's co-founder told us that wage costs in Singapore were a significant motivation behind the company's shift there. Maxtor claimed to have cut its labor costs to one-fourth of what they were in the United States ("Maxtor Corporation . . . Is to Invest," April 3, 1984). In general, during the 1980s, labor costs for drives made in the United States accounted for 15 to 20 percent of a drive; with the move to Singapore that fraction dropped to 5 percent ("Peripheral Mfrs.," October 22, 1984).

Even though wages for these workers were already higher than in other Asian countries, supply was a more important consideration. Moreover, these three countries enjoyed a substantial cost advantage in terms of salaries for engineers, technicians, and operators. Singapore had many managers experienced in electronics manufacturing and a moderately good supply of engineers and technicians. Workers' fluency in English also favored Singapore and Hong Kong over Taiwan, as did communications and transport infrastructure. In the early 1980s, however, Taiwan scored better in terms of size and sophistication of local supporting industries such as precision engineering and PCBA.

Thus, factor conditions alone cannot explain why Singapore was chosen rather than Hong Kong or Taiwan. Moreover, even after Singapore was initially chosen, factor conditions could not adequately explain why production should continue to concentrate there. Singapore experienced increasing labor shortages and rapidly rising wages in the early 1980s, even resorting to importing foreign workers to increase the supply of operators for electronics manufacturing companies. Land prices also escalated during the late 1970s and early 1980s.

THE EVOLUTION OF GOVERNMENT POLICY AND INSTITUTIONS

There is no doubt that the Singapore government has worked to attract and sustain HDD-related investments, but can those efforts be associated with the industry's success? Although it is notoriously difficult to isolate the effect of public policies on industry performance, a comparative analysis of the industry's development in Thailand (chapter 8), Malaysia (chapter 9), and elsewhere (chapter 10) suggests that differences in public policies help account for patterns of investment and industry performance.

Singapore's public policy toward the HDD industry is part of the country's well-known strategy of leveraging MNCs to create high value-added jobs and induce productivity growth through continuous technological upgrading (Wong 1999b, Low et al. 1993). As a result, many of the factors that attracted HDD investments and sustained their expansion were not specific to the industry. Nevertheless, when viewed together from a global and regional perspective, these policies had one important feature: they were in place *earlier* than those in other developing countries both in and outside of the region. Thus, Singapore enjoyed substantial first-mover advantages in attracting foreign investment in both electronics more generally and the drive industry in particular. Only gradually did this advantage erode as other countries converged on Singapore's incentives.

Over time, Singapore's public policy became more industry-specific, seeking to upgrade skills, the capacity of local suppliers, and the nature of foreign firms' operations. These efforts deviated from traditional notions of industrial policy in significant ways. By maintaining a commitment to openness and guaranteeing the involvement of both majors and suppliers through the development of various consultative channels, the government was able to design policy interventions that conformed with industry requirements.

Infrastructure, Business Facilitation, and Tax Incentives. An extensive literature on Singapore's development underlines how the general political and business environment, efficient government bureaucracy, high quality of infrastructure, and generous tax incentives have contributed to Singapore's ability to attract direct foreign investment (see the annual *World Competitiveness Report* and Low et al. 1993). Moreover, the city-state has political and macroeconomic stability, a clean and efficient government, strong protection of property rights and business contracts, and a cosmopolitan living environment. In addition to complete openness to trade and financial flows (essential for the development of a regional production network), the government has directly and indirectly invested heavily in trade- and investment-related infrastructure: transport and communications network facilities, industrial parks, and cost-competitive public utilities. Efficient communications and transport services are of particular importance to a dynamic industry such as HDD manufacturing, where the high volume of procured parts and the importance of speed to market put a premium on effective logistics and supply chain management. Low-cost manufacturing operations can be undone by bottlenecks in both physical infrastructure (such as port handling capacity and frequency of connecting ships or flights) and soft infrastructure (such as customs-clearing procedures).

Customs procedures provide a small but telling illustration of the efficiency of government in Singapore. Asia is the source for more than three-fourths of the parts that Seagate needs, and many are flown in by Singapore Airlines, the national carrier, and expedited by ground crews and customs officials. The time between touchdown and arrival at Seagate's factory is a mere six hours. As the chairman of Maxtor commented, "you can do business in the disk drive industry in Singapore in a more concentrated and streamlined manner than anywhere else in the world. Effectively all you need is right there—and it's not an accident" ("Looking for the Asian Edge," June 17, 1990).

Provision of infrastructure even extends to the physical plant. People in the industry repeatedly cited the country's ability to supply functioning industrial facilities as an aid in rapid ramp-up. The Jurong Township Corporation (JTC), in particular, has been an important part of the industry's success in this regard. In the 1960s, before there was much foreign direct investment in Singapore, the JTC began an aggressive effort to help potential investors, in effect providing a turnkey operation complete with water, power, and regulatory approval. Since then, the JTC has offered American disk drive companies fast availability of property and flexibility in moving.

The importance of these facilitating conditions is difficult to quantify; more transparent are the tremendous tax advantages. The primary tax incentive for disk drive firms over the years, pioneer status exempts holders from corporate tax on profits for five to ten years. This was critical for the young, small American HDD companies: they could accumulate capital offshore to finance their overseas expansions—the equivalent of an interest-free loan. Only when companies repatriated profits back to the United States were they liable for U.S. taxes. Pioneer status, however, was not the only incentive; continual upgrading and expansion of existing assembly operations benefited from tax incentives such as accelerated capital depreciation allowance. Nevertheless, it is important to note that, since the late 1980s, neighboring countries such as Malaysia have imitated many of these incentives, thus eroding their initial advantage.

Labor Markets and Skill Development. The role of labor markets in Singapore's development has been somewhat more controversial. Legislation restricting the independent development of trade unions and a tripartite consultation and wage-setting system dominated by the government have been crucial in creating a nonconfrontational labor relations environment. Early adoption of a liberal immigration policy has not only attracted foreign skills and talents but dampened wage pressures at the lower end of the skill ladder and slowed the pace of real wage growth.

The other side of this restrictive political bargain is extensive government investment in the skills of local workers (see Soon 1993). One early contribution was public investment in a large number of training institutes for precision engineering skills, which contributed to the development of that industry. As industry has demanded higher skill levels, training programs have followed suit with increasing emphasis on training at both the polytechnics and undergraduate and graduate levels at the university. Although they do not target the HDD industry specifically, the institutes' programs have contributed to the reservoir of HDD manufacturing process engineering skills.

The early establishment of the Skills Development Fund (SDF), a compulsory "tax" on payroll that companies can only use by sending their employees to approved training programs, creates strong incentives for firms (Soon 1993). Our interviews with the HDD majors and their suppliers suggest that all have used the SDF extensively for worker training.

Besides training through SDF, HDD majors and their suppliers have used a number of other subsidized skills upgrading programs. In the late 1980s and first half of the 1990s, manufacturers received various incentives through the Industrial Automation Promotion Program to invest in automation and adopt computer-integrated technologies. A study of automation adoption among three HDD majors in the mid-1990s (Wong and Ang 1997) found all of them using the incentives to invest in process automation. One HDD major used another incentive scheme, the Initiative in New Technology Adoption (InTech), to send engineers to the United States to be trained in advanced automation technologies.

In addition, the government has moved to provide a specialized training program for the industry in storage technology conducted by Singapore Polytechnic in collaboration with IDEMA, the international trade association. Although this program is too new to have had any visible impact, it illustrates the continuing public policy effort to innovate new manpower development programs to meet specific industry needs.

Supporting Industry Development Policy. While the Singapore government did not completely overlook local business in its early push to attract foreign direct investment, policies to support these industries began to play a more prominent role after the recession of 1985, when the government paid greater attention to developing the local supply base. Many of the precision engineering firms serving the HDD industry benefited from a variety of financial and technical assistance programs. For example, the Small Industry Technical Assistance Scheme (SITAS), later renamed the Local Enterprise Technical Assistance Scheme (LETAS), and the Local Enterprise Finance Scheme (LEFS) provided public subsidies to small firms to invest in technological upgrading and productivity improvement. A particularly important intervention for the drive industry was the Local Industry Upgrading Program (LIUP) launched by the Economic Development Board (EDB) in 1986.

Through the LIUP, the EDB paid the salary of an experienced engineer employed by a participating MNC. This "LIUP manager" identified local suppliers with the potential to become globally competitive and made recommendations for various upgrades. When possible, the LIUP manager drew on the MNC's resources—for example, inviting suppliers to send workers to attend quality training programs for MNC employees or getting the company to design vendor development programs that address the problems of suppliers. The LIUP managers from the different MNCs are required to meet regularly at the EDB to pool their knowledge of key problems faced by the suppliers under their care. Thus, the managers are able to leverage resources and know-how beyond their own MNCs, while senior EDB officers get a comprehensive picture of suppliers' concerns and can fine-tune existing assistance programs or develop new ones.

A second contributing policy was preferential financing. Many machine shops were so small that banks ignored them, so LIUP provided access to capital that they otherwise would have been unable to raise. One company used such financing to develop a coating process that eliminated contamination in Maxtor drives. As the Maxtor project manager commented, "to our benefit, we will no longer have to buy some items overseas now that our suppliers are expanding their lines" ("Multinational Companies," November 2, 1987). Early in its development, Brilliant, a leading maker of base plates, received grants covering 70 percent of the total cost to build its production and planning control capabilities.[23] Overall, LIUP was important to the development of the HDD industry, and local sourcing of

HDD components and services accelerated after the program's initiation. According to our survey, supporting industry firms that participated in LIUP were satisfied.[24]

R&D Promotion Policy. While early policy efforts to support industry development concentrated on general technological upgrading, they have been complemented by recent efforts to promote technological innovation and R&D and over time have become more industry-specific. Through the National Science and Technology Board (NSTB), the government has initiated a number of R&D incentive schemes such as the Research and Development Assistance Scheme (RDAS) and the Research Incentive Scheme for Companies (RISC) that effectively subsidize private firms' investment in R&D. While these schemes are open to both local and foreign firms and are not confined to the HDD industry, all the HDD majors in Singapore have received an R&D grant from NSTB, although they have not disclosed the actual grant amounts.

In the 1990s, the government began to invest more extensively in a research infrastructure specifically for disk drives as one means to keep the industry in Singapore. In 1992, NSTB established the Magnetics Technology Center (MTC) specifically to build local capabilities in magnetic storage technologies. As with the LIUP, the MTC was encouraged to work closely with HDD companies to establish R&D collaboration. The purpose was to ensure that MTC would both provide technical support service to the HDD majors' operations in Singapore and set in motion a virtuous circle through the enhancement of local R&D capabilities.

Although few R&D activities were actually forthcoming in the initial years, the government nonetheless continued to pour resources into MTC. In 1996, it upgraded the center into a larger R&D institute, the Data Storage Institute (DSI), with a broader mandate to cover R&D in not only magnetic recording technology but also other data storage technologies, especially optical storage. DSI's staff strength rose to 144 by 1998, with an annual budget of about S$28 million. After some false starts and initial groping, DSI gradually began to build strength in selected technology areas, enabling it to attract a growing number of major data storage technology companies to enter into R&D collaboration agreements. As of 1998, DSI had three approved patents and seventeen pending and had spun off one company in laser texturing of magnetic discs and laser microfabrication.

Although it is too early to assess DSI's impact on the product innovation capabilities of the Singapore-based data storage companies, the fact that DSI has been able to attract several leading HDD companies to participate in R&D collaboration projects suggests that it has already developed a certain level of capability. One project involves IBM, Motorola,

Fujitsu, Hitachi, and a local silicon design company, Serial Systems, to develop a superior channel recording technology used in hard disk drives. The government pays for half the project's cost, and DSI contributes half the project's staff ("Local Institute Forms," August 4, 1997). The growing portfolio of patents filed by DSI is another positive indicator. The most important indicator of relevance to the industry, however, is the involvement of the majors in its activities.

In addition to a public research infrastructure, the government has provided direct financial support for corporate R&D. For instance, Seagate Singapore first began to transform its continuation engineering activities into a drive design center in 1992, supported by direct R&D grants from the government. Although the initial design was poor and no volume production resulted, the government continued to extend direct R&D grants to Seagate; and by 1997, R&D staff at Seagate had grown to 140. Seagate's R&D investment effort finally led to the successful introduction of a new low-cost drive (the U4) that began volume production in early 1999, followed by the U8. Government subsidies thus resulted in the local design of one of Seagate's most important drives.

Not all of Singapore's industrial policy efforts have been successful. In 1996, Singapore Technology (ST) Group, a large high-tech conglomerate owned by the government, acquired Micropolis when it ran into financial difficulties. Although the government emphasized that the acquisition was a commercial decision made by the ST Group, some observers saw it as partly motivated by the government interest in having a Singapore-owned company with HDD innovation capabilities. The acquisition proved to be a financial disaster: Micropolis's competitive position weakened after the acquisition, and it eventually had to be liquidated in 1998. Although ST's amount of investment in Micropolis was not disclosed, it was rumored to be several hundred million Singapore dollars. Nevertheless, the important point was that ST did not persist in this effort, nor did the government seek to subsidize a losing enterprise for a long period of time.

AGGLOMERATION ECONOMIES

If Seagate's initial choice to locate in Singapore rather than Taiwan or Hong Kong was somewhat fortuitous, it nonetheless stimulated followers. Despite a well-defined cluster of firms, companies were not truly benefiting from agglomeration effects in the early years. But by the late 1980s, U.S. firms were clearly reaping advantages from agglomeration economies associated with Singapore assembly: a pool of managers and process engineers with industry-specific skills, a local supply base, and technological spillovers.

Seagate played a key role in developing a critical mass of managers and engineers with specific knowledge of disk drives. As the first HDD firm in Singapore, and because it grew so dramatically, Seagate trained a large number of people who went on to populate other U.S. companies entering the country. All of the most successful companies of the period employed ex-Seagate people in their top engineering teams: Maxtor, Western Digital, MiniScribe, Conner Peripherals, Micropolis. Just as IBM was the fountainhead for specialized labor and entrepreneurs in the U.S. technological cluster, Seagate deeply influenced the operational cluster in Singapore. Almost everybody we interviewed had worked for more than one HDD assembler or recording head company in their careers, a fact that reveals companies' ability to recruit ever more specialized labor. As one human resource manager explained, "in the past, when the industry was getting started and technology [was] not so high, we had to be content with taking whomever we could get and train them on the job. We were all learning so we didn't mind getting new people without experience. Now, everything is more focused in the sense that we look for people with industry-specific skills."[25] Experienced personnel came to understand how disk drives were designed, manufacturing yields improved, and unit costs driven down. As a Western Digital manager commented, "the thing about disk drives is we are never 100 percent sure of a solution. You sometimes need intuition, a gut feel. This is where experience matters. And it's not like just one company has it; people move around."[26] In short, the American assemblers benefited from the presence of their competitors because collectively the industry had trained many people who moved freely among firms.

Intermediate inputs are a second factor of agglomeration economies. By the late 1980s, as LIUP projects began to bear fruit, a clutch of local manufacturers achieved economies of scale in base plates and other machined parts by supplying the HDD companies. The process became reinforcing: Singapore-based HDD firms generated growing demand for specialized components that attracted additional local suppliers to the industry.[27] The sheer number of local suppliers (see table 7.2) suggests the range of companies and products.

Supplier proximity also enabled a more efficient and shorter supply chain; Brilliant, for example, delivered base plates three times daily to Western Digital.[28] Supplier proximity was especially important during early stages of ramp-up during equipment changes.[29] Maxtor and other companies made changes to their master schedule (their production output schedule) almost every day. In response, suppliers ramped up or down daily, a critical benefit of a short supply chain. The fact that disk drive assemblers could choose among several companies gave them enormous flexibility in this regard. Proximity of multiple suppliers improved efficiency in other ways as well.

Even something as mature as disk drives "are not perfectly designed. Many things have to be done on the fly. Any change to orders or designs can cause delays and shortages. Being close allows us to respond more quickly."[30] Even in the early 1990s, as wages were rising, new American firms entered Singapore to take advantage of these agglomeration economies.[31]

A third factor is technological spillovers in operations. Within the cluster of firms operating in Singapore, learning and imitation occurred among HDD assemblers, among suppliers, and between assemblers and suppliers. In the first instance, assemblers established benchmarks against each other in the assembly process. Everybody had information about the production and product plans of their competitors because assemblers needed to share that information with their suppliers, who served multiple customers.[32] "Everybody knows one another," said one manager. Information about assembly techniques diffused in a similar way. For example, at the end of the assembly process, drives were burned in as part of testing— an expensive process. Although companies burned in differently, on average it took three days to complete testing using expensive specialized testers. At one point, a Conner Peripheral co-founder invented a way for drives to test themselves without specialized testers. Although he patented the technique, everybody in Singapore copied it, thus reducing the amount of time it took for all firms to test.[33]

Because U.S. HDD firms had demanding production requirements, they aggressively pushed information and knowledge at their local suppliers in order to meet those requirements. Firms learned to make standardized parts because they all wanted to buy the same components from local vendors. The same went for similar machinery. The co-founder of MMI Holdings explained, "The presence of so many HDD assemblers in Singapore really drove our [supplier] learning. One company bought a certain kind of machine because an assembler urged them to. Then everybody in his business bought the same machines. We didn't know really any better—you just copy one another."[34] This kind of information diffused more rapidly and completely in Singapore than in Thailand or Malaysia, which are less institutionally rich and densely packed, and contributed tremendously to rapid productivity growth in the industry.

Agglomeration effects became even more pronounced in the 1990s as the nature of competition began to shift. Time-based competition was an increasingly important characteristic of the industry. While improving yields and reducing costs continued to be important (they are a constant in the industry), a firm needed to ramp up and down quickly to meet shortened life cycles for products that were becoming even more sophisticated, especially at the high end. The presence of a significant number of disk drive firms enabled personnel to accumulate these industry-specific skills, the extensive interfirm movement of engineers and managers carried skills across firms and product generations, and a supporting industry could take a specification and with little direction meet the volumes required by customers on short notice. All have been central to the American industry's success.

Public Policies and Agglomeration Economies.   Although we have discussed various public policies separately, they are extremely interdependent. Singapore's initial advantage stemmed from its early emphasis on attracting foreign direct investment, which required policies that granted firms complete operational autonomy. Once a group of industries developed, Singapore could maintain a locational advantage even if other countries adopted the same incentives. Nonetheless, the government did have some means available to promote the local supply base; for example, LIUP was one way to diagnose areas of weaknesses in local supporting industries. Nevertheless, to rectify these weaknesses, firms needed to draw on complementary resources from programs such SITAS and LETAS. These efforts, in turn, could only be successful by eschewing local sourcing requirements and forcing firms to meet international standards.

Over time, the significance the government gave to developing the local supply infrastructure became more explicit (MTI 1991). The *Strategic Economic Plan* formulated in 1991 explicitly underlined the need to promote integrated clusters linking downstream end-product industries, upstream supporting industries, and enabling capabilities. This strategy required not only interagency coordination in formulating and implementing industrial policies but consultative mechanisms through which government and local firms could understand the requisites of the market. Because of the industry's size and significance, industry players are now represented on the board of government agencies involved in industry and technology promotion, industrial training, and tertiary educational institutions. In particular, senior managers of the HDD majors have regularly been appointed to board membership on the EDB and the NSTB.

Applying this cluster industry promotion approach to the HDD industry went beyond building the precision engineering and PCBA supporting industries. Beginning in the mid-1990s, the EDB focused on attracting disk media-related companies as a way to strengthen Singapore's regional hub role in HDD. Recognizing that only part of the disk media manufacturing process has high value-added qualities, the government has encouraged disk media firms to invest primarily in the chemical production stage and the disk sputtering rather than the disk stamping and polishing stages, which are land- and water-intensive and have lower value-added qualities. The

EDB offered considerable help, such as 100 percent tax holidays and assistance with facility preparation.

Agglomeration economies have also arisen from the proximity of media companies. Seagate set up a media plant to serve its local HDD assembly operations ("Seagate Earmarks $140m," July 12, 1995); and StorMedia claims that "the growth in HDD output in Singapore means that Singapore can attract and retain talent and companies. . . . We need to be close to the customer. Close communication is important."[35] In this case, close interaction between media suppliers and drive assemblers facilitates failure analysis. Moreover, as the executive managing director of Hoya, a Japanese disk maker, stated, "Hoya can take advantage of the skilled manpower available. The Singapore workers have been trained over the years and are accustomed to the rapid pace and demands of the disk drive industry" ("Hoya of Japan," June 15, 1995). Finally, policy has been an important inducement for media companies to locate in Singapore. Conner Peripherals cited the country's favorable tax regime and good infrastructure rather than proximity to its HDD facilities as reasons for investing there ("Conner's Disk Media Unit," August 8, 1995). Hoya shipped its product not to firms in Singapore but to Japanese HDD firms located elsewhere ("Hoya to Produce," June 14, 1995). Although StorMedia's first plant was meant to serve Maxtor in Singapore, all output from a second plant set up in 1996 was dedicated to Seagate assembly locations in Thailand and Ireland.

It is not easy to quantify the precise impact of public policy on HDD industry development in Singapore. Nevertheless, the scope of policy efforts, the involvement of the majors in their formulation and implementation, and interviews, press reports, and public statements provide strong prima facie evidence of the value that American firms place on these policies. These positive evaluations extend to suppliers; as noted in chapter 6, a higher proportion of supplier firms in Singapore than in Penang gave positive evaluations of public policies.

In sum, public policy contributes to the development of agglomeration effects and make operational clusters sticky. Singapore's policies have been structured so that although wages have been steadily increasing, the city-state has been able to attract and retain a more technically sophisticated range of activities. Make no mistake about it: without ongoing tax benefits, many activities currently accomplished in Singapore would likely leave. Nevertheless, the government's commitment to the industry has transcended that minimal requirement. Policies have been directed toward building skills, an unparalleled physical and communications infrastructure, a deep supporting supply base, and responsiveness to the specific requirements of the industry. Public grants have built a human resource base that enhances skills in product and process engineering up through applied research and development. Policy and business behavior have moved in tandem, and the majors that remain in Singapore benefit from the private and public investments that, during the past fifteen years, have resulted in a critical mass of managers, engineers, and suppliers with deep knowledge of the industry and its requirements for success. As an American manager who has worked with both Conner and Seagate says, "why make drives anywhere else? Where else is the environment so supportive?"[36]

8 Thailand

While Singapore has played the central role in Southeast Asia's regional production system, Thailand has been an important complementary actor.[1] Disk drive production in Thailand began modestly in 1983, when Seagate started head-stack assembly with fifty workers. Since then, the industry has become significantly broader and moderately deeper: by 1999, Thailand hosted close to thirty-five HDD firms, making it one of the world's largest sources of disk drives and related components. HDD exports grew from roughly $2.6 million in 1985, to $1.3 billion in 1990, to $5.3 billion in 1998.[2]

This performance made the drive industry a critical part of the Thai economy. In 1998, Seagate was the country's largest employer, with a workforce of 33,000. IBM, Fujitsu, and Seagate are the country's three largest exporters, and the industry as a whole accounts for more than one-quarter of the country's total electrical and electronics exports and 10 percent of total exports.[3] Always competitive in the cost of labor, Thailand has over time developed into a location that contributes directly to the American HDD industry's ability to achieve time-to-volume production with high yields.

The Thai HDD industry includes four different kinds of firms (see table 8.1). Three of the world's five largest drive producers (Seagate, IBM, and Fujitsu) operate large facilities there. Seagate's Thai operations are the "center of assembly in Southeast Asia" and account for nearly half of its global workforce.[4] Thailand was the site of IBM's first volume assembly facility outside of Japan, and IBM and Fujitsu produce finished drives there as well as heads subassemblies. Seagate produced head-disk assemblies for several years, with final assembly and testing in Singapore. Since 1997, it has devoted its Thai facilities to component production.

TABLE 8.1

HDD AND RELATED FIRMS IN THAILAND

Product	Company
Disk drive assembly	Seagate (1987–98); Fujitsu (1991); IBM/Saha Union (1991); IBM-SPT (1997); Avatar Peripherals (1995–98)
Head-related operations	
Head-gimbal assembly	GSS Arrays (1985–92); Acton Computer (1987–88); Seagate (1989); Magtric (1990–98); IBM/Saha Union (1991); Read-Rite (1991); Minebea (1994); Fujitsu (1999)
Head-stack assembly	Seagate (1983); Micropolis (1988–97); IBM/Saha Union (1989); Read-Rite (1989); Fujitsu (1991); Maxtor (1996); IBM-SPT (1997)
Suspensions	K.R. Precision (1988); Magnecomp (1992)
Flex suspension assembly	Boron (2000)
Actuators	Eng Precision (1999); Fujikara (1985); Fujitsu (1994); NMB (1985); Measurex (1998)
Voice coil magnet or assemblies	TDK (Thailand 1992); Hana (1993); Fujitsu (n.d.)
Spindle motors and related components	
Spindle motors	Seagate (1986); NMB (1988); Nidec (1989)
Hubs and related parts (O-rings, sleeves, brackets)	Habiro (1995); Nippon Super (1996); Thai Okoku Rubber (n.d.); Shin-Ei (n.d.); Eiwa (1991)
Bearings	NMB (1985); NHK (1994)
Magnets	Seagate (1994); Daido (1995); NMB (1985); Advanced Magnetic Materials (1998)
Magnetic powder	Advanced Magnetic Materials (1998)
Electronics	
Printed circuit cables	Seagate (1994–98)
PCBAs	Hana (1993); Elec & Eltek (1988); SCI (1988); GSS (1985)
Flex circuit and suspension assemblies	Boron (1995); AdFlex (1996)
Media products	
Polished substrates	Hoya Opto (1991); Asahi Komag (1996); Nikon Thailand (n.d.)
Other components/ general services	
Heat sink	Arrow Mizutani (1998)
Housings/baseplates	Wearnes Precision (1994); T.P.W. (1989); Measurex (1998); NHK Precision (1993)
General machining	Measurex (n.d.); Q.D.P. (1998)

SOURCE: Authors' compilation from industry sources.
NOTE: Date spans indicate entry and exit dates.

Thailand also has an extensive cluster of firms producing read-write heads and related components. In addition to the heads operations of the three HDD majors, the Thai industry includes Read-Rite of the United States, one of the world's major independent head producers, which has located its only mass production slider (the stage before HGA) facility there. The Thai industry also includes two of the world's four independent producers of suspensions (K.R. Precision and Magnecomp) and a well-developed cluster of spindle motor and related parts producers. In addition to Seagate's motor production facility in Rangsit, major production facilities include NMB/Minebea's and Nidec's. These firms have in turn nurtured the growth of suppliers producing parts and intermediate goods. Finally, although far less developed than Singapore, a handful of metalworking firms from Singapore, Japan, and the United States have entered. Although no indigenous Thai suppliers exist in this segment, a significant number of trained Thai personnel has accumulated within the foreign drive firms and suppliers. This has led to a growing capacity for general metalworking within the Thai value chain.

The industry's development in Thailand occurred in tandem with the development of the regional production network, particularly Seagate's. The other two HDD assemblers came to the region later, and their Thai operations are somewhat less embedded in a regional network. IBM's drive operations source HGAs, HSAs, motors, base plates, and voice coil assemblies from Thailand but are part of a chain that includes Japan (drive design), the United States (R&D for heads and disks as well as production of disks and wafers for heads), Germany (production of disks and wafers for heads), Mexico (HGAs), China (HGAs), and the Philippines (PCBs). In addition to sourcing locally, Fujitsu gets components from Japan (disks, suspensions, and tooling) and the Philippines (sliders and disks). The first-tier suppliers—Read-Rite (HGAs), Nidec (motors), and NMB (motors)—also produce for customers elsewhere in the region.

The Thai production complex emerged because of specific conditions that attracted firms and enhanced their competitiveness. As in Singapore, Thai factor costs, especially wage rates, were especially important in the early stages of the industry's growth, as were a large pool of labor near Singapore and favorable tax and tariff policies. But Thailand's political and macroeconomic stability were also important, as was the government's hands-off attitude.

While factor costs, labor availability, and tax subsidies have remained important, agglomeration benefits—specifically, access to trained personnel and industry-related facilities—have grown in significance. As firms trained personnel and established operations near suppliers and customers, they increased both pools. Such agglomeration helped create a set of loca-

tion-specific assets and increased the competitive benefits for firms operating there.

While firm strategies have interacted with public policies to develop the
HDD operational cluster and its agglomeration economies in Thailand, government policies have in general been generic and permissive rather than
industry-specific and proactive. The government's hands-off approach
means that key support services and support for technology development
remain undeveloped. As a Thai quality assurance director at Micropolis
noted, government incentives "are for investors, not technology developers."[5] When support services, failure analysis, and production-related
activities such as tooling exist in Thailand, they are usually part of foreign
firms' in-house operations. Only recently has an independent (although non-
Thai) supplier base emerged.

This chapter traces the evolution of disk drive production in Thailand
through two stages. The first stage, corresponding roughly with the industry's arrival in the region (1983–87), is largely a Seagate story. During this
period, Seagate assembled some of its own components, initiated HDD
assembly, and began developing a local supply base. In the second stage
(1988 to the present), Seagate's early work led to the arrival of a mutually
reinforcing range of suppliers and competitors. The corresponding agglomeration economies were a contributing factor in the industry's success in
both Thailand and the region.

Seagate and the Origins of Thai
HDD Production, 1983–87

Thai disk drive production originated in Seagate's 1983 decision
to shift head-stack assembly out of Singapore to Thailand because of limits on available labor. After looking at a number of possibilities, including South Korea and Mexico, Seagate started assembly in a cramped
Bangkok building formerly occupied by a bank and surrounded by rice
fields. The facility's director collected the finished assemblies himself and
drove them to the airport each evening. In the words of the former
National Semiconductor official who directed the operation, "Seagate
was nobody back then."[6] The company soon introduced motor production as well, starting its first motor line in 1985 in California and
adding a second line in Thailand in 1986. In 1987, Seagate moved to a
much larger facility in Chokchai for high-volume production of HDA,
HSA, and motors. Seagate also began to stimulate the growth of other
firms by contracting the manufacture of key components in motors
and heads. Overall, however, Thailand was important only to Seagate;

it took five years before any producer of main subassemblies invested in the country.

This initial stage of production may seem to be a straightforward result of low labor costs, generic incentives, and proximity to Singapore. With a two- to threefold wage rate differential between Singapore and Thailand, labor costs were clearly central to Seagate's decision to relocate head-stack assembly.[7] During much of the 1980s, labor costs remained low due to the mid-decade recession and because the government kept minimum-wage adjustments below the inflation rate (Nipon and Pawadee 1998: 319). In addition, the democratic movement of the mid-1970s had stimulated educational reforms that resulted in near universal primary education and a significant expansion of vocational training. By the time Seagate entered the country in 1983, these reforms, combined with a serious economic downturn, had resulted in unemployment among vocational and university graduates (Nipon and Pawadee 1997: 311, Anderson 1977). As we showed in chapter 6, however, labor costs are not a sufficient explanation: wages in several neighboring countries as well as Mexico were lower than those in Thailand.

Although generic incentives played a role, they were limited to the relatively modest tax incentives adopted as part of the government's general export promotion policy.[8] Thai incentives were better than those of Indonesia and the Philippines but clearly below those of Malaysia. According to the Seagate official most involved in the decision to set up operations in Thailand, the Thai Board of Investment "had little to offer—no buildings, no electricity, just tax reductions."[9] Nor did Thailand offer much infrastructure support. Certainly, its physical infrastructure was not terrible, ranking well above Indonesia's and somewhat better than the Philippines' on most indicators during the 1980s (see table 6.5). Nevertheless, despite the intention of the 1972 Export Promotion Act, only one export processing zone (EPZ) had been established as of the mid-1980s.[10]

Thailand's only other trade-related advantage was its status as a General Systems of Preferences (GSP) recipient. If Seagate was able to obtain 40 percent of local content, it could obtain significant duty reductions for products exported to Europe. By the time Seagate opened its Chokchai plant in 1987, this had become an important incentive for the company to promote a local supply base.[11] Thailand, however, was not the only country in the region with GSP privileges.

What, then, made Thailand so attractive to early drive firms, especially Seagate? First, throughout the 1980s, the nation exhibited impressive macroeconomic and political stability. With its currency devalued in 1984 and anchored to the dollar, and with state macroeconomic agencies averse to inflationary policies, the factor and product market costs of doing business were predictable (Doner and Anek 1994). Thailand was also attractive in terms of noneconomic costs, especially compared with the Philippines and Malaysia. There was no Thai equivalent to the preferences given to ethnic groups in Malaysia. And whereas martial law under Marcos had devastated the Philippines and undermined its Board of Investment, Thailand was ruled by a relatively efficient, semi-democratic government between 1980 and 1988. IBM's 1988 decision to set up a contract assembly facility in Thailand rather than the Philippines was related in large part to the latter's political instability.[12] While certainly not proactive or well informed about the industry, the Thai Board of Investment was able to pursue its principal objective of attracting foreign investors without much political interference. The board did not officially tailor incentives for specific firms but did have some capacity for discretionary incentives, some of which benefited HDD firms such as Minebea.[13]

Second, the availability as well as cost of labor was a motive behind Seagate's initial HSA and motor production in Thailand. The primary catalyst was a former National Semiconductor (NS) manager who started Seagate's Thai operation. Working through his previous NS contacts, he recruited Seagate's first operators; in fact, in the early days Seagate did not even advertise for workers, preferring to hire relatives and friends through word of mouth. For Seagate's first operation, head-stack assembly, the firm recruited fifty operators on fairly short notice and sent them to Singapore for a weekend of training. Returning to Bangkok, the women immediately began HSA. A similar pattern took place with spindle motors. Seagate established its motor division in 1984 and, as previously noted, set up a manufacturing line in Scotts Valley in 1985. Before Christmas, the firm brought two hundred Thais to Scotts Valley to train on the new line. Between Christmas and New Year's Day, the firm took apart the lines, shipping them back to Thailand in one Boeing 747 aircraft with the two hundred workers in another.[14]

Because semiconductor firms had been operating in Thailand since the 1970s, the country offered a pool of experienced technical personnel. The most important source of personnel seems to have been National Semiconductor.[15] In the words of a Micropolis quality assurance director who had worked for both Philips and National Semiconductor, the firm was "a training ground, a spawning ground for many of Thailand's HDD industry."[16] According to one estimate, close to one hundred engineers eventually left National Semiconductor for Seagate and other disk drive firms such as Micropolis.[17] The former National Semiconductor manager who joined Seagate also convinced its motor division that Thailand's personnel resources made the country the best place to set up its first volume production operation.[18]

Seagate's initial attraction to Thailand was related to cheap labor and tax incentives, a favorable macroeconomic and political environment, and easy access to experienced labor and managerial personnel. These personnel factors were a function of both Thai public policies and previous electronics investments. Seagate benefited from electronics industry spillovers that followed the Singapore pattern, albeit on a much smaller scale.

BENEFITS TO SEAGATE

What specific benefits did Seagate derive from the factors just above? First and most critical, of course, were cost reductions achieved through Thailand's lower labor costs. They allowed Seagate to reduce costs in labor-intensive HSA, a significant part of a disk drive's bill of materials. Moving HSA to Thailand came early in Seagate's overseas expansion, and its success was an early vindication of the strategy. As the firm's president and CEO summarized, "with the shifting of labor-intensive lines to Thailand, our competitive edge has become even stronger" ("Americans Protest," June 25, 1988). Thailand's proximity to Seagate's growing assembly operations in Singapore reduced the company's supply line and gave it more control over delivery times.

The availability of technical managers and a large labor force also enabled Seagate to expand its assembly operations in Thailand to support its vertical integration strategy. While Singapore concentrated on final assembly, Thailand complemented these efforts in HSA, motors in 1986, and HDA in Chokchai in 1987. The HDA operation reached full ramp within six months, a fast pace at the time. This responsiveness was critical to filling enormous orders from IBM, which was buying a large part of Seagate's drives during this period.[19] As a senior Seagate manager commented, "it sure helps ramp-up to be able to get 10,000 workers very quickly."[20] These same factors allowed Seagate to respond effectively to market volatility. Seagate's first Thai director stressed the benefits of "going beyond the normal," getting employees to work extra hours, and being able to call them in the middle of the night to meet special orders.[21] This was a far cry from Seagate's experience with surfer absenteeism in its early Santa Cruz operations.

Thailand also complemented Seagate's incipient product transfer strategy (see chapter 6). The Chokchai facility became the first assembly location to make mature drives transferred from Singapore. When Seagate was making 30- and 40-megabyte drives in volume in Singapore, and even a few 168-megabyte drives, it shifted production of its older 20-megabyte drive to Thailand. According to the president and CEO, "as the drive matures and the process matures, we have the option of sending that to our Thai operations" ("Seagate to Produce," April 16, 1988). Overall, in the words of a Seagate official, Thailand was important during this period for "cost and ramp."[22]

Expansion and Deepening, 1988 to the Present

Seagate's expansion attracted other disk drive and supplier firms. Competing drive makers set up production in Thailand, attracted by the country's low costs and its generally supportive policy environment but also by spillovers from Seagate's expansions. Seagate's growth involved the training of numerous technical workers, many of whom staffed new suppliers; and although the company was committed to a vertical integration strategy for critical components, limitations of captive production led it to promote the development of a few local suppliers, who in turn also produced for some of Seagate's competitors.

Thus, during the 1990s, Thailand developed a fairly large operational cluster. It generated, however, relatively modest agglomeration effects from suppliers and technological spillovers. Because suppliers tended to serve only one HDD major, most of the benefits of proximity were internalized by individual firms rather than spread among HDD firms collectively. The Thai operational cluster also hosted relatively more Japanese suppliers to American firms than did those in Malaysia and Singapore. Because Japanese firms were less likely than their American counterparts to hire technical and managerial talent from other firms, the Thai operational cluster experienced less interfirm movement among personnel. As a consequence, one of the key contributors to the development of agglomeration economies was missing.

Seagate's operations in Thailand provided valuable information to other HDD firms that were considering expansion. In the decade after Seagate started shipping from its Chokchai plant in 1987, a number of HDD producers and first-tier suppliers established assembly facilities in the country (see table 8.2). Among the producers, however, only IBM and Fujitsu joined Seagate to assemble drives.[23] IBM began drive assembly in 1991 through a contract manufacturing arrangement with one of Thailand's largest business groups, Saha Union. In 1997, a facility operated directly by IBM opened, meaning that Thailand now accounted for approximately two-thirds of the company's global output. Fujitsu began producing desktop disk drives in 1991, choosing Thailand for a variety of reasons, including the Board of Investment's incentive program, the fact that it already had a production facility in the country, and the availability of experienced operators.[24] Although Fujitsu soon halted production due to a market slump and a weak local supply base, it resumed drive production in 1994 after prod-

TABLE 8.2

ORDER OF ENTRY OF HDD AND RELATED FIRMS IN THAILAND

Year	HDD Assembly	First-Tier Suppliers	Second-Tier Suppliers
1983		Seagate (HSA)	
1984			
1985			NMB/Minebea; GSS; Fujikara
1986		Seagate (motors)	
1987	Seagate (Chokchai)		
1988		NMB/Minebea (motors); Micropolis (HSA)	Elec&Eltek; SCI; K.R. Precision
1989		Nidec (motors); Seagate Teparuk (HGA); IBM/ Saha Union subcontract (HSA)	T.P.W.
1990		Magtric (HSA)	
1991	IBM/Saha Union subcontract; Fujitsu (temporary)	Read-Rite, Fujitsu	Eiwa; Hoya Opto; Fujitsu
1992			Magnecomp; TDK
1993			Hana
1994	Fujitsu	Seagate Rangsit; Seagate Lad Krabang; Seagate Wellgrow, (HSA)	Wearnes Precision; NHK Precision
1995	Avatar Peripherals		Boron; Habiro; Daido Electronics
1996		Seagate Korat; Maxtor (HSA)	ADFlex; Nippon Super; Asahi Komag
1997	IBM		
1998			AMM; Arrow Mizutani; QDP; Measurex
1999			Eng Precision

SOURCE: Authors' compilation based on industry sources.
NOTE: First-tier suppliers produce heads, disks, or motors. Second-tier suppliers produce all other components.

uct redesign; and Thailand became one of its two high-volume production sites for disk drives.[25]

The industry's growth was accompanied and, in some cases, preceded by the entry or expansion of both independent and captive suppliers, especially in spindle motors and head-related products. In 1988, NMB, a large Japanese producer of bearings and other metal products, which had been in Thailand for several years, began motor production. Nidec, a major Japanese motor producer, set up its first Thai plant in 1989 and its second in 1991. Seagate expanded its spindle motor capacity by establishing a dedicated facility at Rangsit in 1994. The establishment of these facilities was followed by the appearance of smaller firms supplying motor hubs and related parts (Eiwa, Habiro, Nippon Super, Thai Okoku Rubber, Shin-Ei) and magnets and related parts (Daido, Advanced Magnetic Materials) to service Seagate, Nidec, and NMB.

The supply of head-related products also expanded. Each of the three largest HDD assemblers did heads subassemblies for internal use. In 1989, Seagate added a plant to make HGAs, opening a dedicated HSA facility in 1994. Two years later, the firm opened yet another HSA plant in the northeastern city of Korat. IBM started shipping HSAs from its Saha Union plant in 1989 and expanded in 1991 to include HGA. Fujitsu started HSA in the 1990s, and Micropolis began HSA in Thailand in 1986 to feed its Singapore HDD operations. Two independent HGA and HSA firms also set up Thai operations. Read-Rite established a Thai operation in 1991 for sliders, HGAs, and HSAs, making its plant the only mass-production slider operation in the world. In 1990, Magtric opened a facility for winding coils for heads, becoming in 1993 a subsidiary of SAE Magnetics, which used the plant to machine sliders and build HGAs and HSAs.[26]

An important part of building up a heads complex in Thailand was the establishment of two firms producing suspensions, the small but precisely engineered assemblies that maintain the head in position above the disk surface. K.R. Precision began operations in 1988 as a new startup firm to service Seagate. A second suspension producer, Magnecomp, based in California, expanded from its original Chinese facility to set up Thai operations in 1992 with the objective of remaining close to its largest customers, Seagate and Read-Rite. Moving downstream, T.P.W., a precision machining firm based in Singapore, shifted its operations to Thailand in 1989 to manufacture actuators and base plates for motors.

Finally, a number of firms in other product areas appeared during this period. Thailand has three media-related firms making polished substrates (Hoya Opto, Asahi Komag, and Nikon). In electronics, a few producers of PCB and PCBA and flex circuits established operations in the mid-1990s. Among flex circuit producers, Boron set up its Thai facilities to serve Seagate and Read-Rite. For AdFlex, cost reduction was the driving force, although proximity to customers turned out to be an important benefit.[27] Seagate also opened a plant to make printed circuit cables in 1994. A small but growing number of metalworking firms supply the drive industry with components such as housings and actuators as well as with general machining services. They include firms from Singapore, Penang, the United States, and Japan.

Developing and Exploiting Locational Assets

What explains the growing presence of the HDD industry in Thailand during the past decade? Locational assets developed as a result of public policies, changes in factor prices, and firm investments. In addition, changes in the competitive dynamics of the industry affected how firms evaluated locations. While Thailand's factor costs and generic policy incentives remained important to producers through the 1990s, they are not sufficient; cheaper labor, tax incentives, and open trading environments are available elsewhere. Rather, disk drive firms and their suppliers also benefit from proximity within Thailand. Over time, suppliers' need to be close to Seagate, Read-Rite, and other leading companies in the value chain created an operational cluster of HDD, heads, and motor assemblers. Collectively, these investments began to yield some moderate agglomeration economies through the generation of specialized personnel, suppliers, and information spillovers. The interaction of factor costs, public policies, and an emerging agglomeration effect explains the growth of Thai disk drive production in the 1990s.

FACTOR COSTS

As chapter 5 has shown, older, larger, and more diversified assemblers such as IBM and Fujitsu were among the late movers into Southeast Asia. As small form factor drives became a more important part of their business, these firms began to mimic their smaller, more specialized competitors. The relatively high cost structures in Japan and the United States finally became salient to locational decisions. Compared with high-cost Singapore and Malaysia, Thailand's labor costs made the country more attractive for some labor-intensive assembly activities. Once firms made the decision to locate in the region, they had only two lower-cost options: the Philippines and China; and as we have seen, the industry did expand investment in those countries, with the Japanese in particular committing themselves to the Philippines.

Yet to American firms, Thailand was considerably more attractive despite a tightened labor market in the early 1990s when the local economy boomed. Wages increased at an annual rate of almost 10 percent between 1990 and 1994 compared with a rate of nearly 2 percent during 1982–90 (see table 8.3). In the late summer of 1991, Seagate experienced a strike in the Teparuk plant. Although it was in part the result of inept management and was exacerbated by domestic Thai politics, the strike also reflected Seagate's difficulties with high staff turnover.[28] These problems worsened by the mid-1990s. Workers in the electronics industry were

Thailand

TABLE 8.3

REAL WAGES IN THAILAND,
1982–94

Year	Index
1982	100
1983	98.5
1984	110.8
1985	112.3
1986	113.8
1987	114.5
1988	106.2
1989	104.6
1990	116.9
1991	123.1
1992	144.6
1993	163.1
1994	170.1

SOURCE: Thailand Development Research
Institute, cited in Warr (1997: 329).
NOTE: Data are based on an index of nominal wages for the manufacturing sector
deflated by the consumer price index.

receiving annual pay raises of 25 percent before the economic crisis of
1997–98 ("Special Report/Electronics," September 8, 1997). In a search
for more labor (as well as to obtain attractive incentives for investments
outside of Bangkok), Seagate opened a facility in the northeastern Thai city
of Korat.[29] Thus, labor costs were clearly not the sole driver behind
American investment decisions.

GENERIC TRADE POLICIES,
INFRASTRUCTURE, AND INCENTIVES

Generic trade policies, infrastructure, and incentives have also
played important roles. Led by the Thai Board of Investment, the country
improved its physical and trade infrastructure. In interviews, all HDD firm
representatives stressed the benefits of duty reduction for machinery, corporate tax exemption, and duty exemption on raw materials for firms exporting more than 30 percent of their production. The country has expanded
the number of bonded warehouses and EPZs, with the latter occupied by
several HDD firms, including Read-Rite, Seagate, and Nidec. The most
important set of incentives is designed to encourage investment outside of
Bangkok in what is known as zone 3.[30] Indeed, most of those firms inter-

viewed, including IBM, cited zone 3 incentives as an important advantage.[31] If these incentives were not critical to initial location decisions, they became, in the words of one manager, "addicting."[32] The Board of Investment has also maintained a reputation for fairness and a willingness to act as a problem solver in areas such as labor relations (especially the strike against Seagate) and infrastructure bottlenecks. In addition, the board has pushed for continued across-the-board tariff reforms and, before the 1997 crisis, resisted cabinet tendencies to restrict incentives for foreign investors. Thailand has also streamlined customs procedures, reduced electricity costs (Nipon and Pawadee 1998: 319), and expanded sea and air transport facilities, all of which have been important to the HDD industry.[33]

Nevertheless, if the Thai infrastructure offers some advantages, it also has important weaknesses. Thailand's electricity and telephone services, while better than those in the Philippines, are ranked well below those in Singapore and Malaysia (see table 6.5). Thai incentives for firms operating in EPZs are also weaker than those found in neighboring countries. According to a recent minister of industry, Thailand is about ten years behind Malaysia in terms of low-cost funds, tax privileges, factories and equipment, and other forms of government support ("Special Report/Electronics," September 8, 1997). In several cases, lack of government capacity has forced the private sector to play an important role in the provision of zone infrastructure.[34]

Thailand's trade infrastructure also continues to have problems. Suppliers to the disk drive industry can suffer financial losses from delays in obtaining drawbacks on import duties they must pay as indirect exporters (for example, supplying Seagate, which then exports the finished product).[35] The Thai Customs Bureau can also pose problems: a global IBM survey found Thailand to have the worst record for damage of any country in which the firm operates.[36] A World Bank report notes that the logistics cost component in the retail price of traded goods averages between 20 and 25 percent for successful firms with well-established support infrastructure. A conservative estimate in Thailand, however, places the average of such costs at close to 40 percent (Peters 1998).[37] The Thai bureaucracy's implementation and interpretation of regulations is at best uneven, at worst corrupt.

Generally, however, disk drive firms have found ways around these problems. These infrastructure weaknesses are more of a headache than a major obstacle. Although they raise the cost of doing business relative to Malaysia and Singapore, they are not a high price to pay given Thailand's other advantages.

INDUSTRY-SPECIFIC POLICIES
AND INFRASTRUCTURE

While Thailand has made doing business fairly easy for the industry, it has not developed industry-specific expertise in the ways that Singapore has. The Board of Investment has been preoccupied with promoting investment per se rather than encouraging technological upgrading, developing the kinds of related activities found in industry clusters, offering technical training, or promoting local electronics suppliers.[38] An adviser to the Federation of Thai Industries' Electrical and Electronics Club, an individual with more than twenty years of experience in Silicon Valley, said that the electronics industry is "confused by the government's policies" and that various Thai governments have "never had firm policies to develop the electronics industry despite its high potential" ("Industry: Electronics Institute," August 4, 1997). Only in 1998 did the Thai government establish an institute devoted to the electronics industry in general and in 1999 begin to pay specific attention to the disk drive industry's training requirements.

As a result, little ongoing contact exists between firms and Thai government agencies. What does occur is exclusively devoted to the Board of Investment's somewhat uninformed and rigid monitoring of firm compliance with incentive conditions.[39] Even established firms that want to qualify a new project for incentives must state their plans several months in advance of implementation, a difficult requirement for the industry to meet due to rapid changes in product mixes and processes.[40] In general, the government has focused on regulation, not technology. As one HDD official commented, when he worked in Hong Kong, he focused on engineering issues; in Thailand, he spent most of his time on personnel and regulatory issues.[41]

Yet disk drive firms have continued not only to invest in Thailand but to deepen their activities there by expanding the range of tasks and responsibilities performed at their facilities. The reason goes beyond tax incentives and cheap and available labor and land to the fact that public policy has enabled firms to cluster and trade in relative freedom from interference. In turn, U.S. multinationals have developed operational clusters that over time have generated local agglomeration economies while supporting the industry's activities in Singapore.

AGGLOMERATION ECONOMIES: SEAGATE,
MOTORS, AND SUSPENSIONS

Perhaps the most striking feature of this agglomeration has been the presence of a pool of technical labor with experience in or related to the disk drive industry. One measure of this phenomenon is simply the accumulation of Thai expertise within Seagate itself. As of 1999, the firm employed 33,000 people, all but 10 of whom were Thai nationals.[42] Seagate's newest facility at Korat has one expatriate (the director of engineering) out of some 8,000 regular employees.

Other evidence of the buildup of specialized labor is the movement of technical personnel—many of them originally trained by Seagate—among HDD firms, including the president of a suspension producer (K.R. Precision), the director of HSA operations for Read-Rite, and a range of process engineers and managers in a dozen firms. As the president of K.R. Precision has explained, Thailand's key advantage is its "technical infrastructure," the cadre of engineers and technicians that has gradually built up.[43] Note that we do not wish to exaggerate the depth of this pool. Seagate never did final HDD assembly and testing in Thailand even though its Thai facilities were doing head-disk assembly, and K.R. Precision was forced to recruit the core of its new tool and die shop from an institute in India. Nevertheless, the accumulation of Thai technical personnel has both attracted firms to Thailand and generally encouraged them to expand.

Thailand also accumulated a pool of HDD parts suppliers, which by the mid-1990s encouraged reinvestment by Seagate and Fujitsu.[44] Furthermore, newer entrants have extended the range of intermediate inputs available in Thailand, including the supply of precision machined parts such as dies and specific components. For example, Boron, the flex circuit maker, recently began to employ the local subsidiaries of six strong U.S. and Singaporean metalworking firms from the United States or Singapore. It is possible that future location decisions, whether initial investments or project expansions, will reflect the attractions of this kind of supplier base.

Information spillovers have been more limited. They include information about how to operate most efficiently within Thailand, which has diffused across the electronics industry. Local trade associations have typically been the source of information about relocation, poaching, general job descriptions, worker bonuses, and implementing minimum wage increases.[45] Nevertheless, there has been little in the way of technological spillovers within Thailand's operational cluster. In the words of one Read-Rite executive with long experience in Thailand, "Here we don't share anything, not even epoxy."[46] This is not to say that HDD firms have not tried. But each initiative has failed, including Seagate's attempt to promote a center for testing and failure analysis at the Bangkok-based Asian Institute of Technology as well as several attempts to organize an industry training program, K.R. Precision's efforts to establish a tool and die institute, and Micropolis's attempt to set up a center for magnetic testing at King Mongkut Institute of Technology.[47]

While agglomeration economies in Thailand's operational cluster have been more limited than those in Singapore, they have operated fairly strongly in two parts of the value chain: motors and suspensions. We illustrate the emergence of these economies by examining Seagate's development of proximate suppliers in motors and head-related products.

Motors. Thailand has become a global center for disk drive motor production. Its emergence is largely due to Seagate, which, as the largest consumer of motors for desktop disk drives since the mid-1980s, played an important role in pushing motor development. As we have described, once the company shifted motor production to Thailand, it began to transfer motor technology to two key suppliers: NMB and Nidec. Much of the transfer process required face-to-face interactions, which put a premium on physical proximity.

The process began with Seagate's transfer of motor technology to NMB, from whom it had already been purchasing bearings and other important motor components. After building up inventory, Seagate then transferred all of its production lines and operators to NMB, which meant that between three hundred and four hundred Seagate employees actually stayed in NMB's plant for three or four months. As NMB became more proficient at the process, its own employees gradually replaced the Seagate operators. The NMB-Seagate relationship worked so well that in 1989 Seagate transferred new spindle motor technology to NMB and built NMB's cleanrooms, which were required for making the new motors—Thailand's first cleanrooms.

Nidec established its first Thai plant in 1989 under pressure from Seagate to keep the supply chain short. (Nidec established a second facility in 1991 under similar pressure from IBM.) The presence of two suppliers (in addition to Seagate's internal production) became especially important for meeting Seagate's demand for one motor (the ST-3096), which became one of the firm's most successful products. Seagate transferred the ST-3096 from Scotts Valley to its own facilities in Thailand in 1989 and then to both Nidec and NMB in 1990. Originally designed for 80-megabyte drives, this platform was leveraged across twelve product generations, and more than 50 million motors were produced. The proximity among these three production facilities enabled the firms to work through production issues jointly and proved to be an important ingredient in Seagate's ability to achieve enormous scale economies in its HDD assembly by assuring the company of a reliable supply of high-quality motors at low cost.

In 1991, Scotts Valley developed a new motor for a 2.5-inch disk drive along with a highly automated production line. The firm transferred the line to its own Thai facilities. This transfer directly contradicts a labor cost explanation of location because the line was fully automated (almost a "lights out" plant). Why, then, was the line transferred immediately to Thailand? While the primary reason was proximity to Seagate's HDA operation in Chokchai, the move was made possible by the availability of process engineering expertise.

Seagate's completion of a dedicated motor production facility in 1994 was another step in the development of the motor cluster. Because the firm needed a new facility to meet growing internal demand for its motors, it decided to build the new motor within a half hour from Nidec, NMB, and Seagate's HDA facility in Chokchai. The new facility was also necessary to mass-produce Seagate's next technology of spindle motors, which are based on fluid rather than ball bearings. Seagate initiated production in 1997 and is the only firm in the world with the manufacturing technology for this product. Rather than rely on NMB and Nidec to supplement motor capacity, however, Seagate concluded technology and manufacturing agreements with two other Japanese firms: Sankyo Seiki and Seiko Instruments ("Seagate Rides Fluid Motors," October 10, 1997). Seiko has already begun to produce precision parts in Thailand for this motor.[48]

The advantages of proximity in motors go beyond the need for frequent interactions during the transfer of new products. The presence of external suppliers also allowed Seagate to play one against the other, inducing Nidec to reduce its motor prices to Seagate by 40 percent in 1992.[49] Proximity also facilitates problem solving and experimentation in production. Seagate does not allow any product changes without its express approval; thus, the ability of both parties to discuss and even test production modifications on site is critical. Such interaction is supported by the company's Supplier Quality Engineering program, which requires Seagate managers to visit principal suppliers every day. By bringing Seiko Instruments into the motor cluster, Seagate stimulated competition and induced additional R&D in areas of interest.[50] The development of this new technology has expanded and deepened the motor supplier base in Thailand, demonstrating that proximity with key suppliers can serve multiple purposes.

Suspensions. A similar dynamic occurred with heads and suspensions. In the early 1980s, Seagate purchased HGAs from external suppliers and assembled them into head stacks in Thailand. As described in chapter 7, Seagate struck a deal with National Micronetics to supply it with lower-cost HGAs but also used NMI as a vehicle for learning in-house HGA cheaply. Seagate subsequently began to assemble its own HGAs in Thailand and soon attempted to squeeze the prices it was paying for HGA components, specifically suspensions.

At the time, Seagate relied on the world's largest producer of suspensions, Hutchinson Technology (HTI), an American firm. Seagate asked HTI to reduce prices and set up facilities in Thailand so that Seagate could receive better service and engineering support. After HTI refused, Seagate initiated an unsuccessful effort to develop in-house capacity in suspension manufacturing.[51] Seagate then looked to create a new producer of suspensions to gain some leverage on HTI and compel it to reduce its prices. Seagate found a precision etching firm in Japan and, through the Thai Board of Investment, linked it with a Thai partner. The resulting firm, K.R. Precision, was established in 1988 and qualified a year later for a Seagate program. Announced publicly, this qualification led HTI to drop prices 20 percent.

Seagate's support did not stop there. K.R. Precision's first suspension, shipped in 1989, was for Seagate's low-cost, high-volume disk drive—its bread-and-butter product. There were several years of setbacks before the firm developed the capability to make suspensions for higher-end drives. After its initial success, K.R. Precision's lack of manufacturing expertise weakened its ability to win new projects. Seagate responded by brokering a move by one of its best supplier-quality engineers, who helped K.R. Precision ride out this rough period by arranging for the firm to produce less sophisticated floppy disk suspensions. At the same time, he hired experienced American expatriates to improve the firm's manufacturing processes and diversified its client base for HDD suspensions away from its status as a virtual captive supplier to Seagate. In time, K.R. Precision became a second source for IBM/Saha Union in Thailand, proved its reliability, and emerged as the second largest suspension producer in the world.

Seagate thus promoted a Thai-based supplier of a critical component. Equally important is that K.R. Precision, with 2,300 employees, developed into a world-class supplier to a range of customers.[52] Led by such efforts, Thailand developed a technical infrastructure—a cadre of engineers, toolmakers, and technicians—in suspensions as well as precision machining and etching. Far from remaining a source of low-cost labor and tax breaks, Thailand evolved into an operational cluster offering a range of inputs and skills to help the American disk drive industry meet its requirements for speed, flexibility, quality, and low cost in critical pieces of the value chain.

Summarizing Thailand's Contribution

In sum, the benefits of locating in Thailand include the contribution of changing location-specific assets to low costs in operations, rapid plant startup, rapid product ramp-up and -down, dampening supply disruptions, and problem solving in production. At first, of course, firms operating in Thailand benefited from the ability to reduce costs in basic operations. The most important sources of cost reductions were wage rates, including managerial and engineering staff, and investment incentives that, taken together, were at least as favorable as those elsewhere in the region. By the early 1990s, however, Thailand's cluster of internal and external suppliers generated additional cost savings. For Seagate alone, the clustering of HDA with heads (HSA, HGA, and suspensions) and motors (assembly and components) saved transportation and component costs through the presence of multiple suppliers.

The capacity for speed in plant startup was also significant. The availability of workers, experienced technical personnel, and even plant facilities helped cut the startup costs of Read-Rite, Micropolis, AdFlex, Eng Precision, and IBM. In IBM's case, its Saha Union subcontract operation provided experienced personnel as trainers, thus allowing the new facility to avoid the cost of sending new hires back to Japan for training.[53]

The HDD industry in Thailand has also improved its overall capacity for ramp-up and -down. Recall that drives and assemblies typically go through some version of a pilot production process that focuses on the basic manufacturability of the product and then move to ramp-up, which emphasizes the resolution of problems encountered during volume production. The key consideration here is that high volume production of disk drive assemblies and components typically faces a number of unanticipated difficulties (Terwiesch et al. 1999).

Initially, Thailand made products, whether suspensions or disk drives, as they entered the later stages of their life cycle. Until the mid-1990s, for example, Seagate's Thai facilities handled products that had already been debugged in Singapore or had gone through production ramp in the United States. By 1997, however, Thailand was functioning as both a ramp-up and mass-production site. Seagate did all pilot and preproduction work for HGAs in Thailand; and IBM, a leader in entering and then vacating capacity segments before competitors could drive down prices, relied on its two Thai facilities to ramp to volume production quickly and then ramp down during the transition to new products.[54]

The Thai operational cluster also reduced critical uncertainties in production for the American disk drive firms and enabled them to achieve economies of scale with minimal supply disruptions. In disk drives, volatile demand has often led to parts shortages and even failure for firms unable to get critical components. Seagate avoided these problems with its ST-3096 motor, which had been transferred to both Nidec and NMB for production. In this case, having multiple and proximate suppliers kept production on track even as shortages occurred for shafts, magnets, and bearings.

With two suppliers close by, Seagate's motor division director could literally walk into one of the two firms and take parts to the other as needed. In the words of the division director, "without this we would have been dead."[55]

Finally, clustering among suppliers facilitated problem resolution. For example, although the product specifications that customers give to suspension producers suggest fixed parameters, they are in reality only a reference. Even after approving a suspension, Read-Rite or Seagate might subsequently discover that their HGAs have yield problems attributable to the suspension and ask the suspension producer to make some alteration.[56] Tuning these requirements often does not occur until very high volumes have been produced, at which time close interaction between supplier and customer becomes critically important. A suspension maker that does not manufacture locally cannot be as responsive as the customer requires. If based in the United States, for example, they suffer from a twelve-hour time zone delay. But a local producer can be in Seagate's or Read-Rite's plant in an hour and implement a change that same day; the overseas suspension producer might take a week. In addition, the overseas assembler may already have two weeks of unusable product in the shipment pipeline. Although a suspension sells for only forty cents, a delay in its production can ripple through the supply chain, ultimately delaying final assembly of a disk drive.

In sum, agglomeration, combined with consistently low factor costs, attractive trade and investment incentives, moderate infrastructure, and an otherwise hands-off government yielded important benefits. These factors not only helped Thai-based firms cut costs of starting facilities and basic operations but also strengthened the industry's ability to contend with the pressures of rapid ramp-up and -down. Moreover, the operational cluster in Thailand was relatively close to other operations in Singapore and Malaysia, contributing to network benefits as well.

9 Malaysia

Although Malaysia had been a site for foreign direct investment in electronics since the late 1960s, disk drive investment did not come to Penang until 1988—six years after the industry arrived in Singapore, five years after Seagate first invested in Thailand.[1] Although pioneers in Malaysia included both HDD majors and their first-tier suppliers, the country has not developed into a center for drive assembly, for a number of reasons. Nonetheless, the industry's growth in Malaysia has been rapid: a survey conducted by the Penang Development Corporation in 1990 noted the activities of three drive-related firms; in 1997, the survey covered eleven.[2] In less than a decade, the industry grew to account for more than 30 percent of total employment in the electronics sector (see table 9.1).

Who were these pioneer HDD firms? Despite the fact that Penang is not a center for assembly, the American majors were critical to the development of a local concentration of drive-related firms. Their influence was felt in two ways. First, Singapore-based operations developed their regional production networks by extending their operations to Penang and developing close links with suppliers in Malaysia. Second, the entry of the majors and major suppliers developed a local cluster by attracting other firms. Japanese and American firms entered to supply both the region and the majors with media, HGAs, and HSAs. Quite early, Penang developed a specialization in the heads complex, later hosting a number of important media investments. The entry of the assemblers and major suppliers had a ripple effect on the second tier of the supply chain, attracting foreign and local suppliers of intermediates (such as aluminum substrates and chemicals), subassemblies and components (base plates, actuators, flex circuits, PCBA, and turned parts), and engineering services (process equipment).

TABLE 9.1

GROWTH OF THE HDD SECTOR IN PENANG

	1990	1997	Average Annual Growth (percent)
Employment	2,634	37,068	45.9
As a share of the total electronics sector (percent)	4.4	32.2	
As a share of the total manufacturing sector (percent)	2.3	19.3	
	Million Malaysia Ringgit*		
	1990	1996	
Sales	172.0	4448.1	59.0
Capital expenditure	143.3	604.7	22.8
Fixed assets	37.0	1204.7	64.5

SOURCES: *Annual Survey of Manufacturing Industries in PDC Industrial Areas,* Penang Development Corporation, various issues; Economic Report 1997/98, Ministry of Finance, Malaysia.
*1990 Ringgit, using producer price index.

Why did these firms come to Malaysia, come when they did, and stay? As in Thailand, labor costs and generic public policies, such as free trade zones and tax incentives to investors, played a central role. Maxtor and Conner had production operations in Singapore; and as costs rose, both saw advantages in shifting some production to lower-cost sites. As in Singapore, however, Malaysia's advantage did not rest simply on unskilled labor and generic public policies. Indeed, that advantage had already eroded by the late 1980s, when the industry entered; and in the early 1990s, labor markets tightened and wage growth accelerated. Nonetheless, HDD investment continued.

One reason for continued investment was Penang's early development of both network benefits and agglomeration economies. Proximity to Singapore reduced transport costs, increased speed of delivery, and allowed for close managerial oversight and even training, which were important in transferring both product and entire production lines. We thus see strong evidence of the network benefits outlined in chapter 6, particularly those that arise from coordinating relatively proximate locations with complementary or interdependent activities.

Agglomeration economies also developed. First, firms exploited an increasingly deep pool of managerial, engineering, and technical talent. While these resources can be traced to Penang's long history in the electronics industry, industry-specific expertise grew as well. We have already suggested a kind of chain reaction: after the entry of the majors and a number of impor-

TABLE 9.2

INVESTMENT HISTORY IN NORTHERN MALAYSIA:
HDD MAJOR FIRMS AND SUPPLIERS

Company	Year*	Investment Location	Product(s)	Remarks
Maxtor	1988	Perai, Penang	HGA, HSA	Sold facility to Read-Rite in 1992
Control Data	1988	Bayan Lepas, Penang	HGA	Sold to Seagate in 1989
Hitachi Metals	1989	Perai, Penang	HGA, sliders	
Seagate	1989	Bayan Lepas, Penang	HGA	Acquired from Control Data
	1992	Bayan Lepas, Penang	Sliders	
	1994	Bayan Lepas, Penang	Thin-film slider	An expansion of the 1992 plant
	1995	Ipoh, Perak	Magnetoresistive HSA, HGA	
	1995	Perai, Penang	Low end drives	Purchased from Conner Peripherals in 1995
	1996	Ipoh, Perak	Magnetoresistive HSA, HGA	
	1996	Johore	PCBA	To supply to Singapore
Applied Magnetics	1989	Bayan Lepas, Penang	Sliders, HSA and HGA	Shut down operations in early 2000
Conner Peripherals	1989	Perai, Penang	Low end drives	Started with HSA, then sold off operation to Read-Rite in 1991
Dastek	1990	Perai, Penang	Thin-film HGA	Acquired by Komag, later shut down
Read-Rite	1991	Perai, Penang	HSA	Bought Conner's HSA business and Maxtor's plant in 1992, then closed operation in 1998

SOURCE: Authors' compilation from industry sources.
*Year of startup and shipment.

tant heads suppliers, second-tier American, Japanese, and Singaporean firms
entered. Malaysian firms also grew by supplying the industry with, among
other services, engineering and specialized machining capabilities, such as
jigs and fixtures. This local supply base, which consisted of both foreign
and Malaysian firms, developed in response to industry demands and in
turn rooted the industry in Penang. Even though regional rather than
local proximity drove initial location decisions, the advantages of local proximity became more important over time.

As in our analysis of Singapore and Thailand, a central theme for
Malaysia is the evolutionary nature of location-specific assets, which have
developed as a result of the industry's presence. This is also true of public policy. The government began aggressively courting foreign invest-

ment after 1985, and Penang continued to distinguish itself for its ability to provide infrastructure and manage export processing zones efficiently. While Penang lacks Singapore's expertise within industrial policy agencies as well as university-industry links, state officials quickly developed a much more sophisticated industry promotion structure than was evident in other Malaysian states or Thailand. Over time, the state government played a more proactive role in discouraging labor-intensive investment, matching foreign firms with local suppliers and developing innovative public-private partnerships for training.

Although investment has been more or less continuous, two periods correspond roughly with the second and third phases of the evolution of the regional production network outlined in chapter 6. (See tables 9.2 and 9.3 for the investment history of HDD firms and their first- and second-tier suppliers.) For each period, we provide a brief overview of the industry's evolution, the calculations that firms made when entering, and the benefits that Penang provided. The first wave of early entry fell between 1988 and 1991. Although entry was motivated by labor-cost considerations and tax incentives, the majors were also tapping existing technical capabilities. This first wave was followed almost immediately by a range of supplier investments, both foreign and domestic, motivated in large measure by proximity to customers. The majors' second wave of investments in the 1990s included expansions of existing investments, the development of a media cluster, and the failed entry of several firms attempting assembly of advanced drives. These investments were motivated less by factor costs and more by network benefits and local capabilities.

Phase 1: The Pioneers, 1988–91

With the exception of cartridge drive manufacturing, Seagate's assembly operation in Perai (mainland Penang) was the only drive assembly operation in the northern region in 1999.[3] The factory, however, which Seagate had inherited from Conner, was by no means the only investment by drive manufacturers. Maxtor pioneered Penang as a production site for HGA, HSA, and motors; and Digital Equipment, Hewlett-Packard, and Quantum all initiated drive manufacturing but failed to sustain it. Nevertheless, even when these investments were not successful, they affected the development of the industry in Penang and show the position that Malaysia initially occupied in the regional production system.

The early entrants into Penang (1988–89) included Maxtor, Hitachi Metals, Control Data, and Applied Magnetics.[4] Of these, Maxtor and Conner were HDD assemblers, with their move into Malaysia an extension of

TABLE 9.3
THE SECOND-TIER OF THE HDD SUPPLY CHAIN IN MALAYSIA

Company	Year*	Nationality (percent)	Investment Location	Product	Remarks
Eng Teknologi	1988	100 Malaysian	Bayan Lepas, Penang	Actuators	Customers: Maxtor, Micropolis, Seagate, Conner, Quantum/MKE, DEC, Fujitsu
Solectron	1990	100 American	Perai, Penang	PCB, FCB	
Natsteel Electronics	1992	100 Singaporean	Perai, Penang	PCBA	Invested because of Conner Peripherals
MMI Industries	1992	100 Singaporean	Perai, Penang	Voice-coil motors, base plates	Invested because of Conner Peripherals
TransCapital	1992	100 Malaysian	Perai, Penang	PCBA and FCBA	Supplied Read-Rite; now an HDD manufacturer in partnership with Castlewood
Tongkah Electronics (previously known as DME)	1992	51 Malaysian, 49 Singapore	Perai, Penang	PCBA	Invested because of Conner Peripherals
LKT Precision Engineering	1992/ 1993	100 Malaysian	Bayan Lepas, Penang	Process equipment	Customers: Komag, Read-Rite, Applied Magnetics, Seagate
Micro Cut Precision	1995	100 Malaysian	Bayan Lepas, Penang	Turned parts	Customers: Seagate, Micropolis, and Western Digital
Newtechco	1995	60 Malaysian, 40 Singaporean	Bayan Lepas, Penang (for turn parts section only)	Turned parts	Customer: Seagate
Excel Precision	1995	100 Malaysian	Perai, Penang	Process equipment	Customers: Hitachi Metal, Komag (major customer)
Xolox Malaysia**	1995	100 Malaysian (was 100 American)	Perai, Penang	Actuators	Customer: Western Digital
SCI Manufacturing	1997	100 American	Perai, Penang	PCBA	Invested because of Hewlett-Packard

SOURCE: Authors' compilation from industry sources.
*Year of startup and shipment.
**TransCapital has 10 percent equity ownership in Xolox. Xolox Malaysia is a subsidiary of Xolox United States.

their Singapore operations ("Maxtor to Open," April 6, 1988; "Conner to Build," August 1990). Facing component shortages, pioneer investor Maxtor began in-house HGA, HSA, flex-circuit board assembly (FCBA), and spindle motor production in Penang. Within six months of coming on line, however, a glut in heads and falling prices led the firm to abandon HGA altogether. A debate ensued within Maxtor over whether it should also abandon HSA and move drive assembly to Penang.[5] Maxtor began to experience financial difficulties just as these discussions were taking place and had just acquired MiniScribe, which gave the firm substantial capacity in Singapore. As a result, the company sold the HSA operation to Read-Rite in December 1991 and the smaller spindle motor operation to CAM Technologies, a Singapore-based firm.

The story of Conner's 1989 decision to enter bears important similarities to Maxtor's. Conner Singapore experimented in the new location with HSA but within a year started to transfer assembly lines from Singapore to the Perai facility, beginning with the Stubby, a low-end 20-megabyte drive.

This process of building a regional production network out of Singapore was replicated in the heads complex. Applied Magnetics and Control Data, firms that designed their own heads, were pioneers among the major head suppliers. While their investments in Penang were roughly contemporaneous with Maxtor's entry, they were not initially associated with it. Although Applied Magnetics did end up supplying Maxtor's HGA and HSA operations in Penang, it began by supplying Maxtor's assembly operation in Singapore. Control Data was the largest OEM producer of heads in the world, making sliders, HGAs, and HSAs, primarily for its operations in Portugal and Singapore. Shortly after Maxtor's entry, Dastek and Hitachi Metals also came to Penang. Dastek, whose main customer was Maxtor, began with slider machining and HGA, then turning to HSA.[6] Hitachi Metals entered in part to supply Applied Magnetics, which in turn was supplying Maxtor.

The last two major entrants in the heads complex came by way of acquisitions. The history of Seagate's entry into Penang begins with the acquisition of Control Data's drive operations in 1989 and, with it, the Penang facility. Read-Rite's acquisition of Maxtor's HSA operations was followed in 1991 by its acquisition of Conner's HSA business. Under the conditions of the sale, Read-Rite took over the Conner HSA facility, all equipment, and 1,100 employees, while Conner committed to absorb all of Read-Rite's Penang output.

If these investments had been the only occurrences during this phase, local intra-industry links would have been limited largely to the heads complex, which was also closely integrated into the *regional* production system. Conner, however, brought a number of Singaporean suppliers to

Penang, including CAM Technologies, MMI, Natsteel Electronics, Tri-M, and Tongkah Electronics, thus contributing to *local* agglomeration economies as well. Tracing the effect of the industry's development on local suppliers is more complex because most firms had started in some other activity, often in tandem with other foreign electronics firms (Rasiah 1995). The growth of a few, particularly MMI and TransCapital, was tied almost entirely to the HDD industry; but more typically, local firms began with some engineering and machining capabilities, often developed during prior electronics investments, and leveraged them into long-term relations with HDD customers, who helped upgrade local companies' technological abilities.

LOCATIONAL DRIVERS AND BENEFITS

Why and how did this first wave of firms come to Penang, and what benefits did locating in Penang confer? For the two major assemblers, the primary motive was rising wages in their Singapore plants; the primary benefit, a reduction in costs. The availability of land in export processing zones and increasingly generous incentives were also important benefits.

Nevertheless, a closer look at early operations reveals several other advantages. First, labor-cost benefits also arose from the managerial and engineering workforce, which facilitated the easy transfer of operations. Second, locating in Penang linked two relatively proximate sites with different cost structures, while allowing close but relatively inexpensive managerial oversight of the one by the other. Finally, agglomeration benefits similar to those in Thailand allowed firms not only to reduce transportation and inventory costs but to engage in joint problem solving.

Consider the example of the two major assemblers. At the time of Maxtor's entry into Penang, Singapore had become the company's major offshore production site; but rising costs for land and labor limited the possibilities for expansion. Penang, in contrast, was just coming out of a recession that had temporarily dampened wage growth. According to a Maxtor manager, the decision to enter Penang was a "no-brainer": savings on labor costs would allow the company to recoup the entire investment in six months.[7] Conner's story is similar. Rising costs led the Singapore firm's managing director to move HSA to Penang; no other sites were even considered.[8]

Another piece of the story was the changing nature of Malaysia's investment incentives. The country's first experiment with an outward-oriented strategy for the manufacturing sector included generous tax exemptions for export-oriented firms in the Industrial Incentives Act of 1968 and the Free Trade Zone (FTZ) Act (1971) as well as the provision of licensed manufacturing warehouses (LMWs) outside the zones.[9] This strategy clearly sought to emulate Singapore's, particularly in allowing 100 percent of foreign equity ownership at a time when the general thrust of Malaysian industrial policy was to support indigenous Malay (*bumiputera*) interests (for example, through an investment licensing scheme after 1975). The reforms drew the first major wave of export-oriented electronics manufacturing to Penang.

Despite these policies, disk drive investment did not come to Malaysia until the Fifth Malaysia Plan (1986–90). In the early 1980s, Prime Minister Mahathir experimented with his more statist "Look East" industrial policy. But manufacturing's role in realizing the growth, employment creation, and regional development objectives of the Fourth Master Plan (1980–85) was disappointing; and foreign investment in the electronics industry slowed. During the economic downturn of the mid-1980s, the nature of incentives was scrutinized; and in drafting the First Industrial Master Plan, the government undertook a number of reforms, particularly in the 1986 Promotion of Investments Act (see PDC 1988). Some of them, such as the amendments to the 1975 Industrial Coordination Act, eased licensing requirements and provided new opportunities for domestic firms. Others, such as revisions in the Investment Incentives Act of 1968, expanded tax incentives to a number of strategic industries, including electronics. When pioneer status was coupled with additional incentives for high-technology industries, firms were able to get a full tax exemption. Investment tax allowances and reinvestment allowances added benefits connected to capital expenditure incurred during the first five years of entry, and R&D allowances were extremely generous.

Despite these additional incentives, our interviews repeatedly confirmed that the most important financial incentive remained the granting of pioneer status; according to one manager, these tax benefits were more significant than labor savings.[10] Pioneer status granted a partial exemption from payment of income tax for firms meeting changing criteria: companies granted pioneer status pay tax on only 30 percent of their statutory income, with five years of tax exemption commencing from the production date. Among the HDD majors, all that entered Penang received pioneer status, and all that survived longer than the initial five-year period were able to renew it by claiming an upgrade of their product mix. Our survey of suppliers found that they, too, benefited; six of eight foreign-owned suppliers received pioneer status, and three of seven local ones did.

Nevertheless, while Malaysia's convergence toward "Singapore standards" may have had a positive effect on perceptions of the country's investment climate, it did not differentiate Malaysia from its neighbors; the changes simply brought incentives to equivalent levels (Hicken 1997). When we probe the nature of these incentives, we find that the simple cost story of wages and tax breaks must be augmented by an understanding of other assets Penang possessed, including government management of land and facilities, a managerial and engineering labor market that could facilitate rapid entry and startup, and incipient agglomeration economies.

Because of Malaysia's federal structure, basic financial and fiscal incentives were set at the federal level in Kuala Lumpur. In 1969, however, a new growth-oriented state government sought to attract manufacturing investment through the only two instruments fully at its disposal: promotion and marketing of Penang as an investment site, and the provision of basic infrastructure, including FTZs and industrial estates and complementary new township development. As the first state to exploit the new law governing FTZs, Penang gained an important first-mover advantage over other Malaysian states. By 1973, the export-oriented electronics and electrical industry provided one-fifth of all manufacturing jobs in the state and contributed 28 percent of Penang's manufacturing, value added.

Still, while the electronics sector had grown into a sizable cluster by the early 1980s, Penang's dependence on the industry had revealed a number of vulnerabilities, including the narrowness of the industrial base, the dominance of multinationals, and exposure to the highly volatile semiconductor segment. After a shakeout in the electronics industry during the downturn of 1985 created a surplus of managerial, engineering, and semi-skilled labor, the state government directed the Penang Development Corporation (PDC) in 1987 to identify new industries for priority promotion, accelerate their efforts with respect to training, and pay greater attention to opportunities for local links.

By its own admission, the PDC did not have a clear map of the disk drive industry in the late 1980s; nonetheless, it played a crucial role in brokering the entry of Maxtor and Applied Magnetics.[11] It sold not only the advantages of less expensive operatives and the availability of land but the existence of managerial and engineering talent that would facilitate rapid startup. As a result, Maxtor was able to transfer out of Singapore with the participation of only two expatriates. While Conner's entry was initiated by a Singaporean manager and the plant first run by a Singaporean director, that person was quickly replaced by a Malaysian who had worked at Intel.[12] Applied Magnetics' entry was supported by a small group of local engineers, the most senior of whom had worked for Maxtor. According to the original managing director of Control Data's operations, Penang "offered the best combination of desirable attributes, including a skilled workforce with experience in the electronics industry" ("Control Data Announces Addition," May 13, 1988). Dastek's first chief of operations in Malaysia had prior experience at Hewlett-Packard and later went on to become the managing director of Read-Rite's operations.[13] Although examples proliferate, the point is that by the time the drive industry came to Singapore, Penang had already developed a substantial cadre of managers and engineers with experience in the electronics industry who were available to facilitate the majors' entry and rapid startup.

What about the role of agglomeration economies and network benefits during this phase? Although firms with relevant capabilities had developed in conjunction with other electronics segments, these potential suppliers were not a major factor in motivating initial drive investments in Penang. While investments by the majors and the major suppliers did generate a drive-related supply infrastructure and some agglomeration economies, this local agglomeration was tightly integrated into regional production networks as well.

Because Conner's corporate strategy emphasized the benefits of outsourcing and the firm had quickly graduated to drive assembly in Penang, its entry had a wider impact than did Maxtor's on the development of a local industry cluster. A striking feature of Conner's entry was the internationalization of the supply base that it and other drive firms had created in Singapore. Conner brought these firms to Malaysia not only to lower costs but to create proximity benefits, including reduced transit time and greater problem solving.[14] CAM Technologies invested in Penang to supply base plates to Conner, later acquiring Maxtor's spindle motor facilities in its effort to integrate base plates and motors into a single subassembly. MMI also entered to supply Conner, initially with subassemblies but subsequently with base plates as well. Several Singapore-based contract manufacturers followed Conner to provide PCBA: Natsteel Electronics and Tri-M, followed by Tongkah Electronics, a joint venture between Tongkah Holdings (a publicly listed Malaysian group) and Goldtron Electronics (a Singaporean firm). Conner also attracted American-owned contract manufacturer Solectron to follow it into Penang to supply PCBA, and the firm later supplied Maxtor and Read-Rite with FCBA.

The majors' presence also had implications for the development of local suppliers. Although TransCapital began making racks for Conner, it leapt into PCBA with Conner's assistance. Eng Hardware began as an engineering services company to the multinationals, particularly in semiconductors; but its initial work for the HDD industry was in specialized components and automation systems design and production, an area for which proximity is vital. The PDC, however, brokered Eng's initial contact with Maxtor; and Eng exploited its capabilities in machining to supply Maxtor with actuators for high-end drives, first in Singapore and then in Penang.[15]

In the heads complex, Control Data and Applied Magnetics, the two pioneers, did not enter to serve local customers.[16] Over time, however, important agglomeration economies emerged, and firms located with the specific intention of serving local customers.[17] Control Data eventually supplied both Conner and Maxtor in Penang, with advantages that included, in the words of one Seagate manager, not simply lowered transport costs but "quick feedback and efficient joint working of problems."[18] These views were confirmed by an engineer with experience at both Maxtor and Applied Magnetics.[19] Proximity lowered shipping costs, allowed for a daily shipping schedule and weekly meetings with customers' procurement, and offered advantages such as the recycling of packaging materials. But proximity also allowed "ease of quality feedback and control," available through joint engineering sessions and even the presence of a resident Applied Magnetics engineer at Conner. These close interactions allowed the firm to resolve quality issues and "supply the [Maxtor] HSA lines with a continuous supply of HGAs."

Read-Rite's production networks in Southeast Asia evolved somewhat differently. Rather than initially moving to Singapore and expanding into Malaysia from there, Read-Rite began its first Southeast Asian operation in Thailand (see chapter 8). Read-Rite Thailand oversaw the company's forward integration into HSA in Penang through acquisitions from Maxtor and Conner. Proximity was important both with respect to the firm's prime customer, Conner, which initially committed to absorb all of Read-Rite's output, and also to suppliers, including TransCapital and Asian Micro (FCBA) and Xolox and Eng (actuators). According to a Conner manager, the advantages of proximity included shorter transit time, particularly during ramp-up, when products were not completely debugged and there was a constant shortage of materials. But proximity also facilitated "easier problem solving and communication."[20]

Remember, however, that this local agglomeration was firmly rooted in a broader regional network. A reconstruction of Conner's supply chain from the early 1990s (based on interviews with Conner managers) shows a strong revealed preference for proximity only with respect to PCBA, base plates, and other metal parts; other components were sourced widely from within the region and beyond. Even in HGA and HSA, the firm's purchases from Read-Rite were not exclusive; and Conner continued to squeeze life out of an older heads technology by sourcing from firms in the Philippines, China, and Hong Kong as well as Penang.[21] As a former Conner manager explained, "proximity is definitely desirable but it does not mean that things cannot work without it," particularly when cost advantages (such as those derived from sourcing in China) are overwhelming.[22]

In sum, the two pioneering assemblers, Maxtor and Conner, entered through an extension of Singaporean operations, beginning initially with component production but quickly building and exploiting local capabilities to move into more complex subassemblies and, in Conner's case, full drive assembly. Labor costs and incentives played the main role in these investment decisions. Other heads makers, particularly Applied Magnetics and Control Data, independently noted Penang's locational value for similar reasons. Yet shortly after entry, these firms began to influence the investment decisions of other firms in the supply chain, who saw advantages in proximate location and agglomeration. These firms included some of the other major heads suppliers, Singapore-based suppliers of PCBA and metal parts, and a handful of local firms that grew up with the industry by supplying components and engineering services. In the heads complex, proximity between suppliers of heads and HGAs and firms involved in both HSA (Maxtor, Read-Rite, Applied Magnetics) and final assembly (Conner) generated important benefits for both sides, including not only expected logistical benefits but joint problem solving.

Phase 2: The 1990s

As table 9.1 shows, the 1990s were a period of dramatic expansion for the drive industry in northern Malaysia. But Malaysia's position in the regional network also changed in revealing ways. Conner began to use the country for the production of more sophisticated drives while moving low-end desktop products still further offshore. A number of other major drive assemblers chose Penang for production of high-end drives, even though they failed to sustain these activities for fortuitous reasons. The heads complex continued to deepen as did the supporting industry base, and the region came to house important investments in media.

Particularly for more capital-intensive activities, such as those in media, investment incentives continued to play a central role in attracting new entrants. Nevertheless, with the exception of media and heads investments in the neighboring states of Perak and Kedah, the cost advantages of production workers declined in the 1990s. With labor costs rising, quality rather than price of labor became critical; and Penang stepped up into more skill-intensive functions. The supply base also deepened, providing benefits to American firms through the increasing availability of local process engineering services. Government policy played a more sophisticated role in supporting the industry, moving beyond an emphasis on promotion and facilitation to industry-specific measures and the development of the local supply base.

EVOLUTION

The 1990s witnessed a number of new investments in drive assembly. First, in September 1995, Seagate announced that it would acquire Conner Peripherals. Second, three other drive assemblers entered Penang—Hewlett-Packard, Digital Equipment, and Quantum; and while none succeeded, an examination of their activities reveals Penang's changing position in the regional division of labor. Hewlett-Packard initiated high-end drive production in Penang before exiting the industry altogether in 1996. Digital Equipment also entered to assemble high-end drives but sold its storage division to Quantum, which left drive manufacturing shortly thereafter.

In the heads complex, existing firms expanded their operations. The most important development was Seagate's remarkable expansion as the firm gradually concentrated all of its heads operations in the region. After assuming control of Control Data's HGA facility in 1989, Seagate increased its investment in the facility in 1991 and within a year announced yet another expansion to perform machining, grinding, and finishing of heads ("Seagate Expands Thin-Film Head Manufacturing," April 29, 1991; "Seagate S'pore to Get More Work," June 2, 1992). Out of space in Penang, and with labor markets tightening, Seagate Penang oversaw a greenfield investment in the neighboring state of Perak at the Kinta FTZ outside Ipoh. Within a year of that investment, the firm announced an expansion of the facility that more than doubled its capacity.

Finally, northern Malaysia hosted new investments in media in the 1990s, both in Penang itself and in the neighboring state of Kedah. A crucial investment by Komag became operational in 1992, sparking the interest of other producers and their substrates suppliers.

LOCATIONAL DRIVERS AND BENEFITS

The Assemblers. Conner's and Seagate's strategy with the Perai facility, as well as the investments of Hewlett-Packard, Digital Equipment, and Quantum, testify to a shift in these firms' motivations: away from activities solely reliant on low-cost production labor toward those requiring more intensive management and engineering skills and complementary services. Under Conner management, the Perai facility had developed the capability to handle an initial ramp of new product directly from the United States. Before the acquisition, Seagate's Asian assembly operations were concentrated in Singapore (high end) and Thailand (desktop and later mobile); but the acquisition corresponded with a rapid growth in production capabilities beyond these two sites to new facilities in China at Wuxi and Shenzhen (formerly Conner's plant).

Why hold on to the Perai facility? The answer is that Perai graduated to a role previously monopolized by Singapore. Not only did it serve as a stand-alone production facility for certain products, but it functioned as a transfer point for China: drives were initially ramped from the United States to Singapore and Penang and then passed on to lower-cost Chinese operations. To implement this strategy required a substantial strengthening of Perai's technical capabilities in the form of a New Product Introduction Center. Although yields in Seagate's China facilities were actually superior to those in Perai, this was precisely because engineering teams in Penang trained by a group of expatriates from the Longmont design center had done substantial debugging and failure analysis.[23]

The investments of Hewlett-Packard, Digital Equipment, and Quantum also indicate firms' perceptions of capabilities in Penang. Hewlett-Packard's components group was one of the first foreign electronics firms to locate in Penang in the early 1970s. In 1993, its disk memory division was making high-end drives for workstations and servers in Idaho and Colorado, but the firm had gradually moved to greater outsourcing in the Asia-Pacific. Penang was chosen over nine other sites, including Singapore, because of both costs (including use of an existing facility) and the ability to leverage engineering capabilities to debug production problems and provide feedback to the Idaho design team. Hewlett-Packard's plan was to begin with manufacture of a 1-gigabyte and then 2-gigabyte drive but to leapfrog the competition within three years by producing a 10-platter, MR-head, 9-gigabyte drive. The first two products were successfully ramped up to full production, with both regional and local sourcing; only heads came from the United States. In April 1996, however, failure to resolve some key design problems led management to end the project.[24] Nonetheless, the effort shows that, by the early 1990s, a major firm believed that Penang was capable of ramping up production of a drive that, had it succeeded, would have been at or near the technological frontier.[25]

Digital Equipment's story is also revealing. The company approached the PDC about two investments in 1994: one in heads, the other in high-end drive assembly. By this time, the PDC was concerned about the effects of labor-intensive investments on the labor market and discouraged the heads investment, which went to Batam, Indonesia. Although the PDC was interested in the assembly investment and brokered the application process, Digital Equipment's headquarters made a strategic decision to get out of storage altogether, selling the division to Quantum. Quantum proved unable to integrate Digital Equipment's Penang operations. High-end production was ultimately turned over to MKE, which had no use for the Penang facility. Nonetheless, Quantum did open a repair facility that consolidated its entire global repair operations, drawing extensively on local tooling capabilities under the direction of a local manager who had worked at Intel.[26]

Penang's failure to host a larger concentration of HDD assemblers seems largely fortuitous, a function of a general shakeout that resulted in a decline in the number of firms from the industry's mid-1980s peak. Nevertheless, the timing of a given location's entry into the industry also influences its niche. Drive investment in Asia in the mid- to late 1980s was concentrated overwhelmingly in Singapore, with lower-end drives (and later mobile products) assembled in Thailand. Singapore's position as a first mover allowed it to hold on to low-end drive assembly for some time by shifting subcomponent assembly offshore—for example, to Malaysia. By the time this approach was no longer cost-effective, the labor-intensive nature of low-end assembly made Penang relatively costly as a site; and it was passed over in favor of Indonesia, the Philippines, and China. Singapore could hold on to its position in the industry as a whole by graduating to the production of higher-end drives and serving as a regional headquarters. Seagate's Perai facility went through a similar evolution, graduating to a ramp-up site and transfer station. Had the Digital Equipment, Hewlett-Packard, and Quantum investments succeeded, Malaysia would have housed a cluster of higher-end drive assemblers.

The Deepening of the Heads Complex. The motives behind Seagate's expansion out of Penang into Ipoh mirror its earlier investments out of Singapore into Malaysia, including (in the words of Seagate managers) a "cost effective investment package," "the wider pool of workers Perak had to offer [and] cheaper land prices" ("Penang Seagate," March 7, 1995; "Seagate Technology Keen," January 26, 1996). But the heads complex continued to deepen in Penang itself, suggesting the development of higher-order capabilities based on a pool of engineering talent and, to a lesser extent, a local supply base and proximity to customers. For example, Applied Magnetics' original operation focused only on HGA, with virtually nothing sourced locally. Sliders were manufactured in Goleta, California; suspensions were sourced both in-house and from Hutchinson and NHK; and even wire and wire-tubing subassemblies came from the United States and elsewhere in the region.[27] Full slider fabrication began in 1990, still based on wafers from Goleta but with ion milling and photolithography done in Penang. Seagate also located such processes in Penang in the early 1990s; and as a firm manager noted, these processes as well as vacuum technology were too technically demanding to be carried out in either Thailand or the Philippines.[28] Moreover, Penang increasingly took on process engineering tasks for the heads majors. Applied Magnetics built equipment for its slider fabrication and automated lines, and Read-Rite maintained an

Advanced Manufacturing Technology Group that carried out process development. While high-end failure analysis at Applied Magnetics went back to the United States, Penang performed failure analysis with locally made testing equipment.

Although customer specifications drove the sourcing of many HSA components, with much still brought from the United States and Japan, Applied Magnetics had a vendor development program and started to source more components locally. As the heads business evolved into a more integrated head-stack business, firms benefited from proximity to key sub-assembly operations, particularly actuators and flex-circuit assembly. Conversely, the development of such a complex began to attract new investments in these segments, including those from American contract manufacturers. For example, Xolox Malaysia was incorporated in October 1994 and began operation in April 1995 making actuators. Although Xolox was already supplying customers in Penang (including Applied Magnetics and Read-Rite) from the United States, entering in Malaysia not only lowered costs but provided the benefits of proximity. Because of Xolox's strong design capabilities, proximity allowed engineers from customers' firms to visit facilities on a regular basis to discuss issues of design for manufacturing.[29]

A New Media Cluster. Komag's 1992 announcement that it would invest in Penang constituted a major coup. In the words of one PDC official, Komag was the "jewel in the crown"; both its size (as the world's largest independent media manufacturer) and technical sophistication (with highly automated lines that require few traditional production workers) signaled a new phase in Penang's involvement with the industry.[30] By the end of 1998, Komag made three-quarters of its disks in Penang.

Before choosing Malaysia, Komag did not have any operations outside the United States and Japan, and Penang was competing head to head with Singapore to attract the investment. With respect to customer proximity, Singapore had the edge: most shipments were to firms with assembly operations in Singapore. Given that some shipments were also going to Thailand, however, this advantage was not decisive. Products could be trucked easily in either direction and flown in if necessary, demonstrating the advantages of dense regional networks of customers and suppliers. Neither site had an advantage with respect to key inputs (primarily chemicals and substrates) or capital goods, which would be supplied from Japan and the United States. Penang's FTZ matched Singapore in exemption from duties. According to Komag's managing director in Penang, the main considerations were taxes and personnel; costs were rising in Singapore, and studies conducted by Komag indicated that there were adequate personnel with requisite technical skills in Penang.[31]

Komag's Malaysian facilities were expansions out of U.S. operations and manufactured similar products. Originally, new product was ramped up in the United States and then transferred to Penang; but as with Conner, new product was eventually ramped directly into Penang. When Komag launched a major restructuring of its manufacturing operations in 1997, Malaysia was a big gainer because "these facilities [were] closer to customers' disk drive assembly plants in Southeast Asia and enjoy[ed] certain cost and tax advantages over . . . U.S. manufacturing plants."[32] At the time, most of Komag's products were exported to manufacturers in Singapore, with 10 to 20 percent sold to Western Digital in Kuala Lumpur ("Komag to Produce," November 27, 1997). The availability of adequately skilled labor was among the cost advantages of producing in Penang. With highly automated facilities, Komag employed no production workers in the traditional sense; nearly 85 percent of its workforce was made up of technicians.

A closer examination of Komag's operations shows that labor costs and taxes were not the only benefits of location in Penang. Although tooling and new lines were designed by Komag and imported from the United States, local firms played an increasing role in line modification, tooling, and automation. These firms, which included Excel Precision, LKT Precision Engineering, Newtecho Engineering, and Newtecho Tooling, got their start servicing other electronics segments and used their design, engineering, and production capabilities to diversify into the drive industry.[33] Among these firms proximity is vital since the manufacture of production and process equipment resembles a service as much as a freestanding good. In addition, according to a senior vice president, Komag's Malaysian factories "provide real time service and technical support to the drive assembly plants of our customers that are located within the same time zone" ("Komag Enters Volume Production," September 7, 1999).

The effect of Komag's entry and the availability of a new location in the neighboring state of Kedah generated a cluster of media firms. In 1997, Akashic Kubota commenced production of polished aluminum substrates in the science-based industrial park at Kulim in Kedah.[34] In 1997, there was a rapid succession of investment announcements in media-related production in Kulim; and given that many of these firms were Japanese, some follow-the-leader effects were probably operating. The promise of a media cluster was initially interrupted by a glut in the supply of drives that corresponded roughly with the onset of the Asian financial crisis, meaning that at least one investment (by MaxMedia, the media division of Hyundai Electronics) was aborted. By late 1999, however, a substantial group of media firms had located in Kulim, including Fuji Electric and a Showa Denko–Toyo Kohan joint venture in aluminum substrates, Advanced

Disk Technology (a joint venture between Kobe and Nippon Steel), and Ohara in crystalline glass for substrates ("Uemura to Produce," June 11, 1997; "Toyo Memories Plant," December 17, 1997; "Japan's Showa Aluminium," February 11, 1998).

With a few exceptions, such as Kobe, Fidelity Chemical, and a chemicals investment by the Japanese firm Uemura, the motives of the media firms do not reflect the advantages of proximity. On the contrary, one firm manager noted confidentially that the clustering of media investments generated concerns about competition for skilled workers. Rather, firms located as a result of common benefits from tax incentives connected to the Kulim Hi-Technology Park (media firms qualified for special incentives for high-tech firms) and the availability of both land and water. Nonetheless, media firms did exploit Penang's deepening resources in process engineering, a useful service given the reliance of the media segment on highly automated production processes.

THE CHANGING ROLE OF GOVERNMENT

As in Singapore, major and ongoing pressure on the Penang government centered on the labor market. By the early 1990s, rising wages were forcing an uncomfortable dependence on foreign labor in manufacturing and driving the expansion of certain segments of the industry, including media and heads, into the neighboring states of Kedah and Perak.

The PDC first addressed these changes in the draft Penang Strategic Development Plan (PSDP) for 1991–2000.[35] Investment promotion and provision of high-quality infrastructure remained important; and throughout the 1990s, the state government called on Kuala Lumpur to simplify procedures, such as customs, that would ease the activities of foreign investors.[36] Nevertheless, deregulation, liberalization, and provision of infrastructure were seen as necessary, not sufficient, conditions for industrial upgrading. Rather, policy recommendations identified in the PSDP and reiterated in later policy documents in the mid-1990s and after the crisis of 1997–98 began to mirror Singapore in proposing a more activist government role in restructuring the manufacturing sector toward greater intensity in capital, skills, and technology.[37] The PSDP and subsequent documents called for closer inter-industry links and ties between multinationals and local firms, with the ultimate goal of creating an Integrated Manufacturing Center that would have design and R&D capabilities and house not only manufacturing but marketing and support services.

Because of Malaysia's federal structure, however, the government of Penang found itself constrained in implementing these ambitious objectives. The federal government had its own technology policies, which, as Felker

(1998b: chap. 4) has documented, were often imposed from the top down, disconnected from industry needs, and driven by the need to respond to regional inequalities and politics. A first point of policy leverage was to adjust promotional efforts at the margin. The PSDP called for an explicit re-orientation of the government's investment promotion strategy away from labor-intensive manufacturing. PDC officials relate increasing focus on the head count and cite specific examples in which HDD-related investments were discouraged because of their high demand for low-skilled labor.[38] For example, except for Seagate's expansion in the early 1990s, which was some-what controversial because of the demands it raised for operatives, the last heads-related investment in Penang took place in 1991; and both Read-Rite's and Seagate's HGA-HSA operations were consolidated out of Penang in the late 1990s.

A second area in which the Penang government could intervene centered on education: skills development, the public training system, university train-ing, import of skilled technical workers (short term), and workforce planning. Central to this effort was the 1989 launch of the Penang Skills Development Center, whose main feature of success has been its demand-oriented structure. Nominally a private entity, the center was supported by the government both directly and indirectly—for example, through pro-vision of buildings and accreditation, which allows it to tap money from the Human Development Fund, a 1 percent levy on corporate wage bills that can be used for approved training purposes. Firms communicate their training needs to center management and donate (and maintain) equipment and even trainers. Through most of the 1990s, the center pri-marily taught beginning courses designed to prepare individuals for basic assembly work: time management, statistics, information management, positive behavior, and team building. In the second half of the decade, indus-try groups began to organize more focused efforts that concentrated on scarce skills and thus reduced the risks of poaching. For example, in 1998 Seagate led an effort to train workers in tool and die making. Penang, however, still lacked the capability to develop the industry-specific engineering skills seen in Singapore's close government-university-industry partnership. Our conversations with managers indicate that, while many of them are satis-fied and comfortable with the graduates from the local universities, the number of graduates is still too small and their skills too unfocused to meet industry needs. One reason is the location of the Universiti Science Malaysia engineering school in Perak, which indicates the importance of regional pol-icy within the federation.

A third policy area in which Penang had scope for innovation was the development of supporting industries. In the 1980s, the PDC tried to encourage corporations to increase their local inputs; but without the ability to offer grants or even incentives, the PDC's role was restricted to development of serviced industrial areas adjacent to the FTZs and to organizing vendor/procurement exhibitions and meetings. The PDC compiled and produced the first directories of supporting industries, tailored to particular industry needs, to make the capabilities of local industry known to foreign investors.

In 1992, the government established a small- and medium-scale industry center (PIKS) under the auspices of the Penang Industrial Council. The PIKS provided secretariat support to the Penang State Industrial Transformation and Small and Medium Industry (SMI) Development Committee set up to monitor implementation of the strategic development plan, and by the end of 1999 it had approximately two hundred members. PIKS objectives include acting as a means for the government to plan, coordinate, and implement programs and projects for the development of SMIs in Penang. Since its inception, the PIKS has organized programs on finance, market and vendor development, technology enhancement, grants, human resources development, quality management, and occupational safety. A central function is the effort to overcome the informational problems that small entrants might face in seeking to supply the drive industry, including knowledge of relevant regulations, incentives, financial packages, and assistance related to the SMIs. The 1998 PC and Peripherals Task Force report, undertaken in the wake of the financial crisis of 1997–98, called for the creation of a Cooperative Research Center. It is important to underline, however, that vendor development in the Penang region appears to have been largely driven by the private sector, with the PDC playing a facilitative role in the process.

Conclusion

As in Thailand, initial investments into Penang were pushed largely by rising labor and land costs in Singapore and the United States and pulled by tax incentives and basic trade and investment policies that equaled those in Singapore even if the infrastructure did not match Singapore's in quality. From the beginning, Singapore managers saw Penang as an extension of their operations, a proximate location that permitted close oversight and monitoring while offering a different cost structure.

Nonetheless, firms were attracted to Penang because of its skilled managerial, engineering, and technical labor. At the outset, this advantage could not be considered an agglomeration economy since these capabilities developed in conjunction with different electronics industries segments. Over time, however, such economies developed with the movement of personnel among drive firms and the growth of industry-specific skills. Moreover, agglomeration economies and the benefits of proximity were important at the firm level, particularly between limited assembly efforts and in the heads complex, where close links between actuator and flex-circuit makers, HGA producers, and HSA production are important for not only materials management but joint problem solving. Engineering services, particularly in production process capabilities and in the making of tools, fixtures, and jigs, also played a growing role; and the government of Penang used the instruments at its disposal to encourage and deepen this agglomeration.

Nevertheless, the Penang cluster was rooted in the evolving industry division of labor within Southeast Asia and beyond it to China, as can be seen in the close relationships between Malaysian plants and their regional headquarters in Singapore (or, in Read-Rite's case, Thailand). Moreover, investments in Penang were used to extend this network into new proximate areas, as in Komag's and Seagate's management of increasingly far-flung production networks within Malaysia, which benefited from the same advantages initially conveyed by Penang's incorporation into the regional network.

Part _Four_

IMPLICATIONS

10 Policy, Politics, and Location in Developing Countries

Although we have emphasized the benefits of locating U.S. HDD manufacturing activities in Southeast Asia, our study also has important implications for host countries, particularly developing ones. How can Southeast Asia's experience in the disk drive industry help developing countries participate in high-technology industries? Where and how can these countries insert themselves in globalized value chains? More specifically, what role can public policy play in attracting and holding foreign firms and clusters or, alternatively, developing national ones in industries such as disk drives?

With reference to East Asia, these questions take on added significance because of a long-standing and often polarized market-versus-state debate on the efficacy of industrial policy. At one extreme is the market position that governments should not be concerned about the composition of a country's portfolio of industrial activities or the nationality of firms. Rather, by avoiding sectoral interventions and maintaining neutral, stable incentives, a government should act primarily to create an environment in which firms, regardless of nationality, make decisions about how to exploit comparative advantage. In addition to its efficiency arguments, this neoclassical position has taken on a political economy rationale: government intervention inevitably leads to rent-seeking behavior that compounds economic distortions.

At the other extreme is the statist view: governments favor sectors that generate positive externalities of various sorts, such as technological spillovers or the generation of high-wage employment. In this view, advantages can accrue from fostering the capabilities of local firms, even if such fostering discriminates against foreign ones. Advocates suggest that the dangers of rent seeking are exaggerated or at least can be controlled; after all, the advanced industrial states are all democracies that must respond to various constituencies but nonetheless have long histories of sustained growth.

Interestingly, scholars have argued that East Asia's economic development can support either position.[1] Nevertheless, our study of the disk drive industry's concentration in Southeast Asia suggests that these extremes are too crude to capture the range of opportunities and challenges that developing countries face in globalized, high-technology industries. While an open stance toward trade and investment and other generic policies are indeed necessary, meeting such a baseline standard may offer limited opportunities for movement up the value chain. Directed sectoral interventions can help countries increase both value added and efficiency if those interventions conform to what Robert Wade (1990) calls "big followership."[2]

With such a strategy, government officials follow private-sector leads with enough expertise to understand industry-specific market and technology trends but with enough independence to formulate policy without protecting the industry or doling out favors to particular firms. This strategy presumes both beneficial spillovers from the promotion of specific sectors and that sectors can be successfully identified and promoted only through close contact with and incentives for private investors. Moreover, the strategy rests on institutional capacities that, owing to more basic political factors, are often rare in the developing world—and even in the advanced industrial states.

Consider, first, the benefits of the noninterventionist position. The Southeast Asian cases exhibit important commonalities with regard to their policy stance, including liberal trade and investment regimes for foreign firms. These policies were integral to the location-specific assets that proved so important to the competitiveness of American firms. Nevertheless, there is an important methodological problem in drawing inferences only from our Southeast Asian success stories: How do we know that the absence of such policies would have inhibited the growth of disk drive production? Later in this chapter, we examine four countries that were plausible production sites but were either tardy in attracting it from abroad (the Philippines), unsuccessful in their efforts to develop an indigenous capability on their own (Brazil and Taiwan), or a partial exception that proves the rule (the success of Korea's Samsung group).

By demonstrating the positive effects of policy change, the Philippines buttresses the case for a baseline policy environment. Once the government undertook a number of reforms in the late 1980s and early 1990s, the country began to benefit from its position in the region and attracted significant foreign, particularly Japanese, investment. Brazil and Taiwan are more interesting, however, because both attempted to substitute the promotion of indigenous producers for foreign investment, failing to reach their goals because of local firms' inability to keep up with the industry's demanding technological and performance requirements. Moreover, these attempt to work alone actually undermined the ability of local firms to develop relevant capacities in the industry. The Singapore government's own short-lived efforts at direct involvement in disk drive production suggest similar conclusions. Finally, the Korean case suggests a highly limited set of conditions: massive *private* subsidies from other businesses within the Samsung group were required for the disk drive operation to survive.

The failure of Brazil and Taiwan and the uniqueness of Samsung's efforts might suggest that developing countries should walk a relatively narrow policy path to enjoy the benefits of participating in the value chain of industries such as disk drives. This conclusion, however, is misguided. A summary of the Southeast Asian experience suggests that generic policies on their own would probably not have led to the creation of a regional production system. Singapore's industry-specific measures helped create pools of skilled personnel and suppliers who encouraged higher value-added activities to locate there. As a result, Singapore became the anchor of Southeast Asia's disk drive network and a source of positive spillovers to the rest of the region. Although Malaysia and Thailand both benefited from their openness to foreign investment, their relatively weak, sector-specific policies contributed to their proportionately weaker agglomeration economies.

Singapore's achievements suggest that sector-specific policies do not necessarily involve the kinds of protection and subsidies that lead to allocative inefficiency and rent seeking and that the general critique of industrial policy is too sweeping and indiscriminate. Indeed, a commitment to free trade and investment is a crucial component of such market-conforming industrial policies, in part for political economy reasons. These policies constitute an important monitoring device to guarantee that business-government relations do not degenerate into rent seeking and that firms are exposed to the highest levels of market pressures; the Brazilian case demonstrates the costs of removing this check.

It is true, however, that even with such external discipline the implementation of market-conforming, sector-specific policies demands great institutional resources. With a stroke of a pen (to exaggerate only slightly), a government can promulgate successful trade, investment, macroeconomic, and, to a lesser extent, infrastructure policies. In contrast, the formulation and implementation of industry-specific policies such as training and supplier development require governments to mobilize and draw on the specialized knowledge of private actors, which includes the sharing of proprietary knowledge that can expose firms to risks of opportunism. Moreover, these informational requirements are dynamic; policies appropriate to one stage of the industry's growth may not be germane at another.

As the new institutional economics literature highlights, these features result in a number of important institutional problems (Clague 1997a, Drobak and Nye 1997, Burki and Perry 1998). First, transaction costs—the costs of searching, bargaining, and enforcing deals—increase with the number of actors involved, the information intensity of policy, and the extent of policy adjustment required to meet shifting industry requirements. Collective action problems grow with the involvement of larger numbers of actors, each of which may be tempted to take a free ride on the efforts and information of others. Firms' tendency to poach skilled workers rather than contribute to training programs, whether in-house or industry-wide, is an obvious example. Second, so-called principal-agent problems become more acute when policymaking and implementation involve more layers of government and larger numbers of private actors. These problems center on guaranteeing that policies are meeting their objectives and not being captured by private rent seekers.

A key finding of the new institutional economics is that these types of problems typically defy resolution through simple arm's-length or parametric interventions common to generic, baseline policies; they are not resolved by simply freeing trade and investment. Rather, they require institutional resolution (Clague 1997b: 3): rules, norms, and enforcing organizations that facilitate the sharing of information, mutual monitoring, and the implementation of collective goals. Two sets of related institutions are important for achieving these objectives: cohesive, autonomous bureaucracies and mechanisms for public- and private-sector consultation.[3]

As we have suggested in our discussion of big followership, states require expertise and autonomy to appreciate, much less implement, sector-specific policies. Nevertheless, states cannot pursue such market-based sectoral policies without extensive engagement with those most directly involved in the market—namely, firms. Systematic public-private consultation can improve information for public-sector decisions, broaden ownership and enhance the credibility of such policies, improve accountability and transparency, and expand resources for policy implementation.[4]

In some cases, public-private sector exchanges may benefit from a third factor: the encompassing organization of firms in the sector. Industry associations can also provide benefits directly to members. Business organization can limit the pursuit of particularistic benefits by individual firms and facilitate the provision of critical industry-specific information from and among firms.[5] As we will see, however, some policies, particularly those involving highly proprietary information, may require bilateral consultations.

Whether firms act alone or in concert, depth and transparency in business-government relations are key for limiting special favors and promoting firms' willingness to share resources useful to the overall development of an industry. Singapore's ability to implement industry-specific measures suggests that the city-state has much greater institutional strength than do its regional neighbors; as we discuss later in the chapter, differences in disk drive policies among Singapore, Malaysia, and Thailand reflect variations in the countries' broader institutional landscapes.

These observations raise a final but important political question. If certain kinds of institutions can facilitate sector-specific policies that in turn allow countries to expand their role in global value chains, why don't all countries develop such institutions? What accounts for cross-national variation in institutional capacity? Why doesn't the Thai Board of Investment act like the Singapore Economic Development Board?

It is tempting to attribute these differences to differences across countries in the stock of social capital—the capacity for cooperation through networks and trust. An extensive literature on Asia's economic success attributes such capacity to, among other factors, Confucianism and attributes of Chinese culture; but the plausibility of such arguments is belied by intersectoral, interlocal, and temporal differences within countries.[6] For example, Thai officials, commercial bankers, and rice exporters have established long and economically productive patterns of cooperation, while Thai auto parts firms have exhibited little interest in cooperating with the government except for protection. The machine tool firms and semiconductor producers cooperating for skill development in Penang are no less Chinese than those operating elsewhere in Malaysia, and the foreign firms with which the Economic Development Board has established close working connections are for the most part not Chinese at all.[7]

An explicitly political approach is required to account for these institutional difference, and it is particularly important to understand the incentives of politicians in building institutions and devising both generic and industry-specific policies. Our explanation emphasizes two related factors: external pressures and governments' political relationships with domestic private sectors. External pressures, including security challenges from other countries and economic shocks, influence the attention that national leaders give to export-oriented manufacturing as a way of garnering foreign exchange. These shocks, however, are mediated by domestic political calculations, particularly the extent to which governments are beholden to inward-looking domestic business interests that can limit the ability to pursue either baseline economic policies or more demanding sector-specific ones.

Generic Policies and the Baseline for Entry

Clearly, U.S. firms' initial move to Southeast Asia was stimulated by the introduction of small disk drives for the desktop personal computer and pressure from personal computer producers such as IBM for reliable, high-volume, low-cost manufacture. As products began to change more rapidly, however, and the market became more differentiated, drive firms also required the capacity to move large volumes of new products rapidly to market. These pressures to reduce time to market and time to volume, combined with constant price pressures and shifting technologies, generated new demands on local capabilities.

Our case studies have shown how locations in Southeast Asia developed the capability to meet these needs. The first and most basic prerequisite for entry was the cost of labor. A second category of location-specific assets related to the overall business environment: the flexibility of labor markets, macroeconomic stability, and the ability to invest and move product easily, both with respect to infrastructure and customs procedures. A third category involves industry-specific agglomerations of skilled personnel and specialized suppliers that facilitated process innovations while reducing costs, time to market, and time to volume.

To some degree, of course, costs—especially labor costs—are a function of countries' underlying endowments; but both costs and market access are also a function of public policy. Indeed, to be seriously considered as a production site for hard disk drives, a government's policy environment had to meet a number of baseline conditions. Summarized in table 10.1, these constitute what Evans (1995) calls a classic regulatory strategy designed simply to provide stimulus and incentives for foreign investment.

As we have seen, firms repeatedly cited labor costs as an explanation for why they had moved abroad. Nonetheless, many countries had labor costs significantly lower than those in Singapore, Thailand, and Malaysia. Our interviews suggest that labor availability, the flexibility of labor markets, and managerial freedom over shop floor organization (all strongly affected by public policies) were also important variables in firms' calculus.

Free trade policies, at least with respect to the imports of relevant components, were crucial. As product cycles for increasingly high-volume products shortened, the need to move product quickly and with ease also grew. The provision of general infrastructure—telecommunications, customs, transport, energy—was an important complement of the open trade regime. Over time, the importance of time to market and the move toward tighter inventory management, even across borders, required a more sophisticated trade-related and logistics infrastructure.

TABLE 10.1

THE BASELINE POLICY ENVIRONMENT

Policy	Rationale and Importance
Labor market policy	Labor market conditions and costs
	Importance of securing labor and absence of restrictions on management at the shop floor
Free trade	Ability to export and import subassemblies from diverse locations
Infrastructure	Need for developed trade-related infrastructure to move product quickly
Investment regime and incentives	Importance of investment incentives to profitability, ownership control, and freedom to source
Macroeconomic policy	Importance of stability in exchange rate and factor costs

Another important set of policies centered on the general rules governing investment. Given the proprietary nature of technology, the need to integrate operations closely into a global network, and stringent quality requirements for components, foreign firms in industries such as disk drives are unlikely to locate in jurisdictions that place formal or de facto limitations on foreign ownership or impose local sourcing requirements. Nonetheless, competition among jurisdictions for investment means that governments are under pressure to extend additional incentives to firms. Of particular importance are those that affect startup and operating costs—above all, tax holidays but also accelerated depreciation schedules and, for disk drives, incentives based on the technology intensity of production, the use of skilled labor, and other relevant criteria. While the merits of such incentives are a legitimate topic of debate, they clearly had an impact on the industry's entry in the region, particularly on segments such as media in which fixed investments are high.[8]

Finally, it is important that the foregoing policies have been regionally clustered. If only one country in Southeast Asia had offered low-cost and available labor, good infrastructure, free trade, and open investment policies, the U.S. industry would not have benefited from the proximate heterogeneity that contributed to its success.[9]

Roads Not Taken

To assess the actual importance of these generic policies, we examine three cases in which policy deterred rather than attracted entry into the industry. Although the Philippines did suffer from its late entry into the game, its detour proved relatively brief; once basic political conditions became more supportive of open trade and foreign investment, and thus efficient regulation, the country became a major site for Japanese investors. Brazil exemplifies a country attempting to create an indigenous industry largely through a protectionist trade regime, a policy that approximated what Evans (1995) calls a custodial role, in which the state restricted foreign investors and prompted local firms to take the risk of production. Although the strategy worked in the narrow sense of building local production capacity, all of its inefficiencies were manifest in the HDD industry, where the technological frontier has shifted rapidly. Taiwan's initiation but eventual abandonment of disk drive production illustrates even more forcefully the difficulties of attempting to replace the leading disk drive companies. Like Brazil, Taiwan promoted indigenous producers but undertook the effort within a relatively free trade regime and a broader set of both generic and industry-specific policies that have helped it become one of the world's most successful producers of computer parts and equipment. This strategy, however, did not succeed in hard disk drives, shedding light on the broader opportunities for developing countries in high-technology industries. Finally, Korea shows the unusual circumstances under which developing countries might enter this fast-moving industry, circumstances unlikely to be replicated elsewhere.

THE PHILIPPINES

During the 1970s and 1980s, labor costs were low enough in the Philippines to attract substantial foreign investment—for example, in textiles and automobiles.[10] The country also enjoyed reasonable proximity to Singapore; and as we have noted, a number of the American firms that invested in Southeast Asia in the 1980s considered it as an investment site. But the country experienced a full-blown foreign exchange crisis in 1983, followed by a period of profound political instability associated with the collapse of the Marcos regime. As a result, the country missed the first wave of drive-related investment in the region and was able to attract producers only after implementing generic policy reforms consistent with those of its neighbors.

The fall of Ferdinand Marcos paved the way for Corazon Aquino's political and economic reforms and resulted in a handful of early drive-related investments.[11] The momentum of these early investments, however, was interrupted by an attempted coup in December 1989, the well-publicized kidnapping of a Japanese executive, and ongoing problems with basic infrastructure, especially electricity.

Gradually during the late 1980s and the 1990s, the nation's policy environment underwent an important shift. An Omnibus Investments Code passed in 1987 granted an income tax holiday to pioneer status firms, mirroring policies in Singapore and Malaysia. Export-oriented investment received a further boost with the passage of the Foreign Investments Act (FIA) in 1991.[12] According to the World Bank (1993), the FIA made the Philippine foreign investment regime comparable if not superior to its Asian neighbors. The Special Economic Zone Act of 1995 shifted authority over both government export processing zones and privately developed and managed ones to the Philippine Economic Zone Authority. By early 1997, fifty-six such zones (known as ecozones) had been set up; and they became the locations of choice for HDD firms that entered in the mid-1990s.

In the wake of these reforms, the Philippines received a wave of HDD investments; and the dominance of Japanese firms became a distinctive feature of the country's position in the regional division of labor.[13] The investment wave began with Hitachi in 1994, followed a year later with the almost simultaneous entry of Fujitsu and Toshiba for the production of 3.5- and 2.5-inch HDDs, respectively. Less than a year later, NEC Components Philippines set up to produce printed wiring boards (PWBs) mainly for the automotive industry but also for HDDs. Although NEC Hong Kong had been operating in the country through Tsukiden as subcontractor, it also decided to add HDD capacity and in 1999 constructed a new factory to assemble end-of-life 3.5-inch drives designed by IBM. The entry of the four Japanese HDD majors was also accompanied or preceded by the relocation of a number of Japanese suppliers.[14]

The Japanese majors paralleled the American pattern in a number of ways, including a desire to exploit lower labor costs and a strong urge to follow the leader (Tecson 1999). As of 1998, however, they had not generated strong agglomeration economies when compared with their American competitors. Although the Japanese majors derived advantages from proximate local suppliers, they saw considerably less labor mobility, and assembler-supplier relations have largely been bilateral. Moreover, the Philippines shows less evidence of local suppliers emerging. Nevertheless, for our purposes the point is that the Philippines' engagement in the industry came only after it undertook a number of policy reforms that made the country an attractive site for foreign investors. These reforms were the basis of an efficient but minimalist regulatory strategy.

BRAZIL

Brazilian companies were making HDDs before any other developing country had even hosted its first HDD investment and well before Taiwanese and Korean firms entered the market. Other than the United States and Japan, no other country had as many firms making disk drives. By the early 1990s, however, every Brazilian producer had quit the market; and none had been able to produce goods for direct or indirect export. Why did these early efforts come to naught? The answer lies not in unstable macroeconomic and political conditions, as in the Philippines, but in Brazil's heavily protectionist approach to the informatics industry in an attempt to achieve technological autonomy (Evans 1995).

Between 1980 and 1990, eleven Brazilian companies made HDDs. Three began shipping 14-inch drives in 1980 based on U.S. technologies.[15] Although Brazil's transition to smaller form factors was delayed, it occurred nearly as soon as many successful U.S. firms made the transition. Four companies began shipping 5.25-inch drives in 1982 (two based on their own designs using imported components); and in 1988 Multidigit produced Brazil's first 3.5-inch drive, only one year later than Seagate. In the late 1980s, the government estimated that Brazilian firms were producing approximately 40,000 disk drives annually.

All of this activity was a direct result of import substitution industrial policies—specifically, Brazil's Informatics Law, whose predecessors dated to the mid-1970s, when the military government began licensing entry of minicomputers firms and established criteria for granting the permission to import components (Luzio 1996). Companies received preference if their domestic content was high, were majority locally owned, and paid only a small amount in royalties to foreign technology suppliers or for foreign technical assistance. Technology transfer payments could not exceed 3 percent of net sales.

Initially, from fifteen applicants, the government selected four locally owned firms to make minicomputers. They were permitted to import technology but only after a commitment to develop their own technology and introduce original models within five years (Luzio 1996). In 1978, the policy of reserving the market for a select number of firms was extended to other data processing equipment, including disk drives (Tigre 1983). The government tightened the criteria for receiving import licenses, maintained control over production licenses (although, in fact, it greatly stimulated entry), controlled government computer procurement decisions, offered credit lines to domestic firms for the purchase of locally made computers, approved technology transfer agreements, and provided R&D incentives. In 1984, these steps were codified into the Informatics Law, which extended the market reserve until 1992.

Defenders of Brazil's strategy argued that, with nearly four hundred companies, the informatics program created Latin America's biggest information processing industry ("Brazil or Bust," November 11, 1991). In fact, however, the policy resulted in a local industry that suffered from poor quality, high prices, delayed deliveries, and periodic shortages, all of which encouraged smuggling (Luzio 1996: 91–92).[16] Yet despite these inefficiencies, HDD firms maintained a tight grip on the market for ten years.

When protection was removed in 1992, its significance was revealed: in short order, every single Brazilian HDD producer left the market. Although the Informatics Law had been extended in 1991, it was radically modified to eliminate government control over production and import licenses. The Collor administration (1990–93) also introduced a series of trade liberalization measures that slashed import costs and pressured local computer and disk drive producers, but by then the damage had been done. For Brazil, there was little chance of playing an important part in the industry.

TAIWAN

On the surface, Taiwan appeared to be the country most likely to become the site of significant disk drive production.[17] Unlike the Philippines, Taiwan had a stable political system and dependable macroeconomic policies, low wage rates (lower than Singapore's in 1985), and a strong supply of technical personnel as a result of both an efficient educational system and a stream of Taiwanese and other ethnic Chinese from Silicon Valley (Saxenian 1999). Moreover, unlike Brazil, Taiwan's trade regime was relatively open; in downstream industries, the country emphasized export promotion rather than import substitution—a plus because hard disk drive production needs to be acceptable to downstream, globally competitive computer producers. During the 1980s, these strengths had attracted significant electronics investment, making Taiwan the world's seventh-largest producer of computer hardware in 1987. As a major producer of PCs, the country has been one of the world's largest consumers of hard disk drives, undertaking between 1985 and the early 1990s an extensive promotion of drive and component production. As we will discuss, Taiwan also exhibited a number of institutional strengths key to designing sector-specific policies in high-technology industries (Wade 1990, Weiss 1998). These advantages led to a growth in production, especially of major parts, designed to compete in global markets.

Yet Taiwan eventually abandoned its efforts. How can we account for the country's failure in hard disk drives despite its promotional efforts and the fact that it succeeded so well in producing other globally competitive computer products such as motherboards and scanners? Although the answer involves several factors, the core explanation lies in Taiwan's efforts to promote indigenous producers of drives and major components. Despite significant government support for private-sector efforts and impressive technical personnel, local firms lacked the capacity to keep up with the changing technology and competitive strategies of U.S. firms (Noble 2000). In sum, Taiwan got most but not all of the ingredients right.

Before 1985, Taiwan lacked a systematic strategy to promote disk drive production, and the few firms that attempted either failed or shifted to other products.[18] The government did not respond to these failures by emulating Singapore's strategy of reliance on foreign producers. Instead, influenced by its successful promotion of semiconductors, the technocracy suspected limitations to the benefits of foreign disk drive production. As the head of a key government institute noted, "we can't go back to just assembling products" (Noble 2000: 9). Moreover, Taiwan's PC market did not yet attract foreign drive producers since, until the late 1980s, the country specialized in low-end, clone computers, most of which did not carry hard drives.

While these factors were important, none impeded Taiwan's growth as a key player in other areas of the global electronics industry. Nor did Taiwan emulate Brazil in discouraging foreign disk drive producers. More critical was a reluctance to match Singapore in going the extra mile to attract foreign investment. While Taiwan encouraged the return of Chinese scientists and engineers, the government made it difficult for firms to bring in non-Chinese foreign experts. This choice placed Taiwan at a disadvantage in precision machinery, related subspecialties, and head-quarters positions that required strong English competence. Equally important, giving foreign investors extensive financial and tax incentives would have disadvantaged Taiwan's own producers, which was not feasible politically. In Taiwan's ethnic division of labor, the mainlanders who dominated the ruling Kuomintang party held political power, with the result that the economy, with the exception of certain upstream industries, fell to the majority Taiwanese. Given these considerations, the government was unwilling to match Singapore's financial incentives for foreign firms.

Therefore, in the mid-1980s, the government decided to develop indigenous capabilities. Led by the quasi-governmental Industrial Technology Research Institute (ITRI), this strategy involved providing broad development and engineering support to small and medium-sized, high-tech, startup firms in the adjacent Hsinchu Science-Based Industrial Park.[19] In the case of hard disk drives, ITRI's Electronics Research and Services Organization (ERSO) organized a R&D consortium involving five of Taiwan's leading electronics firms. Through in-house research, ITRI completed prototypes of 5- and 10-megabyte drives that, in return for fees, it transferred to the consortium members. The drives, however, were obsolete by the time the prototypes were completed, and none of the members brought product-specific skills to the project. As a result, plans for mass production of hard drives were dropped.

Despite its failure, the ITRI effort attracted six disk drive producers.[20] Because each encountered difficulties in meeting the industry's demand for large capital investments, new designs, and rapid production ramp-up, all failed.[21] In the mid-1990s, Taiwan's efforts shifted to disk drive parts and components; and by 1995, the nation had developed a stronger indigenous base in heads, motors, and media than had any other Asian country outside Japan. At least three of these local initiatives were tied to Japanese component producers, and several benefited from ITRI's technological development efforts.[22] Nevertheless, almost all of the local firms could not keep up with rapid advances in recording density and shortened product cycles.

Unlike Brazil, Taiwan attempted to nurture but did not provide protection or extensive financial support to indigenous disk drive producers. When these efforts failed to yield fruit, the government largely abandoned efforts to provide financial incentives to either domestic or foreign drive producers. Instead, it implemented measures to ensure that local computer producers had easy access to drives produced elsewhere.[23] Forced to choose between a locally based but foreign-dominated disk drive industry and access to foreign drives for Taiwanese computer producers, the government chose the latter.

KOREA: THE EXCEPTION THAT PROVES THE RULE

Unlike those in Taiwan, policymakers in South Korea did not introduce programs to build an indigenous disk drive industry beyond some overall local content requirements and relatively low (10 percent) tariffs. Although half a dozen Korean firms entered the industry in the late 1980s, all but one failed. Oriental Precision, EsPerT, and Hyosung Computer all tried their hand at making disk drives, as did larger companies, including Goldstar Electronics and Hyundai Electronics (through its short-lived ownership of Maxtor of the United States). Even with some policy protection, Korea's computer makers depended almost entirely on imports to meet their demand for HDD; in 1990, approximately 70 percent (or $122.1 million) of total Korean imports came from the U.S.-owned plants in Southeast Asia ("Korea: Disk Storage," July 19, 1991).

An important exception to this general trend, however, is Samsung Electronics, a highly diversified manufacturer of consumer electronics and the world's largest producer of DRAM semiconductors. Until 1988, Samsung's personal computer operations had relied heavily on Seagate to provide it with disk drives. But Samsung then took an equity interest in a small Silicon Valley disk drive company named Comport. In exchange for financing, Comport agreed to have Samsung assemble its drives, and production in South Korea commenced at the end of 1988. Comport failed in 1990, at which point Samsung acquired Comport's disk drive designs and began its own development activity; interestingly, that development activity was located in San Jose, California. Samsung also invested some seed capital in a HDD startup, Colorado-based MiniStor Peripherals, in 1992.

The history of Samsung's presence in the industry can be traced through a series of milestones. By 1992, Samsung's HDD sales exceeded $100 million, almost 30 percent of which went to its in-house personal computer business. In mid-1995, Samsung shipped its first 3.5-inch drive, a 1-gigabyte unit designed by its San Jose R&D center (although this put it at least a full year behind the industry leaders). In 1997, Samsung became the first OEM customer to enter into an agreement with IBM to purchase IBM's MR recording heads for use in its drives. In 1998, the company had more than $1 billion in HDD sales, making it the world's eighth-largest HDD producer. In 2000, the company began shipping drives with 13.5 gigabytes per platter, closing the gap with the other makers of HDD for the desktop market.

Samsung's success, however, has had some detractors; and its lessons for other potential entrants from developing countries are by no means clear. The most important question hanging over Samsung is profitability: most industry observers believe the company makes no money on its disk drive operations. Like other Korean *chaebol,* or conglomerates, Samsung has effectively used its diversified corporate structure to support entry into disk drives—in effect, a kind of private subsidy or industrial policy. Few companies in the world have the luxury to be able to lose money for years at a stretch in an effort to catch up technologically. Moreover, it took ten years for Samsung to reach this point. If industry suspicions about Samsung's financial performance are correct, no other firm has stayed in the business this long without being profitable. As is the case with Korean efforts in a number of other sectors, respect for technological and production capabilities does not necessarily translate into profitability.

POLICY IMPLICATIONS OF THE CASES

The experiences of Brazil and Taiwan illustrate the dangers of attempting to preempt or replace foreign producers in an industry with rapid technological change and time-to-market requirements.[24] Those experiences also raise important political economy questions to which we return. But three policy-related issues remain unanswered. First, are efforts such as Taiwan's to promote indigenous production doomed to failure in any industry? Although a complete answer is beyond the scope of this book, we can gain insight by contrasting Taiwan's failure in disk drives with its greater success in CD-ROMs.

The difficulty of successfully pursuing an autonomous strategy in disk drives reflects the industry's particularly demanding set of characteristics: labor and capital intensity (both high but in different segments), pressures for cost reduction (high), length of product life cycle (short), complexity of value chain (high), level of competition (high), and speed of technological change (high). If Samsung had some success in entering, the company is also quite clearly an exceptional developing country firm—and one with deep pockets.

Taiwan's experience in CD-ROMs, however, suggests that where some of these conditions are relaxed, if only slightly, opportunities for direct engagement are expanded. In the early 1990s, the government undertook the same basic ITRI model of government support for indigenous, private-sector efforts in CD-ROMs. This time, however, the strategy was successful. Not only did it attract dozens of new firms in less than five years, but by 1998 Taiwan became a dominant global supplier of CD-related drives and disks and a promising player in the emerging DVD business. This success did not result from any change in Taiwan's sector-specific strategy or its institutional capacities. Indeed, the government actively promoted local firms' collective action in research and other activities. Rather, the key to success was a better fit between these capacities and the characteristics of CD-ROMs.

First, broad industry shifts allowed Taiwanese firms to gain access to critical technologies. When Japanese firms began to outsource assembly of CD-ROMs to Taiwanese firms, they provided key drive mechanisms with the assumption that the DVD format would take off. When it didn't, however, the Japanese found "that they had armed one of their most dangerous adversaries" (Noble 2000). Second, the technology used in CD-ROM drives is simpler and more stable than that used in disk drives. Unlike disk drives, CD-ROM capacity has been virtually fixed at 640–680 megabytes since its introduction in 1983. Thus, local producers did not have to contend with the rapid product cycles characteristic of the hard drive segment. Moreover, the importance of CD-ROMs in the price-sensitive consumer market for home electronics meant less demand for the innovative capacities so central to disk drive and PC design and manufacture. In short, the strategy of promoting national firms worked in this segment but could not match the more technologically complex and fast-moving hard drive industry.

Nevertheless, it remains to be seen if Taiwan can sustain long-term success in CD-ROMs or make a successful transition to DVD drives. Moreover, even if the country is successful, its achievements are based on the kind of cohesive economic governance we discuss in more detail later in the chapter. Given the political bases of such institutions, it is unlikely that other countries can emulate Taiwan's performance.

Our evaluation of Taiwan's experience raises a second question. If the strategy of "going it alone" is becoming more difficult in industries such as disk drives, do Brazil's and Taiwan's experiences demonstrate the futility of *any* industry-specific policies? The Singapore case indicates that the answer is no. Singapore went considerably beyond generic policies, adding training programs, supplier development efforts, and research consortia. In so doing, the country successfully combined links with foreign producers with the development of an indigenous supplier base and a deep pool of technical personnel, thus making it less vulnerable to external market and technology shifts than are Malaysia and Thailand.

This raises a third question. Why didn't Malaysia and Thailand fully converge on the "Singapore standard" in industry-specific policies as they had done in generic policies? Part of the answer concerns the particular challenges of efficient industry-specific policies, which must address the high transaction costs, principal-agent problems, and collective action dilemmas resulting from high and changing information requirements and the large numbers of private- and public-sector interests involved. Few countries possess the institutional capacities required to address these problems.

Institutions and Industrial Policy in Southeast Asia

Singapore's ability to formulate and implement disk drive–specific policies has depended on a network of well-coordinated agencies led by the Economic Development Board (EDB). These agencies enjoy significant political backing and independence and control substantial economic resources; moreover, they are largely shielded from the normal constraints of democratic politics by Singapore's dominant party system. As a result, officials are able to formulate policies with a view toward longer-term objectives (MTI 1991: 102–6). For example, policies promoting human resource development, supplier links, technology diffusion, and quality standards for the industry nest within a broader strategic vision designed to promote dynamic clusters of related industrial activities.

These efforts are predicated on the assumption that the government's role is largely to catalyze, not replace, the private sector.[25] For some time, the EDB has operated as a client service organization geared toward drawing in and holding multinational corporations. To this end, the board has substantial in-house analytic capacity and some discretion to manipulate incentives to attract high value-added employment and opportunities for technological learning. Beginning in the mid-1990s, it has paid increasing attention to attracting R&D activities as well. For example, Seagate initiated its Singapore design unit, which ultimately produced the U4, in return for new investment incentives.

Catalyzing the private sector requires engagement with it. Because of the proprietary nature of the information that foreign firms share with the EDB, many deals are struck on a bilateral basis, although the foreign firms we interviewed reported that the agency is careful not to allow differences in incentive packages to create unfair advantages in the market. At the sectoral level, however, with regard to human resources, supplier development, and technology diffusion, we see evidence of collective organization and action. In its efforts to promote electronics- and mechanics-related skill development, the EDB has sought out MNCs to establish industrial training centers, institutes, and programs (Wong 2000).

The Data Storage Institute (DSI) also conforms with our model. The DSI has high analytic capacity, both with respect to the industry as a whole and on carefully chosen technical issues. It is also attentive to demands emanating from the industry, which has been drawn into the institute through its governance structure.[26] In effect, the DSI serves as one means through which the HDD industry in Singapore is organized. The Gintic Institute of Manufacturing Technology—designed to help Singapore become a center for precision manufacturing—also draws on groups of firms to define its objectives and support and evaluate its efforts. Singapore's attempts to strengthen local suppliers through programs that tie them to foreign firms (the Local Industries Upgrading Program [LIUP]) or extend direct support for technological upgrading and workforce training are also predicated on multilateral involvement. In the LIUP, representatives of each multinational not only work closely with their firms' particular suppliers but meet with each other to share ideas and information designed to strengthen the overall effort.

In addition, government officials are sufficiently informed and organized to monitor and hold firms accountable for their use of incentives and subsidies. The criterion of accountability is a firm's or industry's capacity to succeed in the market. In the case of state support for local companies in the LIUP, for example, market performance is measured by a local firm's success in supplying export-oriented, foreign firms.[27]

The situation in Thailand contrasts sharply with Singapore's. Several factors undermine the Thai government's capacity to formulate and implement drive-related policies. First, the macroeconomic agencies that until the mid-1990s were the most cohesive and expert part of the government have never believed in the utility of industry-specific policies and thus have not developed competence in them. In their view, macroeconomic stability has been both necessary and sufficient for Thai growth. Second, the government is hobbled by fragmentation between the macroeconomic agencies and sectoral ministries as well as disunity among the latter. The sectoral ministries have traditionally lacked expertise and funds; and any ties to the local private sector tend to be clientelist, with firms either producing for a protected domestic market or receiving government contracts. Although the Thai private sector is filled with business associations, these groups have focused on lobbying for protection and subsidies rather than for public goods such as upgrading.[28] Finally, Thailand's competitive party system, driven by rural-based politicians with little sympathy for industrial promotion, has intensified this fragmentation, politicized the sectoral ministries, and impeded broader political support for industrial upgrading—issues we return to later in the chapter.

These factors have stymied the country's investment promotion agency, the Board of Investment. Traditionally, the board has focused on the provision of generic incentives based on considerations such as employment generation, foreign exchange earnings, and the size of investments. While its main function has been to grant and administer duty exemptions and process associated paperwork, its deployment of investment incentives has been largely indiscriminate due to its lack of sectoral expertise and the influence of private interests.[29]

The board's ostensible mission changed in 1991 following a set of steep tariff cuts and foreign direct investment guidelines that reduced its significance in granting various exemptions. Although the board was reorganized into sectoral divisions with a new focus on industrial deepening and high-technology activities, several factors undermined this effort. Reforms in areas necessary for high-technology foreign investment, including human resource and business infrastructure development, lay outside board authority; and political influence and turf wars exacerbated problems in areas such as standards and testing laboratories, quality control centers, and science park development.

While a 1993 decision to encourage projects in provinces outside the Bangkok metropolitan area had the praiseworthy goal of reducing the city's horrible congestion, decentralization pushed investors to areas with less developed infrastructure and skills. Taking priority over technological upgrading as the chief goal of investment policy, decentralization had the perverse effect of limiting opportunities for geographic clustering and the agglomeration economies associated with the dynamism of the drive industry (Felker 1998b). The result has been a dualistic Thai electronics industry in which export-oriented multinationals operate largely as an enclave in isolation from less efficient, domestically oriented local producers.

Thailand has not implemented any policies designed to strengthen human resources or local suppliers in the disk drive industry.[30]

Malaysia's institutions have been more cohesive and ambitious than their Thai counterparts, particularly at the state level, but less so than those in Singapore.[31] At the federal level, the Malaysian Industrial Development Authority (MIDA) has coordinated investment policy—centered primarily on the approval of projects and qualification for incentives—relatively well. Like the Thai Board of Investment, MIDA has sector-specific divisions, but its staff has developed some familiarity with investor concerns (Felker and Jomo 1999). Since the early 1990s, MIDA has used a variety of incentives to encourage investments that employ more managerial and technical staff, create more links, and provide more technical training. These benefits have been supplemented by efforts to extend promotional incentives to indirect exporters and the development of new infrastructure for high-tech investment, including technology parks and a multimedia corridor.

Nevertheless, Malaysia's goal of promoting high technology and industrial clusters has been hampered by insufficient personnel to monitor compliance with the country's ambitious investment objectives as well as institutional fragmentation within the government. MIDA does not have responsibility for fostering links, enhancing productivity, and promoting exports; and the prime minister's office still exercises discretion over a number of the country's most important industrial initiatives.

Equally problematic are the government's links with the private sector. Although foreign investors are willing to consult with government officials, they are skeptical about the ability of Malaysian agencies to manage training and vendor development schemes effectively. Equally serious are problems between the Malay-dominated agencies and the country's ethnic Chinese manufacturers. Since the early 1990s, the government has attempted to improve these links with a series of public-private consultative mechanisms, including a national-level Malaysian Business Council, dialogues on "smart partnerships," and a range of sectoral exchanges. Although these mechanisms have expanded information flows between government and business, increased trust, and checked some corruption and bureaucratic red tape, their impact has been limited by a lack of monitoring and accountability.

In many ways, weak links between the public and private sectors are a result of the fragmented nature of Malaysian business. Historically, business associations have wielded little power. Instead, individual businesspeople, both Chinese and Malay, have responded to their exclusion from formal policymaking by establishing personal, clientelist ties to politicians and officials.[32] The associations that do exist have been weakened by ethnic divisions; splits between politically connected large firms and smaller, less influential firms; and a single-minded focus on lobbying officials about tax and trade issues.

Nevertheless, these national problems have been offset by the advantages of federalism and innovation at the state level. The Penang state government has been relatively consistent in its efforts to promote export-oriented electronics firms. As chapter 9 has demonstrated, the Penang Development Corporation has been relatively unified, consulting with both foreign investors and local machine tool firms—focusing, for example, on worker training and improving managerial skills through public-private partnerships such as the Penang Skills Development Corporation (PSDC). Although the PSDC lacks the industry-specific capabilities of Singapore's DSI and the city-state's other training and upgrading programs, it is nonetheless able to help investors leverage their own assets.[33]

Explaining Policy and Institutions:
External Threats, Domestic Coalitions

If policy and institutions are so important, where do they come from? What are politicians' incentives for building institutions and devising generic and industry-specific policies? We find two related factors: external pressures and coalitional bases. External pressures, including security challenges from other countries and economic shocks of various sorts, typically have an important influence on the course of national development. In general, they expand the ability of political leaders to build new institutions and launch policy initiatives. More specifically, however, they can influence the attention that national leaders give to export-oriented manufacturing as a way of garnering foreign exchange.

Singapore's national institutions emerged in the 1960s as the country faced a diverse set of external challenges: security threats from Indonesia, the loss of a domestic market and access to natural resources after its 1965 expulsion from Malaysia, and the departure of British military protection. In response, the People's Action Party (PAP) developed a national security strategy with a strong economic component. The country's weak manufacturing base (most indigenous firms were in trade and finance) led the government to emphasize growth led by foreign investment.

As part of Malaysia, Penang did not face Singapore's security challenges. In other respects, however, it resembled Singapore: the state lacked natural resources and lost a key revenue-generating resource when national infrastructure development challenged its entrepôt status and made its port facilities redundant. Penang's political leaders reacted to these challenges by consciously emulating Singapore's development strategy and institutions, albeit under constraints associated with Malaysia's federal structure.

Thailand faced a slightly different combination of threats. Like Singapore but unlike Penang, Thailand has faced significant external security threats—first from colonialism in the late nineteenth and early twentieth centuries and later from the wars in Indochina. Unlike both Singapore and Penang, however, Thailand was able to gain ample foreign exchange through large exports of natural resources, especially rice. National independence and political legitimacy therefore required the presence of a cohesive central bank and a Finance Ministry that could provide the macroeconomic bases for sustained natural resource exports. A bureaucracy focused on promoting manufactured exports was not seen as critical.

The existence of threats, however, does not necessarily mean that institutions will emerge to address them. Political elites' abilities to create institutions is also a function of their coalitional bases. Singapore's ruling People's Action Party came to power partly in opposition to indigenous business interests (Haggard 1990a: chap. 3). Challenged on the left, the PAP needed to expand its support from within the working class. The result has been a regime that, despite its reliance on multinational corporations, is best described as an authoritarian social-democracy. On the one hand, the PAP-led government has had significant leeway to develop institutions that make use of foreign capital, even to the detriment of local firms. On the other hand, its emphasis on increasing value added and developing local skills reflects the importance of satisfying a working-class constituency.

The decision to support local firms after the mid-1980s partly reflected economic considerations: the recent recession and a growing recognition of the value to foreign firms of a strong local supply base. But the shift also corresponded with political changes. In the early to mid-1980s, decline in the party's electoral support reflected working-class frustration about increasing income inequalities and the middle class's resentment at being deprived of political rights. The government responded with programs such as the LIUP that were designed to strengthen indigenous firms, albeit through links with foreign producers. A strong local supplier base has since become one of Singapore's key location-specific assets.

Coalitional factors were equally important in Penang, allowing it to respond to external challenges by promoting both corporate expansion and the growth of an associated group of local suppliers. Because Penang is the only Malaysian state with an ethnic Chinese majority, the state's political leadership is more inclined to pursue a development strategy that promotes the interests of local Chinese firms than are governments in the rest of Malay-dominated Malaysia. In addition, because of its utility as an alliance partner to the ruling coalition, Penang's political elite has been allowed to pursue its own development strategy, which includes promoting industry-specific institutions and policies for advancing the electronics sector. The result is an effort to integrate corporate upgrading with indigenization.

Thailand differs with regard to both coalitional bases and the cohesion of the state elite. Historically, the urban-based banking and industrial sectors were key supporters of Thailand's political leadership, both developing in large part through revenues generated from agricultural exports. Until recently, none of these players were interested in the kind of industry-specific institutions and collective goods evident in Singapore or Penang. While this reasoning seems obvious for agriculture and banking, it is less so for industrialists. Many local manufacturers expanded by drawing on the reservoir of cheap labor in the countryside. Another group of more skill- and capital-intensive local firms (those with the potential to supply disk drive firms) expanded through access to a protected domestic market in areas such as automobiles and consumer electronics. The Thai government has extended tariffs to these segments for revenue purposes but also because of their political strength. Meanwhile the government provides incentives for foreign corporations to operate in Thailand but not for strengthening the country's technological capabilities.

In combination, these factors result in powerful constituencies that do not need industry-specific support and are even suspicious of it. They have accommodated themselves to the bureaucracy's fragmentation and even reinforced the government's disinterest in competitive upgrading. The result is a fragmented industrial structure in which multinational corporations operate in isolation from each other and local suppliers. Unlike Penang, and more recently Singapore, indigenization has occurred at the expense of upgrading.

External threats and shocks and the nature of business-government relations are also useful in understanding why the Philippines, Brazil, Taiwan, and South Korea initially pursued industrial strategies that differentiated them from the Southeast Asian countries where the drive industry initially located. For decades, the Philippines experienced a relatively permissive set of external conditions. The country benefited not only from direct U.S. protection but from American guarantees of financial support, whether in the form of military spending, rescues from balance of payments crises, or assured access to the U.S. market for Filipino sugar. These conditions undermined fiscal caution, allowed economic nationalism to flourish on both the political left and right, and encouraged a set of state institutions that were completely penetrated and weakened by private interests—in Hutchroft's telling phrase, a system of booty capitalism (Hutchroft 1998). Outside of several export processing zones, the combination of protection and corruption was clearly not conducive to the kinds of generic policies required by disk drive producers or even less complicated export industries (Kuo 1995).

Under Ferdinand Marcos, however, corruption reached a peak and contributed to a crisis in 1983–84 that intensified the divisions within the business community between the narrow circle of presidential cronies and those excluded from presidential favors (Haggard 1990b). Although the crisis led to Marcos's replacement by Corazon Aquino, her government was unable to completely break the nationalist mold, in part because of other political preoccupations, in part because of the continued weight of nationalist business interests. But the crisis and development of more internationalized business groups provided the political basis for the wide-ranging reforms of the Ramos administration that moved the country toward at least the generic public policy baseline just outlined.

Brazil's efforts to nurture its own disk drive industry was part of a broader economic nationalism that grew out of the country's enormous size and the ongoing lure of its domestic market. Democratic governments were highly responsive to protectionist business interests, and under authoritarian rule important segments of the military developed an interest in the informatics sector. Over time, however, this "market preserve" policy proved unsustainable both politically and economically. As Peter Evans (1995: 150) notes, "the perception that local informatic firms were being awarded a 'rental haven' undercut political support for further subsidies to local entrepreneurs." This, in turn, impeded the more market-conforming policies required in such an industry (see also Petrazzini 1995). The prolonged crisis of the 1980s and the increasing internationalization of Brazilian business provided the political basis for a gradual economic opening beginning under the Collor administration in 1990 (albeit in the context of a regional integration experiment—Mercosur—that retained some protective elements). Given Brazil's past experience in disk drive production, this opening might have made the country attractive to disk drive producers. But by this time, Southeast Asia already enjoyed first-mover advantages.

The Taiwan case is politically complex. Beyond the oil shocks of the 1970s, the country has not experienced the kinds of economic crises that Brazil and the Philippines have. On the other hand, the country does not have Brazil's large domestic market, lacks the Philippines' natural resources and guaranteed export markets, is exposed to serious threats from the People's Republic of China, and suffers a corresponding political isolation. Under these conditions, developing strong external links through trade and investment is a security as well as an economic strategy.

Then why such an interest in developing local firms? This question becomes particularly puzzling if we consider that the political relationship between the ruling Kuomintang party (KMT), made up of exiled main-landers, and the local private sector, dominated by indigenous Taiwanese, has always been ambivalent. The local private sector long lacked mean-ingful political ties to the government, while the government has explic-itly sought to limit the concentration of private economic power on political grounds (Cheng 1993).

Several related factors, however, have encouraged government support for local producers. Given its initial political isolation from many Taiwanese, the KMT saw support for indigenous producers as an important source of political support. Further, detailed studies of industrial policy in Taiwan have suggested that the links between reformist technocrats within the bureaucracy and the local private sector has always been closer than one might predict (Gold 1981, Kuo 1995). Those within the party who saw the KMT's future on Taiwan have long supported the development of local firms. Beginning in the 1980s, these links developed a wider political rationale as the KMT remade itself as a party of business, a tendency accel-erated by the transition to democratic rule in the mid-1980s (Chu 1994). In general, then, the government's policy stance has been an open one, as befitting a country constantly exposed to both economic and security threats. At the same time, Taiwan's broader political logic has resulted in sector-specific policies that support local firms but not to the point of sub-sidizing activities with little likelihood of long-term profitability.

By contrast, South Korea's political arrangements allowed for precisely such subsidization, as seen in Samsung's sustained and expensive com-mitment to disk drive production. In one sense, of course, the South Korean state was every bit as involved in sector-specific and generally market-conforming policies as Taiwan (Amsden 1989, Haggard 1990a, Woo-Cumings 1998). Yet unlike Taiwan, which depended largely on small and medium-sized enterprises, the Korean state relied on the *chaebol*. Under the authoritarian rule of General Park Chung-Hee, who took power in 1961, this reliance reflected several factors: a belief that, as in Meiji Japan, large enterprises, coordinated and supervised by the state, were necessary for Korean development; a dearth of private entrepreneurs on which to draw as engines of growth; a smaller state-owned sector than the one that Tai-wan's KMT inherited from Japan; and the military's lack of a party appa-ratus capable of providing political support, thus requiring rapid economic growth for legitimacy (Fields 1997: 128).

The state promoted the *chaebol*'s growth and diversification with mas-sive and selective credit at below-market rates as well as state-imposed export and other performance requirements, and groups such as Samsung assumed oligopolistic positions in numerous industrial sectors. Such size and diver-sity were "essential to Korea's success in gaining market share around the world, because losses in one subsidiary could be made up by gains in another" (Woo-Cumings 1999: 18).[34] Diversified groups such as Samsung could draw on both state funds and their own internal resources to gain market share in a range of sectors, including disk drives.

Developing Countries in Other Industries: Many Are Called . . .

What can Southeast Asia's experience with disk drives teach developing countries about other industries? At first glance, the answer seems to be "not very much." Disk drive producers and suppliers must contend with complex supply chains, intense cost pressures, unusually short product life cycles, large capital requirements, and rapid technological change (see chapter 2). Although firms in other industries, such as textiles and autos, must confront some of these conditions (such as short product cycles in textiles and complex value chains in autos), textile and auto producers do not encounter this daunting combination of demands. Evidence for this assertion lies precisely in the regional concentration of disk drive production. The much wider dispersion of manufacturing activities in textiles and autos reflects lower entry barriers in developing countries for those industries as well as other factors, such as auto manufacturers' greater need to customize products to local market demands and higher transport costs due to lower value-to-weight ratios.

Nevertheless, viewed longitudinally, other industries have begun to exhibit at modest levels some of the characteristics so key to the disk drive industry, suggesting that several lessons may be relevant for developing countries seeking to break into other industries (see chapter 11).[35] First, such engagement requires participation in regional or global networks dominated by multinationals who control key technologies, brands, or marketing. The opportunities for expansion through production for protected, domestic markets ("trade policy rents") and indigenous producers, whether state or private, have dwindled substantially. Second, without generic, baseline trade, investment, and labor market policies and adequate infrastructure, successful engagement is unlikely. Infrastructure is particularly noteworthy because it cannot be purchased from another country but is critical for participation in global commerce and for enhancing national productivity (Mody 1998).

Third, diverse levels of engagement and types of benefits are possible. In general, Thailand succeeded in expanding employment and earning foreign exchange, whereas Singapore's (and, to a lesser extent, Malaysia's) engagement has deepened human resources, enhanced local supplier performance, and encouraged local supplier penetration of international markets. Fourth, the nature of and benefits from such engagement depends on new internal capabilities (Mody 1998).[36] In addition to sophisticated infrastructure, successful engagement requires market-oriented, technological support through technical education and institutions catering to small and medium-sized enterprises. Such support often involves measures designed for specific sectors or groups of sectors.[37] Finally, the capacity for such support involves institutions—especially state agencies as well as public- and private-sector links—that can address the kinds of information, distribution, and coordination problems emerging when industries must raise quality, lower cost, and speed delivery, all in a context of technological change. Such revealed institutional advantage (Evans 1995) is not evenly distributed, as shown by the fact that differences among the Southeast Asian countries in the disk drive industry are replicated in other industries.

In sum, the good news is that "many are called." Globalization under conditions of technological change, fast product cycles, and cost pressures creates significant opportunities for developing countries to move beyond inefficient production for domestic markets or simple, turnkey assembly for export. The bad news is that "few are chosen." The chosen countries are those whose institutional context facilitates the diffusion and accumulation of new knowledge. The new context also implies tighter links with foreign producers and, at least during some transition, potentially serious adjustments for local producers. Developing countries can in principle meet these conditions but are often constrained by politics from doing so. As chapter 11 shows, such constraints operate in the advanced industrial states as well.

11 Globalization and Industrial Leadership

    In the past several decades, interest in the spatial dimensions of economic activity has exploded in somewhat contradictory ways. Much of the best work on this topic (from which we have borrowed extensively) has been geographically restricted. Arguing that "all economics is local," this literature examines the dynamics of particular regions, showing how local markets, institutions, cultures, and governments combine to generate growth. Yet this attention to the local has coexisted with an equivalent explosion of interest in the globalization of economic activity: the increasingly extensive and rapid movement of goods, factors, people, and finance across borders and the effects those movements have on households, firms, governments, and countries.

By developing a framework for understanding the role of location in the competitive advantage of both firms and national industries, we have attempted to join these apparently contradictory impulses. In its most general form, our approach emphasizes that investment decisions always have a locational component. Implicitly or explicitly, firms assess how geographically bounded assets complement firm-specific ones and thus contribute to performance. Firms that make the right locational decisions—including when and where to go abroad—increase their likelihood of survival and growth. Those that make the wrong locational choices struggle with their environments and face corresponding difficulties.

Emphasizing factor endowments, economists working in the field of international trade and investment have developed a parsimonious theory of location. In this view, activities that demand a given set of factors should, in both a positive and a normative sense, locate where those factors are most abundant and therefore inexpensive to employ. But access to low-cost factors is not the only motive for overseas investment. As we have shown, firms also seek other locational assets, including proximity to markets and customers or a favorable policy environment. In line with the narrow regional focus just outlined, firms also locate to exploit agglomeration economies that arise out of the collocation of suppliers and competitors. Finally, firms site different activities to exploit the network benefits and externalities that can arise from tapping into heterogeneous location-specific assets across different locations.

To make this framework useful, both social scientists and managers must understand the underlying competitive pressures in specific industries and how the exploitation of location-specific assets helps firms address them. Unfortunately, since different industries have different competitive drivers, understanding those pressures is not a simple task. Indeed, we've needed a whole book for a single industry! Moreover, the framework requires observers to account for the dynamic and reflexive nature of location. In contrast with trade theories, which see countries as endowed with certain relatively fixed factors of production, we see locations as evolving over time, in part as a result of the effects of investing firms. In particular, firms play the lead role in the construction of clusters and regional production systems—in effect, constituting economic space.

Locational Dynamics

Although studies of individual industries have limits, they also possess certain virtues. In this book, we have examined the entire population of firms in the disk drive industry over its forty-five-year history, tracking the location of all R&D and manufacturing operations. Such depth of coverage has enabled us to identify important dimensions of industry evolution that other approaches are likely to miss. Specifically, we have been able to learn more about the relationship among industry evolution, location, and competitive advantage.

EMERGING INDUSTRIES

In an industry's early stages, its geographic pattern is driven primarily by new entrants and where they happen to be located. Over time, the number of firms in an industry increases, competition intensifies, entry rates slow, and the total number of firms peaks. As the rate of exit exceeds that of entry, the number of firms starts to decline. During these intermediate and later stages, the industry's locational pattern is a result of not only entry but expansion, relocation, and exit. Exit can remove locations from an industry's map, often with wrenching implications for households and communities.

Where in the world do new industries come from? The answer depends on prior industrial base, research infrastructure, quality of universities, government policies with respect to R&D and procurement, and a host of other variables. All of these factors, however, are highly correlated with the overall level of development. Innovations generally occur in the core countries of the world economy: the advanced industrial states of North America, Europe, and Japan. The scope and speed of an industry's diffusion rests on the absorptive capacities of the followers. Although industry competition is initially very localized, with each national industry primarily serving its domestic market, international competition gradually intensifies.

Where industries emerge within these economies is equally complex and to some extent random, depending on the location of existing firms that diversify into a new activity or entrepreneurs who launch de novo startups. Over time, however, this random distribution usually changes as a result of firm choices to start up, relocate, or expand in areas where other firms in the industry are already operating. For example, in disk drives, a relatively dispersed pattern of innovation and production gave rise to highly concentrated clusters of collocated innovation and production activities in northern and southern California and a few other places such as Minnesota and Colorado.

GLOBALIZATION AND INDUSTRIAL LEADERSHIP

Our main purpose in this book has been to outline a dynamic model that describes the relationship among the evolution of an industry, location, and competitive advantage in international markets. Although this approach can be applied to any industry that competes internationally, it must begin with the specifics of changing competitive pressures in a particular industry over time, for those changing pressures provide the key to how firms can most effectively exploit location-specific assets.

Several mechanisms drive industries to reconsider their existing locations: a desire to grow internationally, technological changes, changes in competitive pressures, or changes in an industry's environment such as new trade and investment agreements or other regulations. In the HDD industry, locational decisions first focused on firms' effort to reduce costs, primarily by exploiting cheaper labor. In contrast with other industries, these early pressures did not arise from foreign competition but from large customers. As the first firms moved abroad, competitive dynamics in the industry shifted; and those that failed to move found themselves at a disadvantage, thus inducing more firms (including suppliers) to follow.

While relentless cost pressures have been a constant in the industry, firms in the second half of the 1980s were also confronted with incessant technological change and perpetual competition among computer makers to present customers with new, more powerful options. With this pressure came a new urgency to move product to market quickly. Since the 1990s, time-to-volume and yield improvements have been added to these desiderata as manufacturers compete for a relatively small number of major computer makers and customers with ever-increasing demands for storage and speed.

Thus, low-wage assembly workers and tax incentives, while still important, became less central to the requirements of HDD assemblers. As technological change progressed and drive production accelerated, the manufacturing process and supporting activities became more demanding. HDD firms required more from existing and potential investment sites, including managerial and engineering talent for ongoing process engineering and product design modification; skilled workers capable of handling higher tolerances, more complicated manufacturing, and testing functions; and extensive external support services, such as specialists in cleanroom technologies, manufacturers of process equipment, and suppliers skilled in various forms of tooling. Accompanying these demands was a need for a seamless trade-related infrastructure that linked firms to logistics companies, air terminals, and rapid customs clearance.

When unraveling locational dynamics in the industry, however, we concentrate on two factors that other models of foreign investment have underplayed: the advantages associated with clustering and agglomeration, particularly in manufacturing operations; and the advantages firms gained by integrating diverse locations within a transnational regional production system. The first rested on the development of local supply bases, providing advantages of *local proximity,* such as achieving economies of scale, reducing the length of the supply chain, and facilitating joint problem solving. Here, the growing complexity of manufacturing placed a premium on learning in operations. The second rested on the diversity of location-specific assets that the Southeast Asian region could offer, including advantages associated with *regional proximity.*

Throughout, we have emphasized the dynamic and iterative nature of the development of both firm capabilities and locations. By their own investments and sourcing patterns, disk drive firms formed agglomerations and networks. Nevertheless, public policy was also crucial, first in providing the permissive or baseline conditions under which the industry could flourish (see chapters 6 and 10) and then complementing firm activity with more sophisticated supports, including education, training, and the development of national research systems. In other words, states as well as markets contribute to the development of locations.

How can we tell if these factors mattered for performance in the HDD industry? The answer is that firms and national industries making locational choices that matched changing industry needs were more likely to keep up with competitive pressures compared with those that didn't. Other factors such as first-mover advantages, national innovation systems and capacity, and patterns of industrial organization might explain differences in firm and industry performance between American and Japanese firms. Nevertheless, although innovation has been a necessary condition for maintaining competitiveness, it has not been sufficient, and the other factors didn't matter. Within other industries differences in locational strategy and the relative importance of location to competitive advantage may not be as stark. But the burden of proof needs to fall on those who neglect the importance of location. Unless studies of other industries control for the effects of locational choice, it is difficult to tell whether other purported sources of competitive advantage mattered or not.

NATIONALITY, STRATEGIC FOCUS,
AND CONVERGENCE

American disk drive firms were early adopters of the new Southeast Asian location strategy, while Japanese companies followed a different path, making their drives primarily in Japan. This was surprising since both American and Japanese firms faced similar technical requirements and cost pressures and many Japanese companies had considerable experience in Southeast Asia, certainly more than any of the pioneering American firms did. Moreover, Japanese firms felt direct competition in their home market from American exports originating in Southeast Asia. Nonetheless, they were extremely late in copying this assembly strategy.

This difference in collective behavior reveals the relative weight of nationality and industry-specific pressures in international competition. American and Japanese strategies differed because most relationships and skill sets take on national characteristics that influence how firms perceive and act on their competitive environment. Thus, firms of different national origin that are facing the same global market, employing the same technologies, and offering the same products are more likely to act according to nationally specific logics and make social comparisons with and mimic other national firms.

The likelihood of being among the first American HDD firms to shift assembly to Southeast Asia was strongly affected by strategic group membership and similarity of organizational attributes: early movers tended to compete in the same market segments (OEM desktop) and were of similar size (medium) and age (young). These firms emulated successful competitors with similar characteristics. In contrast, none of the new Japanese entrants to the desktop market mimicked the moves of American firms competing in the same segment. Eventually, however, the entire industry converged on this global strategy as the older, larger, and more diversified firms moved their assembly to Southeast Asia (see chapter 5).

These competitive dynamics had implications for the performance of national industry. Timing in adoption of the Southeast Asian assembly strategy affected industry performance for both the small, strategically focused firms that pioneered the global strategy and the American industry more generally. But while American firms were the fastest to learn the emergent global strategy and captured the lion's share of the new desktop market, the incremental benefit of imitation diminished as the number of firms adopting the assembly strategy increased.

Emergent strategies take time to yield collective benefits at the national level. In the early 1980s, 5.25- and 3.5-inch drives represented a small share of industry revenues, and Japan's market share was in fact increasing as it made steady inroads into the market for large-diameter disk drives. But the shift abroad by strategically focused American firms was decisive in turning back the Japanese challenge in desktop drives. By establishing clusters of auxiliary suppliers and specialized personnel in Southeast Asia, the pioneering firms created advantages for adopters of the global strategy and thus benefited the American disk drive industry as a whole.

While imitation of the "right" strategy is an obvious way for competing subpopulations to undermine an initial advantage, inherited organizational structures, practices, and relationships constrain their ability to adopt possibly superior practices quickly (Kogut 1991). Thus, early national differences in global strategic behavior can have long-term consequences.

FUTURE DISECONOMIES OF LOCATION?

While we emphasize agglomeration economies and the rise and stickiness of place, the system we describe is not in steady state. Not only does the industry evolve, but the environment, technology, and competitive pressures change, which in turn affect location decisions. Location-specific assets that were an advantage during one period can become disadvantages during another.

The American disk drive industry exploited the locational assets of Silicon Valley and Singapore to maintain its competitiveness. But since the United States has lost much of its HDD assembly activity, why should we expect Singapore's agglomeration economies to be any more enduring? At some point the benefits of proximity become insufficient relative to the lure of factor cost differentials or public policy benefits of new locations that, in time, emerge to serve the industry better. Although agglomeration economies in operations can be strong, agglomeration diseconomies may set in: congestion, a rising cost of living, escalating real estate prices, salary increases for technical personnel, and, above all, competition among proximate firms for factors and inputs as new industries emerge. In fact, some of these costs have caused firms to shift activities out of Singapore and explore locations such as China.

Nevertheless, Singapore remains the center of the industry's operations, home of the greatest industry-specific engineering and managerial talent outside the United States and Japan. Malaysia and Thailand maintain substantial engineering capabilities as well. Whatever China's advantages with respect to labor costs and flexibility, it is restrained by the absence of other factors central to the industry's growth in Southeast Asia: more skilled labor, agglomeration economies, and the benefits that proximity provides—visible most clearly in the links between Malaysia and Singapore. Moreover, Chinese governments at the central, provincial, and local levels need time to become capable of replicating the industry supports of Singapore and Malaysia. Thus, HDD employment in Singapore will likely continue to decline but primarily in lower-skilled assembly. By continually upgrading skills and various local capabilities, Singapore, Malaysia, and even Thailand should be able to hold production of more sophisticated products, subassemblies, and components; and Singapore will continue to attract some design activities and remain a headquarters for managing offshore assembly operations in the region.

Of course, this locational scenario could be upset if certain basic competitive parameters shift. First, a new competitive logic could emerge requiring firms to produce more customized disk drives rather than exploit economies of scale to make large volumes of a relatively undifferentiated product. If drives are increasingly customized, then proximity to customers will become more important, meaning that market size could emerge as an important reason behind manufacturing or assembly location. This is highly unlikely, however, as customization is likely to be embodied in microcode, which is added after final assembly. Second, a combination of increasingly tight tolerances and the smaller size of key components might force the industry to automate more of the assembly process. In this case, the continuing significance of wage costs would decline more rapidly, and economizing on the cost of communication between development and manufacturing could become more important, possibly luring assembly back to the United States or Japan. But because most operational capabilities reside in Southeast Asia, automation is likely to be introduced there rather than near corporate headquarters.

Our purpose here is not speculation so much as an attempt to underline a central point about locational dynamics. Changes in the terms of competition affect the value of incumbent, location-specific assets, meaning that valuable locations can be rendered obsolete. This has been true through-out the HDD industry's history, as it has in earlier industries. Therefore, locations will find it nearly impossible to immunize themselves against these changing fortunes.

Extensions and Applications to Other Industries

The core of our approach has been to show the following:

- An industry's drivers generate demands for location-specific assets.
- The global distribution of those assets is uneven.
- The geographic configuration of industries varies accordingly, being more or less concentrated internationally and more or less clustered at each location.
- National industries differ in their use of international locations, which can affect their global competitive advantage.

Here, we address the generalizability of our approach by looking briefly at the relationship between industry drivers and location in three other industries, primarily from the perspective of U.S. firms: apparel, autos, and semiconductors. To the extent that the competitive pressures facing these industries differ from those in the disk drive industry, we should see different degrees of international dispersion and local clustering in operations. To the extent they are similar, we should see similar spatial patterns. Obviously, we cannot present detailed information on the geography of these industries; as with disk drives, such data are not routinely collected. But our preliminary comparison underscores the significance of location in competitive advantage.

The first step toward comparative industry analysis is identifying an industry's competitive drivers. Our examination of disk drives identified four industry drivers that influence foreign location decisions. The first driver is pressure on cost, especially pressure that can be relieved by reducing wage costs. Because unskilled and semiskilled production workers are widely distributed across the developing world, we would predict that industries driven to invest abroad to lower their wage bill would, other things being equal, be highly dispersed. Moreover, we would not expect them to reap substantial advantages from clustering within locations; firms do not need to collocate to access and benefit from unskilled, low-cost labor.

A second locational driver, market access can be motivated by transportation costs, the need to be near customers, tariffs, or pressure to tailor products for local markets. Other things being equal, the greater the importance of market access, the greater the dispersion of overseas manufacturing operations to serve them.[1]

The third driver is the length of product cycles. Shorter product cycles entail frequent product introductions, ramp ups, and ramp downs, thus placing a premium on engineering and coordination capabilities. We would thus expect shorter product cycles to imply more globally concentrated manufacturing operations, both for logistical reasons and because of the relative global scarcity of the skills demanded of such manufacturing processes. Short product cycles do not necessarily lead to local clustering in operations if changes to a product are slight; well understood, standardized processes are less likely to generate agglomeration economies. Nevertheless, short product cycles do put pressures on the pipeline and for that reason alone may bring suppliers close together if the value chain involves a large number of inputs.

The fourth and related driver is the speed of technological change. Rapid technological change can significantly influence the production process and create tighter manufacturing tolerances. Producers and their suppliers can become more interdependent because technological change heightens uncertainty and requires ongoing interfirm problem solving and adjustment. These factors can lead to greater global concentration in operations—again because of the skills required to manage the technological challenges—and greater agglomeration economies. The more technologically complex the supply chain, the greater both the geographical concentration of production and the advantages of local clustering among suppliers and assemblers.

We have demonstrated that the disk drive industry is subject to three of the drivers (cost pressures, incredibly short product cycles, and rapid technological change) but, since the 1970s, has not made investments to gain access to markets. These competitive dynamics have resulted in a high level of regional concentration and extensive, albeit varying, levels of local clustering. How do the industry drivers and geographic patterns compare in apparel, autos, and semiconductors?

The international value chain in apparel is complex, involving a diverse set of firms from both developing and developed countries. In fact, of all the major parts of the textile value chain, apparel is "by far the most fragmented" (Dicken 1998: 305). Nevertheless, two types of large firms from developed countries dominate the global apparel industry: branded manufacturers, exemplified by Levi Strauss, Sara Lee, or VF (maker of Lee and Wrangler jeans); and the retailer or buying group, which encompasses a variety of firms operating in different market segments.[2] These include fashion garments (such as gowns from Paris); basics (such as men's white dress shirts or underwear); and fashion basics (basic apparel items with some fashion content, such as stonewashed jeans), a middle category of growing importance. We focus on the latter two categories because they accounted for nearly three-quarters of total shipments in 1992 (Abernathy et al. 1999: 8–9).

Although garments are often produced with specific markets in mind, intense cost pressures have historically pushed developed country firms to source from or invest in countries with low wages rather than locating operations close to or in final markets. Until recently, garment producers have benfited from relatively long lead times conforming to seasonal cycles. New technologies, such as computer-assisted design (CAD), have reduced but certainly not erased the importance of labor costs. The apparel value chain involves fewer steps and requires much looser tolerances than does an industry such as disk drives or autos, and pressure to use low-cost labor remains a central driver in the industry.[3]

As a consequence, production has been widely dispersed globally. Compare the concentration of disk drive manufacturing with the fact that fifteen countries from Western Europe, North America, Latin America, and Asia accounted for two-thirds of clothing exports in 1995, a figure that has not changed since 1980 (Dicken 1998: 291). In 1991, the East Asian "big four" (China, Hong Kong, Taiwan, and Korea) accounted for a dominant share of imports (38 percent) into the U.S. market. Nevertheless, imports came from more than one hundred other countries (Abernathy et al. 1999: 233). In contrast, almost all U.S. HDD imports in 2000 came from only five countries.

Over time, the apparel industry's competitive ecology has undergone important changes, with implications for locational choice. Almost all clothing segments have experienced greater market fragmentation, more seasonal changes, and a shift away from price toward style and quality as a competitive strategy. "As a result of these market changes, the size of production runs has steadily declined along with the time available for manufacturers to respond to product demand" (Winterton and Taplin 1997: 10; see also Mytelka 1991).[4] Technological advances in preassembly processes are in some ways responsible for these changes, but most result from the expansion of demand for fashion-basic products, which are subject to rapid changes in taste and involve "frequent replenishment orders" (Abernathy et al. 1999: 239). Labor cost advantages are increasingly balanced against a new set of desiderata, particularly the need to be highly responsive to major consumer markets.

These changes have reduced the value of simple assembly sites. Apparel producers and retailers are under pressure to move toward full-package sourcing in each region if they are to meet the new pressures for quality, cost, and delivery. As a consequence, firms are increasingly investing in or sourcing from sites that are closer to the dominant consumer markets than East Asia is (Abernathy et al. 1999: 234; Mytelka 1991: 125).[5] Moreover, to be effective, such networks must involve tight links among firms in the textile/apparel value chain and deeper pools of skilled workers.[6]

In sum, even within the highly dispersed apparel industry, geographic concentration and proximity have provided U.S. firms with competitive advantages necessary to address specific sets of pressures. Until recently, East Asian networks have been especially important assets on which U.S. retailers could draw to organize supply and production, meet prearranged deadlines and price terms, and transfer the risks for doing so. As product cycles have shortened, however, American firms have begun to develop more proximate sources of supply in the Caribbean and Mexico. The Italians, leaders in many apparel segments, have demonstrated the possibility of a largely domestic strategy based on high skills, but even they are being pushed toward more subcontracting arrangements with geographically proximate countries in an effort to combine low labor costs with production expertise (Belussi 1997).

In some respects, the automobile industry occupies an intermediate position between apparel and HDD. It is less internationally dispersed than apparel but more so than disk drives, and it is somewhat less agglomerated than disk drives but much more so than apparel. In 1995, eighteen countries accounted for 90 percent of worldwide production, with Europe, the United States, and Japan hosting 75 percent of global output (Dicken 1998: 319).

What drivers account for this particular geographic pattern? Unlike the disk drive and apparel cases, overseas location decisions in the auto industry have been driven more by market access, including the minimization of transportation costs, than by factor cost considerations. Until the 1990s, almost all foreign direct investment decisions in the automobile industry were motivated at least in part by tariff barriers to imports. With few exceptions, there was no foreign investment where there were no trade barriers (Maxcy 1981, O'Brien 1989). Thus, the most important location-specific assets were the size and profitability of markets.

As in disk drives, American firms were much more aggressive than their European competitors in expanding abroad, and they reaped the benefits in global dominance of the industry. As early as the 1920s, Ford, General Motors, and Chrysler had begun to construct a worldwide chain of assembly plants, primarily in Canada, the United Kingdom, France, Germany, and other advanced country markets that extended their competitive advantage.[7]

Between 1960 and 1990, the industry expanded into developing country markets. Because these markets were protected and thus subject to less competitive pressure, economizing on labor costs was peripheral to location decisions. Nor did new automotive technologies play much of a role.[8] More-

over, automotive product cycles were measured not in months, as in disk
drives, or seasons, as in apparel, but in at least two-year periods (Dicken
1998: 326; Sheriff 1993). Finally, although the supply chain of automobiles is composed of thousands of parts, it has not traditionally involved
the kinds of close tolerances and other manufacturing challenges seen in
disk drives; and most components were imported from the home base. As
a result, with the partial exception of Japanese producers, suppliers did not
generally follow assemblers offshore.[9]

Reduction in trade barriers, the influence of Japanese production methods, and shorter product cycles began to shift the auto industry's competitive
dynamics, including the logic of location. By the early 1990s, most auto
majors had adopted just-in-time assembly, which often necessitated closer
geographic proximity of suppliers to assemblers both at home and abroad.
In addition, the majors started to move away from reliance on numerous,
relatively independent assembly facilities producing for national markets
and adopted a "platform strategy." This strategy involved reducing the number of basic vehicle platforms to achieve greater scale economies by stan-
dardizing parts, introducing extensive commonality in components and basic
design, and changing models less frequently.[10] Producing these vehicles created greater supply chain complexity in the context of short product
cycles and increasing R&D costs (OECD 1997; O'hUallachain and Wasserman 1999: 30–38).

Unlike vehicles designed for protected markets, platform cars are produced in several different markets for regional or global export, compelling
the auto majors to integrate more of their facilities into global and regional
networks ("Japan's Carmakers," 1995; O'hUallachain and Wasserman 1999:
25; Belis-Bergouignan et al. 2000; Legewie, forthcoming). As new models are rolled out with increasing frequency, auto majors no longer have
the luxury of waiting months for parts to be shipped around the world.
According to one rule of thumb, auto companies want their suppliers to
locate within 250 miles of the final assembly plant ("House Vote," May
25, 2000). The result is a growing list of supplier-assembler clusters not
just in developed country regions (Hoffman and Kaplinsky 1988, Martin
2000) but also in the larger emerging markets such as Thailand's eastern
seaboard, Mexico's Guanajuato, Brazil's Minas Gerais, and western Turkey
near Istanbul (Humphrey 1998; Tuman and Morris 1998: 14–15; Noble
1999; O'hUallachain and Wasserman 1999).

As a consequence, the role of location in global competitiveness in the
auto industry has changed, and its geographic configuration is becoming
more similar to disk drives. U.S. auto manufacturers previously extended
their advantage by setting up assembly operations behind tariff and non-
tariff barriers. Since the mid-1990s, they have pursued regional produc-

tion strategies involving economies of scale within a region and leveraging regional assets to serve global markets.[11] Public policy still plays an important role in shaping location decisions; but rather than protecting the domestic industry, the governments that are successful in attracting the industry are focusing on macroeconomic stability, an open trade regime, and attractive general investment incentives—precisely the baseline policies that Southeast Asian governments offered the American drive industry.

The semiconductor industry is a high-tech industry that shows a number of similarities to the disk drive industry.[12] It is characterized by rapid technological change and short product cycles, although not as short as those in HDD. Compared to disk drives, however, the competitive advantage of the American semiconductor industry has been due more to leveraging its home-based, location-specific assets, innovativeness, and internalization strategies (especially the use of strategic alliances) than to its overseas operations. Although becoming increasingly globalized, the industry has not yet developed offshore agglomeration economies in production to the extent found in disk drives.

As in all high-technology industries, semiconductor design is intensive in advanced engineering talents and exhibits signs of spatial clustering and agglomeration economies at the home base. Wafer fabrication—the core of production—is also technologically complex and has always been a yield-driven process.[13] Assembly and, to a lesser extent, test have historically been more labor-intensive, especially among American firms, although they are becoming less so. While labor cost pressures were the central locational driver for the HDD industry in the early 1980s, when it began to shift production offshore, yields were always the central manufacturing concern for the semiconductor industry. This difference in competitive ecology between the two industries has had major implications for differences in their location.

Semiconductors and integrated circuits were first developed in the United States, which enjoyed a substantial lead in the industry before European and Japanese firms began to enter in the 1960s (for a concise overview, see Macher et al. 1999). Arita (1996) shows that for integrated companies design and fabrication have traditionally been geographically close: in a 1993 survey, he found that integrated firms located their main plant—which involved both design and wafer fabrication—near corporate headquarters, suggesting some advantages to proximity.

When U.S. firms first ventured abroad in the late 1950s, market access was an important motive, and early overseas investment went to Europe.[14] By contrast, the pattern of globalization in Asia was initially motivated by factors quite similar to those in disk drives (Henderson 1989), namely the search for low-cost labor to perform assembly and test. As in Southeast

Asia, policy was an important attraction; the timing of early Asian investments tracks closely the shift to more outward-oriented policies. Specialized (or merchant) American firms began to move assembly and some testing
to Asia, beginning in 1963 with Hong Kong, the location most friendly to
free trade in the region (Matthews and Cho 2000: 112), and then to Taiwan (1965), Korea (1966), and Singapore (1968).

Despite this move offshore, the U.S. industry faced steep competition
from Japan by the second half of the 1970s, and numerous accounts predicted
its ultimate demise. Why did the aggressive use of offshore sites not contribute
to American competitiveness in semiconductors as it had in disk drives?[15] The
answer lies in crucial differences in the nature of the industry's drivers. In semiconductors, capital-intensive fabrication was the overwhelming determinant
of total production costs, and yields in fabrication were the overwhelming
determinant of competitiveness. Even if assembly and test costs were substantially reduced, they would not have fully offset the differences in yields
and post-test reliability of Japanese and American chips.

Unlike the case with disk drives, offshore locational assets could not solve
these problems. Rather, American manufacturers had to address yield defi-
ciencies in their home-based plants more aggressively, and from the mid-1980s
they did just that. As Angel (1994: 109–14) points out, these efforts had important implications for location. Proximity of design and production gained in
significance; and the major integrated producers began to locate product development, pilot production, and volume production in the same facilities
rather than in a series of separate dedicated ones. Collocation was critical for
moving product rapidly from design to stabilized volume manufacturing.

Improvements in manufacturing were not the only key to the resurgence
of the American industry. Japan faced increasingly stiff competition from
Korea and Taiwan in memory and a dramatic appreciation of the yen, which
eliminated any labor cost advantage they had previously possessed. In
contrast, the changing structure of demand began once again to favor American firms. Their proximity to final product developments in the Internet
and wireless sectors allowed them to shift their product portfolios toward
application-specific integrated circuits (ASICs), microprocessors, micro-
controllers, and digital signal processors. American firms have excelled in
reducing process cycles (which enables the introduction of new classes of
products) from three years to eighteen months or less; interactions with proximate suppliers were important in meeting this challenge.

Although 80 percent of the wafer plants operated by U.S. firms in
1993 were in the United States and an even higher percentage of European-
and Japanese-owned plants were at home (Arita 1996, Leachman and Leachman 1999), American, European, and Japanese firms began to shift some
wafer fabrication to Korea, Taiwan, and Singapore in the 1990s as technical capabilities in those countries rose. Moreover, previous experience

gained from foreign investment, coupled with deepening capital markets, finally permitted indigenous Asian firms to enter fabrication. Korean firms became major players in memory during the 1980s. Fabless American design houses began to exploit the development of semiconductor foundries in Taiwan that specialized in manufacturing.

But in contrast to disk drive assembly, offshore wafer fabrication has been much more gradual (Leachman and Leachman 1999) and continues to be concentrated in a relatively small number of countries. North America, Japan, and the rest of Asia (dominated by Korea and Taiwan) each host between 25 and 30 percent of worldwide capacity, while Europe has less than 15 percent (Leachman and Leachman 1999). Most firms that manufacture their own wafers do so at home.[16] Intel, for example, produces a majority of its wafers in New Mexico, Oregon, Arizona, California, and Massachusetts. Advanced Micro Devices produces its wafers in Austin, Texas; Sunnyvale, California; Dresden, Germany; and a joint venture with Fujitsu in Aizu-Wakamatsu, Japan.[17]

The continuing importance of technological change, the capital intensity of production, and the centrality of yield-driven manufacturing processes has limited the extent of dispersion and kept it primarily in the advanced industrial states, Korea and Taiwan. But with its combination of capacity in basic memory and the success of its foundries, non-Japanese Asia is projected to exceed North American and Japanese production, with more American firms outsourcing fabrication to Asian foundries (Leachman and Leachman 1999: 15–17).

Table 11.1 and figure 11.1 summarize our interpretation of each industry's key drivers and their effect on location. They show that the apparel industry has primarily relied on access to cheap labor and the capacity to meet fairly short product cycles, resulting in extensive dispersion and relatively low clustering. Over the past decade, however, the industry has faced shorter product cycles and pressure to be closer to key consumer markets; these have increased the competitive benefits of greater global concentration and local clustering.

The automotive industry has quite different drivers. Whereas labor costs were relatively unimportant in global competition, access to protected markets was key. These conditions, combined with the size of the advanced country markets, resulted in a level of global concentration higher than apparel but much lower than disk drives. Nevertheless, lower trade barriers, shorter product cycles, and increased technological change have led automobile producers both to concentrate production in fewer locations and to cluster there.

Finally, in semiconductors, rapid technological change and short product cycles have resulted in a high level of global concentration for wafer fabrication. Although agglomeration economies have also been important, they have occurred largely at the home base rather than abroad; colloca-

TABLE 11.1

INDUSTRIES AND LOCATIONAL DRIVERS

	Importance of Drivers Affecting Location Decisions			
Industries	Importance of Labor Costs	Importance of Market Access	Short Product Cycle Pressures	Rapid Technological Change Pressures
Disk drives	Low/decreasing over time	Low	High	High
Apparel	High	Low/increasing over time	Medium/increasing over time	Low
Autos	Low/increasing over time	High/decreasing over time	Low/increasing over time	Medium
Semiconductors				
Wafer fabrication	Low	Medium	Medium-high	High
Assembly/test	High/decreasing over time	Low	Medium	Low/increasing over time

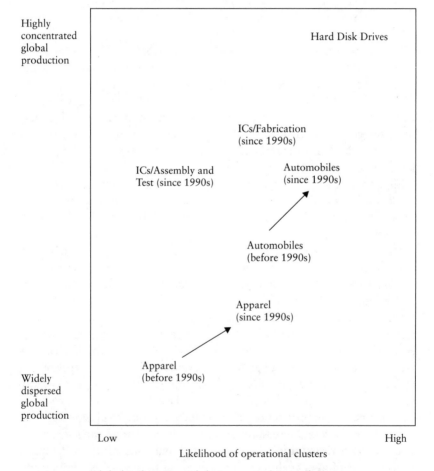

FIGURE 11.1. Global industries and their geographic configuration.

tion of design and manufacturing is still apparently important in time to market and in improving manufacturing yields. Conversely, in assembly and test, lower technological requirements and greater reliance on low labor costs have resulted in a greater dispersion for integrated circuit test and assembly. Over time, the diffusion of manufacturing capacity to East Asia and the need for proximity to end users have increased the benefits of dispersion in both wafer fab and assembly and testing.

The preceding suggests two final points. The first is that manufacturing in the disk drive industry is both more concentrated globally and more agglomerated than in the other industries. The second, however, is that both regional concentration and agglomeration are becoming more important for apparel and autos; semiconductors continue to be agglomerated at home but with gradual shift in production offshore. Finally, generic policies such as open trade regimes and favorable investment incentives are now indispensable to multinational producers. Additionally, market-conforming, sector-specific measures such as those implemented in Singapore will generate increasingly valuable location-specific assets as product cycles shorten and pressure grows to enhance quality.

It is important to underline that these three sketches cannot do full justice to the complexity of the respective industries. But contrary to standard, broad-brush accounts of the determinants of globalization, they demonstrate two key arguments missing from many industry studies: the influence of each industry's specific dynamics on location decisions, and the impact of such decisions on competitiveness at both the firm and national industry levels.

American Industries in International Competition

Our study has important implications for the ongoing debate about the ability of American industries to compete in international manufacturing.[18] If nothing else, this analysis punctures a number of prevalent myths about American capabilities, particularly vis-à-vis their Japanese and other Asian competitors. One common view (although it has eroded since Japan's recent difficulties) is that American firms stay ahead primarily through technological prowess and the capacity to innovate, while Japanese, Korean, and Taiwanese firms are masters of volume manufacturing and cost reduction. Once Asian enterprises reach technical parity, whether through their own investments, technology licensing, or reverse engineering and emulation, American firms will face overwhelming competition, not simply because of factor costs (although they matter in newly industrializing countries such as Korea and Taiwan) but because of superior corporate organization (most evident in Japan, where cost structures are similar or even higher than in the United States). According to this view, when technical parity is reached, American firms can survive by exploiting location-specific assets but primarily through subcontracting manufacturing to more competent, lower-cost producers in the region. The decline of U.S. dominance in consumer electronics in the 1960s and 1970s, the survival of U.S. firms in the computer industry as a result of partnerships with Asian suppliers, and the growth of virtual companies with limited or no in-house manufacturing capabilities are invoked to demonstrate this proposition.

The disk drive industry is a stunning exception to these generalizations. American firms have not only remained competitive but have done so through: manufacturing prowess in an industry characterized by such extreme competition that 90 percent of the firms entering have failed; rapid technological change with extraordinary pressure on manufacturing to make products with ever-tighter tolerances; strong cost pressures; very high volumes; virulent business cycles, recurrent red ink, and limited favor from Wall Street; technically sophisticated, vertically integrated Japanese competitors such as Fujitsu, Sony, and Hitachi, which have dominated a number of other electronics segments, particularly consumer electronics; and the recent entry of at least one Korean competitor, Samsung Electronics, that has endured year after year of sustained losses to establish a foothold. Moreover, the depth of this success cuts across firms of very different sorts, again suggesting the limitations of theories that link competitiveness to particular forms of corporate organization. One common feature of the industry does differentiate it from other electronics segments in which virtual firms have arisen, such as the semiconductor design houses in Silicon Valley that rely on Asian fabs for manufacturing. Nearly all successful HDD firms assemble their own drives, and many also make their own core components, particularly heads. But even this generalization has important exceptions. Quantum no longer does any of its own manufacturing; and IBM, the vertically integrated firm that launched the industry, has successfully outsourced some of its HDD assembly, although it still predominately relies on its own assembly.

What connects these firms is their incredible innovativeness and their ability to exploit complementary location-specific assets. (We will return to this subject later in the chapter.) Our study also punctures a number of other myths about the effects of globalization. First, it is not impossible to go offshore for manufacturing without losing ownership, expertise, or control of manufacturing. All but one of the surviving major HDD firms design, own, and manage their own manufacturing facilities abroad. Thus, going abroad does not mean outsourcing. Indeed, the management of global supply chains has itself grown into a core competence of American drive firms, as we will discuss.

Second, going abroad does not mean that an industry is becoming hollow and losing employment. On the contrary, the disk drive industry shows how foreign direct investment can complement rather than compete with home-based activities. There can be little question that the initial move of manufacturing to Southeast Asia incurred transitional costs for workers in the industry. But had the U.S. industry not shifted assembly to Southeast Asia, it would not have enjoyed its subsequent success. As a result, there would be far fewer highly paid, skilled jobs in the United States in various stages of the industry, especially among the technical equipment and instrumentation firms that enable designers of disk drives, recording heads, disks, and semiconductors to do their work. In 1995, workers in the United States received nearly 40 percent of *all* wages paid in the industry, while 62 percent of the wages paid by U.S. firms went to their U.S.-based workers (Gourevitch et al. 2000).

Implications for Public Policy

These findings do not mean that we should be sanguine about the future or put our faith solely in the market. In chapter 10, we argued that the debate over industrial policy in developing countries has been polarized in less than useful ways. Nevertheless, as Singapore shows, governments can intervene to develop and maintain industry clusters without heavy-handed intervention that either shelters industries from competition (a virtual impossibility) or provides costly subsidies.

While it is beyond our scope to construct a public policy for the HDD or any other industry, we can provide a few guidelines and respond to several common criticisms. The first and most basic point is that advanced industrial states, no less than developing ones, must be able to create the baseline policy environment outlined in chapter 10. Although the eventuality is unlikely, any disruption of the open trade and investment climate that has been a hallmark of U.S. economic policy since World War II would be a disaster for the nation's ability to compete in industries such as hard drives. The issues, however, go beyond platitudes about free trade and investment or even the salutary efforts of American trade negotiators to expand the range and quality of available locations by negotiating liberalizing trade agreements with important countries such as China. Good policy must begin at home; and in many American states, counties, and cities, a baseline policy environment cannot be taken for granted.

Our conversations with managers provided many interesting details about why the United States did not hold on to manufacturing longer than it did, and the reasons were not limited to factors costs. Singapore's infrastructure far surpasses that in many American cities. The U.S. regulatory environment can also be cumbersome; and while this sometimes reflects the benefits of checks and balances and worthy concerns such as environmental protection, it may also reflect political deadlock and bureaucratic inefficiencies. For example, American HDD firms can start up within six months in Singapore, faster than many municipal governments take to approve a building application. For industries such as disk drives, in which both startups and expansions must move quickly if firms are to be successful, such reactions are too slow and inflexible.

Of course, if jurisdictions are to move beyond these generic policies, they must develop industry-specific knowledge. Public managers in Singapore are extraordinarily well versed in the technical and economic aspects of the industry, and industry-specific knowledge is growing in both Thailand and Malaysia. Another striking feature of Singapore's industrial policy apparatus is the fact that public officials spend so much time talking to managers and visiting plants, a process that increases their knowledge of the industry and thus their ability to judge industry claims.

A more controversial lesson is that governments and their constituencies can gain from investments in industry-specific public goods that may have spillovers for other activities but are nonetheless tailored to particular industry demands. Two examples are the investments in training visible in both Singapore and Penang—most ambitiously, in Singapore's university-related activities and the Data Storage Institute (DSI). One principle to guide these investments and act as a check on them is that the private sector should not only participate in defining activities but contribute financially to them. This commitment helps avoid the costs of purely top-down efforts, guaranteeing that the activities actually matter for the industry while limiting the political and economic risks of pork-barrel spending and subsidies. The disk drive companies and their competitors all benefited from participation in the DSI, while shaping the institute's programs and financing its joint projects.[19]

Nevertheless, development of such efforts in the United States may be challenging. First, as a large country, the United States has too many industries for policymakers to monitor. Although Singapore succeeded by remaining focused, Malaysia's federal-level industrial policy agencies and Brazil's efforts at promoting indigenous industry demonstrate that well-intentioned efforts can go awry. Still, the United States has a strong federal tradition with strong state and local governments. While only the very largest firms and industries are likely to receive sufficient attention from national policymakers, at the subnational level, local policymakers have strong incentives to monitor and support local industry. As borders become more open, effective supporting policies such as those we suggest are likely to evolve and flourish at local levels.

A much broader obstacle thrown up by both the political left and right concerns the pressures of globalization on a government's ability to act.

On the one hand, international competition pressures governments to provide the services and conditions that attract firms: a well-educated work force, infrastructure, tax breaks, and regulatory effectiveness. Yet many of these measures require either expenditure (labor training, research, and infrastructure) or forgone revenue (tax incentives). If left to the market, such measures face classic public-goods problems of underprovision; yet if funded by taxes, they are constrained by mobile investment in search of low-tax locations.

Although this debate goes far beyond our scope, we note that the case of Singapore again proves that these tradeoffs may be somewhat less stark than often posed, although the city-state can hardly be said to operate under American political constraints. Singapore does not have a small state: government expenditure is 18 percent of GDP. While contributions to the Central Provident Fund contribute to high labor costs, and the government has invested heavily in education, the nation nonetheless continues to attract substantial investment. Indeed, Singapore confirms the long-standing observation among the advanced industrial states that more open economies actually tend to have larger governments. At the same time, however, the opaqueness of the Singapore approach raises questions about its viability for governments under more public scrutiny. Although the money that Singapore spends on industry-specific training and research programs clearly has benefits, those costs are not published; and whether Singapore taxpayers are the net beneficiaries remains open to question.

Implications for Management: Leveraging
Location for Competitive Advantage

For managers, an improved understanding of the relationship between location and competitiveness is vital, particularly as more competitors take advantage of the expanded range of investment sites available as a result of lowered transportation and communication costs and, most important, favorable policy reforms. A central message of our study is the importance of adopting a nuanced view of costs. Many companies have sought to lower costs by relocating production facilities to low-wage, low-tax, or other low cost-input locations. The importance of the generic policy environment also needs little reiteration. It is also important, however, to look beyond costs and benefits, even though they are easy to measure up front. In industries such as disk drives (and across a wider array as well), companies compete by increasing productivity and yields. Indeed, for such industries, labor costs are a declining share of total costs, and yields may be more important than productivity per se because of the loss associated with throwing away material and rework (Terwiesch et al. 1997).

Improving productivity and yields requires a range of supporting capacities, from decent educational systems to engineering and cleanroom support, which in turn are a function of both public policy (see chapter 10) and agglomeration economies. The significance of agglomeration economies is the second crucial lesson of our work. Locations characterized primarily by low wages and low taxes are poor competitive platforms if they lack efficient infrastructure or fail to generate agglomeration economies composed of suppliers and a production and managerial workforce with industry-specific experience and skills. Locating in an existing or developing cluster can lower total cost and improve time-to-market and time-to-volume production. There is also a certain logic to creating clusters by collocating activities that support manufacturing. Thus, *operational* clusters can be just as important a locational asset as *technological* ones.

For managers, the most difficult task is deciding what corporate functions need to be clustered at home and what can be shifted offshore. While these lessons are less determinant and more industry-specific, a general principle is that companies must continually question their biases about what functions need to be proximate to one another. On the one hand, as Porter (1998) points out, global strategy must harness the advantages of spreading activities across locations while capturing the innovation advantages of a strong home base. We have focused on manufacturing rather than innovation because much outstanding literature already exists on U.S. innovation clusters (Scott 1986, Feldman 1994, Gray et al. 1996), particularly in Silicon Valley (Saxenian 1994, Kenney 2000). It is clear, however, that successful American disk drive companies have tended to locate innovation in clusters that provide the benefits we spell out in chapter 3.

Nevertheless, the HDD industry also shows that firms can separate product development and manufacturing as well as a number of manufacturing processes over long distances and still thrive. Although this approach requires some investment in learning how to handle international supply chains, the investment itself can develop into a core competence that can be used again and again in exploiting overseas, location-specific assets.

Finally, managers need to remember that the attributes of locations can change and that the firm influences at least some of that change. In other words, firms play a role in the development of location-specific assets— for example, through training and vendor development programs or by helping governments implement public policies that contribute to a firm's growth and competitiveness. The development of local capabilities—from skilled labor and suppliers to universities and other institutions—can complement the firm's assets over time and are thus a key component of any farsighted locational strategy. Being a good citizen is also good business.

Industry Origins and Technological Evolution

Hard disk drives originated from magnetic recording research, as have several previous data storage technologies such as magnetic tape and magnetic drums. Because each technology has advantages and disadvantages relative to the others, users have made tradeoffs among technologies with regard to speed of access, storage capacity, and cost.

Core memories, the earliest magnetic memory devices for data storage (as opposed to audio), appeared in the late 1940s. Reliable, fast, and relatively inexpensive, they replaced punched paper tape, quartz, and cathode ray tubes and, by the 1950s, were made from magnetic ferrite materials. Nevertheless, although cores were used into the 1960s, computer users began demanding memory capacities far above what cores could provide at a reasonable price (Monson 1999). Until the introduction of faster semiconductors, magnetic cores held a computer's main memory; but new devices were emerging to provide higher-capacity, auxiliary storage.

Although it was slower than memory cores, magnetic drum storage offered much cheaper storage at higher capacities. Drums consisted of a revolving, magnetically coated drum with information arranged in tracks around its circumference, allowing read-write heads to pick up and record data as the desired site passed under the heads. Drums were the preferred random-access storage device until disk drives offered cheaper storage in the mid-1960s (although drums continued to be manufactured into the 1970s) (Monson 1999). At the time drums were developed, no other technology offered rapid access to the amount of information required for scientific computation or processing. While hard disk drives displaced them for uses requiring greater capacities at lower cost, drums offered faster data access and so continued to serve a purpose until large-capacity semiconductor memories became available (Rubens 1999).

For capacious storage, however, magnetic tape was preferred. Remington Rand brought out the first digital magnetic tape recorder in 1951, integrating it into its UNIVAC computer. Because it was much cheaper and had higher storage densities than disks, magnetic tape was the preferred large-scale auxiliary or extended storage medium throughout the 1950s and much of the 1960s. Tape, however, is a sequential-access technology, making it too slow for online transaction processing. Instead, it became a fast archive storage technology and ultimately a data backup and restoration tool.

Disk drives are direct adaptations of the drum concept but use a flat disk and heads that wait for the desired location to pass under them. As early as 1906, we find suggestions in U.S. Patent No. 836,339 about the storage possibilities of a disk plated with magnetic material. Nevertheless, the difficulty lay in obtaining sufficiently flat disks, and the concept did not gain acceptance until adequate head-positioning mechanisms were developed. Although slower than magnetic drums, disks have had greater room for improvement; their cost has fallen even more rapidly than semiconductors, while their speed has increased dramatically.

Today's hard disk drives take advantage of the latest breakthroughs in a wide range of scientific and engineering disciplines, including mechanical and electronic engineering, chemical engineering, and even aerodynamics. Magnetic recording engineers depend heavily on the semiconductor industry in particular for creating the technical infrastructure, both in education and equipment.[1]

Five Major Events in Disk Drive Development

Five major developments have defined the evolution of the disk drive industry, with the last occurring in the 1970s. Since then, all technological development has essentially been an improvement on these breakthroughs, each of which was pioneered by IBM.[2]

The first was IBM's demonstration in the mid-1950s that random-access storage on disks was practical. The ability to store and retrieve data randomly is the most important reason why during the 1960s disk drives rapidly displaced tape (which stores and retrieves data sequentially) as the primary computer storage technology. Introduced in 1956, IBM's RAMAC 305, the world's first disk drive, had one set of recording heads that read fifty disks and stored about five megabytes of data.[3]

The second major event—and, in the opinion of industry pioneer Al Shugart, probably the most significant—was the introduction of the self-acting air bearing, or slider.[4] In today's disk drives, the platters immediately begin spinning at 3,600 rpm or higher when the computer is turned on and remain spinning until the computer is turned off or loses power. This rapid spinning creates a current of air above each platter, permitting the tiny read/write heads to fly just above the surface. Before this innovation, a recording head flew above the disk by means of an external air supply. Moreover, with an air-bearing slider, a recording head could be put on each disk surface so that the head-positioning mechanism did not have to move from one disk to another in a drive. The result of this innovation was the 1962 introduction of the IBM 1301, which was about the same size as the RAMAC drive but capable of storing ten times as much data.

The third major event was the introduction of the removable disk pack in 1963. For the first time, disk size was reduced to fourteen inches (from twenty-four inches in IBM disk drives and twenty-eight, thirty-one, or thirty-nine inches in some competitors' products). IBM was enormously successful with this product, which became an industry standard and began the IBM plug-to-plug compatible disk drive business. With the disk pack, consumers had, in effect, unlimited storage. All they had to do was replace one pack with another.

The fourth major event was the introduction of a low-mass/low-load head in a sealed environment—a recording system that became known as Winchester technology. Introduced by IBM in 1973, Winchester technology gradually supplanted the removable disk pack as the industry standard. In a Winchester disk drive, which remains the standard today, the heads and disks are sealed into a closed assembly (the HDA) that is never opened, thus lowering particulate contamination. With low mass and low load, the heads can land directly on the disk when power is turned off, eliminating the cost of head-loading mechanisms; and the redesigned head is able to slide along the disk during takeoff and landing. This innovation brought disk drives full circle in concept: from fixed to removable designs, then back to fixed. Although Winchester technology may have ended the unlimited storage of the disk pack, most customers never changed the pack in any case—in effect, using it as a fixed disk drive.

The introduction of the floppy disk drive in the early 1970s was the fifth major event in the history of disk drive development. Given that floppies can store only a fraction of what hard disk drives can, the event may seem like no innovation. But as a small, inexpensive, random-access storage device, the floppy stimulated the first wave of demand for small computer systems. In essence, it democratized data storage. Floppies were initially fourteen inches in diameter but were quickly replaced by 8-inch disks. These disks were followed by the minifloppy drive, 5.25 inches in diameter, whose development indirectly led to small form factor hard disk drives.

Hard disk drives were unsuitable in both size and cost to be used in the first personal computers (from 1975 until 1980). Because the 8-inch hard disk drives (introduced in 1979 by IBM and International Memories) were too expensive, the floppy disk had the PC market largely to itself during these years. (Eight-inch hard drives were used on minicomputers.) By late 1979, users were increasing storage capacity by adding two and three floppy drives, a situation that finally prompted the development of a small hard disk drive. Pioneered by Shugart's Seagate Technology in July 1980, the new drive had the same physical size as the minifloppy but fifteen times the storage capacity at three times the price, with greater reliability and performance. Incorporating both Winchester technology and the minifloppy's "footprint," the world's first desktop disk drive began a new era in the industry.

Technological Improvements

In addition to these five innovations, refinements in materials, mechanics, electronics, and processes have been key to the enormous improvements in performance during the past twenty years. Throughout the industry's history, drive developers have endeavored to pack more data onto the disk while reducing the drive's physical size and increasing the speed of data access.

HEADS

As technology advances, bits are packed more densely on the disk, and the space required to store each bit shrinks correspondingly. As a result, however, the signal produced by the head when reading each bit becomes weaker and harder to read. Thus, a fundamental challenge in packing bits is finding a way to fly the heads closer to the media to increase the amplitude of the signal. The HDD industry has made great strides toward this goal. In 1973, flying heights averaged seventeen microinches; but today's heads fly at less than two microinches.

Underlying these advances have been improvements in materials. The earliest heads were monolithic ferrite heads made of a single block of ferrite, a magnetic ceramic material. Composite heads followed, consisting primarily of nonmagnetic material with a bit of ferrite added. Metal-in-gap (MIG) heads improved on these earlier versions by adding thin metal layers to improve magnetic performance. First introduced in 1979, thin-film heads gradually displaced these earlier technologies. Produced in ways similar to semiconductors, thin-film technology allows for much smaller heads and better control during the fabrication process. A thin-film recording head, for example, is only 1/25 as big as the monolithic ferrite heads, allowing them to record information in less space at less cost. Thin-film heads passively read changes in the magnetic flux on the surface of the disk; and the electronics of the disk drive's circuit boards amplify, filter, and convert those flux changes to digital representation.[5]

The newest head technology, magneto-resistive (MR), was introduced in 1991, followed in 1997 by giant MR (GMR). (*Giant* refers to the technology's high sensitivity, not the size of the head.) Unlike prior head technologies, which were basically tiny inductive electromagnets, MR technology reads using a special material whose electrical resistance changes in the presence of a magnetic field. A small stripe of MR material is deposited on the head. As it passes over the magnetic patterns on the disk, the material senses the strength of the magnetic field and creates electrical pulses corresponding to the flux reversals. Because this mechanism cannot be used for writing, a conventional thin-film write element is deposited alongside the MR stripe. MR heads allow a 30 percent increase in the number of tracks on a disk and about 15 percent more bits within each track.[6]

HEAD POSITIONING MECHANISMS

The mechanical motion of positioning the head and the rotational delay, or latency, while waiting for the disk to pass' account for the time a computer takes to access data. Thus, designers have worked to improve head positioner mechanisms.

In the original IBM disk drive, the stack of fifty discs was mounted on a single vertical shaft and served by a single access arm. Such extensive mechanical motion led to average access times of more than half a second. In the 1960s, second-generation disk drives used a comb of access arms—one for each disk but all moving. Over the years, different approaches were used to move the comb of heads.[7] Among the most significant innovations was voice-coil head-positioning technology, first introduced by IBM in 1965 and later improved in IBM's 3330 drive introduced in 1970.[8] In a voice-coil servo actuator, the head position is given by information prerecorded on a dedicated disk surface during manufacturing (called servo writing). Such fine positioning allowed for great advances in areal density (and thus storage capacity per disk) and a faster seek time of thirty milliseconds. Today's disk drives record position reference information between data sectors equally distributed around the disk rather than on a dedicated disk surface.[9]

DISKS

During the early years, data was magnetically recorded on an oxide-coated aluminum disk. The disks used in IBM's original disk drive were coated on both sides with a magnetic iron oxide (a variation of the paint primer used for the Golden Gate Bridge), which was poured from a cup while the disk was spinning. More recently, thin-film cobalt alloys have replaced oxide coatings; and today making a disk involves depositing extremely thin, uniform layers of metallic film onto a disk substrate using a vacuum deposition, or sputtering, method similar to the one used to coat semiconductor wafers. The industry continues to search for improvements to disk surfaces.

The strength of the magnetic field (known as coercivity), glide height between heads and disk, and the ability of the head to distinguish a signal from background media noise (signal-to-noise ratio) are the primary factors affecting a disk's storage density. Efforts to increase storage density involve a movement toward thinner substrates, harder substrates, textured coatings, new lubricants, and low noise media. As a result, coercivity levels have increased from 800 oersted in the mid-1980s to 2,000 oersted today. Researchers are also exploring the use of alternative materials for the disk substrate: alumina nitride, carbon, graphite, silicon nitrite, magnesium, and titanium. Glass is the only alternative substrate to aluminum currently in use and is already part of most 1.8-inch and 2.5-inch drives.

MOTORS

Mechanical improvements to motors have allowed faster disk rotation and seek time, which in turn contribute to faster access times and data transfer rates and thus larger storage densities. Early drives used motors operating at less than 1,000 rpm. In the early 1980s, disks spun at 2,400–3,600 rpm, and the fastest disk drives today turn at 15,000 rpm.

Motor designers face several impediments to faster speeds, including excessive motor noise, heat, and disk fluttering. As hard disk drives have become smaller, the spindle motors that run them have also shrunk. Developers are increasingly looking at fluid-bearing motors. By eliminating metal-to-metal contact when the motor spins, they can eliminate or minimize vibration, damage, noise, and fatigue while increasing speed and longevity.

ELECTRONICS

Innovations in semiconductors such as digital signal processors and more powerful microprocessors operating at faster frequencies have influenced all aspects of disk drive performance. Electronic drive components include preamp, read channel, hard-disk controller, processor, servo controller, memory, and motor control (spindle motor and voice-coil motor). Custom ASIC devices implement the fastest control functions, such as data caching and error correction. Semiconductor suppliers to the disk drive industry are also searching to reduce the number of chips in a drive, offering a so-called "system on a chip."[10] This level of integration would significantly reduce the overall drive cost (chips are about 30 percent of a drive's bill of materials) and establish an architecture to improve disk drive performance.

INTERFACES

Although the speed of data transfer relies on many elements, among the most important is the disk drive interface to the host computer. A drive interface is a standardized combination of connector configurations, commands, and data transfer protocols that allows the drive to communicate with the host system.

As with the other high-technology developments, drive interface technology has evolved significantly in the past two decades. In the mid-1990s, personal computers commonly used two interfaces. Most IBM-compatible PCs use the intelligent disk electronics (IDE) interface, which can transfer data at .5–1.5 megabytes per second. The second most common interface is the small computer system interface (SCSI, pronounced "scuzzy"). Used on most Apple Macintosh computers as well as high-performance workstations and servers, this high-performance interface can transfer data at up to 20 megabytes per second. To support faster data transfer rates, the standard SCSI is giving way to Ultra2 SCSI, and IDE to Enhanced IDE. Fibre channel, which can handle data-intensive applications such as video editing, is now emerging on some drives, with data transfer rates of up to 200 megabytes per second.

An Innovator's Dilemma?

The evidence presented in chapter 4 also offers insight into an apparent paradox identified by Clayton Christensen, who has advanced a theory about why firms fail based in large part on his analysis of the disk drive industry (Christensen, 1992, 1997; Rosenbloom and Christensen 1994; Christensen and Rosenbloom 1995; Christensen and Bower 1996). Great firms fail, he argues, because they become too closely tied to the needs of existing customers and are ambushed by disruptive technologies.

Disruptive technologies are initially inferior to existing ones in terms of performance, although they offer qualities that customers in emerging markets value. But the market and profit opportunities in these emerging markets are also initially much smaller than those of existing markets, so managers in incumbent firms—precisely the firms that are best at listening to their established customers—are rarely able to build a case for investing in these new technologies. Thus, emerging markets are pioneered by new entrants. Unfortunately for incumbent firms, however, disruptive technologies can progress faster than the market. In efforts to provide better products than their competitors and earn higher prices and margins, firms serving emerging markets give customers more than they are willing to pay for. Over time, the performance of technologies in the emerging markets matches or exceeds that in existing ones, by which time it is too late for industry incumbents. These venerable firms fail.

As applied to disk drives, Christensen identifies the 8-, 5.25-, and 3.5-inch form factors as disruptive technologies. First shipped in 1979, the 8-inch form factor drive was intended for the minicomputer market during a time when incumbent disk drive firms were selling their 14-inch disk drives to mainframe manufacturers. This market, he says, was pioneered by new entrants—Shugart Associates, Micropolis, Priam, and Quantum—that were not tied to the mainframe market. Once introduced, the 8-inch manufacturers were able to gradually enter the bottom end of the mainframe market. Ultimately, every 14-inch drive maker was driven from the industry.

But this characterization is not exactly right.[1] In the first place, minicomputer firms were using 14-inch disk storage for many years before the 8-inch form factor appeared. In 1971, for example, the Raytheon Data Systems Series 700 minicomputer used 14-inch disk pack drives from Information Storage Systems, the leading independent disk drive maker ("Raytheon Data," May 10, 1971).[2] And in 1974, Control Data, also a leading maker of mainframe storage, announced a smaller 14-inch cartridge disk drive for the OEM minicomputer market ("CDC Aiming," March 25, 1974). In fact, CDC became the first computer systems manufacturer to make a major effort to serve the OEM mini-peripherals market. Far from ignoring the emerging market, CDC embraced it almost five years before the first 8-inch disk drive was introduced. CDC and ISS were not alone. Both IBM and Century Data Systems served the new minicomputer market with 14-inch disk drives, and Digital Equipment, the world's leading minicomputer manufacturer, began to make its own 14-inch drives for use with its minicomputer system in 1972. Thus, the makers of 14-inch disk drives were serving the emerging minicomputer market well before the introduction of the 8-inch drive.

Moreover, eight of the first ten companies to introduce the disruptive technology (the 8-inch drive) were incumbents, not new entrants.[3] Contrary to Christensen's claims (Rosenbloom and Christensen 1994: 667; Christensen and Rosenbloom 1995: 245), neither Shugart Associates nor Priam were new entrants; their first hard disk drives were 14 inches.[4] The first two companies to ship 8-inch drives entered at the same time: International Memories and IBM, the latter clearly an incumbent. Both Quantum and Micropolis indeed did well in this segment and were new entrants. But Quantum entered *two years* after the first 8-inch drive was introduced, which, as Christensen points out, was the average time lag for incumbents (Rosenbloom and Christensen 1994: 668; Christensen and Rosenbloom 1995: 245).

By contrast, the emergence of the 5.25-inch drive appears to conform to his model. The 5.25-inch form factor was clearly pioneered by new entrants for a new market—the desktop computer. Of the first ten entrants, eight had never made a disk drive before. The progenitor of the 5.25-inch drive, Seagate Technology, became the market leader, as were other new entrants, although incumbents such as Quantum, Micropolis, and Control Data were leaders in high-capacity segments.

The model, however, does not explain how great firms handled the transition to the 3.5-inch form factor, which accounts for the vast majority of disk drives ever produced. The 3.5-inch form factor, Christensen argues, was intended for the emerging portable computer market, which involved a set of customers entirely different from the set for 5.25-inch drives and offered less performance. Incumbent producers of 5.25-inch drives such as Seagate were too focused on serving the desktop market, which was far more lucrative than the emerging one; and these existing customers showed little interest in the smaller drive. As a consequence, new entrants pioneered the market. The form factor was introduced in 1983 by Rodime, an "entrant," Christensen says, but developed most effectively by Conner Peripherals (which entered more than three years later) for use in Compaq Computer's new portable computers.

As with the emergence of the 8-inch form factor, however, the facts do not support the theory. Incumbents were not laggards: seven of the first ten entrants were incumbents, including Rodime, which previously had shipped a 5.25-inch drive. Moreover, early entrants thought the desktop market would be a likely outlet; the technology was not disruptive at all in that respect. The first two entrants, for example, perceived the 3.5-inch drive as having at least two uses. Rodime's second order in early 1984 was from TeleVideo Systems, a microcomputer maker that wanted the 3.5-inch drive mounted in a 5.25-inch chassis ("Rodime PLC," January 9, 1984). And by 1986, Apple Computer had become a large customer ("Rodime Warns," August 7, 1986). The second entrant, Microcomputer Memories, clearly intended its drive to serve multiple applications, including "mini-computer and microcomputer systems, such as personal and small business computers, portable computers, professional workstations and word processors" ("Microcomputer Memories," January 19, 1984). Indeed, it marketed it in 5.25-inch enclosures.

Moreover, in the case of 3.5-inch drives, the evidence does not indicate that startups "were as unsuccessful as their former employers in attracting established computer makers to the disruptive architecture." Christensen (1997: 46) continues: "Consequently, they had to find *new* customers. . . . Conner Peripherals got its start before Compaq knew the potential size of the portable computer market. The founders of these firms sold their products without a clear marketing strategy—essentially selling to whoever would buy." In fact, when Compaq supported Conner's entry to make 3.5-inch drives, it was well aware of their applicability to portable computers: it had been among Rodime's first customers for the pioneering drive in late 1983 ("Rodime PLC," January 9, 1984). It also seems likely that Finis Conner lined up a customer who knew what product it wanted when he convinced Compaq to put up $12 million in seed money for his firm. In fact, Compaq accounted for 75 percent of Conner's sales during its first six months of production ("Small Drives," August 17, 1987).

But the real paradox is that a whole class of great firms did *not* fail despite often trailing the market in the introduction of disruptive technologies; and despite being early to the market for disruptive technologies, most pioneering new entrants did. Christensen's paradigmatic case in disk drives is Seagate Technology (Christensen 1997; Rosenbloom and Christensen 1994: 669–71; Christensen and Bower 1996: 207–10). Seagate engineers and managers saw the approaching transition to 3.5-inch drives, but management and marketing squashed internal developments of the drive due to the demands of existing customers who wanted more capacity. Seagate belatedly introduced the 3.5-inch drive but had sold "almost none" to portable/laptop makers by 1991; its customers were almost all desktop makers (Christensen 1997: 47). Thus, Seagate missed out on a share of an emerging but rapidly growing market, ceding it instead to startups like Conner Peripherals. For Seagate and other incumbents, "survival was the only reward."

In the HDD industry, as well as many others, survival is a fundamental indicator of success; missing an opportunity to grab a share of the portable computer market, while costly, was not fatal. In fact, Seagate Technology, which is presented as a failure, recovered and went on to be one of the world's two leading disk drive manufacturers. At the time Conner introduced its 3.5-inch drive in January 1987, Seagate was the fifth-largest HDD firm. In 1987 it grew into the fourth spot, was ranked third in 1988, and in 1989 became the world's second-largest HDD firm after IBM, a position it held until 1996, when it became the world's largest. How? Seagate managed to adjust to this presumably disruptive technology in one important way: it used its low-cost, Southeast Asian manufacturing muscle to drive the new entrants out of business. It also prospered to the point that in 1996 it acquired the 3.5-inch success story and arch rival, Conner Peripherals. Yet Seagate is not alone. Other incumbents survived the transition across multiple form factors: IBM, Fujitsu, Quantum, Toshiba, Maxtor, and Hitachi.

The fact that Seagate and others were slow to adopt disruptive technologies but nonetheless survived raises more fundamental issues about organizational change. One branch of organization theory has long assumed that individual organizations cannot change easily and quickly but, when they do change, take great risks (Hannan and Freeman 1977, 1984, 1989). In this view, organizations become increasingly inert over time as procedures, roles, and structures become well established. Indeed, inertia is central to organizational success: firms grow and survive by doing more of what they do, better (Nelson and Winter 1982).

Clearly, there are risks in both changing and not changing. From this perspective, Seagate Technology's very inertia perhaps prevented it from upending a successful model. In discussing the company's strategy for entering the 3.5-inch market, a Seagate co-founder maintained, "It's not who is there first, but who can support the quantities needed with a quality product" ("Smaller Business Computers," June 4, 1984: 1). Seagate had so much production capacity that it could not afford to ship 3.5-inch drives before the market was there. While the company paid a revenue penalty for being late, it maintained the core of its business model (high volume, low-cost manufacture), waited for new entrants to develop the market, and then beat its rivals by producing more 3.5-inch drives than any firm in history.

Notes

CHAPTER 1   WHY LOCATION MATTERS

1. See Piore and Sabel (1984), Goodman and Bamford (1989), Pyke et al. (1990), Harrison (1994), and Saxenian (1994).

2. Even the four-digit SIC code encompassing hard disk drives is too aggregated to tease out these issues: it is for data storage, which includes optical storage, tape storage, floppy disk drives, and disk drive arrays, as well as disk drives. Each of these components has a different competitive ecology.

3. Michael Porter (1998) has begun to focus explicitly on competing across locations. As we elaborate in chapter 4, there are both similarities and differences in our approach.

CHAPTER 2   INDUSTRY BACKGROUND

1. Comments by Steve Luczo, Stanford University Graduate School of Business, November 1999.

2. The most accessible explanation of how a disk drive works can be found on the website of Quantum, a major disk drive company (http://www.quantum.com/src/storage_basics/). Much of this section is adapted from information provided at this site as well as from the website of Read-Rite, a recording head manufacturer (http://www.readrite.com/html/tech.html). For a slightly more technical explanation, see Stevens (1999).

3. Other types of memory include registers, levels 1 and 2 cache, flash or EPROM, optical storage, floppy disks, and magnetic tape.

4. As an example, Western Digital produces 100,000 drives a day with 250 individual parts from multiple suppliers and factories ("WD Plants Sage-Tree," June 21, 2000).

5. Although Quantum and its partner MKE have pioneered a highly automated assembly process, other firms that have attempted automated assembly have moved back to semi-automated assembly processes.

6. The up-tick in growth between 1996 and 1998 was due to Quantum's reintroduction of the 5.25 inch as a viable low-cost desktop drive. The firm folded the 5.25-inch program in 1999.

7. The Herfindahl-Hirschman index (HHI) is the sum of the square of each company's market share. For example, an industry composed of a single monopolist would have an HHI of 10,000; an industry that has five firms, each with a 20 percent market share, would have an HHI of 2,000; while an industry with ten firms with equal market shares would score 1,000 on the index.

8. The pricing pressure, of course, cascades back to component suppliers. The president and CEO of Komag, one of the world's largest independent disk companies, recently noted that the price for a plastic disk—the Frisbee—was higher at a discount store than what he could get for a magnetically sputtered disk holding seven gigabytes of data (comments made at DataStorage99, September 9, 1999).

CHAPTER 3   A THEORY OF INDUSTRY EVOLUTION,
LOCATION, AND COMPETITIVE ADVANTAGE

1. Among some older industries, researchers have observed a resurgence in the number of firms after many years of decline (Hannan et al. 1995, Carroll and Hannan 2000). After declining for almost fifty years, for example, the number of automobile producers in Europe and the United States began to rebound in the mid-1970s, some ninety years after the industry's founding (Carroll and Hannan 1995, Hannan et al. 1995). In this book we do not address the relationship between the resurgence of a mature industry and its location.

2. Sometimes competition is so localized that it occurs primarily within a region or city, as with newspapers, hotels, breweries, and restaurants (Carroll and Wade 1991, Lomi 1995, Baum and Haveman 1997).

3. In modeling the clustering of industry, Arthur (1990) assumes that heterogeneous firms enter a national market in sequence and choose locations based on anticipated profits to be captured from information spillovers. According to Ellinger (1977: 296), the decision to start up near the founder's place of residence results from "spatial ignorance."

4. Standard practice in geography and urban and regional economics distinguishes between localization agglomeration, which refers to the externalities associated with firms in the same industry or sector, and urbanization agglomeration economies derived from the presence of multiple industries or sectors in the same city or region (Harrison et al. 1996). Unless otherwise specified, when we speak of agglomeration we mean localization, which has its origins in Marshall's (1920 [1890]) well-known conception.

5. The literature on clustering emphasizes the proximity of competitors and related firms but generally pays no attention to the different activities and precise functions that a cluster performs from the perspective of the firm. Researchers study either manufacturing (Head et al. 1999) or innovation (Audretsch and Feldman 1996) or refer to firm clusters without specifying the activities that are clustered (Krugman 1991).

6. The idea behind a technological cluster is similar to what Storper (1992) calls a technological district except that the unit of analysis is the industry rather than multiple industries that form the district. Important in the distinction is the relationship of innovative work or interdependence among specific firms within the industry-based technological cluster.

7. The table lists only economies; but congestion, high wages, and scarce land can create agglomeration diseconomies.

8. Firms, of course, also grow through product diversification and acquisition; but our focus here is on internal growth through one product family.

9. See Hall's (1959) excellent and still interesting study of the geographic shift of three New York City industries, part of a series examining the forces shaping metropolitan regions. Raymond Vernon at Harvard University edited the series at the request of the Regional Plan Association. Although he was not one of the authors of the New York study, he did influence the book, and several ideas developed in it bear a striking resemblance to Vernon's later writings about the product life cycle (see chapter 4).

10. Product standardization is often invoked as a reason for dispersion of production and forms the basis for the product life cycle model. Standardization translates into clear and easy to interpret product specifications, which enables the firm to perfect the manufacturing process to such an extent that tasks are routine and production easily replicated to other locations, typically those employing cheaper and less-skilled labor.

11. Drawing on evolutionary theory, Barnett and Hansen (1996) call this kind of self-reinforcing process "Red Queen" competition, in which firms run faster and faster to stay in the same place, much as Alice remarks in Lewis Carroll's *Through the Looking Glass* that she appears to be stationary even though she is running.

12. Chandler (1990) subordinates the benefits of location to a firm's ownership advantages: if a firm does not already have a competitive advantage, overseas activity will not help. We take a slightly different view. If, relative to its competitors, a firm does not have an ownership advantage (in technology, for example), under certain circumstances overseas activity can enable it to gain a competitive position.

13. But see McKendrick (1999).

14. But see Amin and Thrift (1992) and especially Harrison (1994).

15. Students of the multinational firm organize the main influences on (and potential benefits from) foreign investment decisions into several categories. Dunning's categories (1993: table 6.2) are commonly accepted: investments are market seeking, resource seeking, efficiency seeking, strategic asset seeking, or general (tax advantages, slow home market growth). The first two correspond to market access and factor costs in our categorization. We emphasize public policy benefits, part of which falls under general influences in Dunning's account. Studies of foreign investment decisions traditionally have not explicitly addressed agglomeration externalities or international network benefits.

16. Certainly it continues to hold for most service industries such as banking, insurance, trucking, and food services (Shelp et al. 1984, Walter 1988, UNCTC 1989, Nagarajan et al. 1999).

17. Toshiba is fairly representative of the industry. It ships its drives from Japan and the Philippines to its computer assembly plants in Irvine, California; Regensberg, Germany; and Japan.

18. A second important stream of research on networks—social network analysis—is less relevant for our purposes. It examines how structural prop-

erties of firms' internal and external networks, as well as their positions within these networks, influence organizations and their members. Ronald Burt's work (see especially Burt 1992) exemplifies the formal rigor of this approach.

19. Prominent scholars have analyzed intrafirm networks (Brass 1992, Kildruff and Krackhardt 1994, Ibarra 1993), including Ghoshal and Bartlett (1990), who have likened a multinational corporation to an internal network that can be manipulated for competitive advantage.

20. Our research did not turn up much evidence for interfirm learning in international production networks. There was, of course, considerable technology transfer—one-way learning. But we applied a more stringent test: the interaction had to yield a novel synthesis of the information that actually generates new knowledge (Powell and Brantley 1992, Podolny and Page 1998). We found such learning within operational clusters but not cross-nationally within Southeast Asia. By contrast, and without much effort, we identified two innovations that resulted from international transmission of information. The intellectual antecedent of IBM's giant magnetoresistive heads, developed by a team in San Jose, California, was a technical paper written by French academics. More recently, and more modestly, Seagate's low-cost disk drive, the U4, was developed by a Singapore design team in collaboration with engineers in Longmont, Colorado. Based on this admittedly thin comparison, we speculate that network learning in operations is more geographically circumscribed than in innovation networks.

21. Making the multinational corporation a central actor in the formation and management of both locational assets and cross-border networks implicitly challenges research that emphasizes the importance of relations among small firms operating in socially homogenous and historically durable communities. Many proponents of industrial districts and subnational network relationships, for example, see MNCs as manifestations of the global forces they criticize as well as strongly at odds with the small-firm networks they favor. It is useful to point out that while many MNCs are in fact behemoths, variation in their size is quite large. In the disk drive industry, for instance, the early globalizers were both younger and smaller than the industry average.

22. Recognizing the advantages of a multinational network is not a new approach; Kogut (1983) was an early proponent of its advantages (see also Edstrom and Galbraith 1977; Hedlund, 1986, 1993, 1994; and Ghoshal and Bartlett 1990). Ghoshal and Bartlett (1990) extend this line of thinking theoretically by conceptualizing the MNC as an interorganizational network of exchange relationships among distributed and interdependent organizational units embedded in an external network of suppliers, customers, and regulators. Similarly, Gupta and Govindarajan (1991) conceive of the MNC as a network of transactions involving the flow of capital, products, and knowledge among units in different countries.

23. As one example of the industry's increased emphasis on time to market, Micropolis improved its rate of new product introduction from two disk drives in 1988 to five in 1989 and six in 1990.

CHAPTER 4   ALTERNATIVE EXPLANATIONS
            FOR INDUSTRY ADVANTAGE

1. In introducing his product life cycle model, Vernon (1966) used examples of cycles at the industry level. Conversely, in his description of the industry life cycle, Klepper's (1997) evidence was primarily at the product level. A simple analytic difference is that for the product life cycle to hold, pioneering firms need to maintain their leadership position through the mature stage, while industry dominance can be preserved even if the pioneering firms exit.

2. Its core features have been extended to explain cycles of innovation (Utterback and Abernathy 1975, Abernathy and Clark 1985, Utterback 1994) and industry life cycles (Klepper 1996, 1997).

3. Porter (1990: 58) says, "My discussion of locating activities, however, must at this stage remain incomplete. The best location for the activities that constitute a firm's home base, particularly strategy development, R&D, and the more sophisticated portions of production, is after all one of the principal subjects of this book. Suffice it to say that the motivations for locating in a nation go far beyond the classical explanations outlined here." To the extent that international operations are necessary, "the important questions are why and how do multinationals from a particular nation develop unique skills and know-how in particular industries? Why do some multinationals from some nations sustain and build on these advantages and others do not?" (Porter 1990: 18).

4. ICL, Britain's largest computer manufacturer, owned 70 percent of DRI between 1962 and 1972, when it sold its interest back to Grundy, the company that originally financed DRI's establishment in 1956. In 1968, DRI shipped its first disk drive to ICL.

5. A major exception to this tendency was the success of Control Data in selling to European computer manufacturers; it claimed the bulk of the world's shipments of noncaptive drives in the 1960s and still almost half by the late 1970s. IBM's disk drives were solely for use with IBM computers.

6. Global computer market shares were calculated from the *Datamation 100* for various years.

7. An important exception is the printer industry. While the United States lost the impact printer market, it has a huge lead in laser printers.

8. *Keiretsu* are a group of companies federated around a major bank, large industrial firm, or trading company.

9. The two leading U.S. firms, Seagate and IBM, made their own heads and disks, as did the two leading Japanese firms, Fujitsu and Hitachi. Most of the Japanese and U.S. firms that survived longer than a year or two made at least one component. Only Seagate, however, has made its own motors for a sustained period. The combined global market share of the twenty-eight firms was 85 percent in 1983, 91 percent in 1987, 98 percent in 1991, 99 percent in 1995, and 96 percent in 1998.

10. NEC is making IBM drives late in their life cycles and using IBM components. After more than thirty years in the industry, NEC has essentially ceased designing and manufacturing its own disk drives.

11. For a technical history of IBM's first twenty-five years of innovation in the industry, see Harker et al. (1981) and Stevens (1981).

12. Western Digital, another leader in 1998, did not make disk drives until 1988.

13. In the shift to the 2.5-inch form factor, there was little difference between surviving Japanese and American firms.

14. Firms also compete in the desktop market in terms of volumetric density—how much capacity one can cram into the slot allotted to the disk drive. One trick in mechanical design has been the introduction of half-high disk drives in which more disks are stacked closer together. Thus, a company might be a leader in areal density (data on a disk) but a laggard in volumetric density— a distinction that some say IBM has not always understood. Thanks to Frank Mayadas for bringing this issue to our attention.

15. Improvements to inductive technology included proximity or virtual-contact heads, which involved significant enhancements to etched air bearing and transducer technologies.

16. In 1987, a group of leading disk drive companies joined to address common policy concerns. Headed by Maxtor's president and CEO, who had previously played a major role in the organization of the Semiconductor Industry Association, its first goal was to repeal a 3.9 percent tariff on products imported from offshore manufacturing sites. But the group soon expanded its efforts to counter "Japan Inc." and make the U.S. government aware of the industry's strategic importance. It lobbied the government to influence trade legislation and win R&D tax credits to help fund new research. Given the U.S. HDD industry's leadership, however, the group was unable to persuade the government that the industry had a problem that needed fixing.

17. We say "direct" because in both countries the computer and space industries have received substantial public policy support, meaning that the data storage efforts of systems manufacturers may have received some indirect support. For example, HDD firms have employed a technique called partial response maximum likelihood (PRML) to increase areal density and boost transfer speeds. PRML was originally developed for NASA to interpret data from deep-space probes.

CHAPTER 5   GLOBAL SHIFT AND COMPETITIVENESS
IN HARD DISK DRIVES

1. IBM and Honeywell were exceptions: IBM's San Jose lab was set up in 1952 to tap engineering skills in California, which was far from the company's mainframe operations in New York. Honeywell's storage operations were initially located in Massachusetts rather than collocated with its Minnesota systems groups.

2. Internationally, disk drive design and production were mainly diffused through technology transfer arrangements with U.S. firms. NEC, Hitachi, and Hokushin had technical tie-ups with Honeywell, Bryant Computer Products, and Diablo Systems, respectively. In Europe, Compagnie Internationale de l'Informatique was licensed to make Control Data drives, and BASF acquired technology from Century Data Systems. In the late 1970s, Brazilian firms acquired licenses from Ampex, Control Data, and Pertec, among others.

3. Perhaps surprisingly, Oklahoma City has among the longest histories in the disk drive industry. When GE sold its computer business to Honeywell in

1970, its storage business was included. In 1974 Honeywell put all of its disk drive assets, including its Oklahoma City facility, into a joint venture controlled by Control Data. After Control Data assumed sole ownership of the joint venture, Oklahoma City became an important HDD center. Seagate bought Control Data's disk drive business in 1989, and the city remains an important location for the company. Along with Seagate's Minnesota facility, it is the only U.S. location that does any HDD assembly other than prototypes; and today it is responsible for the development of 3.5-inch disk drives intended for use in minicomputers, supermicrocomputers, workstations, and file servers.

4. As a Univac computer engineer who was on the receiving end of these drives wrote, "The 8414 [disk drive] became the only computer storage peripheral known for developing frequent oil leaks. There were a number of other mechanical unreliabilites [*sic*] which, combined with logic errors in early versions of the fantastically complicated controller which interfaced the byte-oriented discs to the 36-bit word mainframe and operating system driver bugs, caused the early adopters of these units an enormous amount of pain" (personal communication, May 22, 1997).

5. Storage Technology introduced disk drive technology to Colorado via its acquisition of Disc Systems, a Silicon Valley startup; it developed STC's 800-megabyte System 8000 series drive designed to compete against the IBM 3330. In 1974, the Disc Systems division was merged into the parent company and the entire operation moved to Colorado ("Disc Syst. Div. Merges," December 12, 1974).

6. By *headquarters* we mean the center of a firm's disk drive operations, not necessarily its corporate headquarters. For example, the core of IBM's disk drive operations are in San Jose, California, not Armonk, New York; Hewlett-Packard's disk drive headquarters were in Boise, Idaho, not Cupertino, California.

7. IBM and International Memories both shipped an 8-inch drive in 1979, but the form factor never became as dominant as the bigger disks or the smaller ones that followed.

8. Europe was a larger market for Control Data than the United States during the late 1960s and early 1970s. Its highest volume during those years went to ICL, English Electric and Siemens.

9. Burroughs set up drive assembly in Winnipeg, Manitoba, in exchange for a large government contract for mainframe computers ("Burroughs' 1st," April 14, 1975).

10. This is not to deny endogeneity in the technology development process, only that the commercialization of the smaller disk drives followed the introduction of the desktop computer. Finis Conner, a co-founder of Seagate Technology, believed that a rigid disk drive that could fit into the slot designed for the floppy disk drive in a desktop computer could fill the memory need for more than one floppy. The result was the first 5.25-inch drive in 1980.

11. These new companies included Seagate, Conner Peripherals, Rotating Memory Systems, International Memories, Atasi, La Pine, Quantum, Maxtor, and Areal Technology.

12. In fact, this part of southern California was called Floppy Valley and became the center of America's floppy disk drive industry.

13. In April 2000, Komag announced it would merge its operations with HMT Technology, another media producer in Fremont, California.

14. In fact, IBM appeared to interpret the environment similarly. The company initially made its 5.25-inch drives in England and Rochester, Minnesota, but soon realized that costs were too high relative to its competitors ("IBM PC AT Plan," April 29, 1985). Looking for a lower-cost location, it began to make them at an existing facility in Fujisawa, Japan. Why? Here's how Fujisawa's plant manager tells the story: "About two years ago IBM's San Jose operation was looking for a manufacturer for the XT drive and thought a Japanese company might be a good source. So we raised our hands and said, 'Let us make it. We are a Japanese company, too.' So we made a study of technical feasibility and cost and came up with a plan that showed we were competitive" ("A Fine Japanese Company," April 8, 1985). Fujisawa became the only IBM plant in the world making drives for the XT computer, shipping all production to the United States.

15. Interview, September 1998.

16. Interview with Fujitsu manager, July 21, 1999.

17. Personal communication from a Hitachi senior manager, May 19, 1997.

18. Like Fujitsu, IBM began some drive assembly in Thailand in 1991 but used a subcontractor rather than managing its own plant.

19. Singapore was responsible for 48 percent of the world's HDDs.

20. Between 1990 and 1995, American firms also extended the global assembly strategy to low-cost areas of Europe (Ireland and Hungary). The high percentage of U.S. assembly in Japan results from Quantum's decision to contract assembly to Matsushita-Kotobuki Electronics.

21. This includes the 3 percent of U.S. drives made in China.

22. As is common in the industry, its facilities and many of its employees became assets of Maxtor, another American HDD company.

23. Through industry consolidations, surviving American firms have found themselves in possession of R&D assets in more than one location.

24. This does not include the travel of the Singapore project manager, who went to the United States six months before the transfer date to provide detailed coordination.

25. Raw data, drawings, and text were shared in real time via the company's corporate electronic network.

26. Interview with a former executive vice president of Conner Peripherals, November 18, 1996.

CHAPTER 6   LEVERAGING LOCATIONS

1. There are two kinds of taxation facing U.S. companies: foreign and American. U.S. income taxes are generally not paid on undistributed earnings of foreign subsidiaries, and U.S. companies generally do not repatriate these earnings but reinvest them indefinitely—in essence lowering their capital costs. Because foreign taxes create potential tax liability in the country where the subsidiary is located, this is where the tax holidays and other incentives come into play.

2. Until Seagate acquired its HDD operations in 1989, Control Data had been assembling components in Portugal, but the quality was poor and the wages

were higher than in Singapore. Interview with a former Control Data manager, September 1999.

3. As of March 1999, Singapore's budgeted spending for major infrastructure projects was roughly $8 billion, following only the much larger China, Japan, and South Korea but leading Hong Kong, Taiwan, Thailand, and India ("Concrete Plans," March 25, 1999).

4. In 1987, CDC had about 33 percent of the $36 million thin-film head market, Read-Rite 32 percent, and Applied Magnetics 30 percent ("Control Data Cashes In," April 15, 1988). This breakdown omits IBM shipments for captive use. By 1990, IBM, Seagate, Applied Magnetics, Read-Rite, and Dastek were the only major thin-film heads makers, and only IBM was not present in Malaysia. Although CDC participated in a joint venture to make heads in Hong Kong and China with Lafe Holdings of Hong Kong, that operation made only the older composite ferrite heads.

5. Kalok was always a small HDD assembler, and Microscience International's plant in China was short-lived.

6. For example, the Economic Development Board facilitated doing business in Singapore through constant monitoring of and coordination among agencies such as the Immigration Department, the Ministry of Labor, and the Jurong Town Corporation. According to one manager, if a competitor begins to intensify the competition for workers by offering significantly higher wages, the manager will not hesitate to call the board and expect help in resolving the issue ("Why Seagate Set Sail," June 1, 1988). Another manager said that establishing operations on the island "is about 10 times easier than anywhere else in Asia" ("MiniScribe, Others," July 13, 1987).

7. Read-Rite closed its Malaysian facility in 1999, and Applied Magnetics went out of business in early 2000.

8. Interview with senior IBM managers, Thailand, July 19, 1999.

9. Interview with senior Fujitsu managers, Thailand, July 21, 1999.

10. This changed with the establishment of a Certificate in Storage Technology program developed and taught by Singapore Polytechnic but administered by the PSDC. IDEMA, the industry trade association, initiated this effort.

11. Singapore suppliers include MMI, Brilliant Manufacturing, Gul Technology, BJ Industries, and CAM Technologies. Penang suppliers include Eng Teknologi and TransCapital.

12. Unfortunately, the survey's results are unclear about supplier satisfaction with these policies. Although almost one-third of the firms refused to comment on this issue, available data indicate that supplier firms in Malaysia are least satisfied with public policies toward the industry (53 percent of Malaysia-based suppliers said they were unhappy), while Thai firms are most satisfied (67 percent). Thailand, however, has only offered tax incentives for locating in the different zones, so the benefits of these narrow policies are easy to see. While Singapore offers a more ambitious array of programs and policies than the others do, 46 percent of its suppliers said they were satisfied. Although this evidence is not conclusive, it mirrors what we have learned through interviews about the policy differences among the three countries.

13. The question is whether Singapore's engineering capabilities will allow it to graduate to a center for some forms of product innovation. Seagate's recent introduction of the Singapore-designed disk drive for PCs below $1,000 suggests that this is possible, at least for lower-end products. We return to this issue in chapter 10.

14. At the time Seagate acquired Control Data's HDD operations, Control Data's highest-capacity drives were made in the United States. The steep slope of the dotted line in figure 6.4 between 1988 and 1989 reflects the fact that Seagate obtained much higher-capacity products with the acquisition. The steep slope of the solid line between 1989 and 1990 reflects the rapid transfer of all volume production of Control Data drives from the United States to Singapore.

15. Seagate quickly shut down Control Data's German assembly facility after its 1989 acquisition as well as its small Singapore HDD plant and component operations in Portugal.

16. Ireland's facility had the highest cost per drive in the company.

17. According to Seagate's CEO, its PCBA operations are among the best in the world. Remarks to an MBA class, Stanford University, November 22, 1999.

18. According to Seagate's senior vice president for worldwide manufacturing, "the consolidation of our Singapore manufacturing operations will provide us with greater operational efficiencies, improved communications, and significant cost improvements through greater economies of scale. Faced with intense global competition, faster product development, and shorter product life cycles, the ability to implement new technologies, to move a product from concept to high volume production quickly, efficiently, and cost-effectively is crucial" ("Seagate Announces," September 7, 1994).

19. Interview at Seagate Malaysia, September 24, 1999.

20. Interview at Seagate Singapore, June 17, 1997; interview at Western Digital Singapore, September 21, 1999.

CHAPTER 7   SINGAPORE

1. When one adjusts for the higher rate of price erosion in HDD compared to manufacturing goods in general, the productivity growth performance in constant prices is even more remarkable.

2. In 1981, Micro Peripherals and Tandon started the first assembly operation of data storage products in Singapore (making floppy disks), but both operations were short-lived.

3. Interview on July 15, 1999. To punctuate his point, he said, "We had too many surfers who were more concerned about surfing than work." Scotts Valley is just up the road from Santa Cruz, a popular surf spot.

4. According to the Seagate co-founder, the new team only had $50,000 in cash in the bank. When he hired the first local manager after only one week of conversation, he gave him a check for that amount "on a handshake." If the manager lost the money, he reasoned, it was better to lose only $50,000 right away than to find out later how untrustworthy his new employee might be. Interview, July 15, 1999.

5. Interview with a senior Seagate manager, June 11, 1999.

6. Tool Products, a Minnesota company that made casings, was one of the few Seagate suppliers to follow. Seagate was able to entice National Micronetics, a heads maker in California, to invest there by promising them business. The information in this section is largely based on interviews with current and former Seagate managers on June 11, 1999; July 15, 1999; September 15, 1999; and a former National Micronetics manager, September 14, 1999. Though not a Seagate supplier, Flextronics, a PCBA company, was one of the handful of U.S. companies that set up a Singapore facility by the mid-1980s.

7. The Rollei closure was a traumatic event for Singapore, so much so that a senior government minister went on television to address the nation. Rollei had been one of the first multinational companies to invest in Singapore in the 1960s, and no company of that size had shut down; Singaporeans were not used to such an event. The minister "turned a negative into a positive" by praising Rollei for all the skills it had developed and the toolmakers it had trained over the years. This was in some ways a seminal event in the government's policy focus, which has always pushed for new skills, an emphasis that has been critical in developing the local labor market. And as it turned out, several Rollei engineers went on to found important companies. Interview with a former General Electric manager then based in Singapore, September 15, 1999.

8. Although Maxtor did not specify the nature of these incentives, in November 1983 it closed its third round of financing, raising a total of $18.25 million through the private placement of preferred stock. Among the new investors was the Development Bank of Singapore ("Maxtor Corp.; Completes Third Round," November 22, 1983).

9. Interview with a former Maxtor procurement manager, September 15, 1999. He joined Maxtor when it started operations in Singapore.

10. Account based on interviews with this manager on September 22, 1998, and September 16, 1999.

11. Rodime cut its cost by $10 to $15 per drive with the move. In retrospect, Rodime's senior managers think the move to Florida was a mistake. The company went to the United States because Apple Computer wanted it there, selecting Florida to "split the time difference" between Scotland and California. But the Apple business lasted for about a year, and expected business from IBM's Boca Raton PC facility never materialized. Rodime therefore found itself carrying a great deal of manufacturing capacity with declining volumes. It compounded its problems by designing HDDs in both Florida and Scotland, thus stretching its managerial and engineering resources. As it turned out, the Singapore move came too late to save the company. Interviews with three former Rodime managers, March 11, 1998.

12. In fact, the Control Data acquisition dramatically expanded the number of locations under Seagate management and increased company employment by 8,500. Seagate soon closed Control Data's HDD and component facilities in Germany; Portugal; and Omaha, Nebraska; but kept important operations in the Twin Cities region of Minnesota, where its largest drives were made and the center of its thin-film heads development; in Oklahoma City, where 5.25-inch drive manufacturing was centered; in Simi Valley, California, headquarters of the 3.5-inch drive efforts; and some smaller U.S. facilities.

13. Interview with an ex-Conner and current Seagate manager, September 21, 1999.

14. Interviews with IBM managers on August 6, 1996, June 16, 1997, and September 21, 1999.

15. Interviews with a senior Seagate manager, September 15, 1999, and a senior IBM manager, September 21, 1999.

16. Comment by a senior IBM manager to a group of investment analysts, Singapore, August 14, 1996.

17. Interview with a senior manager at Supersymmetry, who previously had worked in various divisions in EDB and the Jurong Township Corporation, June 16, 1997.

18. Interview with a former operations director for materials management at Seagate, June 17, 1997. The information in this section also comes from an interview with one of the first Seagate employees in Singapore, who was involved in procurement in 1982–84, September 15, 1999.

19. Interview with a senior IBM manager, September 21, 1999. He was with Conner between 1987 and 1993.

20. Interview with the co-founder and managing director of MMI Holdings, Singapore, September 18, 1999.

21. Interview June 17, 1997; "The American Company Seagate," October 10, 1986.

22. Interviews on September 22, 1998, and September 16, 1999.

23. Interview with the managing director of Brilliant Manufacturing, June 16, 1997.

24. Although the survey covered only thirteen firms and is obviously biased toward survivors, it is instructive nonetheless.

25. Interview with two human resource managers at Maxtor, June 18, 1999. Unfortunately, our notes do not identify which manager is the source for the quotation.

26. Interview with a manufacturing manager at Western Digital, September 21, 1999. As a perfect example of his own point, he had previously worked with Micropolis, Conner Peripherals, Integral Peripherals, Maxtor, and StorMedia.

27. While scale economies are a critical characteristic of agglomeration economies in an operational cluster, we should not make too much of HDD's role in the development of precision engineering in Singapore. This is one weakness of research that draws a boundary around a specific industry. As Wong (1999b) rightly observes, while the clustering of HDD majors facilitated the development of a larger and more varied cluster of precision engineering firms in close proximity, the production capacity of these precision engineering firms were not entirely specific to supplying precision parts to the HDD industry alone. Because the precision and quality requirements of HDD drive components were among the most stringent of all electronics products, firms that had mastered the capability to supply mechanical components to the HDD industry were typically able to supply precision parts to other electronics manufacturing industries as well. Because Singapore has been able to attract a large number of manufacturing firms in a wide range of electronics indus-

tries over the years, the size and diversity of Singapore's precision engineering supporting industry is thus much more than can be sustained by HDD requirements alone. The agglomeration economies of Singapore's precision engineering cluster have thus increased due to the mobility of supply capacity between those serving the HDD and those serving other electronics segments.

28. Interview with the managing director of Brilliant, June 16, 1997.

29. Interview with a senior manager of Cam Technologies, June 18, 1997.

30. Interview with the co-founder and managing director of MMI Holdings, September 18, 1999.

31. When it announced in 1991 that it would build drives in Singapore, newcomer Integral Peripherals attributed the decision in part to the supporting industries available ("Integral Peripherals to Make World's Smallest," August 26, 1991).

32. Interview with a manager at Read-Rite, September 14, 1999.

33. Interview with a senior IBM manager, September 21, 1999, who formerly worked at Conner Peripherals.

34. Interview, September 18, 1999.

35. Plant visit, September 13, 1996.

36. Interview with a senior Seagate manager, September 24, 1999.

CHAPTER 8   THAILAND

1. This chapter draws on Doner and Brimble (1998).

2. Based on these figures, the Thailand's HDD industry was one-fourth to one-third the size of its Singapore counterpart in 1998. Export figures for 1990 are from the Bank of Thailand (cited in Department of Industrial Promotion 1998: 5) and for 1998 from the Thai Board of Investment (cited in Chakchai 1999: 10). Of the 1998 totals, completed disk drives and head-disk assemblies accounted for $3.2 billion, parts (sliders, HGAs, and HSAs) $1.8 billion, and spindle motors $235 million.

3. Chakchai (1999: 10), based on Board of Investment statistics.

4. In 1997, Seagate had 106,000 employees globally, with close to 44,000 in Thailand. After downsizing, the company employed 77,000 in October 1999, of which 33,000 were in Thailand ("Thailand a Hub," October 14, 1999).

5. Interview at Micropolis Thailand, July 23, 1997.

6. Interview, July, 1, 1997. The new plant had little money, and only after a number of rejections did one local bank agree to extend financing.

7. A complementary reason was that Singapore employees did not want to do head-stack assembly. Because HSA is more tedious than many other activities, Seagate experienced much turnover in that function. Wages for HSA were equal to those for head-disk assembly, which HSA workers thought was easier. One consequence of the high turnover was that Seagate's training costs became too high. Interview, Seagate Singapore, September 15, 1999.

8. In addition to typical income tax holidays and exemptions on duties and taxes on capital equipment, special incentives to exporters included exemptions on import duties and business taxes on material inputs, intermediate products, and reexported products. For a review, see Nipon and Fuller (1997: 477–80).

Akrasanee and Tambunlertchai (1990: 117) have assessed Thai export incentives as "modest."

9. Interview, July 1, 1997; confirmed in an interview with Board of Investment officials, June 23, 1997.

10. For a review of early export-linked infrastructure efforts, see Felker (1998a).

11. K.R. Precision interview, July 20, 1999, and an interview with a former senior manager at Seagate, July 15, 1999.

12. IBM (Saha Union) interview, July 19, 1999.

13. For example, the board granted Minebea a lifetime import tax exemption on raw materials and machinery (Nipon and Pawadee 1998: 330).

14. Interview at Seagate Scotts Valley, October 11, 1999.

15. Data General was the source of several T.P.W. employees, which provided actuators and base plates for Seagate.

16. Interview, June 23, 1997.

17. The estimate is from a senior engineer who left National Semiconductor for Seagate in 1985 and has remained with the firm since. Interview, Seagate Teparuk, July 21, 1999.

18. Interviews, Read-Rite, July 1, 1997, and Seagate Scotts Valley, October 11, 1999, from which information in the following paragraph is also drawn.

19. Interview, Seagate Scotts Valley, October 11, 1999.

20. Interview, July 15, 1999.

21. Interview, July 1, 1999.

22. Interview, Seagate Scotts Valley, October 11, 1999.

23. In addition, Avatar Peripherals, a small assembler of cartridge disk drives, made Thailand its sole assembly site.

24. Interview, Fujitsu Thailand, June 26, 1997.

25. The other is the Philippines.

26. Minebea has also tried its hand at slider assembly and HGA in Thailand, building small quantities at its motor facility (NMB) since 1994. It was a late entrant into a declining market, making older-technology heads. Although the firm has had execution problems, it continues to participate in the industry at low volumes (*TrendFocus* 1998b). Acton Computer, an Applied Magnetics spinoff from California, expanded production in Thailand briefly before being acquired in 1987 ("Deal May Be Worth $40 Million," August 25, 1987).

27. Interview, AdFlex, June 24, 1998.

28. The strike itself resulted from a combination of workers' concerns with high exposure to lead, the firm's managerial clumsiness, and support for strikers from a political party faction backing the military government then in power. Seagate began by firing 87 workers who participated in the initial protest and then fired another 621 who demonstrated to get the first group reinstated ("Shut Up," April 1994; "Seagate Asks Government," June 3, 1997). Information on managerial problems was drawn from an interview with a Seagate official, July 1999.

29. Interview at Read-Rite, July 1997. As part of its up-country strategy, Seagate was forced to initiate contact with local vocational institutions,

opened up job placement centers in the region, and set up special two-week training courses ("PC Disk Maker," May 17, 1997).

30. Firms operating in zone 3 receive a 100 percent exemption on duties for imported machinery; eight years of corporate tax exemptions and 50 percent reduction for another five years; 75 percent reduction of import duty on raw and essential materials used in production for domestic sales for five years, renewable annually, provided that inputs comparable in quality are not produced or do not originate in Thailand in sufficient quantity for this activity; double deduction from taxable income for water, electricity, and transport costs for ten years from the date of a firm's first sales; 25 percent deduction from net profits for costs of installation or construction of the project's infrastructure facilities; and five extra years of duty exemptions on raw materials (Thailand Board of Investment 1997). Furthermore, projects in zone 3 can be foreign owned, whereas those in zones 1 and 2 can only be foreign owned if they are export-oriented. Several "short term measures to encourage investment" have also been adopted following the July 1997 economic crisis: eight-year corporate income tax exemption and exemption of import duties on machinery, regardless of location or ownership, for investment in nineteen supporting industries; import duty exemptions for new machinery for investments in sixty-one projects in zones 1 and 2; permission for export projects to locate in any zone; and permission of majority foreign ownership in new projects in any zone, pending approval of the Thai shareholders.

31. IBM had considered the Philippines before selecting Thailand as the site for its wholly owned disk drive assembly facility. Thailand's zone 3 incentives were better than anything the Philippines had to offer. But as described later in the chapter, the accumulated manufacturing knowledge of IBM's contract assembler in Thailand was also an important factor in the decision. Interview, IBM Thailand, June 30, 1997.

32. Interview, AdFlex, June 24, 1998.

33. Interviews at Fujitsu (July 1997, July 1999), IBM (July 1999), and Read-Rite (July 1999). Although Read-Rite established an HSA facility in the Philippines, it has kept its slider fabrication in Thailand in part because of fears about power interruptions in the Philippines.

34. In the case of the Eastern Seaboard Industrial Estate, the private estate manager established an Investors' Club for these purposes (Brimble and Chatri 1994).

35. Interview, Avatar, July 2, 1997.

36. Remarks at the Hard Disk Drive Workshop, Bangkok, July 16, 1999.

37. In fact, Thailand's infrastructure investments during the Seventh Plan (1992–97) were fairly high—more than $10 billion per year—which was nevertheless not enough to meet demand (Warr 1997: 325). A World Bank study has predicted that Thai infrastructure needs for 1995–2004 will total $145 billion (Brooker Group 1997: 20).

38. For a quantitative study showing the board's lack of support for technology transfer, see Westphal et al. (1990). See Brimble and Chatri (1994) for a discussion of the lack of technology support more generally. On the failure to implement a long list of industry-specific measures, including those for electronics, see Felker (1998b) and Lauridsen (1999).

39. For example, several firms mentioned delays in obtaining board permission for tariff exemptions on imported equipment due to its lack of knowledge about equipment function. Officials are known to visit some HDD facilities each month to verify the claims of tariff reductions for used equipment and scrap, often insisting on witnessing a bulldozer crushing the unusable material. In one case, officials insisted on counting scrapped suspensions, which cost between twenty and forty cents apiece.

40. Interviews with Avatar (July 2, 1997) and Seagate (June 27, 1997); remarks at the Hard Disk Drive Workshop, July 7, 1999.

41. Interview, Magnecomp Thailand, August 18, 1997.

42. This does not include U.S. employees temporarily assigned to Thailand for new product launches or specific problems. Within Seagate, for example, its Teparuk facility has tended to have more U.S.-based employees on temporary assignment because that facility has produced newer products than the Korat plant has. Interviews at Seagate Thailand, July 26, 1999; Seagate Scotts Valley, October 11, 1999.

43. Interview, K.R. Precision, July 20, 1999.

44. For example, Fujitsu is now sourcing HGAs from Thai-based Read-Rite.

45. During the mid-1980s, Data General successfully relocated more than six hundred employees from two smaller plants in central Bangkok to a new facility then considered rural; none of the workers quit. When Seagate planned its move into the new Teparuk facility, including employee relocation, it contacted Data General for advice, which shared its models and plans. Seagate knew of Data General's successful move in part because both had participated in earlier monthly meetings of U.S. electronics firms. The most active association seems to be the Ayuthaya Industrial Association (AIA), composed of western firms operating in the Ayuthaya area north of Bangkok. The AIA is concerned primarily with the supply and costs of technicians and engineers. Another is a group of largely Japanese electronics firms in the Ayuthaya area. Interviews, K.R. Precision, July 20, 1997; Read-Rite, July 22, 1999.

46. Interview, Read-Rite, July 1, 1997. In 1999, however, IDEMA initiated an industry training program based on a successful effort in Singapore and Penang. The results of this initiative are not yet clear.

47. Interview, Read-Rite, June 26, 1997; July 22, 1999.

48. In response, NMB strengthened its R&D in fluid-dynamic bearings and expanded its main R&D center in Thailand from four researchers to sixteen ("Japanese Bearing Maker," October 13, 1997). By deciding to hire researchers from Thailand's leading universities in physics and material science, it has signaled to other firms the potential of the local technical labor market.

49. Interview, Seagate Scotts Valley, October 11, 1999.

50. Seiko Instruments' motor division actually originated within Seagate, which sold the unit to Nidec in the early 1990s. The combination did not last, and Nidec later sold the operation to Seiko. But one of Seiko's division heads is located in Scotts Valley, and the company has retained ties to Seagate. Interview, Seagate Scotts Valley, October 11, 1999.

51. During the 1980s, IBM, NEC, Hitachi, Alps, Fujitsu, and Seagate attempted to produce their own suspensions. Among disk drive and record-

ing heads producers, only Fujitsu still makes suspensions. The world leaders are specialists: HTI, K.R. Precision, Nippon Hatusujo Kogyo (NHK), and Magnecomp.

52. The case of Magnecomp, with five hundred employees in Thailand, has parallels. Although an established company when it invested in Thailand, Magnecomp was attracted by the possibility of getting Read-Rite's business as well as Seagate's. To that end, Magnecomp agreed to a self-source inspection process by which Read-Rite trained Magnecomp employees and stationed them in Read-Rite's plant.

53. Interview, IBM Thailand, June 30, 1997.

54. Interviews, IBM Thailand, June 30, 1997; July 19, 1999.

55. Interview, Seagate Scotts Valley, October 11, 1999.

56. One example of this is the correlation problem, which refers to differences in the measurement of a suspension's performance by a producer and a customer. It is very hard to have absolute measurement of some characteristics. Suspensions are very fragile, so even breathing on them will change things. Companies set some measurement standards but then need to agree on periodically calibrating factory equipment with those standards. Proximity facilitates coordination. Interview, K.R. Precision, Thailand, July 20, 1999.

CHAPTER 9   MALAYSIA

1. Much of this chapter is derived from Haggard et al. (1998).

2. The survey does not cover Seagate's investment in Ipoh, new entrants to the Kulim Hi-tech Park in Kedah, or the activities of local suppliers.

3. Western Digital assembles drives in Kuala Lumpur, midway between Penang and Singapore.

4. In September 1988, Control Data transformed its disk drive operations into an independent subsidiary called Imprimis for the expressed purpose of divesting it. Less than a year later, Imprimis announced that Seagate would acquire it. For the sake of consistency, we will refer to Imprimis as Control Data throughout.

5. Penang's management argued that the firm was capable of making the move; Conner had entered by this point and was demonstrating that HDD assembly could be done in Penang. But Maxtor's Singapore management expressed reservations, including concerns about the costs of recertifying the entire Penang facility for its major customers.

6. Dastek was acquired by the media firm Komag in 1991. Although Komag hoped the combination would enable it to optimize the head-disk interface, the acquisition failed to do so. Komag shut down its Dastek subsidiary in 1994.

7. Interview, former Maxtor manager, January 1997.

8. Interview, June 1997.

9. FTZs involve the government's provision of infrastructure and have the advantage for some industries of housing suppliers and customers in close proximity. LMWs provide a mechanism for the government to extend the trade provisions of the FTZs to individual firms by essentially bonding them. The only drawbacks are that an LMW does not have the proximity benefits of the FTZ,

and status must be renewed annually. Nevertheless, LMW status, the development of other industrial parks, and the general lowering of tariffs have gradually eroded the particular advantages of being housed in the FTZ. In Penang, most of the majors and major suppliers are located in the FTZs, while those not in FTZs enjoy LMW status.

10. Interview, Seagate Penang, September 24, 1999.

11. Interview, PDC official, June 23, 1997. Maxtor's interest in Penang was the result of the fact that a senior official in the company had worked in Penang at Advanced Micro Devices, a U.S. semiconductor firm. His connections to the PDC gained Maxtor access not only to the chief minister of Penang but to Mahathir himself. Interview, former head of the PDC, October 15, 1997.

12. That individual later became the managing director of Read-Rite's operations when it acquired Conner's HSA business. Interview, former Read-Rite manager, June 26, 1997.

13. Interview, former Read-Rite manager, November 19, 1997.

14. Interview, former Conner manager, November 24, 1999.

15. Interview, Eng Teknologi group managing director, June 1997.

16. Applied Magnetics was supplying Maxtor in Singapore (interview, Applied Magnetics director, October 15, 1997), and CDC was supplying HGAs primarily to its own operations in Singapore (drive assembly) and Portugal (HSA).

17. As we have seen, Hitachi entered to supply Applied Magnetic's HGA and later HSA operations, and Applied Magnetics was supplying Maxtor. Dastek's main customer was also Maxtor; it tried but failed to secure Conner HSA business and ended up supplying Micropolis in Singapore.

18. Interview, Seagate manager, November 12, 1999.

19. The following draws on an interview with an Applied Magnetics director, November 22, 1999.

20. Interview, former Read-Rite manager, November 24, 1999.

21. Conner sourced HSAs from Kaifa (China and Hong Kong), SAE (China and Hong Kong), Sunward Technologies (Philippines), and Applied Magnetics (Malaysia); HGAs from Read-Rite (Thailand) and Dastek (Malaysia); motors from NMB (Thailand) and Nidec (Japan); media from Conner's media division in San Jose, California, and later Singapore; PCBA from TransCapital (Malaysian-owned in Penang), Tongkah (a Malaysia-Singapore joint venture in Penang), Natsteel (Singapore-owned in Perai), Tri-M (Singapore-owned in Perai); base plates from MMI (Singapore-owned in Perai, also supplying voice coil motors) and CAM (Singapore-owned in Perai); and other metal parts from Leksun (at Sungai Petani in Kedah, Malaysia). Interview, former Conner managing director, October 1997.

22. Interview, former Conner manager, November 24, 1999. Seagate's purchase of Control Data's drive operations was designed to plug a key technological hole in heads technology, and its head operations in Penang subsequently evolved into the largest heads operation in the world. But until Seagate again exploited its capacity to become a merchant supplier in the late 1990s, its slider operations in Penang were wholly dedicated to Seagate and therefore linked to HGA and HSA operations in Thailand; the facility had no local customers.

23. Interviews, Seagate managers, June 12, 1999; September 24, 1999.

24. Hewlett-Packard was reluctant to sell the entire operation because it feared that associated staff would leave with the product.

25. Interview, Hewlett-Packard manager, June 25, 1997.

26. Interview, Quantum, June 26, 1997.

27. Interviews, Applied Magnetics, June and October 1997.

28. Interview, Seagate manager, January 16, 1997.

29. Interview, Xolox managing director, September 22, 1997.

30. Interview, PDC official, June 23, 1997.

31. Interview, Komag managing director, June 24, 1997.

32. President and chief executive officer of Komag ("Komag Announces Restructuring," August 20, 1997).

33. Employment in these enterprises tends to be substantially smaller than in the suppliers engaged in high-volume production, but the number of engineers is much higher. For example, in 1997, Excel Precision had ninety employees, eleven of which were engineers; and LKT Precision had seventy employees, with ten to fifteen categorized as engineers. Many of the engineers at both companies started working for multinationals. Interviews, Excel Precision managing director, August 1, 1997; LKT Precision general manager, August 4, 1997.

34. Akhashic was sold less than a year later to StorMedia and renamed Strates, for the production of substrates. It closed during the second half of 1998.

35. The PDC initiated the draft plan in October 1990 and reviewed it in December.

36. Among the infrastructure bottlenecks that lingered into the 1990s were power supply (which resulted in a series of brownouts and the infamous 1995 power crisis, when Penang Island suffered power rationing for ten days due to a breakdown in the supply coming over the Penang Bridge), impending water shortages (more than 70 percent of Penang's water supply comes from Kedah, and competing demands for water need to be addressed), and facilities to deal with the industry's toxic wastes.

37. See, for example, PDC (1998).

38. Interview, PDC official, June 1997.

CHAPTER 10   POLICY, POLITICS, AND LOCATION
             IN DEVELOPING COUNTRIES

1. Most of these writings consider the region's growth before the 1997 financial crisis. For the noninterventionist position, see Krueger (1995). In support of sectoral interventions, see Chang (1999). For political economy perspectives on the crisis, see Pempel (1999) and Haggard (2000).

2. This is similar to what Peter Evans (1995: 80–81) calls "midwifery" and "husbandry." The former refers to state efforts at stimulating private firms to take the plunge into a new sector; the latter involves efforts to prod firms into more challenging areas of an existing sector. Both can refer to policies aimed at foreign as well as local firms, and both are distinguished from what Evans calls a "demiurge" model in which the state is involved directly in production.

3. The new institutional economics literature is not very helpful at specifying organizational characteristics since it tends to distinguish institutions from

organizations and assume that any organizational involvement in specific sectors will lead to rent seeking, thus implying that organizational (especially government) failure is worse than market failure. For criticisms along this line, see Doner and Schneider (2000).

4. On the benefits of such networks, see World Bank (1993) and the papers presented at the World Bank's meeting on "Business-Government Consultative Mechanisms in Market-Oriented Reforms," Washington, D.C., January 31, 2000.

5. For discussions of business associations and development, see Haggard et al. (1997) and Doner and Schneider (2000).

6. On social capital, see Putnam (1993). On Chineseness, see Lim and Gosling (1983) and Hefner (1998). On the irrelevance of Confucianism for economic growth, see Morawetz (1980).

7. On the different kinds of market success among ethnic Chinese within Malaysia, see Rasiah (forthcoming).

8. Cutting across these labor market, trade, and investment incentives is the significance of macroeconomic policy. All of the foregoing advantages can be undermined by high inflation or exchange rate instability. Uncertainty regarding future costs discourages investors in an industry that requires significant capital costs and long-term planning. On the costs and benefits of such incentives, see Moran (1998).

9. For a useful review of investment policies in Southeast Asia, see Felker and Jomo (1999).

10. This discussion draws extensively on Tecson (1999).

11. American-owned Sunward Technologies began assembly and test of heads in 1988, and Tsukiden Electronics Industries began assembly and subcomponent production for NEC Technologies Hong Kong that same year.

12. The FIA liberalized existing regulations by allowing foreign equity participation up to 100 percent in all investment areas (outside of a small foreign investment negative list) so long as the enterprise was exporting at least 60 percent of output.

13. Only a few American firms also entered the Philippines (see figures 6.2 and 6.3).

14. Suppliers included Nidec Philippines, Luzon Electronics Technology (a wholly owned subsidiary of Hitachi Metals engaged in slider assembly and HGA), Tsukuba Philippine Die-Casting (aluminum base plates), San Technology (voice-coil assemblies, HGA, and HSA), Mette (base plates and covers), Sunpino (flexible circuits), and Precision Technology (spacer rings).

15. The firms were Microlab with a license from Ampex, Elebra using Control Data technology, and Multidigit based on Pertec technology (Hansen 1990, Tigre 1983).

16. In 1986, the computer regulatory agency, the Special Informatics Secretariat, allowed two local HDD companies to import 1,800 drives because of inadequate local production ("Brazil to Import," August 26, 1986).

17. Much of this discussion is based on Noble (2000).

18. A few local producers of traditional electronics attempted to serve as contract assemblers for U.S. disk drive producers, and a startup firm

founded by Silicon Valley returnees began hard disk production in the mid-1980s.

19. ITRI specialized in reverse engineering of the latest foreign products, technology transfer to local firms, organization of R&D consortia, and provision of engineering services but left manufacturing in private hands. By the early 1990s, ITRI's staff numbered more than 6,000, including more than 500 people with doctorates and 2,100 people with masters' degrees (Noble 2000).

20. Two were returnees from the United States, three were locals linked to ITRI, and one was a "pure" foreign investor (from the United States) without prior ties to Taiwan.

21. For example, the most technologically advanced firm, Zentek, began operations with both extensive technical support from ITRI and a strategic alliance with a U.S. design house that promised to buy 50,000 units in the first two years, with Zentek free to market the rest on its own. Zentek's strategy involved low-volume, low-cost manufacturing; and by 1992, the firm boasted that its break-even point of only 2,400 units per month was lower than its American competitors. But Zentek proved unable to meet the industry's grueling product cycles, and both it and other Taiwan producers opted to "cut costs and limit risks by waiting until the next generation of equipment stabilized technically and reached a reasonable price. But by delaying production Taiwan's producers missed out on the most lucrative part of the product cycle" (Noble 2000: 16).

22. These producers included TDK in heads and Mitsubishi Electric and Shinno in spindle motors.

23. This involved attracting investments from UPS, FedEx, and other shipping companies in twenty-four-hour transshipment facilities by upgrading Taiwan's transportation infrastructure and revising its customs procedures, tax laws, and regulation on foreign investments.

24. Singapore's modest efforts at direct involvement support this conclusion. To encourage the introduction of new technology, the government took (but eventually abandoned) ownership shares in several disk drive producers. It acquired all of Micropolis and took equity positions in Rodime and Prairie-Tek, all three of which made drives in Singapore. Micropolis failed soon after the government acquired it; it is unclear how long the government owned shares in the other two before they failed.

25. Note, however, that the government intervenes through state-owned enterprises in a number of sectors. We return to this point.

26. Its management board is led by National University of Singapore faculty, although its chairman is an employee of Hewlett-Packard. The board also includes Singapore-based employees of Mitsubishi and IBM. In addition, the DSI has an international advisory panel that includes American-based technical managers or researchers from Seagate, Maxtor, IBM, and Read-Rite.

27. Two recent cases illustrate these institutional capacities. One concerns industry-specific human resource development: a series of technician-level training courses begun in Singapore in 1999 and leading to a Certificate in Storage Technology. IDEMA, the disk drive industry association, initiated the course. The association's Singapore representative owned a training company, had experience in the electronics industry, and was tied to both government officials and

Singapore's National Trade Union Congress. With backing from both the government and the union (which saw this as an opportunity to address problems of redundant workers), IDEMA's Singapore office was able to draw on foreign disk drive companies for curriculum materials and a local university for instructors (interviews with IDEMA officials, Santa Clara, California, April 1999; Bangkok, July 1999).

A second illustration shows the movement toward commercial collaboration between the Singapore DSI and a Japanese firm in laser cleaning of magnetic head sliders. Until now, cleaning with water has been expensive and difficult. In response to this problem, DSI's Laser Microprocessing Group began working on an alternative, laser-based process in conjunction with foreign firms and engineers. These efforts resulted in the establishment of a commercial spin-off company called LaserResearch that has developed a laser tagging machine for single-sided media. As of the spring of 2000, the DSI, together with Laser-Research and a Japanese firm, have begun to market this technology to U.S. head producers (personal communications with an official from the DSI's Laser Microprocessing Group and a Read-Rite official, April 5, 2000).

28. A partial exception to this pattern occurred during the 1980s when, confronted with a debt crisis and the need to expand manufactured exports, several government officials promoted the growth of a Joint Public–Private Sector Coordinating Committee. The committee has operated only sporadically since then (see Anek 1991).

29. In 1999, the board's secretary general complained that it was unable to reject applications for promotional privileges even in sectors facing overcapacity problems due to the influence of domestic investors (Felker and Jomo 1999: 12). See also the discussion of auto-related investments in Doner (1991).

30. Despite importance of disk drives in Thailand's exports, few (if any) members of the Thai government were aware of Singapore's IDEMA-sponsored training program after the course had been in operation for several months—another illustration of Thailand's weakness in the industry (interviews, Bangkok, July 1999). Since then, an IDEMA-sponsored training initiative has been launched but has received little government support or coordination. Instead, the government is considering financial support for a $1 billion wafer fabrication plant ("State Urged," January 31, 2000).

31. This review draws heavily on Felker and Jomo (1999), Felker (1998a), and Felker (n.d.).

32. This discussion draws largely on Felker (n.d.). For a historical perspective, see Bowie and Doner (1988).

33. See Rasiah (1994: 279–98; and forthcoming).

34. But this policy also increased the state's reliance on the chaebol. Economically, the groups' very size meant that failure would force the government into an expensive role as lender of last resort. Political pressures for democratic opening meant that successive governments faced "increasing demands for political funds that could only be supplied by the rapidly expanding chaebol" (Fields 1997: 128).

35. Many of these points are consistent with recent work by Moran (2000).

36. See also Biggs and Levy (1991).

37. There is a danger that sector-specific measures, such as Singapore's promotion of industrial clusters, will be criticized as incompatible with World Trade Organization rules on domestic and export subsidies. Singapore's response to this criticism merits citation: "While Singapore fully subscribed to the free market mechanism, the Government had never hesitated to exercise its responsibility especially in areas beyond the scope of the private sector. The Government worked closely with the private sector to promote economic development, although finding the right balance had evolved over time" (WTO 1996: 16).

CHAPTER 11   GLOBALIZATION AND INDUSTRIAL LEADERSHIP

1. Although we make no predictions about whether market-seeking investments create clustering, the larger the market, the more likely is it to attract multiple firms. If the industry has a long value chain involving a number of suppliers, however, then a large market may engender agglomeration economies as proximate suppliers achieve economies of scale.

2. Buying groups include firms that vary along two dimensions: whether they are specialists or generalists and whether they are low-cost volume producers or make fewer high-value products. Buying groups thus range from high-value specialist firms such as Gucci, to high-value generalists such as Saks, to high-volume specialists such as The Gap or Benetton, to high-volume generalists such as Wal-Mart (Gereffi 1994; Gereffi and Tan 1998: 32).

3. The supply chain consists of apparel design, marker making (the silhouette for each individual pattern piece of the garment), fabric purchase, fabric spreading, fabric cutting, and actual sewing. See Abernathy et al. (1999, chaps. 8 and 9). Technological change within the industry has occurred largely in upstream textiles and preassembly operations (such as design, marker making, and cutting) rather than in sewing, which remains labor intensive.

4. During the late 1980s, firms such as Liz Claiborne planned their collections with their East Asian packagers at least six months in advance (Mytelka 1991: 129). By the late 1990s, things had changed substantially. For example, during a 1998 meeting, Thai garment and textile producers were told by two leading Hong Kong garment packagers (TAL and Li & Fung) that a polo shirt costing US$28 five to eight years ago could now be purchased for less than $20. Making a profit at this price required sharp cuts in the lead time from order to delivery, often down to six weeks. Inventory had to be reduced from five to six months to six to eight weeks, and non–value-added products had to be dropped. In addition, orders tend to be much smaller. Even with a large volume order, the buyer typically wants a smaller initial delivery to ensure quality ("Textile Exporters," May 28, 1999; interview, Thai Garment Manufacturers' Association, July 30, 1999).

5. An indicator of this shift is the decline in the big four's share of U.S. apparel imports from 38 percent in 1991 to 16 percent in 1997. Mexico alone has increased its share of U.S. imports from 4 to 11 percent during the same period, and the Caribbean Basin Initiative countries have expanded their share to almost 16 percent (Abernathy et al. 1999: 233–34).

6. For example, foreign buyers informed Thai garment producers that meeting new price, quality, and delivery goals would require an improved supply chain strategy involving better coordination with upstream suppliers within the country itself rather than relocating plants from market to market ("Textile Exporters," May 28, 1999; interview, Thai Garment Manufacturers' Association, July 30, 1999). Meeting the new goals also requires the employment of new technologies and management practices and thus more extensive training (Gereffi and Tam 1998, Suphat 1998).

7. By 1920, Ford was assembling cars in twenty countries, while GM made cars in fifteen countries by 1928; Chrysler's first investment abroad came later, in 1927 (Maxcy 1981). Although the U.S. auto industry was the world leader before it invested abroad, globalization extended its advantage: in 1929 it accounted for a remarkable 84 percent of world production.

8. Automakers either added innovations such as new electronics to existing system designs or, in many developing country models, simply omitted the new technologies altogether ("The Future," 1994: 117).

9. U.S. auto assemblers combined exports of high value-to-weight parts to assembly plants in developing countries with local procurement of bulkier items (such as fuel tanks, body stampings, and radiators) and more labor-intensive subassemblies such as wire harnesses (Altshuler et al. 1984; O'hUallachain and Wasserman 1999: 24). By contrast, Japanese production in Southeast Asia was characterized by tighter assembler-supplier ties (Womack et al. 1990; Doner 1993: 178–81).

10. In fact, this is a variation on the "world car" strategy initiated by Ford in the 1970s and an extension of a strategy already implemented in Europe and North America.

11. For example, Japanese car makers have used Thailand as a base since the 1980s, control 90 percent of Thailand's 220,000-car annual market, and are in the best position to exploit the regional market of 450 million people once intraregional tariffs fall below 5 percent after 2002. But General Motors and Ford are attempting to challenge Japanese dominance in Southeast Asia by investing in Thailand's Rayong province and bringing fifty suppliers; Thailand's large domestic market and its central location within the region make large-scale manufacturing economically viable. Both companies are even using Thailand to export cars and trucks to Europe, Australia, and South America ("Southeast Asia's," May 8, 2000).

12. The market for integrated circuits (ICs) can be divided into separate markets for digital and analog devices, with digital ICs accounting for more than 80 percent of worldwide sales (Linear Technology 1999). Linear and mixed-signal integrated circuits are commonly referred to as analog circuits. Analog signals represent real world phenomena, such as temperature, pressure, sound, or speed, and are continuously variable over a wide range of values. Digital signals represent the "ones" and "zeros" of binary arithmetic and are either on or off. Three general classes of semiconductor products arise from this partitioning of signals into linear or digital. Memories and microprocessors operate only in the digital domain. There are linear devices such as amplifiers, references, analog multiplexers, and switches that operate primarily in the ana-

log domain. Finally, there are mixed-signal devices that combine linear and digital functions on the same integrated circuit and interface between the analog and digital worlds.

Compared to the analog integrated circuit market, the digital market has generally been characterized by a narrower range of standard products used in larger quantities by somewhat fewer customers; shorter product cycles; more competition from foreign manufacturers; higher capital requirements for the purchase of new manufacturing technologies (historically, wafer fabrication of analog integrated circuits has not required the state-of-the-art processing equipment necessary for the fabrication of advanced digital integrated circuits); and relatively volatile growth rates that are more influenced by economic cycles.

13. Fabrication involves depositing layers of metal interconnects onto the wafer and patterning them using customized photo masks. Wafers are then tested, cut into die, and sorted. Die that pass initial tests are then sent to the assembly process where the fabricated circuits are encapsulated into ceramic or plastic packages. The finished devices undergo additional testing and quality assurance before shipment.

14. Several producers developed wafer fabs in Europe as a way of gaining entry into the protected European market (Henderson 1989: 45). For example, Texas Instruments' first overseas fab investment was in Britain in 1957; and when Motorola first moved overseas in 1966, it went to France. Japan, by contrast, actively resisted American foreign direct investment. Most U.S. firms could only tap the Japanese market through export or licensing to Japanese firms, which contributed to the development of the Japanese semiconductor industry.

15. It is important to recognize the problem of the counterfactual. The aggressive use of offshore assembly and test may have at least partly offset other competitive failings of American firms, even if they did not fare well overall; declining competitiveness does not, of itself, indicate that location was completely inconsequential.

16. Leachman and Leachman (1999) measure capacity in terms of quadrillions of functions per month and say the shares of capacity in Japan, North America, and Asia outside Japan are each 310–40 quadrillion functions per month, with Europe accounting for 150 quadrillion.

17. Smaller semiconductor firms also maintain production at home. Maxim Integrated manufactures more than 95 percent of its wafer production requirements in its San Jose, California, and Beaverton, Oregon, plants. Linear Technology's wafer fabrication and manufacturing facilities are located at its headquarters in Milpitas, California, and at its wafer fabrication plant in Camas, Washington. LSI Logic makes almost all of its wafers in Gresham, Oregon; Tsukuba, Japan; and Colorado Springs, Colorado. Even companies that outsource often maintain some home-based production capacity.

18. Of course, some analysts believe that the entire concept of national competitiveness is suspect (see particularly Krugman 1994). The Olympian indifference of economists, of course, contrasts sharply with the job that managers do on a daily basis

19. Although its results are not yet widespread, U.S. industry collaboration has recently grown in precompetitive research undertaken through the

National Storage Industry Consortium. The same has been true in Japan (see chapter 4).

APPENDIX A   INDUSTRY ORIGINS AND
              TECHNOLOGICAL EVOLUTION

1. This statement requires qualification. Wafer fabrication and some of the test tools are from the semiconductor industry. But the closer one gets to the finished recording head, the more specific to the HDD industry are the tooling and technology.

2. The most complete descriptions of IBM's technological developments in data storage, including the personalities involved, appear in Bashe et al. (1986) and Pugh et al. (1991).

3. This was equivalent to 50,000 punched cards. In the RAMAC, a head reading from or writing to one disk was removed horizontally from over the disk, shifted up or down vertically to another disk, and then thrust horizontally across it to the proper location.

4. Talk delivered to the One Hundredth Anniversary Conference for Magnetic Recording and Information Storage, Santa Clara University, Santa Clara, California, December 1998.

5. Harker et al. (1981) provide a useful technical overview of innovations in disk drives, heads, disks, and drive electronics.

6. Above ten gigabits per square inch, however, MR heads do not work, and GMR technology displaces them. A GMR head is like a very sensitive MR head, although GMR exploits a fundamentally different effect from MR technology. The property of electrons moving in the metal is different, leading to higher sensitivity, the detection of smaller bits, and dramatically higher areal densities. In April 2000, Read-Rite announced a record areal density of fifty gigabits per square inch using GMR heads

7. In some drives, the head was mounted on a cartridge that slid on rails. Others used a head mounted on a lead screw, and still others used a cam-actuated head movement or employed a flexible metal band to move the heads.

8. Refer to Stevens (1999) and Harker et al. (1981).

9. Actuator materials have also changed. Many observers think the performance of aluminum actuators has reached its mechanical limit and that a new actuator material must be introduced. Companies engaged in advanced metallurgy are working with new alloys such as beryllium-aluminum.

10. For example, companies are trying to integrate the partial response maximum likelihood (PRML) read channel with the disk controller and a core processor, which would mean delivering a nearly complete electronics system for hard disk drives (before adding the preamp, motor drivers, and buffer memory).

APPENDIX B   AN INNOVATOR'S DILEMMA?

1. Christensen omits from consideration the captive disk drive manufacturers, which we do not. They have been a central and powerful direct and indirect competitor to the independent drive makers throughout the industry's history. And, as we have noted, all of the surviving captive makers have significant OEM business except for Toshiba.

2. Note that Christensen acknowledges that both 14-inch disk pack drives and 14-inch Winchester drives were serving the same mainframe computer customers (Christensen and Rosenbloom 1995: 252), so the *technological* distinction between them should not matter for his theory.

3. The incumbents were IBM, BASF (which had made 14-inch drives under license from Century Data Systems), Shugart Associates, Hokushin Electric Works (Japan), Data Recording Equipment (England), Priam, Memorex, and Fujitsu (Japan). The two new entrants among the first ten firms to make an 8-inch drive were International Memories and Micropolis. Two additional new entrants (Hightrack Computer Technik and SLI Industries) fell just shy of ranking in the top ten, as did one incumbent, Hitachi. In addition, there is some uncertainty about when Kennedy Company, an incumbent, entered the 8-inch drive market; the 1980 *Disk/Trend Report* has the company shipping during the first quarter of 1980, but subsequent reports suggest a later shipment date. Similarly, one new entrant, New World Computer, shipped an 8-inch disk drive sometime during 1980, but *Disk/Trend* did not indicate the month or quarter. As a consequence, we do not rank either company among the first ten manufacturers of 8-inch disk drives.

4. This error apparently led him to claim in subsequent research that four of the first six firms to offer 8-inch disk drives were entrants (Christensen and Bower 1996: 205).

References

Abernathy, Fredrick H., John T. Dunlop, Janice H. Hammond, and David Well. 1999. *A Stitch in time: Lean retailing and the tranformation of manufacturing—Lessons from the apparel and textile industries.* New York: Oxford University Press.

Abernathy, William, and Kim Clark. 1985. Innovation: Mapping the winds of creative destruction. *Research Policy* 14, no. 1: 3–22.

Abrahamson, Eric. 1996. Management fashion. *Academy of Management Review* 21 (January): 254–85.

Ahlbrandt, Roger S., Richard J. Fruehan, and Frank Giarratani. 1996. *The renaissance of American steel: Lessons for managers in competitive industries.* New York: Oxford University Press.

Akrasanee, Narongchai, and Somsak Tambunlertchai. 1990. Transition from import substitution to export expansion: The Thai experience. In *Economic development in East and Southeast Asia,* ed. S. Naya and A. Takayama, 104–20. Singapore: ASEAN.

The American company Seagate Technology, a leader in the manufacture of hard disk drives, plans to invest US$20m in its Singapore operations to increase its production and expand its product range. 1986. *Business Times Singapore,* October 10, p. 18.

Americans protest U.S. action toward Singapore. 1988. *Japan Economic Journal,* June 25, p. 16.

Amin, A., and N. Thrift. 1992. Neo-Marshallian nodes in global networks. *International Journal of Urban and Regional Research* 16 (December): 571–87.

Amsden, Alice. 1989. *Asia's next giant: South Korea and late industrialization.* New York: Oxford University Press.

Anderson, Benedict. 1977. Withdrawal symptoms: Social and cultural aspects of the October 6 coup. *Bulletin of Concerned Asian Scholars* 9, no. 3: 13–31.

Anderson, Philip. 1995. Microcomputer manufacturers. In *Organizations in industry: Strategy, structure and selection,* ed. Glenn R. Carroll and Michael T. Hannan, 37–58. New York: Oxford University Press.

Anek Laothamatas. 1991. *Business associations and the new political economy of Thailand: From bureaucratic polity to liberal corporatism.* Boulder, Colo.: Westview.

Angel, David P. 1994. *Restructuring for innovation: The remaking of the U.S. semiconductor industry.* New York: Guilford.

Aoki, Masahiko. 1988. *Information, incentives and bargaining in the Japanese economy.* New York: Cambridge University Press.

———. 1990. Toward an economic model of the Japanese firm. *Journal of Economic Literature* 28 (March): 1–27.

Aoki, Masahiko, and Nathan Rosenberg. 1987. The Japanese firm as an innovating institution. CEPR Discussion Paper 106, Stanford University.

Appold, Stephen. 1995. Agglomeration, interorganizational networks, and competitive performance in the U.S. metalworking sector. *Economic Geography* 71, no. 1: 27–54.

Arita, Tomokazu. 1996. Interactions between the spatial organization of firms and regional industrial systems: Semiconductor industries in the U.S. and Japan. Ph.D. diss., University of Pennsylvania.

Armour, H. O., and D. J. Teece. 1978. Organizational structure and economic performance: A test of the M-form hypothesis. *Bell Journal of Economics* 9 (Spring): 196–222.

Arthur, W. Brian. 1986. Industry location and the importance of history. Center for Economic Policy Research Paper 84, Stanford University. Reprinted in Arthur, W. Brian. 1994. *Increasing returns and path dependence in the economy,* 49–67. Ann Arbor: University of Michigan Press.

———. 1990. Positive feedback in the economy. *Scientific American* (February): 92–99.

Asia's hard drive for an even bigger role. 1994. *Business Times Singapore,* March 18, p. 13.

Audretsch, David B., and Maryann P. Feldman. 1996. R & D spillovers and the geography of innovation and production. *American Economic Review* 86 (June): 630–40.

Balassa, Bela. 1989. *Comparative advantage, trade policy, and economic development.* New York: New York University Press.

Bardai, Barjoyai. 1993. *Malaysian tax policy: Applied general equilibrium analysis.* Petaling Jaya, Selangor Darul Ehsan, Malaysia: Pelanduk.

Barnett, William P., and Morten Hansen. 1996. The Red Queen in organizational evolution. *Strategic Management Journal* 17 (Summer): 139–57.

Barnett, William P., and David G. McKendrick. 1998. The evolution of global competition in the hard disk drive industry. Paper presented at the Academy of Management Meetings, San Diego, August.

Bartlett, Christopher A., and Sumantra Ghoshal. 1989. *Managing across borders.* Boston: Harvard Business School Press.

Bashe, Charles, Lyle Johnson, John Palmer, and Emerson Pugh. 1986. *IBM's early computers.* Cambridge, Mass.: MIT Press.

Baum, Joel A. C., and Heather A. Haveman. 1997. Love thy neighbor? Differentiation and agglomeration in the Manhattan hotel industry, 1898–1990. *Administrative Science Quarterly* 42, no. 2: 304–38.

Belis-Bergouignan, Marie-Claude, Gerard Bordenave, and Yannick Lung. 1996. Global strategies in the automobile industry. *Regional Studies,* 34, no. 1:41–53.

Belussi, Fiorenza. 1997. Dwarfs and giants maintaining competitive edge: The Italian textile clothing industry in the 1990s. In *Rethinking Global Production: A Comparative Analysis of Restructuring in the Clothing Industry,* ed. Ian M. Taplin and Jonathan Winterton, 77–130. Brookfield, Vt.: Ashgate.

Bennett, Douglas C., and Kenneth Sharpe. 1985. *Transnational corporations versus the state.* Princeton, N.J.: Princeton University Press.

Best, Michael. 1990. *The new competition: Institutions of industrial restructuring.* Cambridge, Mass.: Harvard University Press.

Bigelow, Lyda S., Glenn R. Carroll, Marc-David Seidel, and Lucia Tsai. 1997. Legitimation, geographic scale, and organizational density: Regional patterns of foundings of American automobile producers, 1885–1981. *Social Science Research* 26 (December): 377–98.

Biggs, Tyler S., and Brian D. Levy. 1991. Strategic interventions and the political economy of industrial policy in developing countries. In *Reforming economic systems in developing countries,* ed. Dwight H. Perkins and Michael Roemer, 364–91. Cambridge, Mass.: Harvard University Press.

Bowie, Alasdair, and Richard Doner. 1988. Business associations in Malaysia: Communalism and nationalism in organizational growth. Paper presented at the annual meeting of the American Political Science Association, Washington, D.C., September 1–4.

Brass, D. J. 1992. Power in organizations: A social network approach. In *Research in politics and society,* ed. G. Moore and J. A. Whitt, 4: 295–323. Greenwich, Conn.: JAI.

Brazil or bust: The great computer race. 1991. *Business Week,* November 11, p. 162H.

Brazil to import disk drives. 1986. *Journal of Commerce,* August 26, p. 5A.

Brimble, Peter, and Chatri Sripaipan. 1994. Science and technology issues in Thailand's industrial sector: The key to the future. Bangkok, June. Mimeo.

Brooker Group. 1997. BoI investment vision support document. Bangkok, August 25.

Buckley, Peter J., and Mark C. Casson. 1976. *The future of the multinational enterprise.* London: Macmillan.

———. 1998. Models of the multinational enterprise. *Journal of International Business Studies* 29, no. 1: 21–44.

Burki, Shahid, and Guillermo Perry. 1998. *Beyond the Washington consensus: Institutions matter.* Washington, D.C.: World Bank.

Burroughs' 1st Canadian disk plant in works. 1975. *Electronic News,* April 14.

Burt, Ronald S. 1992. *Structural holes: The social structure of competition.* Cambridge, Mass.: Harvard University Press.

Business Monitor International. 1995. *Malaysia: Annual report on government, economy, the business environment and industry, with forecasts.* London: Business Monitor International.

———. 1997a. *Philippines: Annual report on government, economy, the business environment and industry, with forecasts.* London: Business Monitor International.

———. 1997b. *Malaysia: Annual report on government, economy, the business environment and industry, with forecasts.* London: Business Monitor International.

———. 1997c. *Thailand: Annual report on government, economy, the business environment and industry, with forecasts.* London: Business Monitor International.

The *Business Times* reports that Syquest Technology, a California company, is set to go ahead with a S$70m project in Singapore to manufacture computer disc drives. 1984. *Business Times Singapore,* March 17, p. 7.

Campbell, Dennis, ed. 1985. *Legal aspects of doing business in Asia and the Pacific.* St. Paul, Minn.: West.

Carroll, Glenn R., and Michael T. Hannan. 2000. *The demography of corporations and industries.* Princeton, N.J.: Princeton University Press.

Carroll, Glenn R., and James B. Wade. 1991. Density dependence in the organizational evolution of the American brewing industry across levels of analysis. *Social Science Research* 20 (September): 271–302.

Caves, Robert E. 1996. *Multinational enterprise and economic analysis.* Cambridge: Cambridge University Press.

CDC aiming disk drive, drum at OEM mini market. 1974. *Electronic News,* March 25, p. 65.

Chackchai Panichapat. 1999. *Hard disk drive industry in Thailand.* Bangkok: Thailand Board of Investment.

Chandler, Alfred. 1990. *Scale and scope: The dynamics of industrial capitalism.* Cambridge, Mass.: Belknap Press of Harvard University Press.

Chang, Ha-Joon. 1999. The economic theory of the developmental state. In *The developmental state,* ed. Meredith Woo-Cumings, 182–99. Ithaca, N.Y.: Cornell University Press.

The checkered past of Computer Memories. 1988. *Computerworld,* October 31, p. 91.

Chenery, Hollis. 1979. *Structural change and development policy.* Oxford: Oxford University Press.

Cheng, Tun-jen. 1993. Guarding the commanding heights: The state as banker in Taiwan. In *The politics of finance in developing countries,* ed. Stephan Haggard, Chung Lee, and Sylvia Maxfield, 55–92. Ithaca, N.Y.: Cornell University Press.

Christensen, Clayton M. 1992. The innovator's challenge: Understanding the influence of market demand on processes of technology development in the rigid disk drive industry. DBA diss., Harvard University, Graduate School of Business Administration.

———. 1997. *The innovator's dilemma: When new technologies cause great firms to fail.* Cambridge, Mass.: Harvard Business School Press.

Christensen, Clayton M., and Joseph L. Bower. 1996. Customer power, strategic investment, and the failure of leading firms. *Strategic Management Journal* 17 (March): 197–218.

Christensen, Clayton M., and Richard S. Rosenbloom. 1995. Explaining the attacker's advantage: Technological paradigms, organizational dynamics, and the value network. *Research Policy* 24 (March): 147–62.

Chu, Yun-han. 1994. The realignment of business-government relations and regime transition in Taiwan. In *Business and government in industrializing Asia,* ed. Andrew MacIntyre, 113–41. Ithaca, N.Y.: Cornell University Press.

Clague, Christopher, ed. 1997. *Institutions and economic development.* Baltimore: Johns Hopkins University Press.

Concrete plans. 1999. *Far Eastern Economic Review,* March 25, p. 28.

Conner Peripherals could become the fastest growing U.S. company because of its customized approach to disk drive design. 1990. *Los Angeles Times,* May 1, sec. D2, p. 15.

Conner's disk media unit to spend up to $180m on S'pore plant. 1995. *Business Times Singapore,* August 8, p. 2.

Conner to build plant in Malaysia. 1990. *Southeast Asia High Tech Review,* August.

Conner to mass produce new disk drives here. 1993. *Straits Times,* January 29, p. 34.

Control Data announces addition of assembly and test facility. 1988. *PR Newswire,* May 13.

Control Data cashes in on a captive operation. 1988. *Electronic Business,* April 15, p. 120.

Control Data to begin 5 1/4-inch disk drive. 1987. *PR Newswire,* June 17.

Cringely, Robert X. 1996. *Accidental empires.* New York: HarperBusiness.

Davidson, William H. 1980. The location of foreign direct investment activity: Country characteristics and experience effects. *Journal of International Business Studies* 11, no. 1: 9–22.

Deal may be worth $40 million; CCT agrees to acquire Santa Barbara firm. 1987. *Los Angeles Times,* August 25, p. 2B.

Department of Industrial Promotion. 1998. *Study on computer and parts industry: Status, trend, technology and potential.* Bangkok: Ministry of Industry.

Dertouzos, Michael L., Richard K. Lester, and Robert M. Solow. 1989. *Made in America: Regaining the productive edge.* Cambridge, Mass.: MIT Press.

Dicken, Peter. 1998. *Global shift: Transforming the world economy.* New York: Guilford.

DiMaggio, Paul, and Walter W. Powell. 1983. The iron cage revisited: Institutional isomorphism and collective rationality in organizational fields. *American Sociological Review* 48 (April): 147–60.

———, eds. 1991. *The new institutionalism in organizational analysis.* Chicago: University of Chicago Press.

Disc Syst. div. merges into STC. 1974. *Electronic News,* December 12, p. 8.

Disk/Trend report: Rigid disk drives. Various years. Mountain View, Calif.: Disk/Trend.

Doner, Richard F. 1991. *Driving a bargain: Automobile industrialization and Japanese firms in Southeast Asia.* Berkeley: University of California Press.

————. 1993. Japanese foreign investment and a Pacific Asian region. In *Regionalism and rivalry: Japan and the United States in Pacific Asia,* ed. Jeffry A. Frankel and Miles Kahler, 159–216. Chicago: University of Chicago Press.

Doner, Richard, and Peter Brimble. 1998. Thailand's hard disk drive industry. Information Storage Industry Center, Report 98-02. San Diego: University of California.

Doner, Richard, and Anek Laothamatas. 1994. Thailand: Economic and political gradualism. In *Voting for reform: Democracy, political liberalization, and economic adjustment,* ed. Stephan Haggard and Steven Webb, 411–52. New York: Oxford University Press.

Doner, Richard, and Ben Schneider. 2000. The new institutional economics, business associations and development. ILO Discussion Paper. Geneva: ILO.

Dore, R. 1983. Goodwill and the spirit of market capitalism. *British Journal of Sociology* 34 (December): 459–82.

Dosi, Giovanni. 1988. Sources, procedures and microeconomic effects of innovation. *Journal of Economic Literature* 26, no. 3: 1120–71.

Drobak, John, and John Nye. 1997. *The frontiers of the new institutional economics.* San Diego: Academic Press.

Dunning, John H. 1971. *The multinational enterprise.* London: Allen and Unwin.

————. 1974. *Economic analysis and the multinational enterprise.* London: Allen and Unwin.

————. 1981. *International production and the multinational enterprise.* London: Allen and Unwin.

————. 1988. *Multinationals, technology, and competitiveness.* London: Allen and Unwin.

————. 1993. *Multinational enterprises and the global economy.* Reading, Mass.: Addison Wesley.

————. 1998. Location and the multinational enterprise: A neglected factor? *Journal of International Business Studies* 29, no. 1: 45–66.

Economic Development Board. Various years. *Census of industrial production.* Singapore: Department of Statistics.

Edstrom, A., and R. Galbraith. 1977. Transfer of managers as a coordination and control strategy in multinational organizations. *Administrative Science Quarterly* 22 (June): 248–63.

Ellinger, Robert. 1977. Industrial location behavior and spatial evolution. *Journal of Industrial Economics* 25, no. 4: 295–312.

Ernst and Young. 1990. *Doing business in Thailand.* New York: Ernst and Young.

————. 1992a. *Doing business in Indonesia.* New York: Ernst and Young.

————. 1992b. *Doing business in Malaysia.* New York: Ernst and Young.

Evans, Peter. 1979. *Dependent development: The alliance of multinational, state, and local capital in Brazil.* Princeton, N.J.: Princeton University Press.

————. 1995. *Embedded autonomy: State and industrial transformation.* Princeton, N.J.: Princeton University Press.

Feldman, Maryann. 1994. *The geography of innovation.* Boston: Kluwer Academic Press.

Felker, Greg Beauchamp. 1998a. Globalization and the state in late industrialization: The Malaysian and Thai cases. Paper presented at the annual meeting of the American Political Science Association, Boston, September 3–6.

———. 1998b. Upwardly global? The state, business and MNCs in Malaysia and Thailand's technological transformation. Ph.D. diss., Princeton University.

———. n.d. Malaysia's innovation system: Actors, interests and governance. Unpublished paper.

Felker, Greg, and Jomo K. S. 1999. New approaches to investment policy in the ASEAN-4. Asian Development Bank, Manila. Draft

Fields, Karl. 1997. Strong states and business organization in Korea and Taiwan. In *Business and the state in developing countries,* ed. Sylvia Maxfield and Ben Ross Schneider, 122–51. Ithaca, N.Y.: Cornell University Press.

A fine Japanese company. 1985. *Forbes,* April 8, p. 39.

Florida, Richard, and Martin Kenney. 1990. *The breakthrough illusion: Corporate America's failure to move from innovation to mass production.* New York: Basic Books.

Freiberger, Paul, and Michael Swaine. 1984. *Fire in the valley.* Berkeley, Calif.: McGraw-Hill.

Frohlich, Norman, and Joe Oppenheimer. 1998. Some consequences of e-mail vs. face-to-face communication in experiment. *Journal of Economic Behavior and Organization* 35, no. 3: 389–403.

Fujitsu execs stress globalization. 1987. *Electronic Buyer's News,* May 18.

Fujitsu ranked the fastest growing hard drive manufacturer. 1997. *Business Wire,* June 17.

Fujitsu will produce small hard disk drives in Thailand starting this summer. 1991. *IDC Japan Report,* February 28, p. 115.

The future of automotive innovation. 1994. *Japanese Motor Business* (2d quarter): 117.

Gereffi, Gary. 1994. The organization of buyer-driven global commodity chains: How U.S. retailers shape overseas production networks. In *Commodity chains and global capitalism,* ed. Gary Gereffi and Miguel Korzeniewicz, 95–122. Westport, Conn.: Greenwood.

Gereffi, Gary, and Tony Tam. 1998. Industrial upgrading through organizational chains: Dynamics of rent, learning-by-doing, and mobility in the global economy. Paper presented to the Social Science Research Council workshop on industrial upgrading, Geneva, October 30.

Gerlach, Michael L. 1992. The Japanese corporate network: A blockmodel analysis. *Administrative Science Quarterly* 37, no. 1: 105–39.

Ghoshal, Sumantra, and Christopher Bartlett. 1990. The multinational corporation as an interorganizational network. *Academy of Management Review* 15 (October): 603–25.

Gilpin, Robert. 1987. *The political economy of international relations.* Princeton, N.J.: Princeton University Press.

Gold, Thomas. 1981. Dependent development in Taiwan. Ph.D. diss., Harvard University.

Goodman, E., and J. Bamford, eds. 1989. *Small firms and industrial districts in Italy.* London: Routledge.

Gosh, B. C. 1996. *Taxation in Southeast Asia: A comparative study.* Singapore: EPB.

Gourevitch, Peter, Roger Bohn, and David McKendrick. 1997. *Who is us? The nationality of production in the hard disk drive industry.* Report 97-01. San Diego: University of California, Information Storage Industry Center.

——. 2000. Globalization of production: Insights from the hard disk drive industry. *World Development* 28, no. 2: 301–17.

Grabher, G., and D. Stark, eds. 1997. *Restructuring networks in postsocialism: Linkages and localities.* Oxford: Oxford University Press.

Gray, Mia, Elyse Golob, and Ann Markusen. 1996. Big firms, long arms, wide shoulders: The "hub-and-spoke" industrial districts in the Seattle region. *Regional Studies* 30, no. 7: 651–66.

Grieco, Joseph. 1984. *Between dependency and autonomy: India's experience with the international computer industry.* Berkeley: University of California Press.

Greve, Henrich R. 1995. Jumping ship: The diffusion of strategy abandonment. *Administrative Science Quarterly* 40, no. 3: 444–73.

——. 1996. Patterns of competition: The diffusion of a market position in radio broadcasting. *Administrative Science Quarterly* 41, no. 1: 29–60.

——. 1998. Managerial cognition and the mimetic adoption of market positions: What you see is what you do. *Strategic Management Journal* 19 (October): 967–88.

Gupta, A., and V. Govindarajan. 1991. Knowledge flows and the structure of control within multinational corporations. *Academy of Management Review* 16, no. 4: 768–92.

Haggard, Stephan. 1990a. *Pathways from the periphery.* Ithaca, N.Y.: Cornell University Press.

——. 1990b. The political economy of the Philippine debt crisis. In *Economic crisis and policy choice,* ed. Joan Nelson, 215–56. Princeton, N.J.: Princeton University Press.

——. 2000. *The political economy of the Asian financial crisis.* Washington, D.C.: Institute for International Economics.

Haggard, Stephan, Lim Pao Li, and Anna Ong. 1998. *The hard disk drive industry in the northern region of Malaysia.* Report 98-04. San Diego: University of California, Information Storage Industry Center.

Haggard, Stephan, Sylvia Maxfield, and Ben Ross Schneider. 1997. Theories of business and business-state relations. In *Business and the state in developing countries,* ed. Sylvia Maxfield and Ben Ross Schneider, 36–60. Ithaca, N.Y.: Cornell University Press.

Hakansson, H., ed. 1987. *Industrial technological development: A network approach.* London: Croom Helm.

Hall, Max, ed. 1959. *Made in New York.* Cambridge, Mass.: Harvard University Press.

Hannan, Michael T., and Glenn R. Carroll. 1992. *Dynamics of organizational populations: Density, legitimation and competition.* New York: Oxford University Press.

Hannan, Michael T., Glenn R. Carroll, Elizabeth A. Dundon, and John C. Torres. 1995. Organizational evolution in multinational context: Entries of automobile manufacturers in Belgium, Britain, France, Germany, and Italy. *American Sociological Review* 60, no. 4: 509–28.

Hannan, Michael T., and John H. Freeman. 1977. The population ecology of organizations. *American Journal of Sociology* 82 (March): 929–64.

———. 1984. Structural inertia and organizational change. *American Sociological Review* 49 (April): 149–64.

———. 1989. *Organization ecology.* Cambridge, Mass.: Harvard University Press.

Hansen, Dean Lee. 1990. Acquiring high-technology capability: The case of the Brazilian informatics industry. Ph.D. diss., University of Washington.

Hard times for hard drives; Seagate Technology's difficulties affect hard disk industry. 1988. *Electronic Business,* November 15, p. 32.

Harker, J. M., D. W. Brede, R. E. Pattison, G. R. Santana, and L. G. Taft. 1981. A quarter century of disk file innovation. *IBM Journal of Research and Development* 25, no. 5: 677–89.

Harrison, Bennett. 1992. Industrial districts: Old wine in new bottles? *Regional Studies* 26, no. 5: 469–83.

———. 1994. *Lean and mean: The changing landscape of corporate power in the age of flexibility.* New York: Basic Books.

Harrison, Bennett, Maryellen R. Kelley, and Jon Gant. 1996. Innovative firm behavior and local milieu: Exploring the intersection of agglomeration, firm effects, and technological change. *Economic Geography* 72, no. 3: 233–58.

Haug, P. 1991. Regional formation of high-technology service industries: The software industry in Washington State. *Environment and Planning* 23, no. 6: 869–84.

Hayter, Roger. 1997. *The dynamics of industrial location: The factory, the firm, and the production system.* New York: Wiley.

Head, C. Keith, John C. Ries, and Deborah L. Swenson. 1995. Agglomeration benefits and location choice: Evidence from Japanese manufacturing investments in the United States. *Journal of International Economics* 38 (May): 223–47.

———. 1999. Attracting foreign manufacturing: Investment promotion and agglomeration. *Regional Science and Urban Economics* 29, no. 2: 197–218.

Hedlund, G. 1986. The hypermodern MNC—A heterarchy? *Human Resources Management* 25, no. 1: 9–25.

———. 1993. Assumptions of hierarchy and heterarchy: An application to the multinational corporation. In *Organization theory and the multinational corporation,* ed. S. Ghoshal and D. E. Westney, 211–36. London: Macmillan.

———. 1994. The model of knowledge management and the N-form corporation. *Strategic Management Journal* 15 (Summer): 73–90.

Hefner, Robert W. 1998. *Market cultures: Society and morality in the new Asian capitalisms.* Boulder, Colo.: Westview.

Henderson, Jeffrey. 1989. *The globalization of high technology production: Society, space and semiconductors in the restructuring of the modern world.* London: Routledge.

Hicken, Allen. 1997. FDI, tax incentives, and hard disk drives. San Diego: University of California, Globalization Project. Mimeo.

Hill, Charles W. L. 1995. National institutional structures, transaction cost economizing and competitive advantage: The case of Japan. *Organization Science* 6 no. 1: 119–31.

Hoffman, Kurt, and Raphael Kaplinsky. 1988. *Driving force: The global restructuring of technology, labor, and investment in the automobile and component industries.* Boulder, Colo.: Westview.

Hollingsworth, J. Rogers, Phillipe C. Schmitter, and Wolfgang Streeck. 1994. *Governing capitalist economies: Performance and control of economic sectors.* New York: Oxford University Press.

Hoover, E. M. 1971. *An introduction to regional economics.* New York: Knopf.

How Conner Peripherals races to market, boosts quality; sells products first, designs them later. 1990. *Electronic Business,* May 14, p. 79.

Hoya of Japan invests US$30m in disk drive component plant. 1995. *Business Times Singapore,* June 15, p. 2.

Hoya to produce hard disks in Singapore. 1995. *Jiji Press,* June 14.

HP Boise knows business as usual won't work anymore. 1996. *Idaho Statesman,* April 30, p. 1A.

Hu, Yao-Su. 1995. The international transferability of the firm's advantages. *California Management Review* 37, no. 4: 73–88.

Humphrey, John. 1998. *Assembler-supplier relations in the auto industry: Globalization and national development.* Brighton, England: University of Sussex, Institute of Development Studies.

Hutchcroft, Paul. 1998. *Booty capitalism: The politics of banking in the Philippines.* Ithaca, N.Y.: Cornell University Press.

Ibarra, H. 1993. Network centrality, power, and innovation involvement: Determinants of technical and administrative roles. *Academy of Management Journal* 36: 471–501.

IBM PC AT plan: Source drive on availability. 1985. *Electronic News,* April 29, p. 27.

International Labour Office (ILO). Various issues. *Yearbook of labour statistics.* Geneva: International Labour Office.

Imai, Ken-Ichi, Ikujiro Nonaka, and Hirotaka Takeuchi. 1985. Managing the product development process: How Japanese companies learn and unlearn. In *The uneasy alliance: Managing the productivity-technology dilemma,* ed. Kim B. Clark, Robert H. Hayes, and Christopher Lorenz, 337–76. Boston: Harvard Business School Press.

Industry: Electronics institute planned. 1997. *Bangkok Post,* August 4, p. 12.

Integral Peripherals signs lease for Singapore facility. 1992. *Business Wire,* January 10.

Integral Peripherals to make world's smallest disk drive here. 1991. *Business Times Singapore,* August 26.

International Disk Drive Equipment and Materials Association (IDEMA). 1999. *Ingenuity and technology powering today's disk drives.* Santa Clara, Calif. Pamphlet.

Investment surges in Singapore despite levying of US duties. 1988. *Journal of Commerce,* February 24.

Jaffe, Adam B., Manuel Trajtenberg, and Rebecca Henderson. 1993. Geographic localization of knowledge spillovers as evidenced by patent citations. *Quarterly Journal of Economics* 63 (August): 577–98.

Japanese bearing maker Minebea steps up R&D. 1997. *Asia Pulse,* October 13.

Japan's carmakers: Reengineering new model programs. 1995. *Japanese Motor Business* (2d quarter): 100–110.

Japan's Showa Aluminium to invest 107 million dollars in Malaysia. 1998. *Agence France Press,* February 11.

Johnson, Chalmers. 1982. *MITI and the Japanese Miracle.* Stanford, Calif.: Stanford University Press.

Kaplan, David. 1999. *The Silicon boys and their valley of dreams.* New York: Morrow.

Kenney, Martin, ed. 2000. *Anatomy of Silicon Valley: Understanding an entrepreneurial region.* Stanford, Calif.: Stanford University Press.

Kildruff, Martin, and David Krackhardt. 1994. Bringing the individual back in: A structural analysis of the internal market for reputation in organizations. *Academy of Management Journal* 37, no. 1: 87–108.

Kindleberger, Charles. 1964. *Economic growth in France and Britain, 1851–1950.* Cambridge, Mass.: Harvard University Press.

Klepper, Steven. 1996. Entry, exit, growth, and innovation over the product life cycle. *American Economic Review* 86: 562–83.

———. 1997. Industry life cycles. *Industrial and Corporate Change* 6, no. 1: 145–81.

Klimenko, Mikhail. 1998. Competition, search, and agglomeration in high-growth industries. Working paper, European Regional Science Association, August.

Kogut, Bruce. 1983. Foreign direct investment as a sequential process. In *The multinational corporation in the 1980s,* ed. C. P. Kindleberger and D. B. Audretsch, 38–56. Cambridge, Mass.: MIT Press.

———. 1991. Country capabilities and the permeability of borders. *Strategic Management Journal* 12 (Summer): 33–47.

———. 1992. National organizing principles of work and the erstwhile dominance of the American multinational corporation. *Industrial and Corporate Change* 1, no. 2: 285–326.

Kogut, Bruce, and Nalin Kulatilaka. 1994. Operating flexibility, global manufacturing and the options value of a multinational network. *Management Science* 40, no. 1: 123–39.

Kogut, Bruce, and Udo Zander. 1993. Knowledge of the firm and the evolutionary theory of the multinational corporation. *Journal of International Business Studies* 24, 4th quarter: 625–45.

Komag announces restructuring plan; Loss anticipated for third quarter and 1997 fiscal year. 1997. *PR Newswire,* August 20.

Komag enters volume production of next generation disks and demonstrates future technology path. 1999. *PR Newswire,* September 7.

Komag to produce up to 80% in Malaysia by end '98. 1997. *Dow Jones Newswires,* November 27.

Korea: Disk storage devices. 1991. *National Trade Data Bank: Market Reports,* July 19.

Krueger, Anne O. 1995. The role of trade in growth and development: Theory and lessons from experience. In *Sustaining export-oriented development,* ed. Ross Garnaut, Enzo Grilli, and James Riedel, 1–30. New York: Cambridge University Press.

Krugman, Paul. 1991. *Geography and trade.* Cambridge, Mass.: MIT Press.

———. 1993. The current case for industrial policy. In *Protectionism and world welfare,* ed. D. Salvatore, 160–79. Cambridge: Cambridge University Press.

———. 1994. Competitiveness: A dangerous obsession. *Foreign Affairs* 73 (March–April): 28–44.

Kuo, Cheng-tian. 1995. *Global competitiveness and industrial growth in Taiwan and the Philippines.* Pittsburgh: University of Pittsburgh Press.

Kuznets, Simon. 1966. *Modern economic growth.* New Haven, Conn.: Yale University Press.

Labor relations; handful of workers talk about life on the job in '86. 1986. *Los Angeles Times,* September 1, part 2, p. 6.

Lall, Sanjaya. 1996. *Learning from the Asian tigers: Studies in technology and industrial policy.* London: Macmillan.

———. 1998. Thailand's manufacturing competitiveness: A preliminary overview. Paper presented at the Conference on Thailand's Dynamic Economic Recovery and Competitiveness, Bangkok, May 20–21.

Landes, David. 1969. *The unbound Prometheus.* Cambridge: Cambridge University Press.

Langlois, Richard N. 1992. External economies and economic progress: The case of the microcomputer industry. *Business History Review* 66 (Spring): 1–50.

Lauridsen, Laurids S. 1999. Policies and institutions of industrial deepening and upgrading in Thailand, II—The supporting industries with particular emphasis on the downstream plastic parts and mould industries. Vol. 10 of *Institutional Frameworks for Industrial Development: Asian Experiences,* ed. Laurids S. Lauridsen and John D. Martinussen. Denmark: University of Riskolde.

Leachman, Robert C., and Chien H. Leachman. 1999. Trends in worldwide semiconductor fabrication capacity. Working Paper 48. Berkeley: University of California, Competitive Semiconductor Manufacturing Program.

Legewie, Jochen. Forthcoming. Driving regional integration: Japanese firms and the development of the ASEAN automobile industry. In *Facing Asia— Japan's role in the political and economic dynamism of regional cooperation,* ed. Verena Blechinger and Jochen Legewie. Munich: Iudicium.

Lim, Linda, and Peter Gosling, ed. 1983. *The Chinese in Southeast Asia.* Vol. 1: *Ethnicity and Economic Activity.* Singapore: Maruzen Asia.

Linear Technology. 1999. Form 10-K for the fiscal year ended June 27, 1999. Washington, D.C.: Securities and Exchange Commission.

Local institute forms storage R&D consortium with four multinationals. 1997. *Business Times Singapore,* August 4, p. 10.

Lomi, Alessandro. 1995. The population ecology of organizational founding: Location dependence and unobserved heterogeneity. *Administrative Science Quarterly* 40 (March): 111–44.

Looking for the Asian edge; low-cost foreign labor helps a U.S. disk-drive maker lead its industry. 1990. *Washington Post,* June 17, p. H1.

Low, Linda, Toh Mun Heng, Soon Teck Wong, Tan Kong Yam, and Helen Hughes. 1993. *Challenge and response: Thirty years of the Economic Development Board.* Singapore: Time Academic Press.

Lundvall, Bengt-Åke. 1988. Innovation as an interactive process. In *Technical change and economic theory,* ed. G. Dosi, C. Freeman, R. Nelson, G. Silverberg, and L. Soete, 349–69. London: Pinter.

———, ed. 1992. *National systems of innovation: Towards a theory of innovation and interactive learning.* London: Pinter.

Luzio, Eduardo. 1996. *The microcomputer industry in Brazil.* Westport, Conn.: Praeger.

Macher, Jeffrey T., David C. Mowery, and David A. Hodges. 1999. Semiconductors. In *U.S. industry in 2000: Studies in competitive performance,* ed. David C. Mowery, 245–85. Washington, D.C.: National Academy Press.

Macpherson, Neill T. 1992. *The South East Asian investment guide.* Hong Kong: Longman.

"Made in Japan" tag penetrating components market; U.S.–Japan pacts create added equipment sales. 1985. *Computerworld,* December 9, p. 64.

Malaysian Industrial Development Authority. 1992. *Malaysia investment in the manufacturing sector: Policies, incentives and procedures.* Kuala Lumpur: Malaysian Industrial Development Authority.

Manasan, Rosario G. 1988. *A review of investment incentives in ASEAN countries.* Makati, Metro Manila: Philippine Institute for Development Studies.

Mansfield, Edwin. 1988. The speed and cost of industrial innovation in Japan and the United States: External vs. internal technology. *Management Science* 34 (October): 1157–68.

Market share moves seen squeezing disk drive margins. 1990. *Chilton's Electronic News,* December 24, p. 1.

Markusen, Ann. 1985. *Profit cycles, oligopoly, and regional development.* Cambridge, Mass.: MIT Press.

———. 1996. Sticky places in slippery space: A typology of industrial districts. *Economic Geography* 72: 293–313.

Marshall, Alfred. [1890] 1920. *Principles of economics* (8th ed.). London: Macmillan.

Martin, Ron. 1999. The new "geographical turn" in economics: Some critical reflections. *Cambridge Journal of Economics* 23 (January): 65–91.

Martin, Scott B. 2000. Globalization of production, supplier relations and convergence theory: German automotive firms in the American south. Paper presented at the annual meeting of the American Sociological Association, Washington, D.C., January 10.

Mathews, John A., and Dong-Sung Cho. 2000. *Tiger technology: The creation of a semiconductor industry in East Asia.* Cambridge: Cambridge University Press.

Maxcy, George. 1981. *The multinational automobile industry.* New York: St. Martin's.

Maxtor Corp.; completes third round financing. 1983. *Business Wire,* November 22.

Maxtor Corporation, the US disc-drive manufacturer, is to invest S$20m on a factory and machinery in Singapore. 1984. *Business Times Singapore,* April 3, p. 1.

Maxtor Corp. will produce a track-following, closed-loop servo disc drive in Singapore. 1983. *United Press International,* June 20.

Maxtor to open new manufacturing plant in Penang, Malaysia. 1988. *PR Newswire,* April 6.

McKendrick, David. 1997. Sustaining competitive advantage in global industries: Technological change and foreign assembly in the hard disk drive industry. Report 97-06. San Diego: University of California, Information Storage Industry Center.

———. 1998. Dispersed concentration: Industry location and globalization in hard disk drives. Report 98-03. San Diego: University of California, Information Storage Industry Center.

———. 1999. Hard disk drives. In *U.S. industry in 2000: Studies in competitive performance,* ed. David Mowery, 287–328. Washington, D.C.: National Academy Press.

McKendrick, David, and Allen Hicken. 1997. Global strategy and population level learning in the hard disk drive industry. Report 97-05. San Diego: University of California, Information Storage Industry Center.

Microcomputer Memories, Inc. IPO. 1984. *PR Newswire,* January 19.

Micropolis Corp. of the US is to invest S$10M at its Ang Mo Kio factory in Singapore. 1986. *Business Times Singapore,* March 20.

MiniScribe, others answer Singapore call. 1987. *Denver Business Journal,* July 13, p. 10.

Miniscribe's Far East secret. 1989. *Electronic Business,* March 6, p. 88.

Ministry of Finance. 1997/98. *Economic report.* Penang: Ministry of Finance.

Ministry of Trade and Industry (MTI). 1991. *The strategic economic plan: Towards a developed nation.* Singapore: Government Printers.

Mody, Ashoka. 1998. Industrial policy after the East Asian crisis: From "outward-orientation" to new internal capabilities? Unpublished manuscript.

Monroe, John. 1999. Mercurial markets, unprecedented change: Transforming the wastelands of excess inventory. Paper presented at a meeting of IDEMA, Santa Clara, Calif., May 5.

Monson, James E. 1999. Capturing data magnetically. In *Magnetic Recording: The first 100 years,* ed. Eric Daniels, C. Denis Mee, and Mark H. Clark, 221–36. New York: IEEE Press.

Moran, Theodore H. 1998. *Foreign direct investment and development: The new policy agenda for developing countries and economies in transition.* Washington, D.C.: Institute for International Economics.

————. 2000. A new paradigm: Foreign direct investment and development. Unpublished manuscript.

Morawetz, David. 1980. *Why the emperor's new clothes are not made in Colombia.* New York: Oxford University Press.

Mowery, David C., ed. 1999. *U.S. industry in 2000: Studies in competitive performance.* Washington, D.C.: National Research Council.

Mowery, David C., and Richard R. Nelson, eds. 1999. *Sources of industrial leadership; Studies of seven industries.* New York: Cambridge University Press.

Multinational companies bring know-how. 1987. *United Press International,* November 2.

Mytelka, Lynn Krieger. 1991. Technological change and the global relocation of production in textiles and clothing. *Studies in Political Economy* 36 (Fall): 109–43.

Nagarajan, Anuradha, James L. Bander, and Chelsea C. White III. 1999. Trucking. In *U.S. industry in 2000: Studies in competitive performance,* ed. David C. Mowery, 123–54. Washington, D.C.: National Research Council.

Nath, Deepika, and Thomas S. Gruca. 1997. Convergence across alternative methods for forming strategic groups. *Strategic Management Journal* 18, no. 9: 745–60.

National Tax Research Center (NTRC). 1986. *The fiscal incentives of selected countries in Asia and the Pacific: A project of the Study Group on Asian Tax Administration and Research (SGATAR).* Prepared by the Republic of the Philippines, National Tax Research Center, National Economic and Development Authority. Manila: Study Group.

NEC hard disk drive plant in Luzon now operational. 1995. *COMLINE Daily News Computers,* October 9.

Nelson, Richard R., ed. 1993. *National innovation systems: A comparative analysis.* New York: Oxford University Press

————. 1996. The evolution of comparative or competitive advantage: A preliminary report on a study. *Industrial and Corporate Change* 5, no. 2: 597–617.

Nelson, Richard R., and Gavin Wright. 1994. The erosion of U.S. technological leadership as a factor in postwar economic convergence. In *Convergence of productivity: Cross-national studies and historical evidence,* ed. William J. Baumol, Richard R. Nelson, and Edward N. Wolff, 129–63. New York: Oxford University Press.

Newfarmer, Richard. 1980. *Transnational conglomerates and the economics of dependent development: A case study of the international electrical ologopoly and Brazil's electrical industry.* Greenwich, Conn.: JAI.

Nipon Paopongsakorn and Belinda Fuller. 1997. Thailand's development experience from the economic system perspective: Open politics and industrial activism. In *East Asian development experience: Economic system approach and its applicability,* ed. Toru Yanagihara and Susumu Sambommatsu, 466–518. Tokyo: I.D.E.

Nipon Paopongsakorn and Pawadee Tonguthai. 1998. Technological capability building and the sustainability of export success in Thailand's textile and electronics industries. In *Technological capabilities and export success in Asia,* ed. Dieter Ernst, Tom Ganiatsos, and Lynn Metelka, 309–59. London: Routledge.

Noble, Greg. 1999. Developing Asia beckons Japan: The auto industry. Paper presented at the Conference on Asia Beckons Japan. University of California, Berkeley, APEC Center, December 17.

———. 2000. Conspicuous failures and hidden strengths of the ITRI model: Taiwan's technology policy toward hard disk drives and CD-ROMs. Report 2000-02. San Diego: University of California, Information Storage Industry Center.

Nolan, James L. 1996. *Philippines business: The portable encyclopedia for doing business with the Philippines.* San Rafael, Calif.: World Trade Press.

Oakey, Ray. 1985. High-technology industries and agglomeration economies. In *Silicon landscapes,* ed. Peter Hall and Ann Markusen, 94–117. Boston: Allen and Unwin.

O'Brien, Peter. 1989. *The automotive industry in the developing countries: Risks and opportunities in the 1990s.* London: Economist Intelligence Unit.

Odagiri, Horiyuki, and Akira Goto. 1993. The Japanese system of innovation: Past, present and future. In *National innovation systems,* ed. Richard R. Nelson, 76–114. New York: Oxford University Press.

OECD. 1994. *Taxation and investment flows: An exchange of experiences between the OECD and the dynamic Asian economies.* Paris: OECD.

———. 1997. *Science and technology and industry: Scoreboard of indicators.* Paris: OECD.

O'hUallachain, Breandan. 1989. Agglomeration of services in American metropolitan areas. *Growth and Change* 20, no. 3: 34–49.

O'hUallachain, Breandan, and David Wasserman. 1999. Vertical integration in a lean supply chain: Brazilian automobile component parts. *Economic Geography* 75, no. 1: 21–42.

Okimoto, Daniel, and Y. Nishi. 1994. R&D organization in Japanese and American semiconductor firms. In *The Japanese firm: Sources of competitive strength,* ed. M. Aoki and R. Dore, 178–208. Oxford: Oxford University Press.

Oliver, Amalya L., and Mark Ebers. 1998. Networking network studies: An analysis of conceptual configurations in the study of inter-organizational relationships. *Organization Studies* 19, no. 4: 549–83.

Paniccia, Ivana. 1998. One, a hundred, thousands of industrial districts: Organizational variety in local networks of small and medium-sized enterprises. *Organization Studies* 19, no. 4: 667–99.

Patel, Pari, and Keith Pavitt. 1991. Large firms in the production of the world's technology: An important case of nonglobalization. *Journal of International Business Studies* 22, no. 1: 1–21.

Patel, Pari, and Modesto Vega. 1999. Patterns of internationalization of corporate technology: Location v. home country advantages. *Research Policy* 28, nos. 2 and 3: 145–55.

Paul, Catherine J. Morrison, and Donald S. Siegel. 1999. Scale economies and industry agglomeration externalities: A dynamic cost function approach. *American Economic Review* 89, no. 1: 272–90.

PC disk maker finds it hard to attract workers. 1997. *Nation,* May 17.

Peat Marwick. 1987. *Asian pacific taxation.* Hong Kong: Peat Marwick.

Pempel, T. J., ed. 1999. *The politics of the Asian economic crisis.* Ithaca, N.Y.: Cornell University Press.

Penang Development Corporation (PDC). 1988. *Policies and incentives.* Penang: Penang Development Corporation.

———. 1998. *PC and peripherals task force report.* Penang: Penang Development Corporation, March.

———. Various issues. *Annual survey of manufacturing industries in PDC industrial areas.* Penang: Penang Development Corporation.

Penang Seagate sets RM1bn target in 1995. 1995. *Business Times Singapore,* March 7, p. 2.

Penrose, Edith T. 1956. Foreign investment and growth of the firm. *Economic Journal* 60 (June): 220–35.

Peripheral mfrs. making move to SE Asia; cheaper labor, materials draw U.S. firms seeking to be more price-competitive. 1984. *Electronic News,* October 22, p. 53.

Peters, Hans J. 1998. Thailand's trade and infrastructure. Paper presented at the Conference on Thailand's Dynamic Economic Recovery and Competitiveness, Bangkok, May 20–21.

Petrazzini, Ben. 1995. *The political economy of telecommunications reform in developing countries.* New York: Praeger.

Piore, Michael J., and Charles E. Sabel. 1984. *The second industrial divide.* New York: Basic Books.

Plugging into an Asian gold mine. 1993. *Business Times Singapore,* May 3, p. 3.

Podolny, Joel M., and Karen L. Page. 1998. Network forms of organization. *Annual Review of Sociology* 22, no. 1: 57–76.

Porac, Joseph, Howard Thomas, and Charles Baden-Fuller. 1989. Competitive groups as cognitive communities: The case of the Scottish knitwear manufacturers. *Journal of Management Studies* 26 (July): 397–415.

Porac, Joseph F., Howard Thomas, Fiona Wilson, Douglas Paton, and Alaina Kanfer. 1995. Rivalry and the industry model of Scottish knitwear producers. *Administrative Science Quarterly* 40, no. 2: 203–27.

Porter, Michael E. 1990. *The competitive advantage of nations.* New York: Free Press.

———. 1998. The Adam Smith address: Location, clusters, and the "new" microeconomics of competition. *Business Economics* 33, no. 1: 7–13.

Powell, W. W. 1990. Neither market nor hierarchy: Network forms of organization. *Research in Organizational Behavior* 12: 295–336.

Powell W. W., and P. Brantley. 1992. Competitive cooperation in biotechnology: Learning through networks? In *Networks and organizations: Structure, form and action,* ed. N. Nohria and R. Eccles, 366–94. Boston: Harvard Business School Press.

Prairietek selects Edwin Heacox as vice-president of manufacturing operations. 1990. *Business Wire,* November 5.

Pred, Allan. 1965. Industrialization, initial advantage and American growth. *Geographic Review* 55: 158–85.

————. 1966. *The spatial dynamics of U.S. urban-industrial growth, 1800–1914.* Cambridge, Mass.: MIT Press.

Priam goes offshore for automated manufacturing. 1987. *Electronic Business,* October 1, p. 90.

Price Waterhouse. 1985. *Doing business in Malaysia.* New York: Price Waterhouse.

————. 1986a. *Doing business in Indonesia.* New York: Price Waterhouse.

————. 1986b. *Doing business in Indonesia.* New York: Price Waterhouse.

————. 1988. *Doing business in Singapore.* New York: Price Waterhouse.

————. 1989. *Doing business in Indonesia.* New York: Price Waterhouse.

————. 1990. *Doing business in Malaysia.* New York: Price Waterhouse.

————. 1993. *Doing business in the Philippines.* New York: Price Waterhouse.

————. 1994. *Doing business in Malaysia.* New York: Price Waterhouse.

————. 1996a. *Doing business in Indonesia.* New York: Price Waterhouse.

————. 1996b. *Doing business in Malaysia.* New York: Price Waterhouse.

————. 1996c. *Doing business in Singapore.* New York: Price Waterhouse.

Pugh, Emerson, Lyle Johnson, and John Palmer. 1991. *IBM's 360 and early 370 systems.* Cambridge, Mass.: MIT Press.

Putnam, Robert. 1993. *Making democracy work: Civic traditions in modern Italy.* Princeton, N.J.: Princeton University Press.

Pyke, F., G. Becattini, and W. Sengenberger, eds. 1990. *Industrial districts and inter-firm co-operation in Italy.* Geneva: International Institute for Labor Studies.

Rasiah, Rajah. 1994. Flexible production systems and local machine-tool subcontracting: Electronics components transnationals in Malaysia. *Cambridge Journal of Economics* 18 (June): 279–98.

————. 1995. *Foreign capital and industrialization in Malaysia.* New York: St. Martin's.

————. Forthcoming. Politics, institutions and flexibility: Microelectronics transnationals and machine tool linkages in Malaysia. In *The challenge of flexible production in East Asia,* ed. Frederic Deyo, Richard Doner, and Eric Hershberg. Boulder, Colo.: Rowman and Littlefield.

Rauch, James E. 1993. Does history matter only when it matters little? The case of city-industry location. *Quarterly Journal of Economics* 108, no. 3: 843–67.

Raytheon Data "enhances" 700 minicomputer series. 1971. *Electronic News,* May 10, p. 40.

Rodime PLC; starts 1984 with a contract from TeleVideo worth up to $50 million over 18 months. 1984. *Business Wire,* January 9.

Rodime warns of year end loss as results weaken. 1986. *Financial Times,* August 7, p. 26.

Rosenbloom, Richard S., and Clayton M. Christensen. 1994. Technological discontinuities, organizational capabilities, and strategic commitments. *Industrial and Corporate Change* 3, no. 3: 655–85.

Rubens, Sidney M. 1999. Data storage on drums. In *Magnetic recording: The first 100 years,* ed. Eric Daniels, C. Denis Mee, and Mark H. Clark, 237–51. New York: IEEE Press.

Rugman, A. N., ed. 1981. *Inside the multinationals: The economic of international markets.* London: Croom Helm.

Sales of magnetic heads produced by Applied Magnetics Singapore up to US$85m. 1989. *Business Times Singapore,* February 14, p. 2.

Saxenian, AnnaLee. 1991. The origins and dynamics of production networks in silicon valley. *Research Policy* 20, no. 5: 423–38.

———. 1994. *Regional advantage: Culture and competition in Silicon Valley and Route 128.* Cambridge, Mass.: Harvard University Press.

———. 1999. *Silicon Valley's new immigrant entrepreneurs.* San Francisco: Public Policy Institute of California.

Say IBM injects $6M loan to support supplier CMI. 1984. *Electronic News,* December 31, p. 1.

Scott, Allen J. 1986. High tech industry and territorial development: The rise of the Orange County complex, 1955–1984. *Urban Geography* 7 (January–February): 3–45.

———. 1993. *Technopolis: High-technology industry and regional development in southern California.* Berkeley: University of California Press.

Seagate announces multi-million dollar Asia-Pacific expansion plans. 1994. *Business Wire,* September 7.

Seagate asks government to get into information highway fastlane. 1997. *Nation,* June 3.

Seagate earmarks $140m to boost global disk media output. 1995. *Straits Times,* July 12, p. 36.

Seagate expands thin-film head manufacturing capability with new facility in Malaysia. 1991. *Business Wire,* May 29.

Seagate goes East—and comes back a winner. 1987. *Business Week,* March 16, p. 94.

Seagate/Imprimis deal forces industry shift. 1989. *Electronic News,* August 21, p. 1.

Seagate is king of the hill in rough world of disk drives; company beats dismal odds in ever-changing, hockey-like industry. 1995. *Fresno Bee,* May 22, p. E5.

Seagate rides fluid motors as next wave for drives. 1997. *EE Times,* October 10.

Seagate S'pore to get more work with expansion of Penang plant. 1992. *Business Times Singapore,* June 2, p. 2.

Seagate's recording head operations ship 250,000,000th thin film recording head. 1994. *Business Wire,* November 1.

Seagate Technology keen to expand perfect base in Asia. 1996. *New Straits Times,* January 26, p. 26.

Seagate to produce 110 megabyte disk drives at Singapore plant. 1988. *Japan Economic Journal,* April 16, p. 18.

Semiconductor family tree. 1968. *Electronic News,* July 8, p. 5.

Sforzi, F. 1989. The geography of industrial district in Italy. In *Small firms and industrial districts in Italy,* ed. E. Goodman and J. Bamford, 153–73. London: Routledge.

Shelp, Ronald K., John C. Stephenson, Nancy S. Truitt, and Bernard Wasow. 1984. *Service industries and economic development: Case studies in technology transfer.* New York: Praeger.

Sheriff, Antony M. 1993. The next wave in product line strategy. *Japanese Motor Business* (4th quarter): 130–61.

Shut up or shut down. 1994. *Asia, Inc.,* April.

Singapore: Electronics heads the revival. 1986. *Financial Times,* November 3, p. 21.

Small drives, big dreams. 1987. *Computerworld,* August 17, p. 67.

Smaller business computers creating need for half-height, sub-5.25-inch Winchesters. 1984. *Electronic News,* June 4, p. 1.

Smith, David M. 1981. *Industrial location: An industrial-geographical analysis* (2d ed.). New York: Wiley.

Soon, T. W. 1993. Education and human resource development. In *Challenge and response: Thirty years of the Economic Development Board,* ed. L. Low et al., 235–69. Singapore: Time Academic Press.

Southeast Asia's motor city. 2000. *Business Week,* May 8.

Special report/electronics: Warning of decline unless state help given. 1997. *Bangkok Post,* September 8.

Staber, U. H., N. V. Schaefer, and B. Sharma, eds. 1996. *Business networks: Prospects for regional development.* Berlin: de Gruyter.

State urged to back wafer plant proposal. 2000. *Bangkok Post,* January 31.

Stevens, Louis D. 1981. The evolution of magnetic storage. *IBM Journal of Research and Development* 25, no. 5: 663–75.

———. 1999. Data storage on hard magnetic disks. In *Magnetic recording: The first 100 years,* ed. Eric Daniels, C. Denis Mee, and Mark H. Clark, 270–99. New York: IEEE Press.

Storper, Michael. 1989. The transition to flexible specialization in industry: External economies, the division of labor and the crossing of industrial divides. *Cambridge Journal of Economics* 13, no. 2: 273–305.

———. 1992. The limits to globalization: Technology districts and international trade. *Economic Geography* 68, no. 1: 60–93.

———. 1993. Regional "worlds" of production: Learning and innovation in the technology districts of France, Italy and the USA. *Regional Studies* 25, no. 5: 433–55.

Suphat, Suphachalasai. 1998. *Textiles industry in Thailand.* Singapore: APEC Secretariat.

Suppliers ramp up 3.5 Winchesters. 1986. *Electronic News,* December 1, p. 22.

Syed Iftikar: His quest and his drive began with a prophet. 1991. *Business Journal—San Jose,* June 3, p. 10.

Tan, Ging Hoon. 1994/95. The precision machining sector and the national competitive advantage of Singapore in the hard disk drive industry. Advanced study project, National University of Singapore, School of Postgraduate Management Studies.

Tecson, Gwendolyn. 1999. The hard disk drive industry in the Philippines. Report 99-01. San Diego: University of California, Information Storage Industry Center.

Teece, David J. 1976. *The multinational corporation and the resource cost of international technology transfer.* Cambridge, Mass.: Ballinger.

———. 1985. Multinational enterprise, internal governance, and industrial organization. *American Economic Review* 75 (May): 233–38.

———. 1992. Competition, cooperation, and innovation: Organizational arrangements for regimes of rapid technological progress. *Journal of Economic Behavior and Organization* 18 (June): 1–25.

Terwiesch, Christian, and Roger E. Bohn. 1998. Learning and process improvement during production ramp-up. Report 98-01. San Diego: University of California, Information Storage Industry Center.

Terwiesch, Christian, Roger E. Bohn, and Scott Hampton. 1997. The economics of yield-driven processes. Report 97-04. San Diego: University of California, Information Storage Industry Center.

Terwiesch, Christian, Kuong S. Chea, and Roger E. Bohn. 1999. An exploratory study of international product transfer and production ramp-up in the data storage industry. Report 99-02. San Diego: University of California, Information Storage Industry Center.

Textile exporters urged to focus on supply chain. 1999. *Nation* (Bangkok), May 28.

Thailand Board of Investment. 1997. *Incentives and criteria of the BoI.* Bangkok: Thailand Board of Investment.

Thailand: Fujitsu slashed local production of small hard drives as prices collapse. 1992. *Computergram International,* January 13.

Thailand a hub but no disk drive expansion. 1999. *Bangkok Post,* October 14.

Tigre, Paulo Bastos. 1983. *Technology and competition in the Brazilian computer industry.* New York: St. Martin's.

Toshiba develops disk drive of high capacity. 1991. *Los Angeles Times,* August 6, part D, p. 6.

Toyo Memories plant in Malaysia. 1997. *Asia Pulse,* December 17.

Trade Development Board. Various years. *Singapore trade statistics, imports and exports.* Singapore: Trade Development Board.

TrendFocus. 1996a. *HDD recording head information service* (annual study). Palo Alto, Calif.: TrendFocus, March.

———. 1996b. *Rigid media information service* (annual study). Palo Alto, Calif.: TrendFocus, March.

———. 1998a. *HDD recording head information service* (annual study). Palo Alto, Calif.: TrendFocus, March.

———. 1998b. *Rigid media information service* (annual study). Palo Alto, Calif.: TrendFocus, March.

———. 1999a. *Rigid media information service* (annual study). Palo Alto, Calif.: TrendFocus, March.

———. 1999b. *HDD recording head information service* (annual study). Palo Alto, Calif.: TrendFocus, March.

Tuman, John P., and John T. Morris. 1998. The transformation of the Latin American automobile industry. In *Transforming the Latin American automobile industry: Unions, workers and the politics of restructuring,* ed. John P. Tuman and John T. Morris, 3–25. Armonk, N.Y.: Sharpe.

Uemura to produce nickel plating chemicals in Malaysia. 1997. *Comline Daily News,* June 11.

Unesco. 1999. *Statistical yearbook.* Paris: Unesco.

United Nation Industry and Development Organization (UNIDO). 1996. *Industry and development: Global report.* New York: United Nation Industry and Development Organization.

United Nations (UN). 1993. *World investment directory* (vols. 3, 4, and 5). New York: United Nations.

United Nations Center on Transnational Corporations (UNCTC). 1989. *Foreign direct invesment and transnational corporations in services.* New York: United Nations.

———. 1992. *The determinants of foreign direct investment.* New York: United Nations.

United Nations Conference on Trade and Development (UNCTAD). 1997. *World investment report.* New York: United Nations.

U.S. Deptartment of Labor, Bureau of International Labor Affairs. Various issues. *Foreign labor trends.* Washington, D.C.: Government Printing Office.

U.S. OEM vendors fight Japanese with high-capacity drives, bold pricing. 1986. *Electronic News,* July 7, p. 1.

Utterback, James M. 1994. *Mastering the dynamics of innovation.* Boston: Harvard Business School Press.

Utterback, James M., and William J. Abernathy. 1975. A dynamic model of product and process innovation. *Omega* 3, no. 6: 639–56.

Uzzi, Brian. 1997. Social structure and competition in interfirm networks: The paradox of embeddedness. *Administrative Science Quarterly* 42 (March): 35–67.

Vernon, Raymond. 1966. International investment and international trade in the product cycle. *Quarterly Journal of Economics* 80 (May): 190–207.

———. 1974. The location of economic activity. In *Economic analysis and the multinational enterprise,* ed. John H. Dunning, 89–114. London: Allen and Unwin.

———. 1979. The product life cycle hypothesis in a new international environment. *Oxford Bulletin of Economics and Statistics* 41 (November): 255–67.

Wade, Robert. 1990. *Governing the market: Economic theory and the role of government in East Asian industrialization.* Princeton, N.J.: Princeton University Press.

Walter, Ingo. 1988. *Global competition in financial services.* Cambridge, Mass.: Ballinger.

Warr, Peter G. 1997. The Thai economy: From boom to gloom. In *Southeast Asian Affairs,* 317–33. Singapore: Heinemann.

WD plants SageTree subsidiary to manage disk-drive supply chain. 2000. *Electronic Buyers' News,* June 21.

Webber, Melvin. 1972. *Impact of uncertainty on location.* Cambridge, Mass.: MIT Press.

Weiss, Linda. 1998. *The myth of the powerless state.* Ithaca, N.Y.: Cornell University Press.

Wells, Louis T., ed. 1972. *The product life cycle and international trade.* Cambridge, Mass.: Harvard University Press.

Western Digital comes clean on disk crash. 1999. *Wired News,* November 11.

Western Digital opens disk drive plant in Malaysia. 1994. *Straits Times,* October 12, p. 36.

Western Digital's Burger speaks out on state of storage industry. 1995. *Computer Reseller News,* December 4, p. 133.

Westphal, Larry, Kopr Kritayakirana, Kosal Petchsuwan, Harit Sutabutr, and Yongyuth Yuthavong. 1990. The development of technological capability in manufacturing: A macroscopic approach to policy research. In *Science and technology: Lessons for development policy,* ed. Robert E. Evenson and Gustav Ranis, 81–134. Boulder, Colo.: Westview.

Why American high-tech firm recruits in Asian ricefields. 1990. *Los Angeles Times,* June 25, part D, p. 3.

Why Seagate set sail for Singapore. 1988. *Financial Times,* June 1.

Winners and losers in the fifth generation; the race is on in for technologies that will be crucial to information processing in the 1990s. 1983. *Datamation,* December, pp. 193–211.

Winterton, Jonathan, and Ian M. Taplin. 1997. Making sense of strategies for survival: Clothing in high wage economies. In *Rethinking global production: A comparative analysis of restructuring in the clothing industry,* ed. Ian M. Taplin and Jonathan Winterton, 189–98. Brookfield, Vt.: Ashgate.

Womack, James, Daniel Jones, and Daniel Roos. 1990. *The machine that changed the world.* New York: Rawson Associates.

Wong, Poh Kam. 1999a. The dynamics of HDD industry development in Singapore. Report 99-03. San Diego: University of California, Information Storage Industry Center.

———. 1999b. Leveraging MNCs, fostering technoprenuership: The evolving S&T strategy of Singapore. In *Public policy in Singapore,* ed. L. Low and D. Johnston. Singapore: World Scientific Press.

———. 2000. The role of the state in Singapore's industrial development. In *Proceedings of workshop on the role of the state in East Asian industrial development: Reflections in the light of the Asian crisis.* Berkeley: University of California, January.

Wong, P. K., and M. Ang. 1997. Critical success factors in implementing manufacturing automation: Evidence from Singapore's electronics industry. Working paper. Singapore: National University of Singapore, Center for Manufacturing Technology.

Woo-Cumings, Meredith Jung-En. 1998. National security and the rise of the developmental state in South Korea and Taiwan. In *Behind East Asian growth: The political and social foundations of prosperity,* ed. Henry S. Rowen, 319–47. New York: Routledge.

———. 1999. Introduction: Chalmers Johnson and the politics of nationalism and development. In *The developmental state,* ed. Meredith Jung-En Woo-Cumings, 1–31. Ithaca, N.Y.: Cornell University Press.

World Bank. 1993. *The East Asian miracle: Economic growth and public policy.* Washington, D.C.: World Bank.

————. Various issues. *World development report.* New York: Oxford University Press.

World Competitiveness Report. Various years. Geneva and Lausanne: World Economic Forum and IMD.

World Trade Organization (WTO). 1996. Trade policy review: Singapore. Minutes.

Zysman, John, and Laura Tyson, eds. 1983. *American industry in international competition: Government policies and corporate strategies.* Ithaca, N.Y.: Cornell University Press.

Index

Acer, 72
Acton Computer, 302n26
Adaptec, 157, 169
AdFlex, 193
Advanced Disk Technology, 221
Advanced Magnetic Materials, 193
Advanced Micro Devices, 267, 306n11
Agglomeration economies, 6, 7, 11, 38,
   41–42, 46, 133, 232, 269. *See also*
   Operational clusters; Proximity,
   advantages of; Technological clusters
and foreign investment, 54–55, 119–20,
   137, 139–40, 254, 256. *See also*
   Multinational corporations, role in
   industrial clusters
localization, 290n4
in Malaysia, 133, 141–43, 205–06, 210,
   212, 223–24
in the Philippines, 235
in Singapore, 61, 109, 133, 141–43,
   156, 178–81, 300n27
in Thailand, 133, 141–43, 186–87, 191,
   194, 197–201, 304n48
urbanization, 290n4
Akashic Kubota, 220, 307n34
Alps Electric, 77, 100, 304n51
AMP, 169
Ampex, 98, 294n2, 308n15
Amstrad, 73
Anelex, 88
Apparel industry, geographic configuration
   of, 260, 261–63, 267, 311n2, 311n3,
   311n4, 311n5, 312n6
Apple Computer, 61, 285, 299n11
Applied Magnetics, 109

in Malaysia, 129, 135, 207, 209, 212,
   213–15, 218–19, 297n4, 297n7,
   306n16, 306n17, 306n21
in regional production system, 150
in Singapore, 121, 169
Aquino administration (Philippines), 127,
   130, 234, 249
Areal density, 17, 68,
   leadership in, 83–84, 95
Areal Technology, 295n11
Armstrong Industrial, 171
Asahi Komag, 193
Asian financial crisis, 3
Asian Institute of Technology (Thailand),
   198
Asian Micro, 214
Atasi, 295n11
Automobile industry, geographic configu-
   ration of, 40, 251, 260, 263–65, 267,
   312n7, 312n8, 312n9, 312n11
Avatar Peripherals, 302n23

BASF, 72, 73, 92, 294n2, 314n3
Benetton, 311n2
Berg, 169
Big followership, 228, 230
BJ Industries, 168, 297n11
Boron, 193, 198
Brazil
as possible site for disk drive industry, 122
promotion of indigenous disk drive
   industry, 228–29, 235–37, 271,
   308n15, 308n16
Brilliant Manufacturing, 170, 171, 176,
   179, 297n11

Bryant Computer Products, 71, 88, 294n2
Burroughs, 4, 71. *See also* Unisys
  as captive disk drive manufacturer, 77, 88
  as disk drive industry leader, 89
  overseas assembly by, 92, 295n9

CalComp, 72. *See also* Century Data
  Systems
CAM Mechatronics, 169, 170, 171
CAM Technologies, 209, 210, 213,
  297n11, 306n21
Captive disk drive production, 71, 72,
  77–78, 88, 89, 314n1
  as reason for slow move to Southeast
  Asia, 106
Castlewood, 134
Century Data Systems, 89, 91, 284, 294n2,
  314n3. *See also* CalComp
Chaebol, 240, 250
China, disk drive industry in, 4, 5, 33, 34,
  47, 59, 129, 136, 148, 149, 171, 214,
  218, 224, 259, 297n4, 297n5
Chrysler, 263, 312n7
Collor administration (Brazil), 237, 249
COMECON, 72
Compagnie Internationale pour l'Informatique, 72, 294n2
Compaq Computer, 61, 72
  as Conner Peripherals customer, 113, 285
Competition. *See also* Competitive pressures; Technological change
  intensity of, 16, 25, 33, 73, 134, 270
  international, 3, 10, 111, 255
  localized, 11, 39–40, 255, 290n
  price, 29–33
  Red Queen, 291n11
  technological, 27–29
Competitive advantage. *See also* Malaysia,
  and American competitiveness;
  Singapore, and American competitiveness; Thailand, and American
  competitiveness
  and first-mover advantage, 67–69,
  71–74, 257, 291n10, 293n1
  and globalization of production, 5, 11,
  52–59, 64–65, 111–14, 255–57. *See*
  also Location, and competitive
  advantage
  and form of industrial organization, 13,
  74–79, 257, 270, 293n9
  and innovation, 13, 67, 79–85, 257,
  294n13
  and manufacturing capabilities, 13,
  269–71, 273–74
  and national embeddedness, 67, 69–74

and public policy, 8, 67, 85, 294n16,
  294n17. *See also* Public policies
  sources of, 6
Competitive pressures, 16–17, 260. *See*
  also Competition; Technological
  change, and changing competitive
  pressures
  changes in, 49–50, 59–62, 117, 119–21
  and costs, 7, 31–32, 59, 97, 123, 134,
  180, 232, 260. *See also* Foreign direct
  investment, and factor costs
  and manufacturing yields, 7, 61–62,
  134, 180, 256
  and market access. *See* Foreign direct
  investment, and market access
  pricing, 4, 137, 232
  and product cycles, 30, 44, 68, 130,
  180, 232, 261
  and ramping down production, 23, 141,
  179, 180, 201, 261
  and ramping up production, 61–62, 180
  and time to market, 7, 28, 29, 30, 44,
  61, 129, 130, 134, 137, 232, 256
  and time to volume production, 7, 28,
  29, 61, 134, 137, 232, 256
Comport, 239–40
Computer industry, 13, 25, 28, 72–73,
  120, 283–84
  Taiwanese, 237–38
Computer Memories, 4, 95, 97
  influence on other disk drive firms, 98
  in Singapore, 100, 162
  success from producing in Southeast
  Asia, 111
Confucianism, 231
Conner Peripherals, 73, 95, 285
  acquired by Seagate Technology, 134, 286
  autonomy of Singaporean managers,
  151, 163, 170–71
  in China, 171
  competing in Japanese market, 105
  development of suppliers, 109, 142, 169,
  213
  fast to move to Southeast Asia, 4, 127
  in Malaysia, 129, 142, 207, 209, 210,
  214, 216, 306n21
  product development, launch and
  transfer model of, 165–66, 171
  reason for assembly in Southeast Asia,
  104
  in regional production system, 150, 209,
  213
  in Singapore, 98, 163, 168, 182
  success from producing in Southeast
  Asia, 112, 113–14

use of ex-Seagate employees, 179
Control Data, 305n3, 308n15
    assembly in Germany, 92, 298n15
    as captive disk drive manufacturer, 77,
        88
    early disk drive operations of, 71, 72,
        89, 284, 293n5, 294n2, 294n3, 295n8
    in Malaysia, 129, 207, 209, 212,
        213–15, 297n4, 306n16
    in Singapore, 111, 164
Convergence in global strategic behavior,
    9, 39, 62–63, 105–08, 257–58. *See
    also* Mimicry
Core memories, 275
Cybernex Advanced Storage Technology,
    98

Daewoo, 72, 73
Daido, 193
Dastek, 129, 150, 209, 212, 297n4,
    305n6, 306n17, 306n21
Data General, 302n15, 304n45
Data Products, 71, 88, 89
Data Recording Instruments, 72, 88,
    293n4, 314n3
Data storage capacity, 17, 28, 31, 275–76
Data Storage Institute (DSI) (Singapore),
    138, 177–78, 243, 272, 309n26,
    309n27
Diablo Systems, 72, 294n2
Dell Computer, 61, 72
Diffusion, 39–40, 44–45, 294n2
Digital Equipment Corporation (DEC), 4,
    71
    as captive disk drive manufacturer, 77,
        89, 284
    in Malaysia, 134, 207, 216, 217
    slow to move to Southeast Asia, 9, 106
Disc Systems, 295n5
Diseconomies of location, 258–60
Disruptive technologies and the disk drive
    industry, 283–87, 314n1, 314n2,
    314n3, 314n4
Domain Technology, 109
DZU, 72

Economic Development Board (EDB)
    (Singapore), 97, 131, 138, 160, 161,
    164, 166, 176, 181–82, 231, 242–43,
    297n6
Economies of scale, 5, 25, 31, 43, 45,
    49–50, 61, 77, 89, 141, 259, 163,
    179, 199, 202, 256, 264, 265,
    298n18, 300n27, 311n1
Eiwa, 193

Elebra, 308n15
Elec & Eltek, 171
Employment in disk drive industry, 34,
    110–11, 271
English Electric, 295n8
Eng Teknologi, 136, 213, 214, 297n11
Entry of firms, 39–40, 41, 61, 68–69, 73,
    88, 92, 95, 254, 295n11
Epson, 72, 100
EsPerT, 239
European hard disk drive industry, 72, 88
Excel Precision, 220, 307n33
Exit of firms, 29, 39, 41, 61, 68, 73, 134,
    218, 254
Export processing zones (EPZ), 122, 127,
    188, 195, 196, 210. *See also* Free
    trade zones
Export Promotion Act (Thailand), 188

Fairchild Semiconductor, 41, 160, 163
Federation of Thai Industries' Electrical
    and Electronics Club, 197
Ferrite Valley, 11
FerroTec, 157
Fidelity Chemical, 221
Flextronics, 169, 170, 299n6
Floppy disk drive (FDD) industry, 73, 74,
    95, 102, 277, 295n12
Ford, 263, 312n7, 312n11
Foreign direct investment. *See also* Global-
    ization of production; Multinational
    corporations
    and agglomeration economies. *See*
        Agglomeration economies, and foreign
        investment
    and factor costs, 11, 52–53, 119–20,
        123, 130, 136; 172–73, 186, 194–95,
        232, 273. *See also* Competitive pres-
        sures, and costs
    factors explaining, 6
    and market access, 53–54, 91–92, 260,
        291n16, 311n1
    and public policy, 54, 119–20, 123–27,
        130–31, 137, 233. *See also* Public
        policies
    theories of, and location, 50–51, 291n15
Foreign Investment Act (Philippines), 235,
    308n12
Form factor, 25, 26, 28, 80–81, 84, 98,
    106, 118, 163, 194, 236, 277,
    283–85, 286, 295n7
Free Trade Zone Act (Malaysia), 210
Free trade zones (FTZ), 123, 212; 216,
    219, 305n9. *See also* Export process-
    ing zones

Friden, 88
Fuji Electric, 77, 100, 111, 134, 220
Fujitsu, 71, 111, 270, 286, 304n51, 314n3
    and areal density, 17
    and Data Storage Institute, 178
    as exporter from Thailand, 184
    as innovator, 81
    in the Philippines, 106, 235
    reasons for investing in Thailand, 191, 198
    in Thailand, 106, 128–29, 136, 191, 193
    in the United States, 101, 105
    value chain of, 186
    and vertical integration, 76, 293n9

The Gap, 311n2
General Electric, 41, 71, 88, 89, 156, 160, 294n3
General Motors, 263, 312n7, 312n11
General processes of industry evolution, 39–40
General Systems of Preferences, 188
Gintic Institute of Manufacturing Technology (Singapore), 243
Globalization of production. *See also* Foreign direct investment; Mimicry; Multinational corporations
    and competitive advantage. *See* Competitive advantage, and globalization of production)
    difference between Japanese and American firms in, 8–9, 34, 38, 64–65, 100–05, 106–07, 110
    and firm age, 64, 100, 103, 107
    and firm growth, 4, 98, 103, 291n8
    and firm size, 64, 100, 103, 107
    similarity between Japanese and American firms in, 106, 296n14
    and strategic focus, 64, 98, 100, 107
    timing of, 34, 64–65
Goldstar, 72, 73, 239
Goldtron Electronics, 213
Gucci, 311n2
Gul Technology, 171, 297n11

Habiro, 193
Hard disk drives (HDD)
    how they work, 18, 20–21
    innovation in, 24–25, 275–76
    uses of, 18
Hewlett-Packard, 4, 61, 73, 295n6
    as captive disk drive manufacturer, 77
    in Malaysia, 110, 134, 207, 216, 217
    slow to move to Southeast Asia, 9, 106
Hightrack Computer Technik, 314n3

Hitachi, 4, 71, 111, 270, 286, 294n2, 304n51, 314n3
    as captive disk drive manufacturer, 88
    and Data Storage Institute, 178
    in the Philippines, 106, 235
    as innovator, 81, 84
    production in Japan, 101
    and vertical integration, 76, 293n9
Hitachi Metals, 110, 136, 207, 209, 306n17
HMT Technology, 296n13
Hokushin Electric Works, 72, 294n2, 314n3
Honeywell, 71, 88, 294n1, 294n2, 294n3
Hong Kong, 172
Hoya Media, 109, 150, 157, 168, 182
Hoya Opto, 193
Hughes Aircraft, 41
Hutchinson Technology, 201, 218, 304n51
Hyosung Computer, 239
Hyundai Electronics, 72, 73, 239

IBM, 4, 56, 160, 286, 304n51
    and areal density, 17
    as captive disk drive manufacturer, 77, 284
    and contract manufacturing relationship with NEC, 77
    and contract manufacturing relationship with Saha-Union , 76, 128, 191
    and Data Storage Institute, 177
    as demanding disk drive customer, 4, 97, 123, 147, 161, 162, 232
    disk drive headquarters of, 95, 294n1
    as disk drive industry leader, 71–72, 89
    as exporter from Thailand, 34, 184
    in Germany, 92
    in Hungary, 76
    as innovator, 28, 79–80, 81, 84, 88, 91, 276–78, 284, 292n20
    introduction of personal computer by, 72, 92
    reason for assembly in Thailand rather than the Philippines, 189, 303n31
    in regional production system, 150
    in Singapore, 76, 134, 165, 166, 167
    as source for spinoffs, 88–89
    slow to move to Southeast Asia, 106, 296n14
    in Thailand, 76, 128, 134, 136, 191, 193, 201, 202
    value chain of, 186
    vertical integration of, 76, 270, 293n9
ICL, 293n4, 295n8

India as possible site for disk drive industry, 122
Industrial Automation Promotion Program (Singapore)
Industrial clusters, 5, 37, 40, 69, 290n. *See also* Agglomeration economies; Industrial districts; Operational clusters; Technological clusters
benefits of locating in, 12, 41, 70
and collocation of product development and manufacturing, 42–43, 88–92, 95, 118, 255, 266, 294n1, 295n6
Industrial districts, 7, 51, 52, 56–57, 69–70. *See also* Agglomeration economies; Industrial clusters; Operational clusters; Technological clusters
Industrial Incentives Act (Malaysia), 210
Industrial policies. *See* Public policies, industrial
Industrial Technology Research Institute (ITRI) (Taiwan), 238–39, 241, 309n19, 309n21
Industry associations, 198, 230, 304n45
Industry concentration, 29
Industry drivers. *See* Competitive pressures; Technological change, and changing competitive pressures
Industry-specific policies. *See* Public policies, industry-specific
Inertia, organizational, 286–87
Informatics Law (Brazil), 236–37
Information Storage Systems (ISS), 71, 88, 284
Infrastructure, 123, 127, 137–38, 232, 271
Initiative in New Technology Adoption (InTech) (Singapore), 175
Intel, 267
Internalization, 13, 74–79, 259, 270, 293n9
Innovation in disk drives, 24–25, 275–76. *See also* Competitive advantage, and innovation; Technological change
and coordination among designers, 44, 95
in disks, 277, 279–80
in electronics, 280–81, 314n10
in interfaces, 281
in motors, 280
and organizational change, 286–87
in recording heads, 276–77, 278–79, 314n16
Innovex, 109

Institutions, explaining the origins of, 246–51
Integral Peripherals
initial production in Singapore, 98, 165
reason for assembly in Singapore, 109–10, 166, 301n31
in regional production system, 150
International Disk Drive Equipment and Materials Association (IDEMA), 138, 175–76, 297n10, 309n27, 310n30
International Memories
as innovator, 278, 284, 295n7, 295n11, 314n3
success from producing in Southeast Asia, 111
International production networks. *See* Regional production system
Investment Incentives Act (Malaysia), 211
Investment regime, 133, 228

Japan, share of hard disk drives produced in, 95, 101, 107, 108, 296n20
Japanese hard disk drive industry
absence of job-hopping in, 105
absence of spinoffs in, 105
emergence of, 71–72
and weakness of agglomeration economies in Thailand, 191
Joint Public-Private Sector Coordinating Committee (Thailand), 310n28
Jurong Township Corporation (JTC) (Singapore), 133, 164, 166, 174, 297n6
JVC, 100, 111

Kaifa, 136, 306n21
Kalok, 297n5
Keiretsu, 75, 293n8
Kennedy Company, 314n3
King Mongkut Institute of Technology (Thailand), 198
Kobe, 221
Komag, 77, 95, 109, 134, 150, 216, 219–20, 224, 296n13, 305n6
Korean disk drive industry, 229, 239–40, 250–51, 310n34
K.R. Precision, 186, 193, 198, 201, 304n51
Kuomintang (KMT) (Taiwan), 238, 250

Labor costs. *See* Competitive pressures, and costs; Foreign direct investment, and factor costs
Labor quality. *See also* Agglomeration economies
and industry requirements, 11, 140, 256

Labor quality (*continued*)
  and investment in Southeast Asia, 123,
    137
  in Malaysia, 205, 215, 218
  in Singapore, 156, 163–64, 259, 298n13
  in Thailand, 189
Lafe Holdings, 136, 297n4
Lam Soon Engineering, 169
La Pine, 295n11
Latin America as possible site for disk
    drive industry, 122–23
Leksun, 306n21
Levi Strauss, 261
Linear Technology, 313n17
LKT Precision Engineering, 220, 307n33
Local Enterprise Technical Assistance
    Scheme (LETAS) (Singapore), 176, 181
Local Industries Upgrading Program
    (LIUP) (Singapore), 133, 139, 176–77,
    179, 181, 243
Location
  changing dynamics of, 5–6, 7, 10, 12,
    37–38, 46–50, 59–62, 71, 201–02;
    206–07, 255–56, 274
  and competitive advantage, 6, 37, 41,
    51, 62, 121, 253, 274. *See also* Com-
    petitive advantage, and globalization
    of production
  and industry origins, 7–8, 39–43, 87–92,
    254–55
Location decisions. *See* Foreign direct
    investment
Location-specific assets, 5, 7, 12, 253–54,
    255, 258, 260, 263, 265, 270, 274
  and public policy, 228, 247, 269
  in Southeast Asia, 38, 59, 137, 148,
    258
LSI Logic, 313n17
Luzon Electronics Technology, 308n14

Magnecomp, 109, 186, 193, 304n51,
    305n52
Magnetic drum storage, compared to hard
    disk drives, 88, 89, 275
Magnetic tape drives, compared to hard
    disk drives, 17, 275
Magnetics Technology Center (Singapore),
    133, 138, 177
Magtric, 193
Mahathir government (Malaysia), 127,
    211
Malaysia
  and American competitiveness, 210–15,
    216–21
  as center for production, 127, 204, 209.

See also Operational clusters, in
    Malaysia
  disk drive assemblers in, 134, 207, 216,
    217–18
  education and training in, 137, 222
  and generic public policies, 205
  heads assembly in, 209, 216. *See also*
    Operational clusters, in Malaysia
  government of, changing role of,
    221–23, 307n36
  indigenous suppliers to the HDD indus-
    try, 139, 220, 297n11
  industry growth in, 204
  industry-specific policies in, 131,
    138–39, 297n10
  infrastructure in, 127, 138
  investment incentives in, 127, 210–12
  labor costs in, 210, 215
  licensed manufacturing warehouses in,
    210
  media production in, 216. *See also*
    Operational clusters, in Malaysia
  operational capabilities in, 7, 149
  origins of disk drive industry in, 207–10,
    305n5
  rules for foreign investment in, 130
  supply base in, 206
  and wages, 136, 205, 221
Malaysian Business Council, 245
Malaysian Industrial Development
    Authority (MIDA), 245
Manufacturing challenges, 16, 20, 25,
    270
Manufacturing tolerances, 20, 23, 25, 49,
    160, 161, 168, 169, 256, 259, 261,
    262, 264, 270
Marcos administration (Philippines), 127,
    234, 249
Market growth
  revenue, 26
  units, 25
Market shares, 33, 73–74, 89
  of American firms assembling in South-
    east Asia, 111, 112–13
  of firms assembling in Asia excluding
    Japan, 111
Market size, 5, 26, 72, 91
Marshall Data Systems (Marshall Indus-
    tries), 71, 89
Matsushita, 4, 73, 101
Matsushita-Kotobuki Electronics (MKE).
    See Quantum
Maxim Integrated, 313n17
MaxMedia, 220
Maxtor, 4, 95, 286

development of Singaporean suppliers by, 168, 176
fast to move to Southeast Asia, 9, 121
as innovator, 81, 295n11
in Malaysia, 129, 207, 209, 210, 212, 213, 305n5, 306n11
in regional production system, 150
in Singapore, 162, 164, 296n22, 299n8
success from producing in Southeast Asia, 112
use of ex-Seagate employees, 179
Measurex, 171
Memorex, 4, 71, 72, 88, 92, 314n3. *See also* Unisys
Methode, 169
Mette, 110, 308n14
Mexico, disk drive industry in, 33, 186
Microcomputer Memories, 81, 95, 285
Microlab, 308n15
Micro Peripherals, 298n2
Micropolis, 4, 81, 111, 117
  acquisition by Singapore Technology Group, 178, 309n24
  fast to move to Southeast Asia, 127
  as innovator, 283, 284, 292n23, 314n3
  in regional production system, 150
  in Singapore, 98, 164
  sourcing from Singaporean suppliers by, 168–69
  in Thailand, 128, 189, 193, 198
  use of ex-Seagate employees, 179
Microscience International, 4, 81, 297n5
  fast to move to Southeast Asia, 121
  in Singapore, 162
  in Taiwan, 98
Mimicry, 102–105. *See also* Convergence in global strategic behavior; Globalization of production
  among American firms into Singapore, 162–64
  and competitive advantage, 64–65, 258
  firm nationality and, 9, 38–39, 62–64, 257
  role of mental models in, 9, 38, 62–64
  and shift of production to Southeast Asia, 95, 119, 121, 194, 256–58
  strategic groups and, 9, 62–64, 257
Minebea
  in Southeast Asia, 109
  in Thailand, 136, 186, 189, 192, 193, 199–200, 202, 302n13, 302n26, 304n48, 306n21
MiniScribe, 4, 81
  fast to move to Southeast Asia, 121

in Singapore, 98, 104, 162, 163, 172, 209
  success from producing in Southeast Asia, 111, 112, 114
  use of ex-Seagate employees, 179
MiniStor, 73, 117, 240
  fast to move to Southeast Asia, 127
  in Singapore, 98, 165, 166
Mitsubishi, 4, 73, 309n22
Mitsubishi Chemical, 77, 150, 157, 168
MMI Holdings, 169, 170, 171, 180, 210, 213, 297n11, 306n21
Molex, 169
Motorola, 40
Multidigit, 236, 308n15
Multinational corporations (MNC). *See also* Foreign direct investment; Globalization of production
  age of, 4, 9, 139
  role in industrial clusters, 7, 9, 38, 52, 59. *See also* Agglomeration economies, and foreign investment
  role in regional production system, 38, 56–58, 292n22
  size of, 4, 9, 10, 139, 292n21
Myrica, 165

National Micronetics, 109, 121, 129, 150, 200, 299n6
National Science and Technology Board (NSTB) (Singapore), 177, 181
National Semiconductor
  managers who previously worked for, 156, 160, 189
National Storage Industry Consortium, 313n19
National systems of innovation, 79
National Trade Union Congress (NTUC) (Singapore), 309n27
National University of Singapore (NUS), 138, 160
NatSteel Electronics, 169, 170, 171, 210, 213, 306n21
NCR, 88
NEC, 4, 71, 111, 294n2
  as captive drive manufacturer, 88
  as Conner Peripherals customer, 114
  as contract manufacturer for IBM, 77, 235, 293n10
  as innovator, 81
  in the Philippines, 106, 235
  in the United States, 101, 105
Networks, 4, 5, 8, 55–56, 291–92n18. *See also* Regional production system
New institutional economics, 230, 307n3

Newtecho Engineering, 220
Newtecho Tooling, 220
New World Computer, 314n3
NHK (Nippon Hatusujo Kogyo), 218, 304n51
Nidec (Nippon Densan), 22, 306n21
  in Indonesia, 169
  in the Philippines, 110, 136, 308n14
  in Singapore, 157, 169
  in Southeast Asia, 109
  in Thailand, 136, 186, 192, 193, 195, 199–200, 202
  in the United States, 95
Nikon, 193
Nippon Peripherals, 81
Nippon Super, 193
NMB. *See* Minebea

Observational learning, 63. *See also* Mimicry
Ohara, 221
Olivetti, 73, 81
Omnibus Investments Code (Philippines), 235
Operational clusters, 4, 7, 12, 45–46, 118. *See also* Agglomeration economies; Industrial districts; Industrial clusters; Technological clusters
  benefits of locating in, 133, 274
  in China, 33
  in Europe, 33
  in Malaysia, 33, 98, 129, 134–35, 218–21, 297n4, 297n7, 307n33
  in Philippines, 33, 134
  in Singapore, 33, 62, 127, 160–70, 299n6, 299n8
  in Thailand, 33, 98, 128–29, 186, 191, 194, 202–03. *See also* Seagate Technology, motor assembly in Thailand
Optical disk drives, 73, 241–42
Oriental Precision, 239
Otari Electric, 77

Path dependence, 43, 55, 72, 74
Penang. *See* Malaysia; Operational clusters, in Malaysia
Penang Development Corporation (PDC) (Malaysia), 131, 212, 221–23, 246, 306n11
Penang Skills Development Corporation (PSDC) (Malaysia), 138–39, 246, 297n10
People's Action Party (PAP) (Singapore), 246, 247
Perdana Consulting, 169

Peripheral Technology, 95
Pertec, 89, 294n2, 308n15
Philco, 40
Philippine Economic Zone Authority, 235
Philippines
  infrastructure in, 127
  investment incentives, 235
  Japanese presence in, 34, 110, 134, 136, 228, 235, 308n14
  as possible site for American disk drive industry, 127, 129, 130, 189, 234
Philips, 72, 73
Plug-compatible manufacturers, 71, 88–89
Population of firms, 10, 254
Potter Instrument, 71, 89
PrairieTek, 73, 309n24
  in Singapore, 104
Precision Casting, 169
Precision Technology, 308n14
Priam, 73, 111, 283, 284, 314n3
  in Taiwan, 98
  reason for moving production overseas, 103
Product life cycle theory. *See* Competitive advantage, and first-mover advantage
Promotion of Investments Act (Malaysia), 211
Proximity, advantages of, 5, 8, 12, 42–43, 45, 49, 58–59, 61, 64, 110, 115, 120, 130, 150–51, 188, 194, 202–03, 214, 219, 224, 233, 256, 266, 290n5, 305n56. *See also* Agglomeration economies
Public policies. *See also* Competitive advantage, and public policy; Foreign direct investment, and public policy; Malaysia; Singapore; Thailand
  baseline, 8, 228, 232, 256, 265, 271
  evolution of, 173
  foreign direct investment, 123, 229
  generic, 229, 232–33, 269
  industrial, 85, 227–28, 229, 241–42
  industry-specific, 12, 131–33, 138–39, 229, 242, 269, 272
  and institutional capacities, 242–46, 252, 309n27, 311n37
  investment incentives, 124, 130–31, 233, 269
  macroeconomic, 123, 229, 308n8
  regional cooperation and, 13
  role in developing agglomeration economies, 181–83, 187, 229, 256
  trade, 123, 229, 232
Public-private consultation, 230

Quantum, 95, 286
  as innovator, 81, 283, 284, 295n11
  and Matsushita-Kotobuki Electronics
    (MKE) relationship, 76, 77, 217
  and ramp up of production by MKE,
    117
  in Malaysia, 141, 207, 216, 217
  in regional production system, 150
  in Singapore, 134, 165
  success from producing in Southeast
    Asia, 112

Ramos administration (Philippines), 249
Raytheon Data Systems, 284
RCA, 71
Read-Rite, 77, 95
  in Malaysia, 129, 135, 209, 212, 213,
    214–15, 218–19, 297n4, 297n7,
    306n21
  in the Philippines, 136
  in regional production system, 150
  in Thailand, 129, 186, 193, 195, 198,
    203, 224
  sales to firms in Southeast Asia, 109
Regional production system, 8, 13, 119,
  127, 136, 256. *See also* Networks
  and flexibility, 58, 120, 148, 149–50
  and learning, 57–58, 292n20
  leverages multiple location-specific
    assets, 8, 38, 61–62
  and locational heterogeneity, 57, 120,
    148–49, 150–51, 233
  Malaysia role in, 207, 209–10, 215–16,
    223–24
  origins of, 121
  of Seagate Technology, 121, 143–48,
    298n15
  Singapore role in, 156, 165, 170–71
  as source of industrial leadership, 121,
    148
  and speed of execution, 58–59, 120
Remington Rand, 88, 276
Research and Development Assistance
  Scheme (RDAS) (Singapore), 177
Research Incentive Scheme for Companies
  (RISC) (Singapore), 177
Rodime, 73
  as innovator, 81, 285
  in Singapore, 162, 163, 299n11, 309n24
Rollei, 161–62, 299n7
Rotating Memory Systems, 295n11
Route 128, 11

SAE Magnetics, 77, 193, 306n21
Saha-Union, 76, 128, 191

Samsung Electronics, 73, 229, 239–40,
  250–51, 270
Sankyo Seiki, 109, 200
San Technology, 308n14
Sara Lee, 261
SCI, 169, 170
Seagate Technology
  acquisition of Conner Peripherals, 145,
    216
  acquisition of Control Data disk drive
    operations, 144, 146, 164, 209,
    299n12
  autonomy of Singaporean managers,
    170
  in China, 134, 145, 216–17
  competing in Japanese market, 105
  development of Singaporean managers
    and engineers by, 179
  development of suppliers by, 108–09,
    168, 187, 188, 191, 199–201
  disk drive assembly in Malaysia by, 134,
    207
  disk drive assembly in Singapore by,
    143–44, 167, 216
  disk drive assembly in Thailand by, 128,
    171, 187, 190, 198, 216
  as employer in Southeast Asia, 34, 109,
    145, 164, 184, 198, 301n4, 304n42
  as exporter from China, 34, 136
  as exporter from Thailand, 34, 184
  fast to move to Southeast Asia, 3–4, 9,
    97, 121, 160
  headquarters of, 95
  heads assembly in Malaysia, 129,
    134–35, 216, 218, 306n22
  heads assembly in Thailand, 129, 184,
    187, 193, 202, 203
  influence on other disk drive firms, 98
  in Indonesia, 147
  as innovator, 81, 199, 278, 284, 295n10
  in Ireland, 145
  in Italy, 145
  late to market, 114, 286–87
  Longmont design center, 217
  Malaysia as product transfer station for,
    217
  media manufacture in Singapore, 134,
    157, 168, 182
  motor assembly in Thailand, 136, 186,
    187, 192–93, 199–200, 202–03,
    304n50
  origins of operations in Singapore,
    160–62, 299n6
  origins of operations in Thailand,
    187–90

Seagate Technology (*continued*)
    and strike in Thailand, 194, 302n28
    in the Philippines, 110
    research and development in Singapore
        by, 178, 243
    Singapore as product transfer station for,
        171
    size when moving to Singapore, 100
    success from producing in Southeast
        Asia, 111, 112, 114, 286–87
    Thailand as center of assembly for, 184
    and vertical integration, 76, 191, 293n9
Seiko Epson, 72, 100
Seiko Instruments, 200, 304n50
Seksun, 171
Semiconductor industry, geographic config-
    uration of, 40–41, 260, 265–69,
    313n14, 313n15, 313n16, 313n17
Serial Systems, 178
Shin-Ei, 193
Shinno, 309n22
Showa Aluminum, 134
Showa Denko, 77
Shugart Associates, 283, 284, 314n3
Siemens, 72, 73, 295n8
Silicon Valley, 11, 41
    globalization of firms from, 103–04
Singapore. *See also* Agglomeration
    economies, in Singapore; Operational
    clusters, Singapore;
    and American competitiveness, 171–83
    as center for disk drive production, 4,
        98, 127, 134, 155–56, 165
    as center for production of high-perfor-
        mance disk drives, 167
    education in, 137
    generic policies in, 157
    hard disk drives as share of exports in, 34
    indigenous suppliers to the HDD indus-
        try, 109, 127, 133, 139, 157, 168–70,
        297n11
    industry cluster development strategy in,
        133, 138
    industry growth in, 155–56, 157, 298n1
    industry-specific policies in, 8, 131, 133,
        138, 157
    infrastructure in, 127, 138, 173–74,
        297n3
    investment incentives in, 124, 126,
        174–75, 297n6
    labor market policies in, 175
    learning by American firms in, 155
    media cluster in, 134, 157, 168, 182
    multinational corporations' role in skill
        development in, 156

    operational capabilities in, 7, 149, 163,
        165–66
    policies to promote research and devel-
        opment in, 177–78
    policies for supplier industries in, 176–77
    reinvestment in, 108, 165, 166–67
    share of hard disk drives produced in,
        155, 296n19
    skills development policies in, 175–76
    and wage rates, 97, 123, 134
Singapore Polytechnic, 175, 297n10
Singapore Technology Group, 178
Skills. *See* Labor quality
Skills Development Fund (SDF) (Singa-
    pore), 175
SLI Industries, 314n3
Small Industry Technical Assistance
    Scheme (SITAS) (Singapore), 176, 181
Smartflex Systems, 109
Solectron, 213
Sony, 4, 73, 270
Southeast Asia
    presence of suppliers in, 109
    share of hard disk drives produced in,
        33, 100, 107, 111, 296n21
Special Economic Zone Act (Philippines),
    235
Sperac, 72, 88
Storage Technology, 89, 295n5
StorMedia, 109, 150, 157, 168, 182,
    307n34
Sumitomo Special Metals, 110
Sunpino Technology, 136, 308n14
Sunward Technologies, 306n21, 308n11
Sylvania, 41, 71
SyQuest
    decision to establish production in
        Southeast Asia, 104
    in Malaysia, 134
    in regional production system, 150

Tacit knowledge, 44, 49
Taiwan
    and optical disk drive industry, 241–42
    as possible site for disk drive industry, 172
    promotion of indigenous disk drive
        industry, 228–29, 237–39, 308n18,
        309n20, 309n21, 309n22
Tandon, 4, 95
    influence on other disk drive firms, 98
    in Singapore, 100, 162, 163, 168, 298n2
    success from producing in Southeast
        Asia, 111
Technological change. *See also* Competi-
    tion, technological; Competitive

advantage, and innovation; Competitive pressures; Innovation in disk drives
  acceleration with industry age, 17, 68
  and changing competitive pressures, 6, 232, 255–56
  influence on industry location, 48–49, 92, 261
Technological clusters, 8, 12, 43–45, 118, 274, 290n. *See also* Agglomeration economies; Industrial districts; Industrial clusters; Operational clusters
  in Europe, 115
  and innovation, 95
  in Japan, 115
  and product development, 8, 33
  in the United States, 33, 95, 115
TDK, 77, 110, 136, 309n22
TEAC, 77, 101
Technology transfer from technological to operational clusters, 115–18, 296n24, 296n25
TeleVideo Systems, 285
Texas Instruments, 40
Textile industry, geographic configuration of, 251
Thailand. *See also* Operational clusters, in Thailand
  and American competitiveness, 184, 186, 201–03
  as center for production, 127, 134, 136
  education in, 137, 188
  generic policies in, 187
  industry growth in, 184, 301n2
  industry-specific policies in, 133, 139, 187, 197, 304n39
  infrastructure in, 127, 138, 188, 195–96, 303n33, 303n34, 303n37
  investment incentives in, 127, 187, 188, 195–96, 202, 301n8, 303n30
  and low labor costs, 188, 202
  macroeconomic stability in, 188
  operational capabilities in, 7, 149
  and Seagate's competitiveness, 190–91
  supply base in, 191–93, 198, 302n26, 304n39
  trade policies in, 195–96
  and wage increases, 194–95, 302n29
Thailand Board of Investment (BOI), 133, 188, 189, 191, 195–96, 197, 201, 231, 244, 302n13, 310n29
Thai Okoku Rubber, 193
3M, 109, 169
Tongkah Electronics, 210, 213, 306n21
Tool Products, 299n6

Toshiba, 71, 286, 291n17
  as captive disk drive manufacturer, 88, 314n1
  as Conner Peripherals customer, 114
  as innovator, 84
  in the Philippines, 235
  in the United States, 101
Tosoh, 77
T.P.W., 193, 302n15
Trade regime, 133, 228, 269
TransCapital, 171, 210, 213, 214, 297n11, 306n21
Trigem Computer, 73
Tri-M, 169, 170, 210, 213, 306n21
Tsukiden Electronics Industries, 235, 308n11
Tsukuba Philippine Die-Casting, 110, 308n14

Uemura, 221
Unisys. *See also* Burroughs; Memorex
  slow to move to Southeast Asia, 106, 109
United States
  as host to Japanese disk drive firms, 101
  share of hard disk drives produced in, 33, 95, 107, 108
Univac, 71, 89, 295n4. *See also* Remington Rand
Universiti Science Malaysia, 222
Uraco, 168, 169, 171

Value chain, hard disk drives, 16, 21–24, 108–10
Venture Manufacturing, 170, 171
Vertical integration, 13, 74–79, 257, 270, 293n9
VF, 261

Wal-Mart, 311n2
Western Digital, 294n12
  in Malaysia, 134, 305n3
  ramp up production by, 117
  in regional production system, 150
  in Singapore, 127, 163, 166–67, 171
  success from producing in Southeast Asia, 112
  use of ex-Seagate employees, 179
World Trade Organization (WTO), 311n37

Xolox, 109, 118, 214, 219

Zentek, 309n21